The Knicks of t

MW00424914

The Knicks of the Nineties

Ewing, Oakley, Starks and the Brawlers That Almost Won It All

PAUL KNEPPER

McFarland & Company, Inc., Publishers

Jefferson, North Carolina

Library of Congress Cataloguing-in-Publication Data

Names: Knepper, Paul, 1977– author.
Title: The Knicks of the nineties : Ewing, Oakley, Starks and the
brawlers that almost won it all / Paul Knepper.
Description: Jefferson, North Carolina : McFarland & Company, Inc.,
Publishers, 2020. | Includes bibliographical references and index.
Identifiers: LCCN 2020035781 | ISBN 9781476682815 (paperback : acid free paper) ∞
ISBN 9781476641164 (ebook)
Subjects: LCSH: New York Knickerbockers (Basketball team)—History.
Classification: LCC GV885.52.N4 K64 2020 | DDC 796.323/64097471—dc23
LC record available at https://lccn.loc.gov/2020035781

British Library cataloguing data are available

ISBN (print) 978-1-4766-8281-5
ISBN (ebook) 978-1-4766-4116-4

Front cover: Knicks center Patrick Ewing (Chris Johnson);
New York skyline (Luciano Mortula/Shutterstock)

Printed in the United States of America

McFarland & Company, Inc., Publishers
Box 611, Jefferson, North Carolina 28640
www.mcfarlandpub.com

To the memory of my Bubby, Mae Adler,
and to my wife, Stacey.

My Bubby was my biggest fan.
Nobody would have been more proud of this book.
I wish she were here to read it.

This book would not exist without the love, support,
and patience of Stacey. I love her deeply
and am eternally grateful for everything
she does for our family.

Acknowledgments

My wife, Stacey, served as a valuable consultant and helped me manage the ups and downs of the writing process. I am so grateful to have her by my side.

It is not a coincidence that I formulated the idea for this book soon after my son, Brodie, was born. He is my greatest inspiration and brings immeasurable joy to my life.

I am extremely grateful to Martha Cantu for everything she does for my family. Thank you to my father for reading a draft of this book and taking me to Knicks games. I appreciate my mother, Gregg, Sam, Jordyn, Scarlett, Elle, Robbie, Elba and Margo for their love and support. I wish my father-in-law, Andy, were here to read this.

Thank you to my cousin Joe Brofsky for taking me to Knicks and Liberty games and sending me books for this project. I am fortunate to have several friends who took an interest in this book and encouraged me along the way, most notably Daniel Oliver. I would also like to thank Thomas Kremer for encouraging me to pursue writing.

I am deeply appreciative of every one of the sources I interviewed for this book. They include Rand Araskog, Harvey Araton, Stan Asofsky, Barbara Barker, Al Bianchi, Rolando Blackman, Anthony Bonner, Chris Brienza, Clifton Brown, Gerald Brown, Rick Brunson, Curtis Bunn, Dick Butera, Michael Carter, Jr., Bill Cartwright, Dave Checketts, Chris Childs, Doug Christie, John Cirillo, Jim Cleamons, Don Cronson, Terry Cummings, Dave D'Alessandro, Ben Davis, Hubert Davis, Peter DeBusschere, Chris Dudley, Mario Elie, Paul Evans, David Falk, Scott Fiedler, Matt Fish, Corey Gaines, Lewis Geter, Ronnie Grandison, Ernie Grunfeld, Bob Gutkowski, Lori Hamamoto, Said Hamdan, Leonard Hamilton, Tim Hardaway, Derek Harper, Wade Houston, Jaren Jackson, Stanley Jaffe, Mike Jarvis, DeMarco Johnson, Bo Kimble, Travis Knight, Andrew Lang, Ian Mahoney, Brendan Malone, Stephen Masiello, Vernon Maxwell, Xavier McDaniel, Scott McGuire, Carlton McKinney, Charles Oakley, Will Perdue, Dave Robbins, Barry Rubinstein, Bob

Salmi, Wimp Sanderson, Mike Saunders, Rik Smits, Barry Stanton, John Starks, David Steele, Sammie Steinlight, Spencer Stolpen, Erick Strickland, Mark Strickland, Tom Thibodeau, Kurt Thomas, Rod Thorn, Rudy Tomjanovich, Jeff Van Gundy, Stan Van Gundy, Peter Vecsey, Suzyn Waldman, Kenny Walker, John Wallace, Charlie Ward, Gerald Wilkins, Herb Williams, Mike Wise, Dave Wohl, Ronnie Zeidel, and those who prefer to remain anonymous.

I am grateful for my agent, John Rudolph, whose belief in me and this project propelled it forward, and my editor, Aaron Fischman. Thank you to Gary Mitchem and everybody at McFarland who brought this book to life. I also want to thank Adam Criblez and Mick Minas, two authors I have never met who were extremely generous in assisting me with several aspects of this book.

Lastly, I would like to thank the 1990s Knicks for providing me with endless hours of suspense, joy, hope, and heartache. I hope *The Knicks of the Nineties* does them justice.

Table of Contents

Introduction

Basketball is the city game. From the blacktops of Harlem to the "World's Most Famous Arena," the game's beats and rhythms embody the hustle and bustle, ingenuity and artistry of New York City. You cannot walk more than a mile in Manhattan without seeing a basketball court.

The New York Knicks have the ability to inspire and unite the city as no other team can. New Yorkers are divided between the Giants and Jets in football, and the Yankees were forced to contend with the Giants and Dodgers, followed by the Mets. Prior to the Nets moving to Brooklyn in 2012, the Knicks had the five boroughs to themselves for generations.

Suzyn Waldman, the radio voice of the New York Yankees who once covered the Yankees and Knicks for WFAN radio, recalls, "When I was growing up in Boston, the Celtics always won, but the soul of that town was the Red Sox. And when I got here and started covering the Knicks in '87, I saw the reverse." Waldman added, "Not that they didn't love the Yankees. They always did. But the soul was Knicks basketball."[1]

When the Knicks are playing well, orange and blue is splashed across the back pages of the local newspapers and strangers on a train bond over the team's latest victory. Barbara Barker of *Newsday* recalls her introduction to New Yorkers' passion for basketball shortly after moving to the city in the early 1990s: "I'm looking down Second Avenue. I'm coming down from a party or something. This is before you had a phone and everybody could watch TV. There's this basically homeless dude who rigged up this television and plugged it into a light pole. And it's the Knicks and it's a regular season game and there's like 10 people standing all around. The homeless guy, me and my date."[2]

Unfortunately, Knicks fans have endured nearly two decades of ineptitude from their favorite team, featuring a litany of hirings and firings, ill-advised acquisitions, and far too many losing seasons. Yet the fan base has maintained a sense of optimism that belies the results on the court. It is a hope steeped in the past, based on memories and tales of better days.

1

When the media reflects on the glory days of the Knicks, they typically hark back to the great teams of the early 1970s. Countless books have been written about Walt "Clyde" Frazier, Willis Reed, Dave DeBusschere, and Bill Bradley. Those teams operated in harmony like a jazz quintet, seamlessly weaving their bodies and the ball around the court on their way to winning championships in 1970 and 1973.

There was a more recent golden age of Knicks basketball that resonates with a younger generation of fans: the 1990s Knicks. If the Garden was Eden in the '70s, then the '90s version was a sold-out rock concert where the crowd sang along with chants of "De-fense, De-fense!" For more than a decade, the Knicks were the hottest ticket in the hippest city in America.

Unlike the 1973 team, which boasted several future Hall of Famers, the '90s Knicks featured just one star, a proud warrior named Patrick Ewing who carried the franchise on his back for 15 years. The big man was supported by an eclectic cast of characters who took various routes to New York, many overcoming tremendous obstacles along the way. They were led by two brilliant coaches, Pat Riley and Jeff Van Gundy. Although on the surface they may have appeared to be polar opposites, the coaches were equally driven by an obsession with winning.

Ewing and his teammates were underdogs, the David to Michael Jordan and the Bulls' Goliath. Their battles with the Bulls and rivalries with the Indiana Pacers and Miami Heat produced epic moments that helped define the NBA for a decade. Those Knicks teams were tough, relentless, and inspiring. They embodied the working-class spirit of the city in which they played. In turn, the city loved them for it.

The Knicks made the playoffs for 14 consecutive seasons from 1988 through 2001, but they never reached the pinnacle of success. For reasons ranging from Michael Jordan's presence to injuries and ejections, a championship eluded their grasp. Perhaps Charles Oakley, one of the stalwarts of those teams, said it best: "We were always one player away, one possession away, one win away. We should be called 'One Away.'"[3]

Decades later, Van Gundy found it difficult to dwell on the lack of championships, instead extolling those Knicks' achievements. "You'll never convince me that those Knicks teams, from when Pat Riley came until he went to Miami, that even though they didn't accomplish winning a championship that the players weren't champions," Van Gundy said. "They gave championship energy and effort and enthusiasm every day."[4] For Van Gundy, that sentiment extended to the teams he coached in New York as well.[5]

Despite not winning a championship, the Knicks of the 1990s left a lasting impact on the game. In response to New York's physical play and punishing defense, the NBA made several rule changes designed to penalize conflict, decrease contact, and create the freedom of movement that has led to an increase in scoring in recent years.

The longer Knicks fans suffer through dreadful basketball and embarrassing off-the-court incidents, the more they long for the days when gladiators named Oak and Mase roamed the court. This book is for those who lived and died with every shot, defensive stand, and loose-ball scramble. It's also intended to encourage younger generations of Knicks fans to maintain hope that, one day, they will have a team worth loving the way their parents once did.

Prologue

It was May 31, 1991. Dave Checketts was a few months into his tenure as the president of the Knicks and on the verge of signing the hottest coach on the market, Pat Riley. But there was a catch. Riley would not sign on the dotted line until he was assured the Knicks' star center, Patrick Ewing, would remain with the team.[1]

Riley coached the Los Angeles Lakers to four championships in the 1980s and would bring instant credibility and structure to the rudderless Knicks. Ewing was the franchise player. Missing out on Riley would be a disappointment for Checketts and the Knicks; losing Ewing would be a full-blown disaster.

Checketts booked a room at the Mark Hotel on Manhattan's Upper East Side, the same place where Ewing and his agent, David Falk, were staying. Riley shacked up at the Regency Hotel on Park Avenue. The Knicks' president moved feverishly between Ewing's room, where the star center was convening with his wife, Rita, Falk, and his college coach, John Thompson, and the Regency, attempting to secure a commitment from both the center and the coach. Time was of the essence. Ewing intended to file for free agency the following day.[2]

Patrick had been the most promising in a line of supposed saviors for the Knicks in the years following the franchise's two championships. He was widely considered a once-in-a-generation talent when the Knicks selected him with the first overall pick of the 1985 draft, the type of player who would deliver multiple championships to the Big Apple. However, Ewing and the Knicks won just one playoff series in Patrick's first six seasons.

By 1991, Ewing and management had run out of patience with each other and were both considering parting ways. The fans had also grown frustrated with their supposed savior. During a game against the Nuggets on St. Patrick's Day in March 1987, the Knicks provided fans with life-size Patrick Ewing posters. As it became clear the Knicks were going to lose their fourth consecutive game, the fans at Madison Square Garden began ripping up the posters and throwing them on the court.[3]

Ewing had grown disillusioned with the only franchise he had ever played for. Since he arrived, the Knicks had gone through five coaches and three general managers and were about to hire yet another coach. Checketts compared talking to Ewing, in March 1991, to visiting with an orphan who had already lived in several different homes.[4]

Mediocrity was particularly difficult for Ewing, who had experienced so much success at Georgetown.[5] Management failed him by cycling through coaches and surrendering valuable draft picks and young talent for other teams' discarded veterans. Yet, it was Ewing who shouldered the brunt of the criticism from fans and the media for the team's lack of success.

With Patrick's 30th birthday rapidly approaching, there appeared little reason to believe he could win a championship in New York any time soon. Following the 1990–91 season, Ewing rejected a six-year, $5.4 million-per-year contract extension that would have made him the highest paid player in team sports.[6] He was searching for a way out.

Ewing signed a record-breaking 10-year, $32 million contract prior to his rookie year. Before playing an NBA game, he was making 55 percent more than the next highest-paid player in the league, six-time Most Valuable Player Kareem Abdul-Jabbar.[7]

Still, Falk negotiated an early termination clause in Ewing's contract, the first of its kind, in order to protect his long-term interests in a rapidly changing market. The clause stated Patrick could become a restricted free agent if he were not among the four highest-paid players in the league.[8] That meant the Knicks would have 15 days to match any offer he received, though Ewing also had the option of signing a one-year contract with the Knicks for $5.5 million and becoming an unrestricted free agent the following season.[9]

Ewing and the team disagreed as to whether the conditions had been met to trigger the option, which would go into effect on June 1, 1991. Both parties agreed Michael Jordan, John Williams, and Hakeem Olajuwon made more money per year than Ewing. The discrepancy was over Larry Bird's contract. Bird's salary for the '91–'92 season was $2.2 million, but he was scheduled to be paid a total of $7.1 million, the balance consisting of a deferred signing bonus.[10] The Knicks were confident because the wording of the clause in Ewing's contract twice used the phrase "exclusive of signing bonuses."[11]

The Bird argument was a long shot, but Falk had a card up his sleeve. The agent had been in contact with Dan Finnane and Jim Fitzgerald, the president and owner of the Golden State Warriors, respectively. Falk had been trying to convince them to deliver Chris Mullin a new contract that would surpass Ewing's existing deal, effectively making the Big Fella a free agent. Falk would then steer Ewing to the Warriors.[12]

The Warriors and Falk agreed on a 10-year contract for Ewing, even though he was still under contract with the Knicks. Falk pushed Checketts to trade Ewing to Golden State because the Knicks were going to lose him anyway, but the Warriors offered only spare parts for the star center.[13]

Unfortunately for Falk, Mullin's agent, Bill Pollack, also represented Knicks forward Charles Oakley. Pollack did not want his client to be stuck on a bad Knicks team without Ewing. He informed Checketts what Falk was plotting. Naturally, Checketts was furious. He called Fitzgerald and threatened to sue him for interfering with a contractual relationship, litigation that would tie the Warriors up in court for years and prevent them from signing Ewing. Golden State dropped the plan.[14]

The old Knicks regime had entertained dealing Ewing prior to the 1991 trade deadline. Richard Evans, the CEO of Madison Square Garden, offered the Miami Heat Ewing in exchange for Sherman Douglas, Rony Seikaly, and a first-round draft pick, but the Heat turned him down.[15] Al Bianchi, New York's general manager at the time, discussed Ewing with a number of other teams, though was not overwhelmed by any offers.[16]

After being named team president in March, Checketts also fielded calls about Ewing. Checketts flew to San Antonio and offered Spurs owner Red McCombs Ewing and $10 million for David Robinson. McCombs thought it over for a few days before turning Checketts down.[17]

Checketts shifted his focus to keeping Ewing in orange and blue and believed the Big Fella would be more likely to stay with Riley on board. He had been negotiating with Riley for a month. The two had gone out to dinner several times, but Riley had yet to commit to the job.[18]

Unable to make headway with Ewing or Riley on the morning of May 31, Checketts retreated to his hotel room. Martin Davis, the chairman and CEO of Paramount Communications, the company that owned the Knicks, called Checketts to see how the negotiations were progressing. Davis offered his support, but ended the conversation with a crystal clear "Dave, don't you dare fuck this up."[19]

Checketts considered the possibility that he was in over his head. He thought of the back page of that day's *New York Post*, which had a picture of him under the headline "He Should Have Stayed in Utah." Maybe his wife was right when she questioned whether he had that New York edge to him. Then, he contemplated the first lines of "If," a Rudyard Kipling poem his father used to recite to him.

> If you can keep your head when all about you
> Are losing theirs and blaming it on you,
> If you can trust yourself when all men doubt you,
> But make allowance for their doubting too.[20]

Checketts decided to take a stand. He informed Riley he would be holding a press conference at Madison Square Garden (MSG) at 4 p.m. that day, at which point he would either introduce Riley as the new Knicks coach or announce Riley had turned down the job. The negotiations were over. Checketts' final offer was on the table. The coach had 30 minutes to give him an answer. Next, Checketts warned Ewing he would lose in arbitration if he filed for free agency and the massive extension the team offered him would be off the table.[21]

Riley, impressed by his future boss' firmness and confident in his own ability to win over Ewing, called Checketts back and accepted the job. Checketts had his coach. He told Ewing the news, but it did not change Ewing's mind. The center filed for free agency the next day.[22]

1

The Big Fella

"We've had the Mikan era, the Russell era, the Kareem era
... now we'll have the Ewing era."[1]—Pat O'Brien, quoting an
unnamed NBA scouting director

Patrick Ewing graduated college as the most acclaimed prospect since
Lew Alcindor (later Kareem Abdul-Jabbar). The 7-footer dominated the collegiate game with his defense, rejecting shots with an intimidating scowl at
such frequency that opposing guards were terrified of driving to the basket.
College and professional coaches, as well as National Basketball Association
scouts, compared him to Boston Celtics great Bill Russell.[2]

Patrick won three state championships at Cambridge Rindge and Latin
High School, before becoming a three-time All-American at Georgetown
University. The big man guided the Hoyas to three appearances in the NCAA
Championship game, winning the title in 1984. He was named College Player
of the Year in 1985 by several media outlets.

In the spring of 1985, *Sports Illustrated* referred to Ewing as possibly "the
most recognized athlete ever to enter a major professional league."[3] Conse-
quently, the '85 draft lottery was regarded as a major news event and aired
by CBS Sports. The lottery was held in the glamorous Starlight Room of the
Waldorf Astoria in New York City. There was a dais at the front of the room
where a representative from each team sat. The Knicks were represented by
their general manager, a member of their two championship teams, Dave
DeBusschere. Big D was sharply dressed in a powder blue suit.[4]

Team officials and fans were filled with anticipation at the prospect of
the Knicks landing Ewing. There was also a great deal of curiosity around the
lottery itself in its first year of existence.

Prior to 1985, the NBA flipped a coin between the teams with the two
worst records to determine the draft order. The winner received the first pick,
the loser the second, and the rest of the teams picked in inverse order of their
record. However, during the '83–'84 season, several teams, including the Hous-

ton Rockets, who ended up winning the coin flip, intentionally lost games in order to gain a chance at drafting Hakeem Olajuwon. It was embarrassing to the league and bad for competition.[5] There was an assumption the problem would repeat itself in 1985 with Ewing as the prize, so the league attempted to remedy the problem by replacing the coin flip with a lottery.

Under the lottery system, the logo of each of the seven teams that did not make the playoffs was placed in an envelope. All of the envelopes were placed in a hopper. The envelopes were selected one by one by the commissioner of the NBA, David Stern, who then read their contents aloud to determine the draft order. The team represented in the last envelope selected would have won the first pick. Each lottery team had an equal 14.3 percent chance of winning the first pick.[6]

John Cirillo, the Knicks' vice president of communications, heard that some of the teams were bringing lucky charms to the lottery so he called one of Yonkers Raceway's leading harness drivers, Buddy Gilmour, and secured a horseshoe from champion pacer On the Road Again. Cirillo picked up the horseshoe and stopped at St. Patrick's Cathedral to offer a prayer that the Garden become a different Patrick's cathedral, before delivering the lucky charm and a No. 33 Ewing Knicks jersey to DeBusschere at the Waldorf.[7]

The Knicks had lost star forward Bernard King to a career-threatening injury during the '84–'85 season and finished with the third-worst record at 24–58. With just three envelopes remaining, New York had yet to be selected. DeBusschere was so nervous he could barely watch. He put his hands in his mouth, then covered his eyes. The third pick went to the Los Angeles Clippers, leaving just the Knicks and Indiana Pacers remaining.

At that point, Ewing thought, "Oh my God, I hope it's New York."[8] He received his wish. The second-to-last envelope went to the Pacers, giving the Knicks the first pick in the draft. Pat O'Brien, who was announcing the draft for CBS, shouted, "Basketball is back in New York City, my friends!"[9]

The crowd in the Starlight Room erupted. Even members of the New York media were delighted, though the best reaction came from DeBusschere, who stood up and pounded his fist on the table in front of him. DeBusschere made no secret of whom the Knicks intended to select. He pulled out the No. 33 Knicks jersey with Ewing's name sewn on the back.[10]

Fans, members of the media, and officials from other teams immediately called foul. They believed the lottery was fixed. Cynics pointed out that the NBA's $91.9 million television contract with CBS was set to expire the following year, and it seemed way too convenient that the biggest prospect in a generation would end up in the league's largest market.[11] The Knicks

Dave DeBusschere (right) and the Knicks left no doubt that they would be selecting Patrick Ewing with the first pick in the 1985 draft after winning the first NBA draft lottery. The outcome of that lottery would become the subject of conspiracy theories that persist to this day. Commissioner David Stern is at left (AP Photo/ Marty Lederhandler).

were desperate for a spark. King had blown out his knee, and the Garden was half-empty most games during the recently completed season.

Conspiracy theorists developed what became known as the "Frozen Envelope" theory. They claimed the league froze the Knicks' envelope beforehand so the person selecting the envelopes knew not to choose it. Others argued the corner of the Knicks' envelope was bent or had been placed in the hopper in a different direction.[12]

After the lottery, DeBusschere told O'Brien, "We just became a very good team."[13] Ewing was expected to make the Knicks an immediate contender.

It did not work out that way. New York went 23–59 in Ewing's rookie year under coach Hubie Brown, and the big man was asked to play out of position at power forward because the Knicks had another, less agile 7-footer in Bill Cartwright. In Ewing's second season, the Knicks won 24 games, and Brown was replaced early in the season by Bob Hill.[14]

In addition to the losing and instability, Ewing struggled to grasp the complexities of being a superstar in New York. He yearned for affection and endorsements, yet was unwilling to open up to the media or fans. Later in his career he cluelessly complained to ownership about not receiving as many endorsements as Michael Jordan.[15]

Unfortunately, Patrick never had an opportunity to play with King, who was one of the elite scorers in the league before he tore his ACL in March 1985. The injury was deemed career ending. King missed the entire '85–'86 season and returned for six games at the end of the following season before the Knicks released him in the summer of '87.[16] King later defied the odds by making an All-Star appearance with the Washington Bullets. To this day, he and Ewing both wonder what might have been had they had the chance to play together.[17]

In 1987, the Knicks hired a young, rising coaching star named Rick Pitino. Fresh off a Final Four run with Providence College, Pitino quickly established a winning culture and brought excitement back to New York basketball. He handed the reins to Mark Jackson, a cocky rookie point guard from Brooklyn, and encouraged him to push the ball up the floor.[18] New York applied full-court defensive pressure, trapped ball handlers, and launched so many three-pointers that the perimeter players came to be known as the "Bomb Squad."

The result was a 38–44 record and a trip to the playoffs. Buoyed by the acquisition of power forward Charles Oakley and the addition of another local rookie point guard, Rod Strickland, the Knicks won 52 games in 1988–89. They were upset by Michael Jordan and the Chicago Bulls in the second round of the playoffs.

Then, Pitino, who had contemplated a return to the college game within months of taking the Knicks job, bolted for the University of Kentucky.[19] Suddenly, it was back to the doldrums for the Knicks.

Jackson put on weight, and his performance no longer resembled that of the All-Star from the previous season. The Knicks traded Strickland to San Antonio for an aging Maurice Cheeks who was on the downside of his career. Ewing averaged a career-high 28.6 points per game in 1989–90, but New York slipped to 45 wins under Stu Jackson, who was fired 15 games into the following season and replaced by John McLeod. The Knicks won just 39 games during the '90–'91 campaign and were swept in the first round of the '91 playoffs.[20] Enter Riley.

In July, an arbitrator ruled against Ewing's claim for free agency. That did not stop Falk from pushing the Knicks to trade his client.[21] Riley flew to Washington, D.C., in August to meet with Ewing in person. He informed Patrick he would be the focal point of the offense, something Ewing had shockingly never heard before.[22] He then shared with Patrick and his wife, Rita, a dream he had of riding in a parade down Lower Manhattan with confetti falling all around them. Patrick responded by providing Riley a list of seven teams to which he would like to be traded.[23]

Ewing's desire to leave New York was fueled by his hunger to win a championship.[24] Riley and his four rings ultimately won him over. Checketts offered Ewing the same two-year extension that was previously on the table, which Patrick signed, making him the highest-paid player in the league.[25]

The Ewing Riley inherited was a different type of player than he had been in college. Patrick consistently ranked among the NBA leaders in blocked shots, but he did not dominate the paint defensively the way he had at Georgetown, nor did he average double-digit rebounds until his fifth season. To the surprise of basketball insiders, his offensive game had surpassed his defense.

Patrick had a few go-to post moves, which forced opponents to double-team him, leaving shooters open on the perimeter. He loved to operate on the left side of the floor, where he could uncork a turnaround fadeaway toward the baseline over his right shoulder, or take two long strides into the lane for a runner.

Ewing was anchored to the post at Georgetown. To the surprise of many, he became a deadly shooter from 15 to 20 feet from the rim for the Knicks. Patrick claims he could shoot in college, but coach John Thompson would not let him. "Son, get your ass in the post," Thompson would say. "I need a bull, not a butterfly."[26]

There were some flaws in Ewing's game. The 7-footer was too dependent on his jump shot at times rather than attacking the basket. His hands were average, at best, and he never excelled at moving the ball. Ewing's unwillingness to pass frustrated teammates at times. Derek Harper said, "Patrick shot with two or three guys hanging on him some nights. And there were times when people were wide open." Patrick's post moves were somewhat limited as he relied mostly on athleticism to beat his man.[27]

If there were such a thing as "sweat equity," Ewing would own Madison Square Garden. His oversized wristbands were no match for the perspiration that poured from his face. Jack McCallum of *Sports Illustrated* aptly dubbed him the "lunchpail superstar."[28] Nobody outworked the Big Fella.

In that sense, Patrick was the ideal franchise player. His commitment to winning and willingness to be coached set the culture for the team. Ewing was not a vocal leader. He led by example. His teammates rave about how hard he practiced, especially given the knee pain that hampered him throughout his career. "You had to get to practice four or five hours early to beat Patrick," according to John Wallace, who played two seasons with Ewing.[29] When the best player on the team works as hard as Ewing did, the rest of the players fall in line.

Patrick's knees were bothering him as early as his rookie year when he had surgery to remove tissue from his right knee. Early in the '86–'87 season, he was in so much pain that he had trouble bending to shoot free throws.[30] Knicks fans grew accustomed to the oversized white knee pads the center wore over the more traditional black pads. He iced his knees down after every game. There were times when the man his teammates called "Beast" was in so much agony he could barely walk. Still, he refused to sit out practice.[31]

Despite earning the respect of his teammates and coaches, Ewing was perceived by the public as a detached underachiever. In addition to the outlandish expectations that followed him to New York, he had a cold, at times contentious, relationship with the fans. Ewing's public persona must be viewed within the context of his background.

Patrick Ewing is the American dream. From his birth in Kingston, Jamaica, his journey to the NBA was the ultimate immigrant success story before such stories were common in the league. Many reporters falsely portrayed him as an entitled superstar. The Knicks and advertisers failed to capitalize on his unique background and brilliant smile. Instead, New York's first major advertisement of Ewing featured the unimaginative and racially insensitive image of the Big Fella standing among skyscrapers looking like King Kong.[32]

Soccer and cricket were Ewing's first sports. "I wanted to be the next Pele," he once said.[33] Ewing's mother, Dorothy, immigrated in 1971 to the United States, where she worked double shifts as a hospital maid for two years in order to raise enough money to bring the rest of her family to the States. Ultimately, Ewing, his father, and his six siblings came over, one or two at a time.[34]

In 1975, at the age of 12, Patrick settled with his family in Cambridge, Massachusetts. The Boston area had a history of racial tension, which boiled over at that time over forced school busing. A young Patrick was on the receiving end of the "N" word on several occasions.[35]

It was in Cambridge that he started playing basketball. Initially, he appeared to be a fish out of water on the court. Patrick was tall, gangly, and spoke with an accent, which led other kids to tease him. They called him all kinds of names, like Kermit the Frog, because he was all arms and legs when he rode a bicycle.[36]

The basketball coach at Patrick's junior high school, Steve Jenkins, asked Mike Jarvis, then an assistant coach at Harvard University, to train Ewing. The boy needed friends, and Jenkins thought being on a team would help. Patrick's mother had formed a bond with Jarvis' mother-in-law, who was also from the West Indies, and Dorothy put her trust in Jarvis, who ended up becoming Patrick's high school coach his sophomore year. Boasting his mother's work ethic, Ewing stayed after practice to work on his skills.[37]

Patrick also had a big heart. His high school team had a manager/ball boy named Stephen Clark who was intellectually and developmentally challenged. Ewing often put his arm around Clark and helped him pick up the balls after practice. The Big Fella did not tolerate anybody making fun of Stephen. Even when he became the most sought-after high school player in the country, the Jamaica native never demonstrated an ego off the court. Every teacher at Cambridge Rindge and Latin loved Patrick because he never missed a class and was always polite.[38]

Unfortunately, the court was not a safe haven from discrimination. Children threw rocks and slashed the tires of his team's bus, and Ewing faced racist taunts at games.[39] The hurtful remarks intensified after Ewing disappointed Bostonians by choosing to attend Georgetown instead of Boston College. Word leaked that Jarvis informed college recruiters Ewing would need extra academic assistance due to his poverty and immigrant background. In Patrick's last high school game, Cambridge Rindge and Latin faced Boston College High School in the 1981 Massachusetts State Championship game. The Boston College High fans chanted, "Ewing can't read" throughout the game.[40]

Patrick seriously considered attending Georgetown, the University of North Carolina, and UCLA.[41] Georgetown's coach, John Thompson, went to see him play on the suggestion of Red Auerbach, the legendary coach and general manager of the Celtics. "I said to my assistant, 'Get me that kid and we'll win the national championship,'" Thompson recalled.[42]

Patrick's mother wanted her son to play for a strong black coach. On several occasions, she told Jarvis she wished he could coach Patrick in college. Thompson fit the mold. Ewing wanted to move away from home and committed to Georgetown, in large part because he could relate to Thompson, who had played the same position as him. Thompson was Russell's backup for the Celtics for three years in the mid-'60s.[43]

The hateful barbs followed Patrick to Georgetown, where opposing crowds held up signs comparing him to an ape.[44] Ewing was shy by nature and sensitive about his Jamaican accent. The racism he faced led him to be guarded in public and distrustful of the media.[45]

Many in the media attributed Ewing's reticence to Thompson. The coach kept a tight lid on his players.[46] Reporters dubbed it "Hoya Paranoia." Thompson could have better prepared Ewing for the spotlight, however, Georgetown big men Alonzo Mourning and Dikembe Mutombo appeared comfortable in front of the camera upon entering the league. Patrick was simply a private person.

There was no hiding in New York City for a 7-foot savior. Win or lose, Ewing answered questions at all mandatory media sessions, which was no easy task for the lone superstar on a New York team. Yet, the reluctant superstar did not cozy up to reporters or smile for the camera.

At a time when the league was experiencing a massive growth spurt and most stars were pining for publicity, Ewing set strict rules about when he would talk to reporters. He refused to meet with the press before games and rarely granted one-on-one interviews. He spoke to the press in his bathrobe for a few minutes after each game and would abruptly end each session by saying, "That's it, fellas."[47] Many reporters interpreted his aloofness as rude and portrayed him as such. His unwillingness to sign autographs for children did not help his image.[48]

With few exceptions, reporters, fans, and his opponents were not privy to Ewing's sense of humor and friendly nature, which was reserved for those closest to him. Patrick also had a sensitive side, which surfaced during his career in the form of professional pride. He enjoyed drawing in his free time, often pictures of his late mother, and began painting landscapes during his final year at Georgetown.[49]

Doc Rivers captured the dichotomy between the two sides of Patrick in his autobiography: "When I played against Patrick, I had the impression he was one mean, unhappy man," wrote Rivers. "Patrick isn't anything like what people think. He is a very nice guy, a very smart guy, a very thoughtful guy, and the best leader there is."[50] However, there were times when Ewing irked teammates by refusing to take up their cause with management.

Mike Wise, who was a Knicks beat writer during the '90s, experienced Ewing's humor firsthand. One year, a beautiful Cleveland Cavaliers cheerleader approached Wise during the game and said, "Are you Mike Wise from the *New York Times*? Oh my God, I read everything you write." Wise spent the rest of the game trying to decide his next move. He tried to talk to the cheerleader after the game, but she blew him off. When Wise walked into the Knicks locker room, Ewing looked up with a smile from ear to ear and said, "April fools."[51]

2

Riley Does Broadway

"Character is like a tree and reputation its shadow. The shadow is what we think it is and the tree is the real thing."
—Abraham Lincoln

Eighteen minutes into the Knicks' first practice of the 1991–92 season, fists were flying. What began as a non-contact rebounding drill turned into a brawl between veteran forward Xavier McDaniel and a bruising journeyman named Anthony Mason. McDaniel started pounding on Mason's head. Mason responded with haymakers of his own. Each player landed at least a half a dozen blows that would have floored most men. The battle began near the baseline and made its way toward the sideline before eventually coming to a close near center court. It was a draw.[1]

That fight set the tone for the season, and those in attendance would talk about it for years to come. The Riley era in New York was underway.

Pat Riley arrived in New York a star. "He was a Hollywood big man. Pat Riley was iconic," said Bob Gutkowski, president of Madison Square Garden at the time. "He was above us all in so many ways. His stature was just at a different level and I think we all kind of knew that and respected that."[2]

Tall and handsome, with impeccable style, Riley coached the Lakers to four championships in the 1980s. The coach parlayed his team's success into feature articles, sponsorship deals, and $20,000 speaking engagements.[3] Yet, like much of Hollywood, Riley's slicked-back hair and $2,000 Giorgio Armani suits were a facade. The coach was a scrapper at heart, and he wanted his players to adopt his personality. He was pleased to see McDaniel and Mason carving out their turf.

Riles, as some of his friends and former players refer to him, hails from Schenectady, New York, a blue-collar town about 150 miles north of New York City. His father, Lee, was a career baseball minor leaguer turned coach. The elder Riley worked as a janitor and battled an alcohol problem after baseball.[4] It was Lee who taught his son to always look well-groomed in public.[5]

Pat's family did not have much money. He wore hand-me-down clothes. There was a period when he only had one pair of khaki pants, which he dried in the oven. On one occasion, he left them in too long, forming grill marks on the back side. He had to wear them to school like that, but Pat did not receive any ribbing from other kids. They knew better than that.[6]

He was tough, the kind of kid who hung out on street corners and hustled people in pool. He played quarterback in high school and was recruited by the likes of Bear Bryant and Joe Paterno to play college football. The Dallas Cowboys drafted him even though he didn't play a down of college football.[7]

Riley chose to play basketball at the University of Kentucky for legendary coach Adolph Rupp, whose drill-type mentality made an impression on the future coach.[8] At just 6-foot-3, Riley played power forward and even jumped center at times, battling bigger players on a nightly basis for the team known as "Rupp's Runts." He was part of the Kentucky team that lost the historic 1966 National Championship game to Texas Western, the first championship team with an all-black starting five.[9]

Riley was selected in the first round of the 1967 NBA draft by the San Diego Rockets. He was a tweener, too small to play forward and not quick enough to play guard. The native New Yorker forged a nine-year NBA career out of sheer determination.

The Lakers signed Pat in 1970 merely for his intense practice habits until injuries to others cleared a path for him to become the third guard on the '71–'72 championship team that won a record 33 consecutive games.[10] Riley, who came to bear a striking resemblance to Sonny Bono with his mustache and long hair, retired after the '75–'76 season.

Fortuitous circumstances led to Riley's foray into coaching. When the position of color man/traveling secretary for the Lakers became available, the team's broadcaster, Chick Hearn, thought of him. Early in the 1979–80 season, Lakers coach Jack McKinney was seriously injured in a bicycle accident. Paul Westhead succeeded him, and needing some help on the bench, he too, turned to Riley. Westhead coached the team to a championship in 1980, but soon alienated his star player, Magic Johnson, and found himself without a job early in the '81–'82 season. Riley replaced him.[11]

Riles knew he had a thoroughbred in Johnson and set him loose. Johnson and the "Showtime" Lakers ran their way to four championships over the next seven seasons, including back-to-back titles in 1987 and 1988.

As the pressure to repeat and then "three-peat"[12] mounted, Riley cracked the whip harder. Practices grew longer, and the coach alienated his players by attempting to keep their wives and girlfriends away from the team.[13] By his own admission, Riley's ego had grown "totally out of control."[14] The Lakers lost their edge, falling to the Detroit Pistons in the '89 Finals, before failing to reach the Finals in 1990. The players stopped responding to Riley's demands, and he resigned after the '89–'90 season.

Despite his success and high profile, Pat fancied himself a simple man. "I'm just a basketball coach," he liked to say. Riles accumulated some Hollywood friends over the years, such as actor Michael Douglas (whose Gordon Gekko character from the movie *Wallstreet* Riley was often compared to) and director Jerry Bruckheimer, though his best friends remained his buddies from high school.[15]

On the rare occasions when Pat was not obsessing about basketball, he enjoyed spending time with his family, collecting antique cars and listening to music, especially Motown. He traveled the world to see his favorite singer, Bruce Springsteen, in concert.[16]

If "The Boss" was "Born to Run," Riley was born to coach. Within weeks of leaving the Lakers, Pat began fantasizing about coaching the Knicks while running on the beach in Los Angeles. He thought about the style of play he would implement and how he would coach individual players like Ewing, Oakley, and Jackson. He even imagined riding a championship float down the Canyon of Heroes in Lower Manhattan. Riley worked as a commentator for NBC that season in their New York City studio and covered as many Knicks games as possible, providing him with an opportunity to scout the team.[17]

The Knicks fired general manager Al Bianchi in early March and hired Dave Checketts as team president the same day. Checketts, a devout Mormon, grew up in Bountiful, Utah, a suburb of Salt Lake City. He played basketball at BYU while earning his MBA. Standing 6-foot-5 with a thick head of blond hair, blue eyes, and rosy cheeks, he made everybody he talked to feel like the most important person in the room. Checketts befriended Commissioner Stern as a young man while working for the Boston consulting firm Bain Capital. On Stern's recommendation, he was hired as president of the Utah Jazz at just 28 years old. He later ran NBA International for a couple years.[18]

When Checketts took the Jazz job, his older brother Larry helped him move. Larry rode in the back of the pickup. He lost his balance, fell out of the truck and landed on his head. Larry died six days later. Checketts was devastated and decided to live his life in tribute to his brother.

Checketts wanted to rebrand the Knicks and turn them into the hottest ticket in town. He imagined a courtside celebrity row that rivaled the one at Lakers games during the Showtime era. His first move was to spruce up the in-game entertainment with the addition of the Knicks City Dancers.[19]

Checketts also wanted to win, and his bosses at the Garden and Paramount were fully on board. Two weeks after hiring Checketts, Paramount named movie producer Stanley Jaffe president of the company. "When I got there, the Knicks' five-year plan said they would reach round two in five years," said Jaffe. "It was all about how do we look good and not spend money, and of course, you can't do that." Jaffe, a lifelong Knicks fan, and Garden president Bob Gutkowski allowed Checketts and his underlings to do their jobs and take risks.[20]

Checketts became acquainted with a number of NBA coaches during his time in the league's front office, Riley being one of them. The two had lunch together two months before Checketts landed the Knicks job, at which time Riley asked Checketts, "Why don't you go fix the Knicks?" Checketts countered by asking if Riley would join him, and Riley said he would think about it. When Riley called Checketts to congratulate him on being named president of the Knicks, Checketts reminded him of their conversation. Riley said he might be interested if the coaching job were to become available.[21]

A couple of months later, Riley ran into Pitino in Lexington, Kentucky, at a celebration for the 25th anniversary of the 1966 Kentucky team. The former Knicks coach asked Riley if he planned to coach again, and Riley said yes. Pitino called his friend and former neighbor, Jaffe, and informed him Riley was available.[22]

The Knicks finished the season 39–43 and were swept in the first round of the playoffs. MacLeod was subsequently let go. Tom Penders, Doug Collins, and Paul Silas were considered for the job, though Checketts had his eyes set on Riley.[23]

Jaffe recalls walking down Park Avenue with Riley after one of the early meetings with the coach and seeing several cab drivers roll down their windows to scream, "Come to New York, Pat."[24] After a series of negotiations, the Knicks offered Riley a five-year, $6 million contract with limousine service and other perks that would bring his salary close to $2 million per year.[25]

It was the job Riley had been fantasizing about for a year, an opportunity to coach one of the league's marquee franchises. He had a chance to quiet the naysayers who attributed the Lakers' success to players such as Kareem, Magic, and James Worthy, rather than their coach.

Still, Riley was apprehensive about taking the job without a guarantee Ewing would be there. He was not interested in a full rebuilding job. Ultimately, it was an opportunity he could not pass up.

Riley held his first training camp in Charleston, South Carolina. His biggest challenge was rebuilding the team's shattered confidence. Over the previous year, the players had endured two coaching changes, bickering in

Dave Checketts (left) presented Pat Riley with a silver apple from Tiffany's at the press conference introducing Riley as the new coach of the Knicks on May 31, 1991 (AP Photo).

the locker room, and near-constant trade rumors. Riley believed discipline and professional work habits would foster a winning culture.

Jaffe recalls attending that first practice: "I'll never forget observing it and watching him [Riley] and watching the players. And they were rapt. They were hanging on every single word he said and he spoke softly to them. And at that point I knew this was the right guy."[26]

The first thing Riley told his new players was "We were gonna become the hardest-working, best-conditioned, most professional, most unselfish, toughest, nastiest team in the league."[27] Unlike most coaches, Riley had the resolve to hold his players to that standard. He demanded complete focus and effort at all times.

Dave Wohl, who served as an assistant under Pat in Los Angeles, recalls the Lakers having the best practice he ever witnessed until they ran out of steam in the last 10 minutes. Wohl commented to Riley about what an incredible practice it was, and Riley replied, "They just didn't bring it today." An incredulous Wohl asked Riley what he meant. Wohl recounted how the players fought for rebounds, talked on defense, and ran the break to perfection.[28]

Riley said, "They didn't have it in the last 10 minutes. Dave, those were the most important minutes. Those are the fourth quarters of playoff series and the Finals, and you've got to fight through to bring it in those minutes."[29]

Riley abandoned the fast-paced style he had so much success with in Los Angeles in favor of a grind-it-out, half-court offense that best-suited his personnel in New York. The coach wanted his new team to emulate the "Bad Boys" Pistons that dethroned his Lakers. New York's forte would be defense, and they would intimidate the rest of the league with their effort and physicality. Riles instituted a "no layup rule," which he first used against the Celtics in the 1984 Finals. If an opposing player attacked the basket, he was to be fouled and earn his two points at the foul line, rather than be allowed an easy layup or dunk.[30] Riley did not want his players fraternizing with their opponents, on or off the court. He fined them $500 for helping up a player on an opposing team.[31]

Prior to the '92–'93 season, the Knicks' marketing department showed Riley pictures from a proposed advertising campaign that depicted an overhead view of the basket and a chalk outline of a dead body in the lane. The image and accompanying slogan, "Tough town, tough team," had gone too far, Riley told them.[32]

The coach led marathon practices, which often ran three or four hours and were scripted down to the minute. Training camp included two practices per day and typically involved several consecutive "17s" (a grueling conditioning drill, which required players to run from sideline to sideline 17 times in a minute). Rookies faced an initiation ritual known as the "gauntlet," in which veterans formed a path and delivered forearms and other shots to them as they ran through.[33]

Bill Sharman, a Celtics legend and the coach of Riley's Lakers in the early '70s, invented the morning shootaround, a light walkthrough the day of a game intended to discourage players from staying out too late the night before.[34] Teams still use them. Riley did not even allow his players to use the term "shootaround."[35] Instead, he led full practices on game day.

The controlling coach instilled an "us vs. them" mentality in his players, which depicted the media and management, in addition to their opponents, as the other. He was obsessive about preventing players from leaking information to the press.[36]

Practices were closed. Reporters were not allowed in the locker room at the team's practice facility at SUNY Purchase. Beat writers had to wait in the parking lot and try to talk to the players as they walked to their cars after practice. Riley also banned reporters and broadcasters from the team bus and plane.[37]

The coach ramped up the intensity at practice by verbally challenging his players, which often led to altercations. According to point guard Greg Anthony, "We had a fight minimum once or twice a week in training camp."

Those clashes built respect and prepared them to fight together when they faced other teams.[38]

Riley planned team-building activities, such as gatherings at his house for the players and their families. He often referred to the team as a family, and guard John Starks credits the coach for creating a family-like atmosphere in the locker room, with relationships that exist to this day.[39] Corey Gaines, who spent one season with the Knicks, said of his teammates, "We were close to everybody. It was you against the world."[40]

Pat was also a master motivator. Jim Cleamons, who was a teammate of Riley's with the Lakers and coached against him as an assistant with the Bulls, said of Pat, "If it's in you, he's going to get it out of you."[41] Riley gleaned psychological tactics from his wife, Chris, a therapist, for maximizing the productivity of his players.[42]

Sometimes he played mind games, like turning his back on a player in an elevator, or sending messages through the media.[43] After one loss late in the 1993–94 season, Riles ranted about how "abominable" his team played, then stormed out of a press conference without taking questions.[44]

Other times, he challenged his players directly. During a game in Philadelphia, Greg Anthony took an ill-advised three-point shot early in the possession. He missed, resulting in a long rebound, which led to a 76ers fast break and two points for the home team.

Riley immediately called a 20-second timeout. His players sat on the bench, looking at their coach for instructions, but Riley did not say a word. He just glared at Anthony. Finally, as the timeout was coming to an end, Riley screamed at Anthony, "What the fuck were you thinking?"[45]

Then there were Riley's memorable speeches. Unlike Gene Hackman in the movie *Hoosiers*, NBA coaches do not deliver stirring speeches before every game. Players would grow tired of that and tune them out. Coaches save their motivational talks for special occasions.

Riley delivered a passionate, riveting address for 10 to 15 minutes before each and every one of the team's 82 games. "Riles was like listening to Martin Luther King or Gandhi speak every game," said point guard Doc Rivers.[46] He frequently had notes for his speeches, which included a moral purpose related to the game.[47] The coach often used war metaphors, comparing the team dynamic to being in the trenches.

Sometimes, he opted for symbolic gestures to make his point. Prior to a game against the Portland Trail Blazers, Riley chastised his team repeatedly during practice for being soft. Instead of a pregame speech, he put on a video of violent images, including car crashes, rams butting heads, and boxing knockouts. Then, he turned it off and left the room without saying a word.[48]

One night after a loss, with his suit and tie still on, he talked about trust, then submerged his head into a bucket of ice water. Finally, after what seemed to everybody in the room like an eternity, assistant coach Dick Harter pulled the coach's head out. His eyes were watering and there was snot all over his face. Riley said he was not going to pull his head out until somebody saved him and he knew somebody would.[49]

Knicks broadcaster Mike Breen said, "Riley was the most focused person I think I've ever met in my life."[50] The coach was meticulous in his preparation, scripting every second of practice on a piece of stock paper he kept in his pocket. Every drill had a purpose. He tallied a variety of statistics, ranging from shots made to unconventional pieces of data, such as how often players boxed out or whether they ran down the court in transition.[51]

Riley's greatest strength was convincing players to buy into his vision for winning a championship. He encouraged his players to learn their role, then "become a superstar at their role."[52] That role might be nothing more than an effective practice player. Riles took the time to explain why he wanted his players to play a certain way, a detail many coaches neglected.[53] Even those who rode the bench bought into Pat's approach because of his pedigree and honesty.

Doug Christie was unhappy when the coach informed him on his first day with the team that he would not be in the rotation that season. However, he came to appreciate Riley's forthrightness, did not complain about playing time, and worked his butt off to find his niche in the league.[54]

Pat's players also responded to his exhortations because everything he said and did, from his rousing speeches to hours of film study, was geared toward winning.[55] Derek Harper, who played two seasons under Riley, said of his former coach, "He would give one of his arms to be a champion. And the way he went about it was he worked and worked and worked." Harper continued, "If you see a guy as a coach work like that, it forces you to want to do the same thing, put forth the same effort, challenge yourself the same way, going about things the right way."[56] Gaines believes Pat's players worked so hard because they did not want to disappoint him, the way a son does not want to disappoint his father.[57]

All Riley asked of his players was that they be "all in" and sacrifice everything they have for the team. He frequently lectured about the importance of players sharing a spirit of togetherness and subjugating their egos. Otherwise, he argued, the "Disease of Me" or "Disease of More" would destroy the team.[58]

At a team party at Riley's house, several of the guys entered a pool tournament for money. Harper was victorious and gifted his winnings to one of the ball boys. Riley was impressed by the gesture and took the opportunity to espouse his belief that success is not achieved by one person, but by trying to make those around you successful and by working together as a unit.[59]

In return for his players' sacrifices, Riley ensured everything for his team was first-class. Most teams stayed at Marriotts on the road. The Knicks rested their heads on pillows at the Four Seasons. Riley told journalist Mark Kriegel: "I want to treat my players to the best. If I'm having a team party, I want white tablecloths, I want china, and I want silverware. I don't want fuckin' plastic plates. And I want a flower arrangement in the middle. And if the towels are hotel white, hey, put some color in there, I don't give a shit. I want my team to fly first-class, to stay in first-class hotels. I'm gonna ask them to do a lot. So tell me, is that wrong, wanting them to have the best?"[60]

3

Riley's Runts

"Plant your feet, stand firm, and make a point about who
you are."[1]—Lee Riley

Riley set a theme for his first season in New York: "Awaken the Giant."
He took the slogan from his friend Tony Robbins' book, *Awaken the Giant
Within*.[2] The giant Riley was referring to was New York City. New Yorkers'
love and appreciation for the game goes beyond that of most fans.

Bill Bradley once said, "I feel that they understood the game. They ap-
plauded the pass that led to the pass that led to the basket. It wasn't just the
basket."[3] Herb Williams, who played 18 seasons in the NBA, recalled, "When I
came here [New York], it was the first time I played on a team when I left the
game fans said, 'we won' or 'we lost.' He continued, 'Here, you always felt the
fans were a part of the team.'"[4]

With its rich history and prime location in Midtown Manhattan, Madi-
son Square Garden retained an aura that was evident to all who played there.
B.J. Armstrong of the Bulls once said, "There's nothing like a playoff game in
New York in the spring time."[5]

Riley played in the Garden during the Knicks' glory days. He understood the grandeur of the building and the way basketball could captivate
the city. If his team played inspiring basketball, the fans would carry them to
greater heights.

Riley saw Ewing, Oakley, and Jackson as the building blocks of the
team.[6] Ewing and Oak were two warriors in the prime of their careers. They
had exemplary work ethics and commanded the respect of their peers. Riley
liked Jackson's bravado and was confident the point guard would benefit from
a fresh start under his tutelage.[7]

Jackson starred at Bishop Loughlin High School in Brooklyn before attending St. John's University in Queens, where his Redmen advanced to the
Final Four in his sophomore season. The Knicks selected the point guard with
the 18th pick in the 1987 draft, and he flourished in Pitino's fast-paced offense.

Jackson's agent, Don Cronson, used to say Mark "turned the lights back on in the Garden," with his exuberance and flashy passes.[8] The local kid averaged 13.6 points, 10.6 assists, and 2.5 steals per game and was named Rookie of the Year. The following season, he averaged 16.9 points and 8.6 assists per game, good enough to earn an All-Star selection.

Jackson struggled in a much slower offense under Stu Jackson that exposed his poor shooting. During the '90–'91 season, he was benched by John MacLeod in favor of Maurice Cheeks. The point guard requested a trade and was suspended in March after engaging in a shouting match at practice with MacLeod and general manager Al Bianchi.[9] He was anxious to prove he could still play at an All-Star level.

Rounding out the starting five were Gerald Wilkins at shooting guard and McDaniel at small forward. Wilkins, the younger brother of Hall of Famer Dominique, was a second-round pick of the Knicks in 1985, out of the University of Tennessee at Chattanooga. His teammates called him "Dougie" after his favorite rapper, Doug E. Fresh.[10] Gerald was a great athlete who participated in a couple of slam dunk contests, but his shot was inconsistent, despite continuous efforts to improve it.[11]

McDaniel, known around the league as "X-Man," had a chip on his shoulder and never backed down from a fight. He had a shaved head, which was not yet in vogue that made him look particularly menacing. X-Man once strangled Wes Matthews, Sr., of the Lakers during an in-game altercation and tussled with Oakley during a game in 1989.

Throughout the NBA, rookies are assigned to a veteran and must do whatever that veteran asks of them, from carrying his bags to picking up a hamburger. In Gary Payton's rookie season with the Seattle SuperSonics, he was assigned to McDaniel. One day, the feisty point guard decided he was tired of McDaniel's demands and refused to do what he was told. X-man grabbed Payton by the neck during practice and put him in a sleeper hold with all of their teammates watching. He did not let go until the rookie was about to pass out. Payton never talked back to McDaniel again.[12]

At 6–7, X-Man could score down low with a strong post game or step out and hit the jumper. Put a power forward on him, and X would use his quickness to beat him off the dribble. If he was covered by a small forward, he would outmuscle him in the post. He also posed a threat on the fast break.

X was the first player to lead the nation in scoring and rebounding during his senior season at Wichita State, and the Sonics selected him with the fourth pick in the 1985 draft. He averaged better than 20 points per game in four of his first five seasons, before being traded to the Phoenix Suns during the 1990–91 season.

X never had the same lift after undergoing knee surgery in 1988 and had drifted farther from the basket, though he still averaged 17.0 points and 6.9 rebounds during the '90–'91 season. The day before training camp, New York acquired him for Jerrod Mustaf, Trent Tucker, and two second-round draft picks. Riley envisioned X-Man as the consistent second scorer Ewing lacked throughout his career.

McDaniel was apprehensive about playing with Oakley because of their fight. On the first day of practice, Riley showed the team a highlight reel and in the middle of it was the battle between X and Oak. The team started laughing. Riley said, "Now we fight together." X and Oak were cool after that.[13]

By the time the regular season began, the Knicks were a confident and hungry bunch. The games seemed like a vacation compared to Riley's three-hour practices. New York's goal was to win the Atlantic Division, and an aging Celtics team appeared to be the only thing standing in their way.

The Knicks established their identity on defense, where they played an aggressive, attacking style designed by assistant coach Dick Harter. They blitzed pick-and-rolls, double-teamed the low post, and used their hands to direct ball-handlers where they wanted them to go.

The offense ran through Patrick, who made the players around him better by drawing double-teams. McDaniel provided an additional post threat, and Riley relied on Jackson's leadership at point guard. New York's glaring weakness was shooting. Jackson's shot was unreliable and the two shooting guards, Wilkins and John Starks, were streaky.

New York received a boost from its second unit, which was led by three fiery competitors, Starks, Mason, and Greg Anthony. Starks and Mason were journeymen trying to carve out a niche in the league. The three youngsters impressed the coaching staff during summer league and training camp and carried the bulk of minutes off the bench.

Starks was born and raised in Tulsa, Oklahoma. His father left home when he was a little boy. One of seven siblings, his family was often on welfare and moved a lot. He slept two to a bed on bunk beds and wore hand-me-down shoes that were too small for his feet. John often had to steal food to keep from going hungry.[14]

There was a rule in the Starks home: Never back down from a fight. If John lost a fight as a kid, his older brother, Monty, would make him track down the kid and fight him again until he won.[15]

Riley could relate. When Pat was nine years old, his father told his brothers to take him to Lincoln Heights, a park in Schenectady where they played baseball, football, and basketball. His brothers threw him into a game. Pat struggled to compete and was beaten up. He was so ashamed that he ran home, hid in the garage, and cried.[16]

This went on day after day, until one night Pat stayed in the garage and did not come to dinner. His father asked where he was, and Pat's brothers explained what had been going on. Pat's father told his older sons to get Pat.[17]

Pat's oldest brother, Lee, said, "Dad, why do you make us take him down there? He doesn't want to be there. He's only nine years old. He doesn't like the game. Every day, he goes down there, gets beat up, and runs home crying."[18]

Pat's father said, "I make you take him down there because I want you to teach him not to be afraid." He explained that everybody at one time must take a stand and make a point about who they are and what they believe in. And they must do it alone. Mrs. Starks also wanted her son to take a stand.[19]

John was 5-foot-10 and had only played two games of high school basketball when he graduated. (He quit his senior year in order to get a job and help support the family.) He enrolled in five colleges over the next five years, playing ball at three of them. Two of the schools kicked him out for stealing a stereo and smoking marijuana.[20]

In between stints at Northern Oklahoma College and Oklahoma Junior College, Starks worked the graveyard shift at Safeway supermarket in Tulsa for $3.35 an hour. The NBA could not have seemed further away, but his love of the game propelled him forward.[21]

Starks sprouted to 6-2 in college. There was no denying his athletic ability, and he played with tremendous determination. The shooting guard was so dedicated to basketball that he cut his wedding short to play in a junior college game. "I drove from the reception in Tulsa to a small town about an hour and a half away," Starks recalled. "Picked up a speeding ticket, scored about 30 points in that half."[22]

Leonard Hamilton, then the coach at Oklahoma State University, saw one of Starks' games at Oklahoma Junior College and offered him a scholarship, even though he had only one year of eligibility remaining. Starks averaged 15.4 points per game in his lone season at OSU, but was not drafted.

Larry Brown coached the Kansas Jayhawks to the national championship in 1987–1988. The Jayhawks played Starks' team three times that season. Brown, who was hired by the San Antonio Spurs after the season, was so impressed by Starks he invited the guard to play for the Spurs' summer league team. After summer league, Brown extended Starks an invitation to training camp, but Starks turned him down because there was no guaranteed money.[23]

Don Nelson invited the young guard to the Warriors' training camp, and Starks made the team, but was stuck on the bench behind rookie Mitch Richmond. Nellie cut Starks at the end of the season, calling the shooting guard "too wild." Starks spent the '89–'90 season playing for the Cedar Rapids Silver Bullets of the CBA, where he was suspended for five games for bumping a referee, a move that damaged his reputation in the eyes of many NBA front offices.[24]

Bianchi liked what he saw from Starks in the 1990 Summer League and invited the guard to training camp. Starks was a long shot to make the team. New York had five guards signed to guaranteed contracts. During a scrimmage on the last day of training camp, John stole the ball and drove down the right wing, with a streaking Ewing chasing him down. He was having a strong training camp, but thought he needed to do something spectacular to impress the coaching staff, so he tried to dunk over the big man. Ewing met him at the rim and blocked his attempt. Starks landed awkwardly and sprained his knee.[25]

The Knicks were forced to place Starks on injured reserve, and by rule, a team cannot cut a player who is on IR. Jeff Van Gundy, then an assistant coach with the Knicks, later told Starks that Stu Jackson and his coaches planned on cutting him that day. They viewed him as a CBA journeyman. Then, fate intervened.[26]

In late December, another injury aided Starks. This time, Trent Tucker injured himself just when Starks was ready to return, providing him a shot with the team. The shooting guard contributed 20 points, six rebounds, four assists, and two steals against the Hawks in his second game with the Knicks. Given the chance to stick with the team for the rest of the season, the guard averaged 7.6 points per game.[27]

Starks' game was raw. He played at full speed all the time, had questionable shot selection, and was reckless with the ball. Still, Riley recognized his talent and loved his competitive spirit. Accordingly, he gave the gunslinger free rein, and Starks fired away with his shot and his mouth. The Tulsa native who was laid back away from the game talked trash constantly whether in practice, games, the locker room, or on a bus or plane. If he won a shooting drill in practice, his teammates would hear about it for the next week.[28]

Riley called Starks "Feast or Famine," because he could shoot you in or out of a game. However, the coach stuck with his protégé even when he was not hitting shots because of his intensity, particularly on the defensive end. Riley praised him so often Starks' teammates began referring to him as "Riley's son." The coach admitted years later Starks was the player he coached who reminded him most of himself.[29]

Ewing called Starks "Pinky," because he had pink lips and the nickname caught on with some of their teammates.[30] John also had a baby face, which endeared him to the younger Knicks fans. Director Spike Lee, the team's unofficial mascot, began wearing a Starks jersey courtside. His was just one of many No. 3 jerseys sprinkled throughout the Garden crowd.

Anthony Mason took an even more roundabout journey to the league. Mason grew up playing football and baseball in Springfield Gardens, Queens. He first dreamed of becoming a "mean, black left-hand pitcher with a nasty hook and a scowl" for the Yankees. When the high school he attended didn't have a football team, he took up basketball during his junior season. He was the sixth man on a team that won the New York City championship.[31]

Mason was one of the hardest workers his high school coach, Ken Fiedler, had ever seen. If Fiedler told him to do 80 push-ups a night, Mason would do 160. However, Fiedler never imagined the lanky, relatively unskilled forward would go on to play basketball professionally.[32]

Mase played college ball at Tennessee State University, where he averaged 28.0 points per game in his senior season, when his chest and shoulders ballooned to cartoonish proportions. He was drafted in the third round by the Portland Trail Blazers in 1988, but failed to make the team, which already boasted Jerome Kersey and Mark Bryant at power forward.[33]

Willis Reed, then the general manager of the New Jersey Nets, invited Mason to camp in '89, and the burly forward played 21 games for the Nets that season. After that, Mase played in Turkey, Venezuela, Denver (for just three games during the '90–'91 season), Tulsa (in the CBA), and finally, Long Island as part of the USBL.[34]

Mason credited his world tour with making him a better player. He learned his ball-handling skills on the streets of New York City, how to play physical in Turkey, where they did not call fouls, and the finesse game in Venezuela, where hand-checking was illegal.[35]

In the summer of '91, Ed Krinsky, GM of the Long Island Surf, informed longtime Knicks scout Fuzzy Levane that he had something special in Mason. Levane scouted the forward and invited him to play for the Knicks' summer league team. Prior to summer league, Knicks assistant coach Paul Silas coached Mase in the Maurice Stokes charity game at Kutsher's Hotel and pushed Ernie Grunfeld to sign the massive forward. Grunfeld and Checketts inked Mason to a two-year deal before summer league to prevent another team from poaching him.[36]

The journeyman came to training camp wanting to prove he belonged in the NBA. In addition to slugging it out with X-Man, he refused to back down from Ewing and Oakley.[37] Mase wore a nasty scowl on the court to go with his intimidating physique. His tenacity made quite an impression on Riley.

Mase was ahead of his time, a "position-less player" before the term was invented. He had remarkable handles and excellent court vision for a big man, which enabled him to initiate the offense in the backcourt or out of the post. At 6 feet 7 inches, 250 pounds, the massive forward was a load on the low block, could finish with either hand, and moved with the agility of a man 50 pounds lighter. Mase's rare combination of size, strength, and quickness allowed him to defend all five positions. Riley would later compare him to LeBron James, for his multiple skills and ability to play all over the floor.[38]

The most glaring weakness in Mason's game was his awkward jump shot and poor free-throw shooting, both of which he worked diligently to improve upon throughout his career. He pushed the ball upward like a shot putter before snapping his wrist.

New Yorkers related to Mason and Starks because of their humble backgrounds and scrappy demeanor. They were not blessed with the talent of many of their NBA peers, nor were they doted upon since the moment they reached puberty. Mase and Starks were underdogs who came to represent the grit of Riley's Knicks.

Media outlets began doing feature stories on their journeys to the league. Every Knicks fan knew Starks was bagging groceries a couple years earlier. Meanwhile, Mason's latest haircut was a regular topic of conversation. The New York tabloids even did pieces on Mase's barber, Freddie Avila, in Jamaica, Queens. Mase gave Avila free rein to use his head as a canvas. In turn, Avila shaved different messages such as Dogg Pound, Whatyagonna Do?, Point God, Mase, Knicks, In God's Hands, Back to D, and an image of the NYC skyline.[39]

Mason's hair even made it into a song by the New York rap group Beastie Boys on the track "B-Boys Makin' with the Freak Freak." Mase also appeared in an episode of the Fox television show "New York Undercover." Starks received a shout-out of his own in the Beastie Boys track "Get it Together," when Mike D compared his own heart to that of the Knicks guard.[40]

Starks and Mason bonded over their difficult journeys to the league, which Starks believes gave them a different perspective than most NBA players. They were able to see through the often-cutthroat nature of life in the league and keep their teammates loose with humor.[41]

Mason was like a big kid who enjoyed pulling childish pranks on his teammates. He once told ball boy Steve Masiello to turn the showers at the Garden on in a specific order after the game. It was too late when Masiello realized he had closed himself in. Doug Christie recalls Mase standing behind Coach Riley and making funny faces at Christie while Riley was talking to him.[42]

Starks and Mason were joined on the bench by rookie point guard Greg Anthony. Anthony was the Knicks' first-round pick in 1991, selected 12th overall. He registered a stellar collegiate career at the University of Las Vegas, Nevada, where he, Larry Johnson and Stacey Augmon won the NCAA Tournament in 1990. They went on to win their first 34 games the following year before being upset by Duke in the Final Four. Greg, Stacey and Larry all wore No. 2 in the NBA in honor of their college coach, Jerry Tarkanian.[43]

Anthony's shot needed work, he struggled to finish around the basket, and he occasionally made poor decisions with the ball, but he was a relentless defender, and the Knicks were a defensive team. The point guard also embodied the competitive spirit for which Riley was looking. Anthony broke his jaw in two places during a game against Fresno State in his junior season at UNLV. He showed up to practice the next day with his jaw wired shut and played in the team's next game a few days later.[44] New York traded Cheeks to the Atlanta Hawks at the beginning of training camp and turned over the backup point guard duties to Anthony.

New York started the season slowly, and in late January, Riley addressed an issue that had been festering in the locker room. When he took the job, Riley heard that the Knicks players did not get along with one other, and he noticed different cliques within the team.[45]

Riley brought his players to a conference room at the hotel where they were staying for a game against the Warriors and asked them to sit down in chairs in the middle of the room. Then, he sent each player to a corner of the room according to that player's clique. The coach then led an hour-long discussion about the "Disease of Me," how selfishness can destroy the spirit of tolerance, openness, and understanding that make up a functioning team.[46]

Riley didn't allow issues in the locker room to fester. "It was one of the qualities that made Riley an excellent leader. He always tackled issues within the locker room head on, rather than looking the other way," said Van Gundy, who served as Riley's assistant for four seasons. "And unlike most coaches, he preferred to air his grievances out in the open instead of calling a player or players into his office."[47] The Knicks won eight of their next nine games after Riley's conference room talk.[48]

New York played the type of defense Riley demanded, suffocating ball-handlers and punishing anybody who dared enter the paint. The Knicks finished second in opponents' points scored at 97.7 per game, and Ewing, Oak, Mase, and McDaniel controlled the defensive backboards. Scoring was a different story.

Ewing played in typical all-star form, averaging 24 points, 11.2 rebounds, and 3.0 blocks per game, and Jackson bounced back with 8.6 assists per game, but the team lacked a consistent second scorer. Starks placed second on the team with 13.9 points per game, though "Feast or Famine" was not reliable.

X-Man contributed 13.7 points per game, yet there were stretches when you forgot he was on the court. Veteran Kiki Vandeweghe could still fill it up, but Riley refused to play him significant minutes because he was a defensive liability.

Still, the Knicks appeared to have the division locked up in March. They were up seven games on the Celtics three quarters of the way through the season, and five ahead with eight games remaining. Then, New York lost five of its final eight. The Knicks and Celtics both finished the season 51–31. Boston won the tiebreaker, having taken the season series from the Knicks, 3–2. As the fourth seed in the Eastern Conference, the Knicks landed the Detroit Pistons in the first round of the playoffs.

Detroit was the ultimate matchup for a Knicks team that prided itself on being the toughest, most physical, best defensive team in the league. Chuck Daly's team had earned the moniker "Bad Boys" for its aggressive play. The Pistons' core players were beginning to show their age by the '91–'92 season. Most prominently, Bill Laimbeer and Mark Aguirre missed many games due to injury. Yet Detroit still managed to surrender the fewest points per game that season and a hall of fame backcourt of Joe Dumars and Isiah Thomas, the league's leading rebounder in Dennis Rodman, and the team's championship pedigree, made it a formidable foe.

The Knicks sent a message in Game 1 of the series, demolishing the Pistons, 109–75, at the Garden. The proud Pistons bounced back two days later to steal Game 2, 89–88. Neither of the first two games at Madison Square Garden sold out. That would soon change. Ewing shot a dismal 5-of-20 from the field in Game 2, though he rebounded in Game 3, dominating Laimbeer with 31 points and 19 rebounds, while carrying the Knicks to a 90–87 overtime victory.

New York opened Game 4 with a 31–21 lead, a promising chance to close out the Pistons at the Palace at Auburn Hills, when Detroit erupted with a 28–4 run, led by Dumars. The Pistons held on for an 86–82 win, sending the series back to New York for a decisive Game 5. Detroit hung around in the final game, pulling within two points with eight minutes remaining. Then, Ewing sparked a 9–1 run with two easy buckets and a big blocked shot, which gave the Knicks some breathing room. They finished ahead, 94–87.[49]

Isiah and Laimbeer recognized the Bad Boys had been beaten at their own game. Thomas said the Knicks were the more physical team, and Laimbeer was uncharacteristically complimentary of his opponent. "This series established that they are a big, giant, monstrous, physical basketball team," the 7-footer said.[50] New York held Detroit to just 84.8 points per game, the fewest points scored by a team in a five-game series since the inception of the shot clock in 1954.

Ewing led the way with 23.4 points, 11.0 rebounds, and 3.0 blocks per game. The emergence of McDaniel was a pleasant surprise for the Knicks. X, who had been inconsistent all season, played with a newfound ferocity. He averaged 19 points and grabbed 9.0 boards per game for the series.

4

Running with the Bulls

"We were either gonna win the game or win the fight."
—Anthony Mason

Next up for the Knicks were the defending champion Chicago Bulls, led by the game's premier player, Michael Jordan. Jordan left UNC after his junior season and was selected by the Bulls with the third pick in the 1984 draft. Since then, he had transcended the game of basketball with the help of a brilliant Nike advertising campaign, becoming an international icon with his own Jumpman insignia. Jordan was a tremendous athlete with remarkable talent, excellent footwork, and an assassin's mentality, who put constant pressure on defenses by relentlessly attacking the basket. And he was arguably the best defensive player in the game, to boot.

MJ won his sixth consecutive scoring title in 1992, at a clip of 30.1 points per game and had just been named MVP for the third time. He validated all of his individual accomplishments the previous season by winning his first NBA championship. Still, he was hungry for more.

Jordan and Ewing were old friends. They first met while visiting UNC at the same time during their senior year in high school. UNC coach Dean Smith planned it, hoping to land both recruits. MJ knew of Ewing, the most sought-after high school player in the country, but Ewing had never heard of the cocky, skinny kid from North Carolina.[1]

The two hit it off immediately and played some pickup ball during the visit. Ewing remembered years later that Michael's legendary competitiveness was already on display. MJ attended UNC, but Ewing was scared off by a Ku Klux Klan rally that took place in North Carolina during his visit. The Big Fella opted for Georgetown.[2]

It did not take long for Michael and Patrick to meet again. UNC faced Georgetown in the 1982 National Championship game during Jordan and Ewing's freshman season. The Tar Heels trailed by one with 15 seconds remaining before Jordan hit an 18-foot shot from the left wing to give Carolina the lead. Georgetown brought the ball up the court, but Hoyas guard "Downtown" Freddie Brown accidentally passed it to the wrong team, essentially ending the game. Ewing had the better individual numbers—23 points and 11 rebounds, to Jordan's 16 points and nine boards—but Jordan came away with the win.

Two years later, Ewing and Jordan were teammates for the first time on the U.S. Olympic team. They played a lot of cards together that summer. A bunch of the players enjoyed wrestling during their free time, and one day Ewing and Jordan went at it. Jordan held Ewing in a headlock and would not release him until Ewing submitted. The following morning, Patrick could barely move his neck. He had to explain to his coach, the notoriously strict Bobby Knight, that he couldn't practice because he injured himself wrestling. The Big Fella recovered, and he and Jordan went on to win their first gold medal together.[3]

Ewing briefly contemplated skipping his senior season to enter the 1984 draft with Jordan. However, Patrick had promised his mother, who died of a heart attack during his junior year, that he would complete his education. Jordan and Ewing hired the same agent, David Falk, and pooled their resources in a few profitable business ventures.[4]

Bulls forward Scottie Pippen had developed into MJ's ultimate sidekick. Pip did not receive any scholarship offers coming out of high school as a 6-foot-1 point guard, so he walked on to the University of Central Arkansas team and sprouted to 6–8 during college. The SuperSonics selected him with the fifth pick in the 1987 draft and immediately traded him to the Bulls for Olden Polynice and future draft picks.

Pippen worked tirelessly on his skills and by the early 1990s had emerged as one of the premier all-around players in the game. He was a fantastic finisher in the open court with a versatile offensive game, who was willing to defer to MJ, though also capable of taking over for stretches. Scottie had an enormous wingspan, huge hands, and the foot speed of a guard, which enabled him to smother perimeter players. He was selected to the first of eight consecutive NBA All-Defensive First Teams that season.

Chicago also had two strong post defenders in Horace Grant and Bill Cartwright, and spot-up shooters who fed off of Jordan's double teams in John Paxson and B.J. Armstrong. Coach Phil Jackson had established a winning culture in Chicago by convincing MJ to share the basketball.

A trade between the Knicks and Bulls in the summer of 1988 would prove instrumental in shaping both squads. Chicago sent Oakley to the Knicks in exchange for Cartwright. The teams also swapped first- and third-round draft choices. The 7–1 Cartwright had been with the Knicks since the team selected him third overall in the 1979 draft. He had an unusually high release on his shot, but was an efficient scorer who averaged better than 20 points per game in each of his first two seasons.

Cartwright missed all but two games of Ewing's rookie season and some of the following year with a broken foot. When he returned, much to Ewing's chagrin, Knicks coach Hubie Brown tried a "Twin Towers" lineup that included them both, with Cartwright at center and Ewing at power forward. The latter disliked having to chase around power forwards like Xavier McDaniel and Terry Cummings.[5]

Pitino turned Cartwright into a backup center in 1987. The young coach wanted the Knicks to run up and down the floor and had little use for the slow-footed, oft-injured Cartwright.[6] The Knicks were in need of a power forward who could help Ewing on the boards.[7]

Oakley spent the first 10 years of his life in Alabama. His father died when he was nine years old, and his mother moved the family to Cleveland. Charles' maternal grandfather, Julius Moss, became his role model. Julius was the rock of the family, a hard-working farmer who never made excuses and always got the job done.[8]

"Charles literally made himself into a player," Loren Olson, his high school coach, told William Rhoden of the *New York Times*. "Natural athletic ability was not there. He learned from his mistakes, he worked, he worked, and he worked. We had no weight machines here, so he did push-ups, he did leg squats with someone on his back. He jumped rope, he jumped over chairs. He made himself into what you see today."[9]

Michael Jordan (left) and Patrick Ewing were friends dating back to their senior year in high school when both visited the University of North Carolina at the same time. On the court, they were fierce competitors (AP Photo/Fred Jewell).

Charles' options for college were limited because of academic issues, and he landed at a small school in Richmond, Virginia, named Virginia Union. The school's weight room was reserved for the football team, so Oakley used a barbell in the hallway outside of Coach Dave Robbins' office. If the team practiced for two hours, he would lift weights for an hour or two afterward.[10]

By Oakley's senior year, he had become an NBA prospect and as Robbins put it, "too big for his britches." Prior to a road game, Robbins stepped onto the team bus and asked the coaches if everybody was there. One of them answered, "Oak's not here." Not wanting to leave without his best player, Robbins stepped off the bus to make a phone call in order to buy some time. When he returned, Oak was on the bus. Robbins told Oakley after the game that if he were ever late again, he would leave without him. Oak laughed incredulously and said, "Yeah, okay, Coach."[11]

The next game, Robbins asked if everybody was on the bus. Once again, he was told Oakley was not there. The coach said, "Let's go." All of Robbins' players started yelling about Oak, but Robbins told the bus driver to keep going. The players thought Robbins was bluffing and would turn the bus around, but the coach did not relent. Oak has returned to Virginia Union several times since he left school and always tells that story, adding that he was not fined once for being late for practice or a game during his 19-year NBA career.[12]

"Big Fella," as Robbins called Oakley, averaged 24.3 points and a remarkable 17.3 rebounds per game for his senior season and was named Division II National Player of the Year. The Cavaliers selected him with the ninth pick in the draft and immediately traded him to the Bulls.

Oakley quickly emerged as an elite rebounder and excellent help defender for Chicago. He led the league in total rebounds in his second and third seasons, averaging 13.1 and 13.0 per game, respectively. He also served as Jordan's chief enforcer. Opposing players knew if they took a shot at Jordan, they would have to take it up with the Oak Tree.

Jordan took Oakley under his wing during Oak's rookie year. He invited him to be his guest during All-Star weekend, and the two started driving to games together. Oakley also grew close to Pippen, who was assigned to him as a rookie. Pippen came to view Oakley like an older brother.[13]

Bulls management believed Oakley became expendable after a strong rookie season by one of their first-round picks in the 1987 draft, Horace Grant, and Chicago desperately needed a starting center. Oakley and Jordan were at the Mike Tyson–Michael Spinks fight in Atlantic City when they heard about the deal. Reporters asked the two friends what they thought of the trade, and both responded, "What trade?"[14]

Jordan was furious the Bulls dealt his close friend and voiced his concerns publicly. "I don't know about trading a 24-year-old guy for a 34-year-old," he quipped. (Cartwright was actually 31 at the time.) Years later, Oak surmised that MJ must have known the deal was going down. He believes the Bulls would not have made a trade of that magnitude without consulting the greatest player on the planet.[15]

Oakley's mother, Corine, is a fabulous cook, and MJ and Pippen continued to go to her house for dinner after the trade when the Bulls played in Cleveland. Oak and MJ remained close. Oakley called Jordan when he was disappointed he did not make the All-Star team the following season.[16]

Meanwhile, MJ took out his frustration on Cartwright. He zoomed passes at the center to accentuate his poor hands and then complained about his inability to catch the ball. Cartwright eventually earned Jordan's respect and became a leader in the Bulls locker room. He fought through a bad knee to start at center for the Bulls and was particularly effective at bothering Ewing in the post, perhaps from insight gleaned from their time together in New York.[17]

In New York, Oakley became a franchise cornerstone for the next 10 years as the Garden crowd fell in love with the man who collected as many floor burns as baskets.

Oak's ability to control the defensive glass and whip outlet passes to the guards kick-started the Knicks' fast-paced offense during the lone season he played for Pitino. A succession of Knicks coaches never called a play for Oak, who made teams pay for double-teaming Ewing with a consistent outside shot. Despite a lack of athleticism, Oak was an elite help defender, relying on anticipation and effort to cut off angles to the hoop. "He protects the basket as well as anybody who's ever played the game," Jeff Van Gundy once said.[18]

Oakley stood 6-9, but due to poor balance and a negligible vertical leap, the sight of Oakley dunking was as rare as finding a parking spot in Midtown Manhattan—something his teammates teased him about mercilessly. He seemed to prefer diving into the stands or onto the court after a loose ball.

Oak once said, "If you want to win a championship, you need some thugs on your team." He was the Knicks' thug. Mike Breen noted, "He [Oakley] was one of the few guys that other players were scared of."[19]

If Oak felt you had disrespected him or one of his teammates, you were going to receive a hard foul or punches would be thrown. He took the no layup rule to an extreme, getting whistled for a league-high 10 flagrant fouls in the '92–'93 season alone, at a time when you had to practically rip a player's head off to be called for a flagrant.[20] (A flagrant foul was defined in 1992–93 as an "unnecessary and excessive foul" that could lead to injury.[21])

Charles Oakley was the Knicks' enforcer and vocal leader. He was also a fan favorite throughout his 10 seasons in New York (Al Messerschmidt via AP).

Oak's belligerence was not limited to games. He routinely engaged in scuffles during practice—after which he often grabbed a drink with his opponent—and had his share of altercations before and after games, including a brawl with teammate Sidney Green at 35,000 feet on a team flight.

During the 1994–95 season, Oakley knocked Tyrone Hill of the Cavaliers unconscious with one punch during pregame warm-ups. He then stood over Hill's prone body and yelled, "Listen, motherfucker, you better pay me and you better pay me soon." Hill owed him money from cards. Knicks assistant coach Bob Salmi was in the vicinity and described the punch as a "take a two-by-four from Home Depot and hit anything in the store with it kind of sound." (Gambling, especially on cards, was a regular activity among the Knicks. Spades, tonk, and blackjack were three popular games. Anthony claims there was sometimes as much as $50,000 to $60,000 in the pot. "There might be more pressure on the card games than what you dealt with on the floor."[22])

Despite his toughness, Oakley was very sensitive and has been described by numerous people in and around the Knicks organization as a "sweetheart." For Oak, no favor was too big for a teammate or friend. He provided ball boy Steve Masiello with his car and a driver for his eighth-grade dance.[23] When Doug Christie joined the team in 1994, Oak picked up the youngster and gave him a tour of New York City, pointing out all of the hot spots.[24]

In 1997, with the NBA All-Star Game in Oak's hometown of Cleveland, he played host to all of the Knicks writers in attendance. He retrieved them at their hotel in a white, stretch limousine and took them to Club Togo, a spot he purchased in his old East Cleveland neighborhood. After that, the reporters continued on to Oak's mother's house for an enormous, home-cooked meal. "He just wanted people to see who he was," said Barbara Barker of *Newsday*, who was touched by the gesture. "He showed us his prom picture. He didn't have any airs. He wasn't a snob."[25] Oak went out of his way to make female reporters Barker and Suzyn Waldman feel comfortable in the locker room. He once put a security guard up against a wall for giving Waldman a hard time about entering the Knicks' locker room prior to a road game.[26]

Riley appreciated Oak's work ethic and commitment to the team. One of his first moves upon taking over the Knicks was naming Oakley and Ewing co-captains. The coach said every coach needs "two or three allies, two or three guys who say yea to everything the coach says, even if, deep inside, they're thinking nay. Clearly, Patrick and Oak are our yes guys." Whereas Ewing led by example, Oakley would not hesitate to get in a teammate's face. His personality reflected his style of play: tough and straightforward. He held everybody accountable.[27]

Oak and Ewing got along well throughout their time together in New York, but they were not close friends. Not once did they have lunch together without others there. Oak held a bit of jealousy toward Ewing. Patrick was the face of the franchise, the first person reporters spoke to in the locker room after games. He received the most money and put up the most shots. Oak devoted as much work as Patrick, but received none of the accolades that came his teammate's way.[28]

Oak had a bit of a Yogi Berra quality to him. He had a unique way of talking, which more than one reporter referred to as "Oakspeak," with a slight accent from his early years in Alabama and a tendency to jumble metaphors. The forward also mumbled at times, which made him difficult to understand, though there was often wisdom in his words.

One of his favorite lines was "If it ain't broke, don't break it." Another Oakley-ism was "You know what they say about spilled milk—clean it up, go into the kitchen and get some more."[29]

His response to receiving the most flagrant fouls in the league was, "It's just like driving on a highway. The speed limit is 55 or 65, and you do 70, they'll pull you over. It's one of those things. I'll just have to keep my eye on the speed limit, keep my eyes on the road, and keep my eyes looking out for the cops. In my case, I have to keep my eyes looking out for the NBA."[30]

When asked about attacking Tyrone Hill for owing him money, Oak responded, "Like the IRS, they going to freeze your credit card, hold your passport, or put a freeze on your bank account. So after two, three years, I got fed up."[31]

Regardless of the delivery, Oak got his point across and teammates listened because they appreciated his loyalty and knew how respected he was throughout the organization. Van Gundy, who later became Oak's head coach, liked to know what Oak was saying to the media because the forward always had his finger on the pulse of the team.[32]

Oak also brought his teammates together with bonding activities off the court, such as inviting the guys to his house for dinner, where he did the cooking. Every time the Knicks traveled to Cleveland, the entire entourage, including the ball boys, equipment manager and any family members, were invited to Mama Oak's house for a massive home-cooked meal.[33]

Oak mentored new players on the team and particularly enjoyed teaching the younger guys how to dress. He took great pride in possessing the most eclectic Knick wardrobe since Walt "Clyde" Frazier, which featured loud colors such as fuchsia, crimson, and bright yellow. At one point, he had 18 pairs of exotic leather shoes in his closet, including two in green alligator. One day on the road, he and teammate Chris Childs came out of their hotel rooms wearing the same pastel peach suit. Furious, Oak went back to his room and changed.[34]

Nobody loved being a Knick more than Oak, and he enjoyed showing his teammates a good time in his adopted city. Bo Kimble, his teammate for one season in New York, called him "Mr. New York" because Oak knew everybody who was anybody and was a welcome guest at all of the hot clubs. You never knew whom you were going to meet when you went out with Oak.[35]

On one occasion, he took teammate Anthony Bonner out on a Sunday night to a popular club called Chaz and Wilson on the Upper West Side. They skipped the line because Oak was friends with the owner. Oak and AB ordered a bottle of champagne, but were told the bar had run out. Tupac Shakur had ordered every bottle of champagne in the place. The bartender told them if they wanted to drink champagne they had to talk to Tupac. So Oak and Bonner popped bottles of Crystal with Tupac. Oak hung out with Pac a few other times and regularly partied with Hip Hop personalities LL Cool J, Grand Puba, Kid 'n Play, and Chuck D.[36]

The Bulls-Knicks matchup also showcased two of the game's elite coaches: Riley versus Jackson. Both were excellent communicators and master motivators who experienced tremendous team success as players. Instead of controlling every aspect of the game and his players like Riley, Phil encouraged self-discovery on and off the court. He allowed his team to play through rough patches, rather than call a timeout when they appeared to come undone.[37]

Phil bought his players books and led group meditation sessions, an activity that earned him the nickname "Zen Master." His triangle offense, which was invented by Bulls assistant coach Tex Winter, was predicated on player and ball movement. It integrated the principles of interdependence Jackson admired in Buddhist and Native American cultures, as well as the style of play of his unselfish Knicks teams of the 1970s.[38]

That's right. Jackson had deep roots behind enemy lines. He was drafted the same year as Riley, 1967, in the second round by the Knicks. Like Riley, he was a marginal NBA player. All arms and legs, the gawky forward was a defensive specialist who came off the bench for the Knicks for 11 years before finishing his career with the New Jersey Nets. Jackson missed the entire '69–'70 season, the year of the Knicks' first championship, after undergoing spinal fusion. There were no assistant coaches at the time, so he served as Red Holzman's unofficial assistant, as well as the team's unofficial photographer. "He is the reason I am a coach, obviously," Jackson said of Holzman.[39]

Unlike Riley, Jackson did not begin his coaching career with a plum job. Holzman's protégé landed his first head coaching gig with the Albany Patroons of the CBA or "Cockroach League," as Jackson called it. The Patroons won a championship in 1984, Jackson's first year on the job. Still, no NBA team came calling. NBA executives were scared off by Jackson's reputation as an unorthodox hippie.[40]

When Jerry Krause became general manager of the Bulls in '85, he tried to secure Jackson a job on Stan Albeck's coaching staff. Jackson attended the interview in jeans, sandals, an Ecuadorian hat with a macaw feather in it, and a scruffy beard. Albeck wanted nothing to do with him. Two years later, Krause set up another interview for Jackson with then-coach Doug Collins. The Zen Master dressed to impress and received the job. It was just in the nick of time. With children to feed and a minuscule CBA salary, Jackson had been considering going to law school. Two years later, Phil was the head man in Chicago.[41]

There was still a piece of Phil's heart in New York. The coach owned a reversible leather coat with the Bulls' logo on one side and the Knicks' on the other. On a couple occasions, his name surfaced regarding coaching vacancies in New York before he became the head man in Chicago.[42]

When Jackson was named president of the Knicks in 2014, he addressed rumors about him coaching the Knicks in the late '80s. Phil interviewed for the job in '87 when the Knicks hired Pitino, and Pitino endorsed him as his replacement when he left the Knicks in '89. As Jackson told it, "[Bulls owner]

Jerry Reinsdorf approached me [because] there was some rumors that I was going to come to New York and take the job in '89 after Rick Pitino left, and he said, 'Would you rather coach the Knicks or would you rather stay here and coach the Bulls?'" Jackson concluded, "The Knicks could win a championship with Patrick Ewing. But the Bulls could win two or three with Michael Jordan." Three years later, Jackson was trying to guide Jordan to his second ring, while denying Ewing his first.[43]

Chicago went 67–15 during the 1991–92 regular season and swept Miami in the first round of the playoffs, behind 45.0 points per game from MJ. The Bulls appeared to be coasting on cruise control to back-to-back titles. To make matters worse, they had beaten the Knicks the last 14 times they played, including all four contests during the regular season and a sweep in the previous postseason. The Bulls held home-court advantage, and the Knicks had not won once at Chicago Stadium in their last 16 tries. Prognosticators did not give the Knicks much of a shot at knocking off the defending champs.

The Knicks couldn't match the Bulls' athleticism, so they had to rely on their size and physicality to control the backboards, clog the lane, and intimidate Jordan and company. Laimbeer was one of the few people to predict the Knicks would have a real chance of winning the series, with a caveat. "Hopefully, they'll be allowed to play that way against Chicago because that's their style of play," said Laimbeer. "And I think they'll beat Chicago if they're allowed to play like that."[44]

Riley and Jackson knew the officiating would be crucial to the series and both attempted to gain a psychological advantage with the referees through public statements. Riley tried to get inside the head of his own players as well, particularly Wilkins, who drew the assignment of trying to slow down Jordan. Wilkins called Riley "my biggest nightmare and best mentor." The coach told Wilkins he was the key to the Knicks beating the Bulls, then repeatedly accused him of being scared of Jordan, including once in front of the whole team. Wilkins was so obsessed with stopping Jordan that he kept a picture of the Bulls guard on the mirror in his bathroom so he could look at him every time he brushed his teeth.[45]

Riley liked to say, "You give a team respect by giving them no respect at all. And you go at 'em." His players showed Chicago the ultimate respect. New York singled out Pippen as a target for intimidation. There had been questions about Pippen's mental toughness dating back to the Bulls' showdowns with the Pistons, especially after he sat out Game 7 of the 1990 Eastern Conference Finals with a migraine.

McDaniel began his assault on Pippen before the series started, calling the Bulls a "one-man show." In Game 1, X talked in Pippen's face, connected on a hard forearm to Scottie's chest, and continued to bump, shove, and elbow the Bulls forward at every opportunity. Pippen complained to the refs to no avail, which only led to further taunts. "Quit whining and play the fuckin' game," McDaniel said.[46]

Oak contributed to the cause by hammering Cartwright for a flagrant foul early in the first quarter of Game 1. Ewing tallied 34 points, including a runner in the lane to put the Knicks up for good with 33 seconds left. New York took the first game in Chicago, 94–89, as Pippen walked off with a gimpy ankle.

MJ came out gunning in Game 2, scoring 15 straight points for the Bulls over a five-minute span in the first quarter. He finished with a game-high 27. Armstrong chipped in with 18 points off the bench, including two consecutive big buckets in the final two minutes after the Knicks had cut their deficit to one. The biggest difference between Games 1 and 2 was Chicago's defensive pressure, which forced the Knicks into 23 Game 2 turnovers. The Bulls emerged victorious, 86–78, despite 2-of-12 shooting from Pippen.[47]

Game 3 in New York saw more of the same, with Chicago winning, 94–86, behind 32 from Jordan. MJ had received some criticism from the media for not driving the ball to the basket against the hostile Knicks defense. On a breakaway, late in the first half, he took off from just inside the foul line. Only, he misjudged his jump and instead of throwing down a monstrous slam, Michael clanked the ball off the back of the rim so hard it landed at midcourt. The MSG crowd taunted Jordan with chants of "Michael."[48]

Jordan made up for it later in the game. With just over four minutes left in the fourth quarter, he recovered a loose ball, drove to the rim, and took off about five feet from the basket. Ewing shoved him, while X popped him in the face. Undeterred, MJ still managed to dunk the ball. After slamming it, he charged toward the fallen McDaniel and Ewing, emphatically pumping his right fist in the air. Pippen bounced back with 26 points, as the Bulls appeared to take control of the series.[49]

New York responded in Game 4 by returning to its hard-nosed style. The Knicks outrebounded the Bulls, 52–33, and knocked around the men in red at every opportunity. Jackson was ejected late in the third quarter for contesting the Knicks' aggressive play. McDaniel delivered 24 points and held Pippen to 4-of-13 shooting. New York evened the series with a 93–86 win. Through four games, they'd held the Bulls to an average of 88.8 points per game, 21.1 below their regular-season average.[50]

The verbal sparring between Riley and Jackson escalated after Game 4. When asked about his ejection, Jackson said, "They were tackling the dribblers. That's football, not basketball. So we tried to get that point across." The

Zen Master added, "I don't like orchestration. It sounds fishy, but they [the league office] do control who sends the referees. If it goes seven games, everybody will be really happy. Everybody will get the TV revenue and the ratings they want."[51]

Not wanting to cede an edge to his rival, Riley responded, "He's not respecting the fact that this team is playing with as much heart as any team has ever played with. What championship teams are all about, they've got to take on all comers. They don't whine about it." Riley was so insulted by Jackson's remarks about his team that he sent a note to the Bulls locker room before Game 6, informing Jackson that if his Bulls win the series he should not expect the customary congratulatory handshake from Riley.[52]

Michael was angry for Game 5. At one point in the second quarter, he and Ewing went face-to-face and exchanged words. MJ scored 37 points to Ewing's 14. Jackson's whining paid off. Chicago took 38 free throws and won the game 96–88.

In the playoffs a year earlier, Jordan spun baseline to escape a Starks and Oak trap and threw down a vicious dunk over Ewing. Prior to Game 6, Riley showed his players that dunk on a loop for several minutes. Then he ordered them to knock MJ down and take what they wanted.

The Knicks came out swinging. Pippen was driving to the basket in the third quarter when Starks clotheslined the Bulls forward, knocking him to the floor. It was a violent image, with Pippen's head going one way and his body another. Such a blow would result in an immediate ejection in today's NBA. Then, Starks was merely assessed a flagrant foul and a $5,000 fine.[53]

Pippen stayed down for a few minutes and looked woozy when he rose to his feet. When the Bulls went to the bench during a stoppage of play, Jordan pushed Phil aside and pointed his finger in Pippen's face. With controlled rage, Jordan exclaimed, "The next time you get the ball, you're going to jam it down their throat. Otherwise, you're going to answer to me."[54]

Ewing sprained his left ankle late in the third quarter, causing the Garden crowd to hold its collective breath as he was helped to the locker room.[55] The Knicks trailed by two at the end of the third quarter, with their star player nowhere to be seen. Minutes later, Ewing reappeared in a scene reminiscent of Willis Reed exiting the tunnel for Game 7 of the 1970 Finals. He scored 11 of his 27 points in the fourth quarter, and the crowd was as loud as it had been since the days of Reed. "Patrick played like a thoroughbred," said Jordan. X-Man added 24 points and 11 rebounds, and Starks outscored Jordan 27–21. New York won, 100–86.[56]

After the game, McDaniel criticized Pippen, who scored 13 points on 5-of-16 shooting: "He [Pippen] didn't want to drive because he felt myself or

Oak or Pat or someone was gonna knock the shit out of him. Just like the hit John Starks put on him."[57]

The Knicks had done the unimaginable, pushing the Bulls to a seventh game. Before the game, Riley unleashed one last psychological ploy. He told reporters, "There's no chance we can win Game 7. The sponsors, the fans, the press love the drama and exposure. Now, though, they don't want the lowly New York Knicks to beat the marquee-value world champion Chicago Bulls in seven games."[58]

Game 7 was played at Chicago Stadium, one of the most intimidating atmospheres in sports. The Bulls were the first NBA team to entertain the crowd with a theatrical introduction of the starting lineups. They featured the song "Sirius," a mysterious and menacing instrumental tune by the Alan Parsons Project, while flashing a spotlight on the Bulls logo on the Jumbotron.

Bulls public address announcer Ray Clay would begin, "Aaaand now, the starting lineup for your Chicago Bulls!" The crowd noise reached a crescendo as Clay finished the starting lineup with, "From North Carolina, at guard, 6–6, Michael Jordan!" Jordan once said, "I've never heard a word after 'Carolina.'"[59]

The entire scene came to represent the aura of greatness that surrounded the Bulls championship teams, striking fear into the hearts of their opponents, while galvanizing the home team and its fans. Jackson noted, "The Bulls, without question, used that intro as an intimidation factor against other teams. It was like giving spinach to Popeye."[60]

Michael shot early and often in Game 7. He scored 18 in the first quarter, had 29 by halftime, and ended the game with 42. He also settled all scores that night. X-Man was roughing Pippen up, as he had all series. McDaniel had outscored Pippen, 74–41, in Games 4 through 6, during which Pippen connected on just 13-of-39 shot attempts. Pippen's ankle had been bothering him, though McDaniel also took up space in his head.

Finally, in Game 7, Jordan stood up for Pippen as if he were his younger brother. Jordan and McDaniel stood forehead to forehead, exchanging heated words. Jordan could be seen on camera screaming, "Fuck you X!" as he walked away. Pippen had his best game of the series, turning in a triple-double with 17 points, 11 assists, and 11 rebounds.[61]

Riley claimed in his second book, *The Winner Within*, that he told Checketts, "Jordan will collect 10 free throws in the first period. And they'll suddenly put Patrick Ewing on the bench with a third foul early in the second period or else a fourth foul early in the third period." He was close.[62]

MJ was awarded eight foul shots, and with the Knicks down three early in the second half, Ewing drew three fouls in a minute and 35 seconds to give him four. By the end of the quarter, the Knicks trailed by 18. Ewing finished with 22 points, nine rebounds, and five fouls. Chicago won the game easily, 110–81.[63] The Bulls then eliminated the Cavaliers in the conference finals and went on to win their second consecutive championship by defeating the Portland Trail Blazers in six games.

That summer, Jordan and Ewing were Olympic teammates once again on the "Dream Team," the first group of professional basketball players to represent the United States, and possibly the greatest basketball team ever assembled. Jordan and his fellow lords of the rings, Magic Johnson and Larry Bird, enjoyed teasing Ewing, Charles Barkley, and Clyde Drexler about not winning an NBA championship. Jordan laid it on especially thick for his old friend and rival, Ewing. Patrick had lost to Michael in the National Championship game and three times in the NBA playoffs, though he remained confident he would, soon enough, beat Jordan and the Bulls en route to an elusive championship.[64]

5

Arranging the Pieces

"[Greg] Anthony should be suspended for the rest of the year. How can some scrub come off the bench in street clothes and take a cheap shot?"[1]—Kevin Johnson

Early in the 1992–93 season, Knicks rookie Hubert Davis showed up right on time for a team shootaround before a game against the SuperSonics. Riley pulled Davis aside and pointed to Sonics veteran Ricky Pierce, who was putting up shots on the other side of the court. Davis asked when the Sonics' shootaround was, and Riley said it was after the Knicks'. Pierce woke up early to shoot extra shots hours before his team's shootaround. Riley said to Davis, "Pierce is an All-Star, and it's his 12th or 13th year in the league. You're a rookie, and he's here before you." Then, he walked away.[2]

Riley once said of his Knicks: "The players have to understand that to win a championship is going to be the most difficult thing you've ever done in your life."[3] The coach expected his players to provide a level of focus and effort above and beyond that of the average NBA player. The Knicks bought into his message. They carried themselves like professionals, taking care of their bodies, putting in extra practice time, and remaining focused on their goal of winning a championship.[4]

New York was ahead of schedule, pushing the world champions to seven games in Riley's first year on the job. They expected to build on their success and make a run at a championship in 1993. The core was in place, and youngsters Mason, Starks, and Anthony had room for improvement. Management had two main personnel goals for the offseason: re-sign free agent Xavier McDaniel and add some shooting.[5]

McDaniel proved his worth in the playoffs after an up-and-down first season in New York. He scored consistently and embodied the aggressive attitude Riley was seeking. McDaniel had paid $500,000 to buy out the final two years of his contract during the previous winter in order to become a free

50

agent. He believes the team reduced his playing time during the second half of the season in order to keep his value down.[6]

New York was intent on signing X. Teams were allowed to go over the salary cap to re-sign their own players, so the Knicks attempted to acquire talent from other teams first before dealing with McDaniel. It was a decision they would come to regret.[7]

Ernie Grunfeld worked with Dave Checketts on the Knicks' personnel moves. Grunfeld is Jewish, and his parents were Holocaust survivors who resided in Romania. Each year, a certain number of Jewish immigrants were selected through a lottery system to leave Eastern Europe, where they were still treated like second-class citizens. The Grunfelds' year was 1964. Ernie was eight years old and did not speak a word of English when his family relocated to the United States. He learned the language while playing basketball on the playgrounds of Queens. Occasionally, his father took him to Knicks games at the Garden.[8]

After attending Forest Hills High School, Ernie teamed up with Bernard King to form a devastating scoring tandem at the University of Tennessee, known as "The Ernie and Bernie Show." Between his junior and senior seasons, Grunfeld won a gold medal as a member of the U.S. Olympic team. He was drafted by the Milwaukee Bucks in 1977 and spent nine seasons in the league as a marginal player, the last four with the Knicks.

After his playing career, Ernie worked as a color man on the Knicks radio and television broadcasts. Then he served briefly as an assistant coach under Stu Jackson after losing out to Jackson for the head job. Al Bianchi moved Grunfeld to the front office in 1990, and Checketts elevated Grunfeld to vice president of player personnel in '91. Two years later, he was named general manager.[9]

The mustachioed Grunfeld was bright and personable. He was direct with his subordinates, though always courteous, and was well respected throughout the Garden. Ernie could usually be found smoking a cigar at a desk in his office while contemplating the team's personnel. His first few moves—drafting Anthony, signing Mason, and trading for McDaniel—paid off. In the summer of '92, Grunfeld had his eyes set on a shooting guard.[10]

Starks and Wilkins, who was a free agent, were too inconsistent. Riley needed at least one shooting guard whom he could rely on to knock down an open shot when opposing teams double-teamed Ewing. The Knicks did not have the cap space to sign a starting-caliber shooting guard, so any significant veteran addition had to be acquired via trade.

Grunfeld targeted Sacramento's Mitch Richmond, Orlando's Dennis Scott, Dell Curry of the Charlotte Hornets, and Rolando Blackman of the

Dallas Mavericks. Once he discovered he would have to surrender at least one of the Knicks' core players to acquire Richmond or Scott, his focus shifted to Blackman and Curry.[11]

New York discussed Blackman with Dallas twice over the previous two seasons, but the Mavs' asking price was too high. When the Knicks began their pursuit of Blackman in 1991, Dallas wanted two first-round picks. In February '92, the Mavs asked for a first-round pick and Starks. The waiting game worked to the Knicks' advantage.[12]

The Mavericks finished the '91–'92 season with a 22–60 record and their core group of players, which had a great run in the mid- to late '80s, had either moved on or were on the downside of their careers. The Mavs were rebuilding and planned on selecting shooting guard Jimmy Jackson out of Ohio State University with the fourth pick in the draft. With the 33-year-old Blackman no longer part of their future, Dallas lowered its asking price to one first-round pick, and the Knicks pounced.[13]

Blackman was old school, from his professionalism to his tight shorts. He prepared for every game as if it were Game 7 of the NBA Finals. Ro attacked the basket frequently in his younger days, though over the previous few seasons operated primarily in the mid-range, where he was a knock-down shooter spotting up and coming off screens. Ro played 11 seasons for the Mavs, during which he was selected to four All-Star teams, and averaged over 20 points per game three times.[14] His 18.3 points per game average led the Mavs in '91–'92. Once a solid, if not spectacular, defender, his lateral quickness had begun to decline at age 33.

Blackman lived in Panama City for the first eight years of his life before beginning his basketball career at William E. Grady Career and Technical High School in Brooklyn. He became Kansas State University's second all-time leading scorer and was a starter on the United States' 1980 gold medal-winning Olympic team. Now he was coming back to New York.[15]

The same day the Knicks acquired Blackman, they added another shooter through the draft, selecting Hubert Davis, the nephew of All-Star Walter Davis, out of the University of North Carolina with the 20th pick. The 6-foot-5 shooting guard averaged 21.4 points per game in his senior season and remains UNC's all-time leader in three-point percentage. The knock on Davis was that he could not do much beyond shoot, though shooting was what the Knicks needed.

Davis said that upon being drafted, "I thought I was going to get broken in half. Just looking on TV and seeing how physical Mason, Oakley, Charles Smith, Patrick, John Starks, and Greg Anthony were."[16] New York was three deep at shooting guard (Starks, Blackman, and Davis) with free agent Gerald

Wilkins being the odd man out. Wilkins signed with the Cavaliers, and Riley wrote him a letter thanking him for his professionalism.[17]

Blackman restructured his contract when the Knicks acquired him, leaving New York with about $2 million in space under the salary cap. The Knicks were hoping to add a backup center and a small forward to pair with McDaniel. Then, they would address retaining McDaniel.[18]

New York's main target was Washington Bullets forward Harvey Grant. At 6–9, 225 pounds, Harvey was a little more slender than his twin brother, Horace. He showed steady improvement over his four years in the league and averaged 18.0 points and 6.7 rebounds for the Wizards in '91–'92. Grant was a restricted free agent, so the Wizards would have 15 days to match any offer sheet he signed with another team.[19]

On July 1, the first day of free agency, New York offered Grant a six-year, $17 million contract. The offer included a 15 percent increase in salary if Grant were traded during the life of the deal, which the Knicks hoped would dissuade the Bullets from matching. Grant desperately wanted the Wizards to let him go. He was excited about the idea of playing in New York City alongside Ewing. Alas, the Wizards matched the offer.[20]

The Knicks moved on to Plan B, Los Angeles Clippers forward Charles Smith. In late August, New York reached an agreement with the Clippers and the Orlando Magic on a three-way trade, which would send Smith, point guard Doc Rivers, and shooting guard Bo Kimble to the Knicks. New York would surrender Mark Jackson, its first-round draft pick in 1993, and a second-round pick in 1995. However, there was a snag in the deal.[21]

Center Stanley Roberts, who was supposed to go from the Magic to the Clippers as part of the trade, had a no-trade clause in his contract and refused to agree to the deal. Orlando and Los Angeles spent the following weeks trying to persuade Roberts to acquiesce.[22]

While the Knicks were waiting on Roberts, X-Man stunned the front office by signing with the rival Celtics. Checketts thought he had an agreement with X-Man and his agent, David Falk. He expected they would work something out once they took care of other business. When Falk did not even give the Knicks an opportunity to match the Celtics' offer, Checketts was shocked.[23]

McDaniel had a different take on the situation. Free agency began on July 1, and he'd waited until after Labor Day. Training camp was set to start in a few weeks, and he had to take care of his family. He also took New York's pursuit of Grant as a troubling sign. The Knicks could have reached a tentative agreement with X-Man behind the scenes before seeking out other players, but they did not so much as make McDaniel an offer.[24]

Frustrated by the lack of interest, McDaniel and Falk met with Celtics president Red Auerbach, who offered McDaniel $8 million guaranteed, take it or leave it. Red wanted an answer before McDaniel left the room. McDaniel was supposed to meet with the Bulls next, but Falk was not able to ascertain how much they were willing to offer him. Falk had been negotiating with Checketts about an extension for McDaniel for a year. Checketts was concerned about X-Man's knees, and he convinced Falk there was no way the Knicks would go over $2 million per year.[25]

X-Man called Ewing and explained he had an offer for $8 million from the Celtics and had still not heard from the Knicks. Ewing said if the Knicks were going to make him an offer they would have done it by then and that he should do what was best for his family. That is what McDaniel did.[26]

Assistant coach Bob Salmi called Riley the most prepared and organized person he has ever been around. In the four years they worked together, the only time he saw Riley caught by surprise was when X-Man signed with the Celtics. McDaniel had been a big part of the coach's plans.[27] Riley sent X-Man a letter after the fact apologizing for the way the Knicks handled his free agency.[28]

McDaniel's departure increased the Knicks' urgency to land Smith. Roberts eventually relented, and the Knicks had their coveted new forward on September 22. Riley did not want to lose Jackson, but Smith was a tremendous talent, and the addition of another veteran point guard in Rivers softened the blow.[29]

Kimble was a throw-in, best known as one of the two stars on Paul Westhead's fast-paced Loyola Marymount teams. The shooting guard led LMU to the Elite Eight in 1990 and shot his first free throw in each game of the tournament left-handed, in honor of his co-star, Hank Gathers, who had collapsed on the court and died earlier in the season. He shot his first free throw left-handed in each of his three NBA seasons as well.[30] Kimble shot below 40 percent in each of his two seasons with the Clippers and was considered a bust.

Days after losing out on McDaniel, New York traded a second-round pick to the Minnesota Timberwolves for veteran forward Tony Campbell. Campbell won a ring as a bench player with Riley and the Lakers in 1988. He averaged over 20 points per game in '89–'90 and '90–'91 with the expansion T-Wolves, but lost his starting job late in the '91–'92 season. He was a versatile scorer, and with X gone, the only true small forward on the Knicks roster.[31]

A couple of weeks into the season, New York added free agent Herb Williams. The former Maverick gave them a formidable backup to Ewing for the first time since Cartwright was sent packing for Chicago.

The Knicks opened training camp two deep at every position. They had seven new players on the roster, and questions about how Riley would make the new pieces fit together. Who would start at guard? Blackman or Starks? Rivers or Anthony? What would Smith's role be? How many players would be in the rotation?

Riley announced at the start of training camp that Ewing was the only guaranteed starter. The other four positions were open for competition. Oak, in particular, was concerned about his playing time.[32] Oakley's minutes diminished the previous season, and he did not average double-digit points and rebounds for the first time in his career. Then, New York traded for Smith, a power forward, and brought another forward into the mix in Campbell.

Oak responded the only way he knew how: with hard work. On one of the first days of camp, Oakley took a charge from Mason and dove on the floor eight times over a short stretch during an intrasquad scrimmage.[33] The effort paid off, as he found himself in the starting lineup opening night.

Riley selected Rivers, Starks, Campbell, Oakley and Ewing as his starters. Blackman injured his back weightlifting in training camp, clearing the path for Starks.[34] However, there was no guarantee Starks would keep his spot once Blackman returned or that Riley would not make other changes to the lineup.

New York started the season slowly. Ewing did not trust his new teammates, and Riley hadn't yet settled on a rotation. Campbell started the first 13 games before Riley benched him in favor of Smith at small forward. Smith struggled with the new position, particularly chasing around perimeter players on defense, and was unaccustomed to being the third scoring option.[35] Blackman played the entire season in pain with a herniated disc pressing against his sciatic nerve, yet he replaced Starks as the starter after seven games, only to lose the starting job in February.[36]

Riley was so unhappy with the point guard production that New York contemplated trading for Dallas' Derek Harper in December.[37] Before one game, Bob Gutkowski, the president of Madison Square Garden, popped his head into Riley's office, where the coach was sitting in complete darkness, except for the light from his cigarette. (Riley often smoked cigarettes in his office and the hallways of the Garden.)

Riley looked at Gutkowski and said, "What we really need, Bob, is a point guard that can go like this," and he quickly zigzagged his right hand.[38] Riley was frustrated by Doc's lack of quickness. Anthony took over the starting spot when Doc injured his shoulder in early January, but the second-year guard's poor decision-making infuriated Riley and he eventually landed back on the bench.

Anthony was one of the younger Knicks who demonstrated a lack of maturity at times, particularly one night in November against the Clippers and their old teammate, Mark Jackson. Starks, Mason, and Anthony were jawing with Jackson all night. Late in the first half, Jackson walked over to the Knicks bench and said something to Starks. Starks threw his cup of water at Jackson and looked as if he was going to charge the point guard before his teammates held him back.[39]

New York lost the game, and Riley was not amused. He benched Starks for the entire second half, and Starks, Mason, and Anthony did not see the court in the next game. The message was clear: Your focus should be on winning. Anything else is a distraction.[40]

The Knicks continued sputtering into January. They fell to 21–14 after blowing a 10-point, fourth-quarter lead to the Houston Rockets on January 16. After the game, Ewing and Oakley called a players only meeting. Ever since, the Knicks took off, winning 39 of their last 47 games. Finishing with 60 wins, they secured the No. 1 seed in the Eastern Conference, while enhancing their reputation as the league bullies.[41]

Oakley was fined $10,000 for leveling Reggie Miller in the lane during the Knicks' 94–90 win over the Pacers on December 30. Rod Thorn, the league's chief disciplinarian, noted that Oak had committed six flagrant fouls in just 30 games. Pacers general manager Donnie Walsh claimed Riley had "gone from an orchestra leader in LA to Hannibal Lecter with this team."[42]

On March 1, Starks injured Nets point guard Kenny Anderson. Anderson drove to the basket in the third quarter and elevated before Starks shoved him in the face and chest while he was airborne. Anderson landed awkwardly on his left wrist, breaking it in the process. The Nets pointed out to the league that Starks delivered a similarly violent blow to Pippen in the playoffs the year before. Thorn fined Starks $5,000.[43]

Riley walked a fine line with Starks and Mason. Both played with tremendous emotion, which gave them the edge they needed to succeed. However, that much emotion could be detrimental. Mason and Starks made a pact before the season that they would attempt to calm each other down if one of them became too emotional.[44] The agreement, however, did not stop them both from hurting the team by losing control in key moments over the next couple of years.

Glenn "Doc" Rivers grew up in Chicago at a time when the city boasted the richest crop of basketball talent in the country. Isiah Thomas, Mark Aguirre, Terry Cummings, Craig Hodges, Darrell Walker, and Rod Higgins were just some of the 14 future NBA players Rivers competed against on the blacktops of Chicago.[45] Doc was the rare Chicago kid who rooted for the Knicks because he loved Walt "Clyde" Frazier and Earl "The Pearl" Monroe.[46] He was given the nickname Doc when he wore a Dr. J shirt to a basketball camp run by Hall of Fame coach Al McGuire. Coach Rick Majerus was looking for one more player for a pickup game and said, "Where's that kid, Doc?" The other campers caught on, and the name stuck.[47]

Doc spent his first eight seasons with Atlanta before being traded to the Clippers in 1991. The point guard was a scrappy defender with quick hands. Offensively, he utilized an efficient jump shot and ample strength to finish around the hoop. Doc was accustomed to feeding a superstar like Ewing from his days playing with Dominique Wilkins.

Rivers was 31, with his game in decline, when the Knicks acquired him. He also missed 23 games the previous season due to leg ailments. He was an upgrade over the slow-footed Jackson defensively, though he was neither the floor general that Jackson was nor as quick as the younger Anthony.

Doc was an affable guy and popular among his teammates, though he was a feisty competitor, willing to mix it up on the court if pushed. During his rookie season, Rivers competed with Wes Matthews for the Hawks' final roster spot. Matthews was pushing him around in training camp. Finally, Doc picked up Matthews during a scrimmage and body-slammed him. Coach Mike Fratello informed Rivers five minutes later that he made the team.[48] Doc exchanged punches with Oakley while playing for the Hawks in '88, despite giving up five inches and seventy pounds.

On March 23, the Knicks faced the No. 1 team in the Western Conference, the Phoenix Suns, led by Charles Barkley. The game, which was hosted by Phoenix, was being hailed as a possible Finals preview.

The contest was physical from the start, and with seconds remaining in the first half, Rivers was called for an offensive foul on Kevin Johnson as the Knicks attempted to inbound the ball under their own basket. Rivers then shoved KJ, and both benches emptied onto the court. Two possessions later, Rivers dribbled the ball up the court, guarded by Danny Ainge, and Johnson, who appeared to be setting a screen on Rivers (a strange play for a defensive player), lowered his shoulder and bowled Rivers over. Doc chased KJ down and started throwing punches.

Both benches cleared. Oakley was in the thick of it shoving around Suns players. Once things appeared to settle down, Greg Anthony, who didn't play in the game due to a sprained ankle, rushed onto the court in a hideous Hawaiian shirt and sucker-punched KJ with a left hook. Players and coaches from both teams piled on top of Anthony. Riley ripped a pant leg on his Armani suit while trying to break up the fight. Rivers, KJ, Anthony, Mason, Starks, and Ainge were ejected.[49]

The Suns blew out the Knicks in the second half. After the game, the Knicks closed their locker room and refused to talk to the media. Rivers, KJ and Anthony were suspended, and the league doled out over $160,000 in fines.[50] Doc engaged in a scrum with another All-Star, Isiah Thomas, a few weeks later.[51]

Riley wanted to send Anthony home for the rest of the road trip, but some of the veterans talked him out of it. (Riley was furious when word leaked to the press that the players changed his mind, asking each player individually if they were the leak.[52]) The coach was fed up with Anthony, who demonstrated a lack of maturity throughout his tenure with the Knicks.

Anthony was a bit of an enigma. He was named captain of his college team and aspired to be the first African American senator from Nevada after his playing days. He interned for Nevada congresswoman Barbara Vucanovich on Capitol Hill, during the summer between his sophomore and junior years at UNLV and worked for the World Economic Summit the following summer. His UNLV teammates already called him "Senator."[53]

Anthony also began supporting his mother, who was battling cancer, and his sister, a hemophiliac, after his grandfather passed away while he was in college. He worked as a public relations representative for a real estate company, then formed his own T-shirt and silk-screening business called "Two Hype." He expected to make so much money that he voluntarily paid UNLV back $12,212 for his scholarship his senior year. (The NCAA ultimately forced Anthony to relinquish the business in order to remain eligible.)[54]

However, his sophistication was coupled with volatility and poor judgment on and off the court. More than once during his junior season, he was accused of kicking other players on the court. He also received his share of untimely technical fouls for running his mouth or making excessive contact at UNLV and with the Knicks.[55]

One day, Bob Salmi walked into the weight room at the Knicks' training facility and found a loaded nine-millimeter Glock sitting on top of a dehumidifier. He knew it belonged to Anthony, who was lifting weights at the time and always carried a gun.[56]

Salmi brought the gun to Riley's office, where the head coach was sitting in the dark watching film. Salmi knocked on the door and Riley told him to come in. Riley looked up and all he could see in the light coming through the open doorway was Salmi with a gun in his hand. Riley was terrified. He thought Salmi might have lost his mind.[57]

6

Seeing Red

"I didn't follow him in the CBA. I didn't know about him in college. But I know about him now."[1]—Michael Jordan on John Starks

Charles Smith's parents were separated when he was a child. He lived with his mother, though his father remained an integral part of his life. The Smiths were not a sports-obsessed family. Growing up in Bridgeport, Connecticut, Charles never had a favorite player or team and pursued many interests outside of sports, including the chess club, library club, and yearbook staff.[2]

Smith was a skinny kid, standing 5-foot-11 during his freshman year at Warren Harding High School. He played guard for the freshman team that year. The following season, varsity coach Charles Bentley considered cutting Charles, who had no discernible strengths on the court. However, Smith impressed with his determination, earning a spot on the JV team.[3]

Charles ran cross country to improve his stamina while mastering the basketball drills Bentley taught him. He sprouted to 6–10 by his senior season and led his high school to two state championships. He played his college ball at the University of Pittsburgh, where he earned the nickname "Mr. Fluid" for his smooth game.[4] In 1988, Charles was named Big East Player of the Year.

Smith had blossomed into a tremendous talent with superb quickness and athleticism for a man standing 6-foot-10. He could block shots, beat his defender off the dribble, and knock down an open 15-footer. The Clippers selected him with the third pick in the '88 draft. In his second and third seasons, he averaged 20 points per game, highlighted by a 54-point performance against the Nuggets in 1990.

However, there were a number of question marks surrounding Smith when the Knicks traded for him in '92. He was a finesse player who had received the dreaded "soft" label[5] and appeared to be an awkward fit on a team known for its physicality. Charles would also be playing small forward, a new position that did not match his skill set, and there was concern about his knees. He underwent arthroscopic surgery in October 1991 and missed 32 games that season with various knee ailments.[6]

Riley envisioned Charles as another interior offensive force, but that description neither fit Smith's game nor his personality. The Knicks tried to toughen him up, to no avail.

Early in Smith's first training camp with the team, he drove the ball to the basket, where he was met with an Oakley elbow to the jaw. One of Smith's front teeth fell out, and he picked it up off the floor before running out of the gym. Lewis Geter, an undrafted rookie who was trying to make the team recalls, "I think he [Oakley] was trying to send a message, like, 'Charles, if you come in here, you gotta come stronger or you gonna get it.'"[7]

Smith is highly intelligent and was always intrigued by the marketing aspect of basketball. He was kind to reporters and team employees and created a foundation to support kids in Bridgeport. He was also well-liked in the locker room, but his coaches and teammates questioned whether he was "all in," to use Riley's term. According to assistant coach Bob Salmi, "Pretty much everyone on the team, including coaches, would have stepped in front of a train for Pat ... everyone except Charles Smith."[8] Smith's lack of physicality and unwillingness to play through pain grated on some of his teammates and Riley.

Charles was sensitive to comments about his toughness, too. Starks once confronted him about not being more physical after a game. In response, Smith threw his shoe at Starks, and a scuffle ensued.[9]

On another occasion, Riley suspected Smith was capable of playing in a game he was sitting out due to injury. The forward walked into the locker room before the game sporting a fancy wool suit. Riley, who had been writing on the blackboard, turned around and asked in front of the whole team, "Hey, Charles, if I asked you to give me one minute, just one tonight, to win a championship, could you do it?" Smith replied, "Sure, Coach." Riley resumed writing on the chalkboard. A couple of seconds later, he spun around and screamed at Smith, "Then, why the fuck are you wearing that suit?"[10]

Riley's reaction may not have been as personal as it appeared. The coach often singled out individuals in order to send a message to several players or the team as a whole.[11]

Smith didn't want to miss games. He was a competitor. When he was with the Clippers, he took the constant losing so hard that he developed a medical condition called alopecia areata, which caused him to lose patches of hair.[12]

The Knicks publicly revealed in early '94 that the forward had a bone-on-bone condition in his right knee.[13] Riley admitted years later, "He [Smith] was injured the entire time he was here. He really was. Charles had a very chronic problem with his knees, and it prevented him from doing the yeoman type of work everyone else did."[14] Yet, some of his teammates and coaches still questioned whether he did everything he could for the team.

To make matters worse, Smith did not respond well to Riley's criticism. Instead of taking out his anger on opponents, he lost confidence in his game and played tentatively on offense at times. Despite the disappointment and frustration, Smith was the Knicks' third-leading scorer in his first season with the team. He would play a pivotal role in the 1993 playoffs.

New York and Chicago appeared destined to be on a collision course for a rematch, this time in the Eastern Conference Finals. First, the Knicks had to dispose of the Pacers in the first round. Indiana, led by sharpshooter Reggie Miller, went 41–41 and had not yet developed the chemistry and team identity that would vault them into contention. Still, they had talent with Miller, forward Detlef Schrempf and the 7–4 Rik Smits. They were a formidable first-round opponent.

The story of the series became the animosity between the teams' two shooting guards, Starks and Miller. Starks set the tone by refusing to shake Miller's hand before the opening tip of Game 1. Miller was always looking for a psychological edge over his opponents and felt he could get under the skin of the temperamental Starks, whom he goaded with pushes, elbows, and a barrage of trash talk.[15]

Miller led all scorers in Game 1 with 32 points, but Starks' team emerged victorious, 107–104. Starks had a solid performance with 16 points and six assists, and Ewing led New York with 25 points and nine rebounds.

The Knicks' 45–26 rebounding advantage accounted for their 101–91 victory in Game 2. Starks was brilliant with 29 points and 11 assists. Meanwhile, Reggie contributed 25 points and four assists for Indiana.

For Game 3, the series shifted to Indiana, where the Pacers were desperate to avoid a sweep. Miller and Starks talked smack all game, and the conversation heated up as Reggie caught fire in the third quarter. Miller hit a floater in the lane, and the two guards jawed at each other on the way back down the court. Then, Starks abruptly headbutted Miller. Miller, an Oscar-worthy actor, went flailing backward, and Starks was ejected from the game.[16]

Doc Rivers has an expression: "He who angers you, owns you."[17] Reggie, whose sister, Cheryl, referred to him in the documentary *Winning Time* as a "maddening human being," owned the excitable Starks during the mid–1990s, even though Starks outshined him on many occasions. During a regular season game in '95, Starks and Miller went nose to nose. When a reporter asked the Knicks guard after the game why he allowed Miller to get inside his head, Starks got a frightening look in his eye and said, "I'm going to cut his dick off and make him eat it."[18]

Starks' teammates were furious about the headbutt, and the two captains, Oak and Ewing, gave him hard shoves of disapproval.[19] An incredulous John "Johnny Hoops" Andariese, who was calling the game for MSG Network, exclaimed: "Look at Ewing and Oakley, they're beating Starks up!" Starks' mother, Irene, did not appreciate anybody putting their hands on her boy. She told Starks that night she was going to hurt Oak and Ewing and warned Ewing a few days later that he better not ever put his hands on her son again.[20]

After the ejection, the Pacers went on a 30–11 run and won the game, 116–93. Miller finished with 36 and received ample help from Schrempf and Smits, who added 29 and 25 points, respectively.

Game 4 went to overtime. Rivers hit a couple of crucial threes to ice it, 109–100, and close out the series. Doc converted 4-of-6 three-pointers for the game and finished with 21 points and 11 assists. Ewing contributed 28 points and 13 rebounds, and Mason had a huge game with 25 points and 10 boards.

New York's second-round opponent was the Charlotte Hornets, a talented young team led by Alonzo Mourning, Larry Johnson, and Kendall Gill. Mourning was coming off a spectacular rookie season, in which he averaged 21.0 points, 10.3 rebounds, and 3.5 blocked shots. Johnson scored better than 22 points per game and was selected to the All-Star team in just his second season. The Hornets stung an

John Starks was the ultimate underdog and always had a chip on his shoulder because of the long road he traveled to the NBA. Sometimes he had difficulty controlling his emotions on the court (AP Photo/John Swart).

aging Celtics team in the first round when Mourning drained a 20-foot game-winner at the buzzer in the decisive fourth game. Charlotte appeared headed for a very bright future, but was not ready to match up with one of the league's elite teams in New York.

The Knicks took the series in five games, marking the first time they advanced past the second round since 1974. Their depth and experience were too much for Charlotte. The Hornets' lone win came in Game 3 in Charlotte behind 34 from Alonzo and 31 from LJ. Zo averaged 23.8 points, 9.8 rebounds and 3.0 blocked shots for the series, compared to Ewing's 26.0, 10.6, and 2.2, respectively. Oakley taught the young Johnson a lesson or two, delivering 14.4 points and 11.2 boards per game, including 21 points and 11 rebounds in the clincher, while holding Johnson to just 10 points.

Chicago was waiting for the Knicks in the conference finals. Many basketball fans and insiders viewed the matchup as the de facto Finals, believing the Knicks and Bulls to be the two best teams in the league. The Eastern Conference was considered the stronger of the two conferences. New York was also seen as the team with the best shot at defeating Chicago because it had pushed the Bulls to seven games the year before and was the best defensive team in the league, surrendering a mere 95.4 points per game.

For their part, the Bulls viewed the Knicks as serious contenders. Riley had instilled in his team the belief they could beat Jordan and company.[21] The matchup between the two teams had turned into a chess match. Jackson instructed the Bulls to strictly use the Triangle offense and avoid running any plays against the Knicks in the regular season, because he did not want to give Riley and his assistants a chance to scout them. The Bulls also tried certain things like not reversing the ball to see how the Knicks would react come springtime. Even in the playoffs, Jackson saved certain plays for the final minutes of the game.[22]

The Bulls had not lost a game in the playoffs, sweeping the Hawks in three games before doing the same to a 54-win Cavaliers team the following round. Still, the Knicks had reason to be confident. New York outpaced Chicago, 60 wins to 57. If there were to be another Game 7, it would be in New York. The Knicks took the season series from the Bulls, 3–1, including a win in Chicago. Riley's team was also more experienced and deeper than the year before.

The Bulls had a lot to say prior to the series. Pippen was dismissive of the Knicks, saying, "They're not the team the Pistons were." Jordan correctly noted: "The Knicks have trouble scoring." And Jackson continued moaning about the Knicks' style of play, referring to it as "basketbrawling."[23] Riley instructed his players not to read the papers or listen to the news, though it is a safe bet that the Bulls' messages were received.

Animosity between the two teams who were meeting in the playoffs for the fourth time in five years was inevitable, particularly on the part of the Knicks, who lost the first three matchups. Starks spoke for many of his teammates when he said he hated the Bulls.[24]

That hatred was coupled with significant respect for the two-time champions. The Knicks knew how great the Bulls were and relished competing against them. Mason embraced the challenge of matching up against a superb athlete like Pippen.[25] The former's combination of quick feet and a bulky frame made him uniquely qualified for the job.

Starks idolized Jordan before he made it in the NBA. While in college, he recorded all of MJ's games and studied film of No. 23.[26] Now he was the Knicks' starting shooting guard and was going toe-to-toe with Jordan. He made the most of what he learned in the first two games of the series.

Starks and the Knicks held MJ to 10-of-27 shooting in Game 1, including 3-of-13 in the second half. (The Knicks typically played Jordan one-on-one for most of the game, then double-teamed him down the stretch.) The three-time MVP was held scoreless in the final 6:32. Meanwhile, Starks dropped in 25 points on 8-of-14 shooting, including five three-pointers. Ewing added 25 points and 17 rebounds, and the Knicks jumped out to a 1–0 lead, 98–90.

Game 2 saw more of the same. Jordan scored 36 points, but the output required 32 shots. He missed 20 of them and shot just 1-of-7 from behind the three-point arc. All five Knicks starters scored in double figures. Ewing led the way with 26 points, and Oak chipped in 14 points and 16 rebounds.

New York's pestering defense rattled Pippen in the fourth quarter of Game 2. After being called for a double dribble, he threw the ball at referee Billy Oakes, who tossed him from the game. Minutes later, Oakes kicked Greg Anthony out of the game for a flagrant foul on Jordan.[27]

However, the night belonged to Starks. In addition to playing great defense on Jordan, No. 3 dished out nine assists and scored an efficient 12 points, including the last two, which would be talked about for years to come. Starks had the ball on the right wing with the Knicks leading, 91–88, and one minute remaining. He and Ewing ran a pick-and-roll from the same spot a few times that night and Starks drove toward the middle of the floor each time. So, on this occasion, his defender, B.J. Armstrong, overplayed him up top. Ewing saw Armstrong's adjustment and set the screen on the baseline side.

Starks took two dribbles, then exploded toward the rim like he was shot out of a cannon and threw down an emphatic slam with his left hand over Grant and a late arriving Jordan. It was reminiscent of that iconic dunk by Jordan himself a couple of years earlier over Ewing.

The Garden crowd erupted. The Knicks' bench players leapt out of their seats, and Oak slapped Starks on the back as he regained his footing and made his way down the court. The dunk was an exclamation point on a huge victory for the Knicks and the culmination of Starks' arrival as a star in the league he'd worked so hard to crack. More than 25 years later, Starks' brilliant slam is still referred to by Knicks fans simply as "The Dunk."

More than any individual performance, it was the Knicks' aggressive team defense that was responsible for their 2–0 lead. New York held a Chicago team that averaged 105 points per game to 90 and 91 points in the first two games, respectively. The Knicks blitzed the ball handler in certain spots on the court, and any time a Bulls player penetrated the lane, Oakley or Ewing waited for him with a charge, blocked shot, or "Don't come in here again" foul. New York's help defenders were also quick to recover and challenge shots on the perimeter after clogging the lane.[28]

The Knicks had the defending champions on the ropes heading back to Chicago, with Michael Jordan embroiled in controversy. The *New York Times* reported Jordan was still at the Bally's Grand Casino in Atlantic City gambling at 2:30 a.m. the night before Game 2, which meant that he could not have been back to his hotel before 4. MJ swore he was in his room by 1 a.m.[29]

Basketball players live a different lifestyle than most people. They often travel to a new destination late after a game and are accustomed to going to sleep in the middle of the night. Many of them take a nap on game day.

Bulls center Will Perdue claims he and his teammates were not concerned about Jordan's trip to Atlantic City, because they knew Michael was nocturnal. The stories of MJ playing cards all night, then a round or two of golf before the Dream Team's games the previous summer were legendary. David Robinson, one of MJ's Dream Team teammates, joked that Michael made a deal with the devil.[30]

However, the Atlantic City story was particularly inflammatory, because it surfaced around the time a known gambler, Richard Esquinas, wrote a book titled *Michael and Me: Our Gambling Addiction*, in which Esquinas claimed he once won $1.3 million betting on golf with Jordan.[31] "His Airness" had also testified in court earlier that year that a check in his name for $57,000 found in the possession of a drug dealer named Slim Bouler was to cover gambling losses in golf and poker.[32]

There were three days between Games 2 and 3, which allowed plenty of time for the story to gain steam. NBC's Bob Costas asked David Stern about it during a halftime interview. The Bulls stopped talking to the media after Game 2, resulting in a $25,000 fine.[33]

The Knicks blew a huge opportunity to all but end the series in Game

3. With the Atlantic City controversy hanging over him, Jordan shot 3-of-18 from the field. But the Knicks came out flat.

For all of the attention paid to Jordan's offensive skills, the Bulls' greatest strength was their ability to clamp down defensively. Chicago trapped the ball from the opening tip and forced New York into 20 turnovers. The Knicks were down by 19 at halftime and lost the game, 103–83. Despite his poor shooting, Jordan contributed 11 assists, eight rebounds, two blocks, and two steals. Pippen picked up the slack for Jordan with 29 points on 10-of-12 shooting.[34]

Game 3 was testy, beginning with Starks barreling into a Pippen screen and then getting in Scottie's face. That was followed by a few minor skirmishes, including a shoving match between Ewing and Bulls forward Stacey King. Early in the fourth quarter, Starks took a swipe at the ball, but connected with Jordan's face instead. The two players went face-to-face, as both were assessed a technical foul. Starks was being guided away by a couple of teammates when he charged toward Jordan screaming, "You wanna go, Mike?" Jordan tried to make his way to Starks, but his teammates held him back, and Starks was ejected for his second technical.[35]

Game 4 was a vintage Jordan performance. MJ dropped 17 on the Knicks in the first quarter and finished with 54 points, including 6-of-9 shooting from downtown. The Knicks were able to hang around until late in the fourth quarter behind 24 each from Ewing and Starks, but the Bulls eventually pulled away for the 105–95 win. The series was tied at two heading back to the Garden.

The Knicks were confident before the pivotal Game 5. They had won 27 consecutive games at MSG and took the first two games of the series at home.[36] They fought all season to gain the No. 1 seed and were being rewarded with home-court advantage in what amounted to a best-of-three series.

Game 5 was close from the start. Neither team could pull away. Jordan found his groove in the third quarter and scored 17 straight points for the Bulls. He finished the game with 29. Ewing tallied 33 points and connected on a rare three-pointer, which started a 16–7 run that put the Knicks up by one with 90 seconds remaining. New York led by two with 30 seconds on the clock when Armstrong connected on a huge three to give the Bulls a 95–94 lead.

The next possession ended in an exchange that would live in infamy for Knicks fans. Riley called for a Starks-Ewing screen-and-roll on the right side of the floor. Starks pulled up as if he was going to shoot, but changed his mind and passed it to Ewing at the top of the key. Patrick took a couple of dribbles toward the basket, then lost his footing and had to shuffle the ball to Smith.

The 6-10 Smith was in the paint, just a few feet from the basket, but surrounded by a sea of red jerseys. He went up for the layup, and Grant blocked it. Smith retrieved the ball and tried again. Jordan swiped it away from behind. Smith tried another layup. This time, it was Pippen who got a piece of it. The ball came back to Smith, and Pippen rejected his shot once again. Grant recovered the ball and passed it to Jordan, who pushed it up to Armstrong. B.J. laid it in as time expired. The Knicks lost, 97–94.

Charles Smith (center) was rejected four times by the Bulls in the closing seconds of Game 5 of the 1993 Eastern Conference Finals. The sequence has come to symbolize the Knicks' futility against Michael Jordan and the Bulls (AP Photo/ Ron Frehm).

The Knicks and the crowd were stunned. It was inconceivable that a player Smith's height could be rejected four times so close to the basket in a span of six seconds. The Knicks knew they had squandered their best opportunity to finally defeat the Bulls and faced an elimination game in Chicago Stadium. Doc, who was certain the Knicks would win the series, had tears in his eyes as he answered questions after the game.[37] He later compared the feeling to "the sudden death of a family member who was perfectly healthy."[38]

Rivers eventually drove home to Connecticut. Overwhelmed by the magnitude of the loss, he stopped for some air at a gas station on a dark highway at about 2 in the morning. There was one other person at the gas station standing toward the rear of his car with his head in both hands as the nozzle pumped gas into his car. It was the image of a broken man. That man was Herb Williams. Herb said he felt like throwing up after the game.[39] Rivers continued on his journey until he noticed a police car and another car pulled over on the right shoulder. As he passed the two cars, he realized the driver who was showing his identification to the cop was Charles Smith.[40]

Game 6 went as expected. Jordan and the rest of the Bulls were not going to allow the series to go back to New York for a Game 7. The Knicks fought valiantly, but the Bulls were victorious, 96–88, behind 25 from Jordan and 24 from Pippen. Oakley believes Jackson outmaneuvered Riley in the closing minutes of games during the epic matchups between the two teams. More often than not, however, the difference was sheer talent.

In the aftermath of Game 5, enraged Knicks fans flooded sports talk radio with derogatory comments about Smith, often raising the question: "Why did the 6–10 forward not attempt to dunk the ball?"

Smith believes he was fouled on the sequence.[41] Van Gundy and many Knicks fans agree with him.[42] The Bulls watched the footage several times in slow motion and concluded "he just got his ass blocked," as Cartwright put it.[43] Television networks did not provide as many camera angles in 1993 as they do now. Based on the footage available, Cartwright appears to be correct.

Xavier McDaniel believes he would have made the difference in that series. The NBA is a league of matchups, and X-Man matched up very well with Pippen. He said of the Smith sequence, "If you block me once and I get it back, I'm going to try to tear that rim down."[44]

Smith was an easy scapegoat. The play was not even called for him. More importantly, the Knicks would not have needed a bucket in the closing seconds if they had hit their free throws. New York shot a dismal 20-of-35 from the line. Additionally, the Knicks team that prided itself on toughness was outrebounded by the Bulls, 48–37. As Riley was fond of saying, "No rebounds, no rings."

Ewing received his share of criticism after the Knicks were eliminated. He had a great season, finishing fourth in the MVP voting, but superstars are judged by championships. The center had been in the Big Apple for eight years and had yet to reach the Finals. However, Patrick did not have a wingman like Pippen, whose athleticism and superb all-around play in Games 3 through 6 was the difference in the Chicago series.

The rap on Ewing was that he did not make big shots or take over close games as superstars are supposed to do. Critics pointed to Game 5 of the Bulls series when he had the ball in his hands in the final possession with Stacey King—not exactly the second-coming of Bill Russell—on him and stumbled over his own feet before passing the ball to Smith. Ewing's naysayers conveniently overlooked the many crucial shots he had connected on during his career.

Van Gundy, who spent close to 15 years with the club as an assistant and head coach, believes the 1992–93 Knicks were the best team he coached in New York.[45] Riley had a saying: "Humiliation before honor."[46] New York was as determined as ever to come back stronger and win the championship the following season.

7

Jordan Opens the Door

"I told Michael repeatedly that I want him to be there for my championship so I can rub it in his face the way he's rubbed it in mine many times."[1]—Patrick Ewing

On October 6, 1993, Michael Jordan shocked the sports world by announcing his retirement from basketball at the age of 30. He cited a loss of desire to play and later admitted it had a lot to do with the death of his father. James Jordan was murdered in June of that year while resting in his car on the side of the road in North Carolina. Jordan delivered another surprise months later, when he announced that he had signed a minor league contract to play baseball for the Chicago White Sox.[2]

Many basketball fans believed Jordan's departure cleared the path for the Knicks to advance to the Finals, but the people in the locker room did not look at it that way. "I didn't feel within our team we ever said, 'Now, this is our opportunity.' I think we were still smarting from the lost opportunity the year before, when we thought we had the best team in basketball," said Van Gundy.[3]

Even before Jordan retired, the Knicks' brass was optimistic about the '93–'94 season. The Checketts, Grunfeld, and Riley trio had only been together for two seasons, and the climb to a championship is typically a slow, painful process. The Bulls lost to the Pistons in the conference finals in '89 and '90 before beating the Bad Boys and winning a championship in 1991. Detroit lost to the Celtics in the conference finals in '87 and then the Lakers in the '88 Finals[4] before winning back-to-back titles in '89 and '90.

Blackman and Campbell were the only players on the team who had competed in a conference finals prior to 1993. Now, the rest of the team was better equipped to handle the pressure of performing on such a big stage.

The only addition of note that the Knicks made during the 1993 offseason was signing forward Anthony Bonner right before training camp. Bonner was a 1990 first-round pick of the Sacramento Kings who averaged 8.6 points and 6.5 rebounds per game in '92–'93. He was a solid fit for the Knicks, a physical, defensive-minded player with a terrible jump shot. At 6–8, he could play either forward position.

New York's big offseason move was re-signing Smith to a seven-year, $26 million deal. Charles had a disappointing first season in New York and chronic knee problems. He underwent arthroscopic surgery on both knees that summer. Toward the end of the previous season, the forward was not even on the floor in crunch time of most games, having ceded those minutes to Mason.

Still, Smith was an asset who started 68 games in 1992–93. The Knicks did not want to lose him via free agency without receiving something in return. Knicks fans were apoplectic at the size and length of the deal after the Game 5 debacle, as was Oakley, who publicly stated the Knicks should have re-signed McDaniel.[5]

Oak signed a five-year extension during the '91–'92 season, which did not go into effect until '93–'94. The contract was below market value, and he was jealous of Smith's deal.[6] Dating back to his days with the Bulls, it was an annual rite of passage for Oak to complain publicly about his role, his minutes, the number of shots he was taking, or his salary.

He began grumbling about playing time as soon as the 1993 playoffs ended. "I don't know if I'll be here next year," he said. "I want to play more, but I'm not going to kiss no one's butt." He said the Knicks play three big men, but he does all the dirty work.[7] When Riley first joined the Knicks, he told Oakley he was cutting his minutes for the betterment of the team. Oak went along with the plan. His minutes per game dropped from 36.0 in '90–'91 to 27.2 in '92–'93. He told Riley and Checketts before the start of the 1993–94 season that he believed he should be playing at least 35 minutes per night.[8]

Oak's complaints weren't limited to basketball. He was an equal opportunity curmudgeon. Doc Rivers said of the power forward, "He has to tell you how his sneakers are tight, his uniform is stiff, his locker is dirty, the chicken has too much salt, the bus is leaving too early, the plane is leaving too late. You just put up with him because he's Oak and somehow he's still lovable."[9]

Oak's biggest source of agitation was food. The amateur chef in him could not accept anything less than a perfect meal. He frequently sent his food back two or three times at a restaurant and always had something to say about the meals on the team plane. John Wallace, who played with Oak in New York and Toronto, recalled, "He'd be like 'This is missing paprika. This is missing some salt. This is missing some pepper. You ain't season this long enough. You ain't marinate this.' He was always saying how they should have cooked it a little bit better."[10]

Teams were allowed to begin practicing on October 8, 1993, so Riley called New York's first practice for 12:01 a.m. that day. "We wanted to be the first team to hit the floor in '93, the last to leave it in '94," he said of the workout, which lasted an hour and 40 minutes. Riley wanted the pain of losing in the playoffs the previous season to drive his team, so he harped on it constantly.[11]

Riley's club started the season strong, winning its first seven games. Then, it was tested by a rash of injuries in December. Smith tried to battle through cartilage damage in his left knee, but ended up going under the knife for another arthroscopic surgery.[12] Davis, who won the backup shooting guard spot over Blackman, broke his right hand in late December.

The most devastating injury happened to Rivers when he tore the anterior cruciate ligament (ACL) and meniscus in his left knee during the Knicks' December 16 win over the Lakers. Rivers was ruled out for the season with what was considered to be a career-threatening injury.[13] As a result, Riley was left without a starting point guard. Anthony had not progressed as the team had hoped.

The Knicks' depth helped them absorb their losses, but they desperately needed to add a veteran point guard if they were going to compete for a championship. Grunfeld pursued Detroit's Isiah Thomas. The Pistons' glory days were behind them, and the Knicks hoped the future Hall of Famer would jump at the opportunity to play for one more ring in the twilight of his career. Grunfeld offered the Pistons Tim McCormick, Tony Campbell, and a first-round draft pick for Isiah. Detroit was unimpressed.[14]

Pistons owner William Davidson asked Thomas, with whom he had a great relationship, if he would like to be traded to a contender or finish his career with the Pistons. Thomas chose the latter, and the deal was dead.[15] He ended up suffering a career-ending torn Achilles tendon in April.[16]

Checketts and Grunfeld zeroed in on their second choice, Derek Harper. The point guard could score off the dribble or from behind the arc and had been named to the NBA All-Defensive Second Team twice. Perhaps, most importantly, he knew how to run an offense, something Anthony struggled with. New York sent Campbell and a conditional first-round draft pick to Dallas in exchange for Harper.[17]

Derek was raised in a poor neighborhood of West Palm Beach, Florida. His mother, Wilma, was a single parent who worked two jobs while Derek and his nine siblings grew up. Derek led North Shore High School to a state championship in 1980. When he wasn't working on his game, he was working to put food on the table. At an early age, he had jobs washing dishes at a hotel and as a hospital custodian.[18]

Harper attended the University of Illinois, where he led the Fighting Illini to their first NCAA Tournament in 18 years as a freshman, and the Elite Eight as a junior. He declared for the draft after being named a Second-Team All-American his junior season, and the Mavericks selected him at No. 11.

Harper played ten and a half years for Dallas. Naturally, he had mixed feelings about the trade. He had so many wonderful memories in Dallas, so a part of him wanted to finish his career there. At the same time, he felt reinvigorated by the opportunity to go from the worst team in the league to a contender.[19]

Herb Williams, who had played with Harper in Dallas, was thrilled to be reunited with his former teammate. He referred to Harper as "one of the toughest, most competitive guys I've ever played with in my life. And it's not just game day. It's practice. Whatever you're doing."[20]

In many ways, Harper was the perfect replacement for Rivers. They had similar offensive games and both were fiery competitors who commanded respect in the locker room. Like Rivers, Harper was 32 years old and had lost a step.[21]

However, Harper came to the Knicks with some red flags. His production declined precipitously over the first two months of the season, a troubling sign for an older player. The veteran averaged just 11.6 points and 3.5 assists in 28 games for Dallas, down from 18.2 points and 5.4 assists the previous season.

It was also concerning that Harper was coming from a Mavs team that suffered a dreadful 11–71 record in '92–'93 and were 2–27 at the time of the trade. Athletes tend to pick up bad habits in losing situations, and Harper was no exception. The point guard arrived in New York overweight and displaying sloppiness on his defensive rotations.[22] Still, he was the best option available in the middle of the season for a Knicks team that did not want to surrender a major asset. They just had to hope he had something left in the tank and would round into shape by the playoffs.

During one of Harper's first practices with the team he chased after a loose ball. As he bent over to pick it up, his legs were taken out from under him by Oak and Mase who both dove through him onto the floor in pursuit of the ball. That's when it clicked for Harper that he was not in Dallas anymore and had to pick up his effort.[23]

The NBA announced the 1994 All-Stars on February 2, and Ewing and Starks were among those selected. It was Ewing's eighth All-Star selection. For Starks, the nod was validation of everything he had worked so hard to achieve.[24] His last All-Star game had been in the CBA. Now, he was being recognized among the game's elite as the first undrafted player to ever become an

All-Star. Leonard Hamilton, Starks' coach at OSU, said, "You read about this kind of story about a good person making it good. He did it by fighting and scrapping all the way. It's kind of like the American dream."[25]

Starks was averaging 19.5 points per game, though more than scoring earned him the All-Star selection. The shooting guard was racking up seven-, eight-, nine-assist games with Rivers out and Harp still acclimating to the team. In addition, he was a defensive standout. A couple years later, Riley said of Starks, "He had a run of two or three months the year he made the All-Star team when he was as good as any 2-guard in the league."[26]

As happy as Starks was, he and his teammates were disappointed the Knicks did not have three All-Star representatives. Oakley was having perhaps his best season in orange and blue, and New York stood at 33–13 at the break. Oak's minutes rose back to 35.0 per game and he took full advantage, averaging 12.3 points and 12.5 rebounds, though as always, it was his defense that made him special. Any time a Knick defender was beaten, Oak seemed to be there to protect the basket.

A few days later, Oakley received the call. Alonzo Mourning had to pull out of the game because of a torn left calf muscle, and David Stern named Oakley to the team.[27] The truculent warrior finally received his due. Rivers summed up the elation of Oak's teammates when he said, "Now we're sending our heart. Oakley is our heart."[28] It was the first time the Knicks had three All-Stars since Bill Bradley, Walt Frazier, and Dave DeBusschere in 1973. Oak received further recognition after the season when he was named to the NBA All-Defensive First Team.

The Knicks hit a road bump in February. After starting 32–11, New York lost eight of 12, including four in a row to end the month. They were scheduled to play in Sacramento on March 1, but Riley surprised his players by having their plane touch down in Reno, Nevada. Limousines were waiting for them, and Riley handed each player $500 worth of casino chips when they arrived at the Peppermill Casino. The Knicks responded with 15 consecutive wins.[29]

Such detours were not unusual for Riley. On another road trip, the Knicks suited up for practice in Seattle and boarded the team bus, only to be taken to see the movie *Tombstone*. Riley had his finger on the pulse of his team and knew they needed him to ease up a bit. He believed such activities brought the team together.[30]

Riley also dangled a carrot in order to jumpstart his struggling team in early 1994, offering a $100 reward every time a player took a charge. He upped the ante by $100 during each game of their 15-game win streak, so that players were earning $1,500 a charge by the end of the period.[31]

Even when he was not doling out cash, Riley had his assistant coaches keep track of "hustle stats," including loose balls, deflections, charges, contested shots, and rebound effort (a statistic Riley devised to determine how often a player pursued a rebound on offense and defense. For an elite rebounder like Oakley, that number was typically just under 80 percent on defense and approaching 50 on offense.). Riley posted the statistics in the locker room and praised those who excelled in the hustle categories, while chastising those who lagged behind.[32]

The dapper coach embraced analytics long before the term became part of the sports lexicon. In fact, it was not until the 2016–17 season that the NBA began keeping hustle statistics like Riley's. While with the Lakers, he created his own ratings system for every player in the NBA based on position and performance, which was similar to the Player Efficiency Rating currently used by ESPN and other basketball websites. He also developed his own formula for quantifying what is now known as "plus/minus," a means of measuring how much a player's production impacts winning and losing.[33]

Riley was also an adherent of the Bob Knight quote: "The box score accuses, the videotape indicts." The coach did not trust the statistics by themselves. The information had to pass the eye test. Tape put the statistics into context and allowed the coach to understand why a player or the team was producing certain statistics. If a player averaged eight points per fourth quarter, Riley wanted to see if the majority of those points were scored in close games or when the team was up or down by over 20 points. Salmi compiled film of plays that supported the advanced statistics he provided to Riley. In turn, Riley spent hours each day poring over the footage.[34]

It took more than casino chips and a little extra cash to get the Knicks rolling again. Riley made three changes to the starting lineup. Two months after joining the team, Harper replaced Anthony as the starting point guard. Starks moved to the bench in favor of Davis, and in the biggest surprise, Bonner was named the starting small forward, in place of Smith. Bonner, in particular, brought tremendous energy to the starting unit, and he, Davis, and Harper remained starters for the rest of the regular season. New York finished the year winning 21 of its last 27 games.[35]

It also helped that the Knicks were finally healthy. Smith was back in the lineup on January 20, and Davis returned from his broken hand on February 15. Then, New York's luck changed for the worse when Starks tore cartilage in his left knee in a game against the Hawks on March 14, requiring surgery.[36]

The prognosis was that the shooting guard would be sidelined for six to eight weeks. The playoffs started in five. There was no telling how effective Starks would be upon his return, and the Knicks had no shot at winning a championship without Starks at least near the top of his game. When the playoffs started five weeks later, No. 3 was in the lineup, coming off the bench as he had been prior to the injury.[37]

The Knicks ended the regular season with unexpected drama between Riley and Mason. The coach benched Mason for the entire second half of the team's 87–84 loss to the Hawks on April 19, in favor of Smith, who was working himself back into form following knee surgery. Smith's playing time had been limited and his performance was so poor that the Garden crowd booed him mercilessly during the Hawks game.[38]

Mason complained to reporters about being benched after the game. When asked about playing Smith over Mason, Riley said Smith was the team's best offensive option at small forward, and he wanted to give him an extended run to see if he could be counted on in the playoffs.[39]

Mase took exception to Riley's comments and responded to the press the following day. "That's his opinion," said Mason. "He always has his opinion, and we have ours." Riley was furious when he heard what Mason said and suspended the forward indefinitely for conduct detrimental to the team.[40] Mason's agent, Don Cronson, advised his client to lay low until the incident blew over, but Mason showed up Riley by attending the Knicks' next game against the 76ers at the Garden. The crowd cheered him on as he gave high fives to fans. Riley fumed on the bench.[41]

A couple of days later, Mason arrived at the Knicks' practice facility for a workout. Riley was irate when he found out. He called Mason and started screaming, "Don't you get it? You're banned! You're barred! You're not part of the organization!"[42]

Riley told Checketts several times that he was going to leave Mason off the playoff roster. Checketts had two copies of the playoff roster made, one with Mason's name on it and one without. Fifteen minutes before the deadline to submit the roster on April 25, Checketts and Grunfeld called Riley and asked him once more. They told Riley it was his decision. Once again, Riley said he did not want Mason on the roster. Grunfeld argued that the Knicks needed Mason, particularly against the Bulls, and Riley finally relented. The Knicks sent in the roster with Mason's name on it one minute before the deadline.[43]

Riley had another difficult roster decision regarding Rivers. Typically, it takes about a year to recover from a torn ACL, but Rivers healed at a miraculous speed. Doctors told Riley that Rivers would most likely be ready to play in the Eastern Conference Finals and definitely by the Finals. Currently, coaches can activate or deactivate players on a game-by-game basis in the playoffs. However, in 1994, coaches had to submit a roster for the entire playoffs and could not make any changes. Riley opted for journeyman Corey Gaines over Rivers.[44]

The Knicks won the Atlantic Division with a 57–25 record and once again finished with the No. 1 ranked defense, surrendering just 91.5 points per game. They tied with the Hawks for the best record in the East, but by virtue of the Hawks' superior win-loss record in conference, Atlanta received the No. 1 seed. Ewing averaged 24.5 points, 11.2 rebounds, and 2.7 blocked shots per game and finished fifth in the MVP voting.

8

Road to a Ring

"If Scottie hadn't fouled him, I wouldn't have called it."[1]—
Hue Hollins

Madison Square Garden had become the fashionable destination Checketts envisioned when he began working for the team. The Knicks were the hottest ticket in town. The team reserved a section of courtside seats for celebrities, which came to be known as "Celebrity Row" and was always occupied by some of the most popular entertainers. Tom Cruise and Nicole Kidman, Richard Lewis, Jerry Seinfeld, Woody Allen, John F. Kennedy, Jr., newscasters Tom Brokaw, Maury Povich, and Connie Chung, and, of course, Spike Lee were among the regulars. The boisterous crowd provided New York one of the best home-court advantages in the league with chants of "DE-FENSE, DE-FENSE!"

Management continued its mission of enhancing the live arena experience by introducing a theme song called "Go New York Go," which was written by a 22-year-old Long Island native named Jesse Itzler. Itzler had been writing jingles for a living and did some work for Ernie Grunfeld's wife, Nancy, who owned a clothing store at the time. He put together a demo of a Knicks song for Nancy and Ernie. They both liked it, and the Knicks hired him. Itzler wanted the song to be something simple and interactive, a call and response song so the fans could sing along.[2]

Early in the 1993–94 season, the Knicks introduced the song at the Garden. Itzler produced an accompanying video with appearances by several of the Knicks. By the 1994 playoffs, fans were singing the song at games and it had become the No. 1 requested song on several local radio stations.[3]

The Knicks decided on a new unifying look of black socks and black sneakers for the playoffs, while every player on the team shaved his head except for Ewing, Starks, and Blackman. New York's opponent in the first round was its neighbor to the west, the Nets. New Jersey was a dangerous team. They took four out of five from the Knicks during the regular season, including two blowouts.

Chuck Daly, the coach of the "Bad Boy" Pistons, was now the head man in New Jersey. He had two young All-Stars in Derrick Coleman and Kenny Anderson, but not much else. The franchise was still reeling from the shocking death of Drazen Petrovic a year earlier.

The Knicks continued with the same starting lineup they used to finish the season: Harper, Davis, Bonner, Oakley, and Ewing. They took the first two games at MSG, 91–80 and 90–81. Ewing was ejected from Game 2 after his second technical foul, which was called when he and Coleman jostled up the court in the second quarter. Oak bailed him out with 25 points and 24 rebounds.[4]

The series shifted to the Meadowlands, where the Nets eked out a one-point overtime victory in Game 3 behind 25 points and 17 rebounds from Coleman. Ewing helped the Knicks close out the series in Game 4 with a clutch 36-point, 14-rebound, five-block performance.

The Knicks prevailed on the strength of their defense, which held New Jersey to 36 percent shooting in the series, including 26 percent from downtown. Coleman posted prolific numbers, averaging 24.5 points and 14.3 rebounds per game, but he and Anderson were lacking in efficiency. Both shot under 40 percent. For the Knicks, Ewing led the way with respective averages of 24.8 and 11.8, while Oak chipped in 16.3 and 14.3.

Riley slowly worked Starks back into the lineup, increasing his playing time each game. The shooting guard looked tentative during nine minutes of play in Game 1. In Game 4, he was on the floor for 32 minutes, in which he scored 16 points on an efficient 5-of-8 shooting. While his comfort level increased, it was evident he had no lift in his legs.

Next up for the Knicks was their old nemesis, the Bulls. The Knicks had a score to settle after the previous season's devastating defeat. This time, there was no Michael Jordan, but the three-time defending champions were not to be taken lightly. They won 55 games without MJ, just two fewer than the Knicks, and boasted the league's third-ranked defense.

Scottie delivered a magnificent season, stepping out of Michael's shadow and proving he was one of the top players in the league, not merely a sidekick. Scottie averaged 22.7 points, 8.7 rebounds, 5.6 assists, and 2.9 steals per game, was named MVP of the All-Star game, and finished third in MVP voting.

The Knicks could have had their hands on Pippen in the 1987 draft. The Bulls traded up three spots from the No. 8 pick in order to select Pippen.[5] At one point, the Knicks had the rights to both of those picks. The fifth pick was their own and the eighth had belonged to the Nuggets.

New York acquired Denver's pick just before the start of the '86–'87 season in exchange for guard Darrell Walker. A few weeks later, they sent the pick to the Bulls for a mediocre 7-footer named Jawann Oldham.[6] New York already had one of the best centers in the league and an overqualified backup in Cartwright. Oldham averaged 3.9 points per game for the Knicks before he was sent to the Kings for a second-round pick a year later.[7] Early in the '86–'87 season, the Knicks traded their own pick to the SuperSonics for guard Gerald Henderson and the Bucks' first-round pick in 1987. The Knicks cut Henderson early the following season.[8]

New York could have drafted Pippen with the fifth pick or possibly the eighth. Instead, the one player who was best equipped to slow down Jordan ended up being his teammate. Those Ewing-Jordan matchups might have ended differently if Pippen had been on the other side.

Jordan left the Bulls with little time to prepare for his absence when he retired days before training camp, though general manager Jerry Krause made the best of the situation. He had already lured Toni Kukoc, considered by many to be the best player outside of the NBA, to Chicago. The Bulls drafted the 6-foot-11 Croatian in the second round in 1990, though he remained in Europe, where he would ultimately win three Euroleague championships.[9] Kukoc could play either forward position and score from anywhere on the court. He was also an excellent passer and ball-handler for his size. Jackson brought him off the bench as the sixth man.

Journeyman Pete Myers replaced Jordan in the starting lineup, and though not much of a scorer, he and Pippen formed an excellent defensive tandem. Sharpshooter Steve Kerr, who signed as a free agent, helped spread the floor. Chicago also added depth up front with centers Luc Longley and Bill Wennington. Horace Grant turned in his best season, averaging 15.1 points and 11.0 rebounds per game, and Jackson pressed all the right buttons in what amounted to a brilliant coaching job.

Heading into the series with the bigger, stronger Knicks, the Bulls planned to use quickness to their advantage. Chicago spread its Triangle offense out a couple of feet in each direction in order to create driving lanes for Pippen, B.J. Armstrong, and Kukoc. Games 1 and 2 followed a similar pattern. Chicago penetrated to the basket through the first three quarters, but New York's defense clamped down in the fourth and suffocated the Bulls' attack.[10]

Chicago held a 15-point lead in Game 1 until it abandoned the Triangle and went to more of a pick-and-roll offense, which the Knicks were able to snuff out. Ewing paced New York with 18 and 12, and Starks earned 11 free throws, which was a good sign for the Knicks. Mason scored five of his 11 points and grabbed five rebounds in the final period, sparking the Knicks' 90–86 win.[11]

New York took Game 2, 96–91, despite over 20 points apiece from Pippen, Grant, and Armstrong. Mason had 15 points, 14 rebounds, and six assists and shut down Kukoc in the fourth quarter. Starks hit two momentous threes down the stretch to help seal the win.[12]

Jackson resumed his complaints about the Knicks' rough play after the second game. "The Chicago Bulls are a basketball team. They're not a mud-wrestling team or a rugby crew or anything else." His endless whining continued to irk Riley.[13]

The Bulls played with desperation in a Game 3 rife with controversy. Harper and Bulls backup point guard, Jo Jo English, were talking trash and bumping each other toward the end of the second quarter. With 2:41 left in the half, the two guards went head-to-head and simultaneously shoved each other. Harper threw a punch, and as English tried to retaliate, Harper body-slammed him to the floor. Players from both teams attempted to break up the fracas as it spilled over into the stands near midcourt, four or five rows in front of where David Stern was sitting.[14]

English and Harper were both tossed from the game, a trade-off that clearly favored the Bulls. English was suspended one game and fined $10,000. Meanwhile, Harper received a two-game suspension and $15,000 fine. "That's the deal of the century for them," Oakley said.[15] Several other players on each team were fined for leaving the bench, and each organization was fined $50,000.[16]

Chicago jumped out to a 22-point lead late in the third quarter, but Ewing brought the Knicks back. He finished with 34 points and nailed a three-foot hook shot with 1.8 seconds remaining to tie the game at 102. Chicago called timeout and Jackson designed a play for Pippen to inbound the ball at midcourt to Kukoc for the final shot. Pippen was upset about not taking the last shot and exchanged some words with Phil. Scottie said, "I'm tired of this," then sat down at the end of the bench. A few of his teammates tried to convince him to reconsider, but the forward refused to enter the game.[17] "It was a painful, painful, painful moment," Grant said decades later.[18]

Pippen was sensitive about how he was perceived around the league after lingering in Jordan's shadow for so long. He believed he should be treated as a star, and stars take the final shot. Scottie also had a history of resentment toward Kukoc. A couple of years earlier, Krause aggressively wooed Kukoc with a lucrative contract offer at the same time Pippen was in contentious negotiations with the team. Scottie, who made $3 million a year, resented that Kukoc's contract could exceed his if certain incentives were met.[19]

Pippen and Jordan, who was no fan of Krause, took out their frustration on Kukoc when the Dream Team played Kukoc's Croatia squad in the '92 Olympics. The two Bulls trapped Kukoc every time he touched the ball with such intensity that Kukoc's teammates asked him what he had done to make them so angry.[20]

Jackson called another timeout when he realized he only had four men on the court. Myers replaced Pippen in the lineup and delivered a pass to Kukoc, who calmly knocked down a 22-foot shot to win the game. It was Kukoc's fourth game-winning buzzer-beater of the season.[21]

Pippen's refusal to participate was the lead story after the game. Jackson was tight-lipped about the incident, other than to say Pippen took himself out. It is the delicate handling of NBA egos, not X's and O's that often separates the great coaches from the rest. Instead of chastising Pippen, the Zen Master allowed Pip's teammates to handle it. Cartwright, the team's elder statesman, confronted Pippen in the locker room. "How could you?" Cartwright asked with tears in his eyes. Scottie apologized to his teammates, but the incident tarnished his reputation for years to come.[22]

Anthony replaced the suspended Harper as a starter for Game 4, and Riley inserted Starks and Smith into the starting lineup for the first time since February.[23] Starks scored 11 points on 5-of-11 shooting, but turned the ball over five times. He had still not regained the lift on his jump shot or the quickness to drive by defenders.[24] Anthony struggled with Chicago's ball pressure, turning it over four times and connecting on just 2-of-13 shot attempts. Meanwhile, Pippen returned to form after the Game 3 drama, contributing 25 points, eight rebounds, and six assists. The Bulls evened the series at two with a 95–83 victory.

Like the previous year, Game 5 hinged on a controversial play in the final seconds. This time, the basketball gods favored the Knicks. The Bulls took an 86–85 lead when Armstrong nailed a 15-foot jumper with 44.7 seconds left. Ewing missed two free throws on the ensuing possession. Then, Armstrong missed a three-pointer with 10 seconds left to give the Knicks one more chance.[25]

The play was designed for Ewing. Oakley inbounded the ball to Starks, but he was trapped on the sideline, unable to deliver it to the big man, so he found Davis at the top of the key. Hubert let it fly with 2.1 seconds left. The ball clanked off the back of the rim, but the whistle blew. Referee Hue Hollins said Pippen, who ran at Davis as he took the shot, caught the Knicks shooting guard on the wrist after the release.[26]

Pippen and Jackson were irate. Davis calmly knocked down the biggest free throws of his life. This time, Jackson designed the final play for Pippen, but Mason knocked away the inbounds pass, and the Knicks escaped with an 87–86 win.

Everybody was talking about the call on Pippen after the game, except for Pippen himself. He continued a media boycott, which began after the Game 3 scandal. Jackson refused to take any questions, though he made a brief statement: "I've seen a lot of plays in the NBA, but I've never seen what happened at the end of the game like that."[27]

Davis contends he was fouled after the release, though he admits that type of contact is typically not called. He was quick to add that Smith was fouled the previous year so as far as he is concerned the teams are even.[28]

Bulls fans believed there was minimal contact by Pippen and that officials should not have "decided the game" by making a call like that in the closing seconds. The counterargument? A foul is a foul regardless of when it occurs, and Davis decided the game when he knocked down those free throws. Hubert's foul shots saved Ewing from being the goat. The center scored only six points after the first quarter and missed two crucial free throws seconds before Davis hit his.

Darell Garretson, the league's chief of officials, was one of the three referees working the game. He issued a statement that said in part: "I think it's important to define what a shooter is. A shooter remains a shooter until he regains his balance on the floor." He added, "The call was within the context of how they had been calling them all game."[29] Upon retiring months later, Garretson admitted, "It was a terrible call."[30]

New York returned to Chicago for Game 6 intending to close the doors for good on Chicago Stadium, a sight of so much heartache for the orange and blue. The Bulls would be moving across the street to a new arena, the United Center, the following season. The most memorable moment of Game 6 occurred in the third quarter, with the Bulls up 15. Myers delivered a pass to Pippen on the break, and Pippen soared over Ewing for the dunk. Then, in a blatant sign of disrespect, Chicago's star stepped over Ewing's fallen body. Pippen was hit with a technical for taunting, and Patrick tried to restore his pride by chasing after Pippen. The Bulls forward was too busy screaming, "Sit the fuck down!" to Spike Lee, who made the trip to Chicago for the game.[31]

Pippen's emphatic dunk and the aftermath represented the primal scream of a championship team showing its mettle. The Bulls played with an unmatched sense of desperation that night. They were the aggressors, and the officiating seemed to be in their favor. Chicago shot 15 of the game's first 16 free throws. Ewing scored eight points in a row after being embarrassed by Scottie to cut the deficit to seven, but that was as close as the Knicks would get.[32]

Game 7 had enormous implications for the Knicks beyond just the '93–'94 season. If they couldn't beat the Bulls without Jordan, then Jordan was not the problem. The issue was with the Knicks themselves. In such a scenario, management likely would have broken up the team. Naturally, the most pressure fell on Ewing. The kid from Georgetown who had joined the Knicks with so much promise was now 32 years old and had not even sniffed a championship.

The big man came up small in the first half. Foul trouble glued him to the bench for much of the half. He was scoreless at halftime. Still, the Knicks held a one-point lead at intermission. Ewing found his groove in the second half, and the Knicks pulled away. The Big Fella finished with 18 points, 17 rebounds, and six assists, and Oak delivered 20 points and 17 rebounds, 11 of them offensive. New York even received a boost from Anthony, who hit a couple of big threes.[33]

The Garden crowd erupted when the floor-bound Oakley dunked the ball with 32 seconds left and serenaded the Bulls with "Na Na Na Na, Na Na Na Na, Heeeeeyyy, Goodbye." As the buzzer sounded, Mason spiked the ball at midcourt.[34] It was a symbolic stake in the heart of the Bulls. The Knicks had finally beaten their archnemesis and were on their way to the conference finals to take on the Pacers.

Standing 6-foot-5, Reggie Miller was as thin as a piece of paper. His stature and ears that jutted out from the side of his head prompted Pacers play-by-play man Mark Boyle to say he looked like "Mr. Potato Head on a stick."[35]

Pacers fans were devastated when general manager Donnie Walsh selected Miller instead of native son Steve Alford in the 1987 draft.[36] When he graduated from UCLA, Miller was known more for being the younger brother of Cheryl Miller, one of the greatest women's basketball players ever, than for his jump shot. But Indiana soon fell in love with the gunslinger from California.

Reggie was a long-range assassin who excelled at moving without the ball. During the '93–'94 season, he joined Larry Bird as the only members of the 50/40/90 club (players who shot 50 percent from the field, at least 40 percent on three-pointers, and 90 percent from the foul line). He often used his gift for gab to unnerve opponents, as he did when Starks headbutted him the year before. Reggie once had Jordan so riled up that the Bulls star tried to claw his face off.

The Pacers were a different team from the one the Knicks defeated in the playoffs the previous year. Bob Hill was fired at the end of the '92–'93 season and replaced by Larry Brown, who had won everywhere he coached, including the ABA, NBA, and NCAA. He guided Kansas to a national championship in 1988 and would later become the only coach to win championships in college and the NBA when his Pistons won the title in 2004.

Brown was born in Brooklyn and starred as a point guard at the University of North Carolina. Despite standing just 5-foot-9, he made three ABA All-Star teams before transitioning to coaching. Brown, like Riley, was a perfectionist who demanded a lot out of his players, especially his point guards. His players found his constant criticism both irritating and motivational.[37] With Brown on board, the Pacers were more disciplined offensively and carved out an identity as a hard-nosed defensive team.

Indiana swapped small forwards with Seattle at the start of the season, acquiring veteran Derrick McKey in return for Detlef Schrempf. The Pacers also added a promising, high-energy forward to their bench in Antonio Davis. Davis had been playing in Europe since the team drafted in 1990. In addition, newly acquired Byron Scott won three championships with Riley in Los Angeles and could still stroke it from outside.[38]

The Pacers-Knicks matchup was billed as "Hicks vs. Knicks," the country versus the city, the origins of the game versus "the Mecca." But in fact, the teams were mirror images of each other. Each played a slow, physical, grind-it-out game.

Each team featured a foreign-born 7-foot center with a soft touch. Smits, of the Netherlands, was selected by the Pacers second overall in 1988. He could not match Ewing's athleticism, but had excellent range for a 7–4 player. Smits' problems came on the defensive end, where the plodding center often ended up in foul trouble.

Each team had a talented, though inconsistent small forward, Smith for the Knicks and McKey for the Pacers. McKey was a good athlete and versatile offensive player. Year after year, the Pacers hoped he would develop into a consistent second or third scoring option. The Davis boys, Dale and Antonio, were Indiana's answer to Oak and Mase, two physical forwards who did the dirty work in the paint. Then there was the matchup between Miller and Starks, two brash shooting guards without a conscience.

New York and Indiana were equally hungry for a ring. Both teams won their last championship in 1973, New York in the NBA and Indiana in the ABA. The Knicks witnessed how much danger Reggie could pose when he went off for 31.5 points per game in their playoff series the year before. Brown's club won 47 games as the fifth seed in the Eastern Conference. Indiana then swept the upstart Orlando Magic in the first round before defeating the top-seeded Hawks in round two.

The Knicks took the first two games of the series at MSG behind two superb performances by Ewing. Game 1 featured a duel between the two centers. Smits had the touch and finished with 27 points and 10 rebounds. Not to be outdone, Ewing scored 28 points, grabbed 11 rebounds, and added six blocked shots in New York's 100–89 victory.

The Knicks were trailing 62–57 late in the third quarter of Game 2 when they went on an 18–2 run to take a 75–64 lead with just under eight minutes remaining. The Pacers never closed the gap to less than seven points. Ewing scored 10 of his 32 points during the third-quarter run and added 13 rebounds. Harper contributed 18 points, eight assists, and six rebounds. New York came away with a 89–78 win and a 2–0 lead.[39]

Miller was conspicuously quiet during the first two games. The notorious trash-talker decided to keep his lips zipped due to the importance of the games. Miller scored just 14 points in Game 1, and it took him 21 shots to compile 23 points in Game 2.

After Game 2, Reggie received a phone call from his older sister, Cheryl, who told him he was playing too nice. She wanted to know why he was showing the Knicks so much respect. They had not won a championship. The conference finals was no time to dial it back, she argued. Miller's teammates, Vern Fleming and Sam Mitchell, echoed Cheryl's message. The team needed his fire. It was time to play nasty.[40]

Foul trouble limited Reggie to 14 points in Game 3, but the Pacers defense carried them to victory. Indiana held New York to 68 points, a playoff record for the least points scored in a game during the 24-second shot clock era. New York shot 34 percent from the field and 54 percent from the line and turned the ball over 20 times. Ewing shot 0-of-10 and scored just one point, while his counterpart, Smits, contributed 14.[41]

Ewing bounced back in Game 4 with 25 points and 13 rebounds, but the Knicks continued to cough up the basketball and their shooting remained cold. They had nearly as many turnovers (24) as converted field goals (26). Reggie erupted for 31 points. Still, the Knicks had an opportunity to tie the game, down three with 6.8 seconds left, but Hubert Davis dropped a pass out of bounds. Indiana evened the series.[42]

The Knicks were essentially now locked in a best-of-three series with a well-coached team that was as intense and hard-working as they were. Indiana was even the superior defensive team over the previous two games. The Knicks' advantage remained their home court, where they had gone a perfect 8–0 that postseason.

The first three quarters of Game 5 went according to plan with the Knicks leading, 70–58. Then, Miller had the kind of fourth quarter basketball players dream of but rarely ever achieve. He started off by losing Starks on a Kenny Williams screen for a three. Then, Reggie hit another three with Davis guarding him. Riley switched Anthony onto Miller, but it did not make a difference. He knocked down a pull-up from 15 feet, then drilled a jumper from 20 feet, followed by a bomb from five feet behind the three-point line that capped off a 14–0 run and gave the Pacers a 75–72 lead.[43]

Riley was furious. The Garden crowd chanted, "Cheryl," as it had all series, but the taunting had little effect on a man who later penned a book titled *I Love Being the Enemy*.

Reggie and Spike Lee had been yapping at each other all series. Lee, a Brooklyn native, directed numerous films, such as *Do the Right Thing* and *Malcolm X*, though he was perhaps best known from a Nike campaign in which he reprised the comical, Air Jordan-loving character, Mars Blackmon, from his movie *She's Gotta Have It*. In the commercial, Blackmon, who was wearing big glasses and a Brooklyn hat with the brim turned up, repeatedly asked Jordan what made him the best player in the universe. After Michael shot down all of his suggestions, Blackmon concluded, "It's gotta be da shoes."

The diminutive director grew up a Knicks fan during the team's glory days and was anxious to see another championship up close. He bought his first season tickets in 1985 in nosebleed territory the day after the Knicks won the lottery to draft Ewing and gradually inched closer to the court over the years, until he purchased courtside seats across from the opposing team's bench. When Oakley came out for warmups, he threw the ball to Spike, who tossed it back to Oak to start the layup lines. The director was usually clad in his favorite Knicks jersey—in those days, it was Starks'—and loved to heckle the opposition.[44]

Lee and Miller did not know each other well prior to the series. They made a bet during a joint appearance on a news show before the start of the series: If the Knicks won, Miller had to visit Mike Tyson in prison. (The former heavyweight champion was convicted of rape in 1992.) If the Pacers won, Lee had to cast Miller's wife, Marita, in his next film, *Clockers*. The trash talking between the two escalated during Game 5.[45]

After Miller connected on that long-range bomb to give the Pacers the lead, he turned to Spike, gave him the choke sign, and grabbed his crotch. Lee said in the ESPN 30 For 30 documentary *Winning Time*, "I didn't mind the choke sign, but to grab his nuts. My wife's sitting right there. C'mon."[46]

Reggie continued to launch away, and none of the Knicks guards could stop him. He finished the night with 39 points, including 25 in the fourth quarter. Of those 25 fourth-period points, 15 came from three-pointers. Indiana won the game, 93–86, to take a 3–2 series lead with a chance to clinch at home in Game 6. The Knicks were stunned to be on the verge of elimination.

The New York media seized on Miller's performance and his feud with Lee. The back page of the next day's *New York Daily News* had a picture of Miller doing the choke sign with the headline "GAG CITY." The *New York*

Post went with "CHOKERS" in bold letters.[47] Fans called into New York sports radio station WFAN and blamed Lee for Miller's heroics, claiming the director egged him on.

Lee made the trip to Indiana for Game 6 and visited Tyson in prison, where Tyson (also a Knicks fan) and Lee were heckled by other inmates. Then, Lee received a security escort to his front-row seat at a hostile Market Square Arena. "I've never been to a Klan rally," Lee said, "but that was close to it."[48] Few people gave the Knicks a chance after losing Game 5. They were 1–6 on the road in the playoffs, and the Pacers were 6–0 at home.

Starks called a team meeting. The players all gathered in Ewing's hotel room in Indiana and watched the fourth quarter of Game 5. Harper believes, "It was the greatest thing a player could have done. It brought us together as a team."[49]

The Knicks answered the bell in what Riley would later deem the biggest game of his tenure in New York.[50] Ewing, who had guaranteed victory for the first of many times, had a quiet 17 and 10. It was Starks, who was still not 100 percent after knee surgery, who came out aggressive with the season on the line. The shooting guard connected on 5-of-6 from beyond the arc for a total of 26 points. He added six assists and three steals. For Indiana, Reggie scored 27 points, but on an inefficient 8-of-21 shooting, including 2-of-7 from downtown.[51]

The Knicks shot 52 percent for the game and won, 98–91, staving off elimination. After the final buzzer sounded, Starks walked across the court and gave Lee a big high five. The series was heading back to New York for Game 7.

Nobody felt the pressure of Game 7 more than Ewing. He received the brunt of the criticism for the team's inability to defeat the Bulls and developed a reputation for not producing in big games. Jordan was out of the way, and the Knicks had home-court advantage in the final game against the Pacers. There were no excuses left.

The Knicks trailed by as many as 12 in the third quarter of Game 7, but Mason and Harper led the charge back, and New York closed the quarter on a 14–4 run to pull within two. Then Ewing put the team on his back. The star center ran past the bench and yelled at Riley, "Call 'em for me." Riles obliged.[52]

When Ewing was not fed the ball, he retrieved it off the glass. Eleven of his 22 rebounds came on the offensive end, which he converted into 11 second-chance points. The Knicks dominated the Pacers on the glass, 51–29, including 28 offensive rebounds, 19 more than they had in the previous two games combined.

Patrick snatched his biggest rebound of the night in the final minute of the game. Dale Davis put the Pacers up one, 90–89, with 34.5 seconds left on a dunk off a nice dish from Haywoode Workman. Riley called the next play for Ewing to set a high screen for Starks. Starks, with Miller on him, drove hard right and tried a twisting layup, which rolled off the front rim. Ewing dunked the follow-up to put the Knicks back on top with 26.9 left.[53]

Indiana did not call timeout. Everybody knew whom the ball was going to. Reggie came off a pick with Starks trailing him, but Oak closed out on him and put a hand in his face. Reggie's game-winning attempt from 20 feet was an airball. He then fouled Starks, in what was ruled a flagrant foul, which sealed the game. New York won, 94–90. Ewing finished with 24 points, 22 rebounds, seven assists, and five blocks. Reggie had 25 in the losing effort.[54]

The moment belonged to Patrick. He carried the team to victory in the biggest game of his professional career. Coach Brown said in defeat, "As a coach, I'm in awe of him [Ewing]."[55]

After the final buzzer, Ewing gave high fives to the fans sitting courtside and went into the crowd to hug his college coach, John Thompson. Then the big fella waded through the throng of people on the court, climbed on

Patrick Ewing raised his arms in victory after going into the crowd to hug his college coach John Thompson when the Knicks advanced to the 1994 Finals. Ewing posted 24 points, 22 rebounds and seven assists in Game 7 of the Eastern Conference Finals against the Pacers (AP Photo/Charles Rex Arbogast).

top of the scorer's table, and victoriously raised his arms in the air. For a moment, the tension between players and fans melted away. Ewing was one step away from fulfilling the lofty expectations he'd been carrying around for nine years. The Knicks were heading to the Finals for the first time since 1973.

9

A Dream Matchup

"It was the most bizarre telecast I've ever been involved in."[1]—Marv Albert on Game 5 of the 1994 NBA Finals

The Knicks' opponent in the 1994 Finals was the Houston Rockets, who were led by the MVP and back-to-back Defensive Player of the Year, Hakeem Olajuwon. Hakeem was born and raised in Lagos, Nigeria, and did not play basketball until he was 17 years old. He was accustomed to running up and down the court in pain with his toes folded at the knuckle because the biggest sneakers he could find in Lagos were size 13, three sizes smaller than his feet.[2]

Olajuwon came to the United States in 1980 as a relatively unknown prospect to play for Guy Lewis at the University of Houston. On one occasion, Olajuwon dunked so effortlessly the coach commented, "it was like a dream." From that moment on, the spectacular center was known as "Hakeem the Dream."[3]

The Dream was quiet and had a regal air about him, befitting of a man who was admired and feared by his opponents. A devout Muslim, Olajuwon fasted during daylight hours for the month of Ramadan. Initially, he ate and drank on game days during the holy month, but fellow Muslim Mahmoud Abdul-Rauf convinced him to begin fasting on game days as well in 1995.[4]

The marquee matchup between Olajuwon and Ewing was the biggest storyline of the series. The two met for the first time while in college in the summer of '83 at an NCAA-sponsored anti-drug event in Phoenix. Ewing heard Peter Tosh playing from another hotel room on his floor, so he stopped in to say hello. Patrick and Hakeem quickly discovered they had a lot in common.[5] Both were immigrants who grew up playing soccer, not basketball, in their native countries.[6]

They faced off for the first time less than a year later in the NCAA championship game. Although Olajuwon outscored Ewing 15–10, Georgetown beat Olajuwon and his "Phi Slama Jama" teammates, 84–75. Ewing was named the Final Four's Most Outstanding Player.[7]

The two star big men's careers followed similar trajectories. Both suffered their share of heartbreaking losses, Hakeem in the 1984 NCAA Championship game and the 1986 NBA Finals, and Ewing in the 1982 and 1985 NCAA Championship games. They were selected first overall in the NBA draft, in consecutive years, and each played alongside another big man early in their careers. Hubie Brown copied Houston's "Twin Towers" lineup of Olajuwon and Ralph Sampson when he paired Ewing and Cartwright together. And like Ewing, Olajuwon grew frustrated with the franchise for which he played.[8]

The Rockets were successful early in Hakeem's career, though his supporting cast rapidly crumbled. Sampson's knees gave out on him, and John Lucas succumbed to a drug problem. A year after Ewing pushed to become a free agent in 1991, Olajuwon asked the Rockets to trade him.[9]

Finally, at age 31, the two men were meeting in the NBA Finals, each in search of a long-awaited championship. Olajuwon had revenge on his mind 10 years after losing to Ewing in college. While toying with the inferior Felton Spencer in the conference finals, Hakeem's mind wandered to the thought of meeting Ewing in the Finals. He was obsessed with beating his old foe by the time the series began.[10]

Hakeem was the better player. Ewing possessed a smoother outside shot, but Olajuwon was superior at every other facet of the game. The Dream had balletic footwork in the post and was a better passer out of double teams,

Two of the premiere centers in the game, Hakeem Olajuwon (left) and Patrick Ewing, faced off in the 1994 NBA Finals (AP Photo/Tim Sharp, File).

though the biggest difference between the two was quickness and agility. Olajuwon was listed at 7–0, though he was more like 6–10 and moved like a guard. Hakeem dominated Patrick in their two meetings during the regular season, averaging 33.0 points, 16.5 rebounds, and 2.5 blocked shots to Patrick's 12.0 points, 9.5 rebounds, and 1.0 blocks.

Ewing and Olajuwon had remarkably similar teams around them. Houston and New York each ranked among the top five in team defense and played inside out through its talented big man. Each team lacked a consistent second scorer and was overly dependent on a streaky shooting guard with no conscience and a short temper.

Houston's answer to Starks was the man they called "Mad Max," Vernon Maxwell. "It's like we were twins on the basketball court," Maxwell said of Starks.[11] Unlike Starks, who was generally mellow off the court, "Mad Max" could explode at any moment with little or no provocation, sometimes leading to confrontations with teammates.[12]

The Rockets had their own workmanlike power forward in co-captain Otis Thorpe, and both teams relied on a veteran point guard, Harper and Queens product Kenny "The Jet" Smith. The Finals were bittersweet for Smith, who was thrilled to compete for a championship in the Garden but resented being treated like an enemy in his own city. Smith recalls walking into a CVS in Manhattan during the Finals and hearing an employee state over the intercom, "Cleanup on Aisle 4. There's a Rocket spill. Please get it out of the store." Worse yet, some of his childhood friends rooted against him in favor of their hometown team.[13]

At 6–10, Robert Horry was the prototypical Stretch 4 before the term existed, a long-armed forward who could do damage from behind the arc. His range enabled him to play small forward, where he was matched up against the equally long Charles Smith. The Rockets agreed to trade Horry and Matt Bullard months earlier to the Pistons in exchange for Sean Elliott, but the deal was rescinded when Elliott failed his physical because of a kidney ailment.[14] Horry, who was reluctant to shoot during his first couple of seasons with the Rockets, would go on to have a unique career, earning the nickname "Big Shot Bob" for knocking down numerous clutch shots while winning seven championships with three different franchises.

Like Mason, Mario Elie was a New York City kid who played all over the world before making it in the NBA. He and Carl Herrera were the energy guys on Houston's bench, which also featured a pugnacious rookie point guard named Sam Cassell.

The Rockets were coached by Rudy Tomjanovich, who starred at the University of Michigan. Rudy T. had been with the Rockets for 24 years, as an

All-Star player, scout, assistant coach, and head coach. His No. 45 jersey hung in the rafters at the Summit.

Unfortunately, Tomjanovich was best known to most NBA fans as the victim of "the Punch." During a melee in the Rockets-Lakers game on December 9, 1977, Lakers forward Kermit Washington punched Tomjanovich in the face so hard that he shattered his jaw and other bones in his face, resulting in life-threatening injuries. Rudy T. made a full recovery and resumed his career.[15]

Upon firing Don Chaney in 1992, the Rockets named him head coach on an interim basis. At the end of the '92–'93 season, the title became permanent. Tomjanovich was known to work himself to exhaustion in preparation for games, though he was much more easygoing than his counterpart, Riley. He had a self-deprecating sense of humor and earned a reputation as a players' coach.[16]

Tomjanovich marveled at the size and strength of New York's frontcourt and had been following Riley since Riley first started coaching the Lakers. Rudy was intrigued by the plays Riley drew up, particularly the way he carried them all the way through to a third option.[17]

Houston tied a record by winning 15 consecutive games to start the '93–'94 season, with the record-tying win coming against the Knicks at MSG.[18] They finished with 58 wins, and like the Knicks, placed second in their conference.

The Rockets lost the first two games at home in their second-round series against the Suns, blowing a 20-point lead in each. The front page of the *Houston Chronicle* read "Choke City" after Game 2.[19] The city of Houston was still reeling from a devastating playoff loss by the Houston Oilers a year earlier, in which they surrendered a 35–3 lead to the Buffalo Bills.

The Rockets fought back to win the series in seven games, leading the *Chronicle* to create a new moniker, which has stuck with the Rockets and other Houston teams since: "Clutch City." Next, Houston disposed of the Jazz in five games in the conference finals.[20] The Rockets took both games from the Knicks during the regular season and held home-court advantage in a city desperate for a title. At the time, Houston was one of only two cities with an NBA, MLB, and NFL franchise that had yet to win a championship.

Neither team looked sharp in Game 1. The Knicks were tired after their grueling seven-game series with Indiana, and Houston was rusty from not playing for over a week. Both teams shot poorly, setting records for offensive futility. Their combined 28 points in the fourth quarter and 63 in the second half marked all-time Finals lows.[21]

The Knicks, in particular, shot dreadfully from the field, connecting on just 34 percent of their shots, including an atrocious 12-of-50 in the second half. Starks shot a dismal 3-of-18, while the rest of the Knick guards converted on 7-of-23 attempts. Patrick delivered 23 points and grabbed nine rebounds, and Oak turned in a double-double, but it was not enough. New York posted just 78 points, compared to Houston's 85. Hakeem led the way for the Rockets with 28 points and 10 rebounds, and Thorpe grabbed 16 boards.[22]

Still, the Knicks were encouraged. They played extremely poorly on the road and were still within three points with two minutes remaining. Their most significant takeaway from Game 1 was Mason's defense on Olajuwon. Despite giving up four inches, Mase held the Dream to 1-of-9 shooting in the second half and frustrated the center into receiving a technical foul.[23]

Houston double-teamed Ewing in many instances, but the Knicks chose to play Hakeem straight up. Ewing, Oak, Smith, and Williams all took their turn at trying to slow down the league's MVP, though nobody defended him as well as Mason. This, just weeks after Mase was the team's most effective defender against Pippen, highlighted the forward's versatility and value to the Knicks.

Derek Harper was considered by many in the game to be the best player not to make an All-Star team. He achieved impressive individual accomplishments during his Mavs tenure, including being named to the NBA's All-Defensive Second Team twice, though his most memorable moment was a monumental gaffe in Game 4 of the 1984 conference semifinals. The Mavs were down 2–1 to the Lakers in Harper's rookie season when he dribbled out the final six seconds of the clock in Game 4, thinking his team was up one. The score had actually been tied, and the Lakers ended up winning in overtime.[24]

Harper played on some great teams in Dallas, which included Blackman and Mark Aguirre. They advanced to the Western Conference Finals in 1988 but were unable to get over the hump against the Lakers. Ten years after Harper's gaffe, he had an opportunity to redeem himself in the Finals.

The Knicks point guard was the difference in Game 2, scoring 18 points and serving up seven assists. He connected on a three with the Knicks trailing 81–79 and 4:23 remaining, then knocked down another to give New York an 87–81 lead with two minutes left.[25]

However, his greatest impact came on the defensive end, where Harp used his strong hands to direct the ball-handler where he wanted him to go. Hand-checking was legal at the time, and according to Cassell, Harp was "the king of the hand check."[26] He was also a master thief. Harp used an unusual technique in which he would count the ball-handler's dribbles in his head to capture the rhythm of the bounces as he moved closer and closer to the ball. Then, he swiped at the ball on its downward motion.[27]

Harp had owned Kenny Smith since his days in Dallas and smothered the Houston point guard in Game 2, limiting him to two points.[28] Tomjanovich went with the rookie, Cassell, for the entire fourth quarter. Rudy T. viewed his point guards in baseball terms, with Smith as the starter who spread the floor for Hakeem with his three-point range, and Cassell, the feisty closer who came in to finish off the opponent.[29]

Starks bounced back with a 19-point, nine-assist performance, and Ewing blocked six Rocket shots. The Knicks shot 52 percent as a team and evened the series with a 91–83 win.

In 1994, the Finals followed a 2–3–2 format, so the series shifted to the Garden for Games 3 through 5. The atmosphere was electric before Game 3 for the first NBA Finals game at the Garden in 21 years. The fans started chanting "De-fense, De-fense" long before player introductions.

The Knicks fell behind 11–2 to start Game 3. They trailed by as many as 16 in the second quarter but clawed their way back to take an 88–86 lead on a Harper jumper with 53 seconds left. On the ensuing possession, Olajuwon spun into the lane. Unable to shake Ewing, he kicked the ball out to Cassell at the top of the key. The rookie confidently stepped into a three-pointer and nailed it with 32.6 seconds remaining to put the Rockets up 89–88.[30] Many years later, Van Gundy would say it was the biggest shot of the series.[31] After Ewing was called for a moving pick the next trip down the floor, Cassell sealed the game with four free throws. The Rockets won, 93–89.

Patrick finished with 18 points, 13 rebounds, and seven blocked shots, but Olajuwon and a series of double-teams limited him to a paltry 9-of-29 shooting. Olajuwon was one of five Rockets in double figures with 21 points, 11 rebounds, seven assists, and seven blocks. Harper and Starks were the Knicks' leading scorers with 21 and 20 points, respectively.

Olajuwon and Ewing both struggled through the first three games. Hakeem had just two made field goals in the fourth quarter, and Ewing was shooting 35 percent from the field. It was the players around them who were knocking down the big shots.

After forfeiting home-court advantage in Game 3, the Knicks faced two must-win games. Oakley took care of Game 4. The Knicks power forward corralled more offensive rebounds than the entire Rockets team.[32] Two, in particular, stood out. The game was tied at 74 with less than five minutes remaining when Olajuwon rejected Ewing in the lane. Oak snatched the rebound and laid it in as he drew contact. His free throw gave New York a three-point lead.[33]

Moments later, the vertically challenged Oakley reached over Thorpe to tap a missed Ewing free throw. The ball was heading out of bounds on the left side of the court when Oak dove for it, cupped it in his left hand, and somehow whipped a pass behind his back as he crashed to the floor. The recipient, Starks, was standing behind the three-point line on the right side of the key and calmly knocked down the shot to extend the lead to six. After that, the Knicks never looked back.[34]

Starks delivered in the fourth quarter, scoring 10 of the team's last 13 points. Meanwhile, Harp recorded another strong outing, netting 21 points, while holding Smith scoreless. New York survived a 22-point second half from Olajuwon and evened the series with a 91–82 win.

Madison Square Garden was the epicenter of New York City in the spring of 1994, with the entire city buzzing about the possibility of winning two championships. For it was not just the Knicks who were chasing a title, but the hockey team they shared a building with, the New York Rangers, were competing in the Stanley Cup Finals.

The Rangers were one of the original six NHL franchises and thus had a loyal fan base that dated back generations. They were heckled for years by fans of their rivals, the New York Islanders, for not winning a title since 1940. Accordingly, they were desperate to see the Stanley Cup back in New York City. Like the Knicks, the Rangers overcame a 3–2 deficit to win a grueling conference finals, theirs coming against the New Jersey Devils.

Mark Messier famously guaranteed victory in Game 6, then backed up his words with two goals. The Rangers won Game 7 in double-overtime on a goal by Stephane Matteau, during the Knicks-Pacers series. As the Knicks battled the Rockets in the Finals, the Rangers were locked in combat for the Cup with the Vancouver Canucks.

The night before Game 4 of the Knicks' series, the Rangers ended their 54-year title drought by defeating the Canucks, 3–2, in Game 7 at the Garden. Messier brought the Cup into the Knicks locker room for inspiration prior to Game 4 and sat with it courtside during the game.[35] The city threw the Rangers a ticker-tape parade down the Canyon of Heroes in Lower Manhattan on the morning of Game 5 of the NBA Finals. Spontaneous chants of "Let's Go, Knicks" broke out, and Checketts and Grunfeld, who made an appearance at the festivities, were assured by throngs of fans the Knicks would be next.[36]

The Rangers' parade was just one of several noteworthy sporting events in the country that day. Arnold Palmer played his final round of his last U.S. Open, the World Cup kicked off in Chicago, and, of course, Game 5 of the NBA Finals would be played that evening at the Garden. However, the biggest story on June 17, 1994, both in and out of the sports world, was the news that NFL legend, O.J. Simpson, was a fugitive from justice.[37]

Fifteen years after his retirement, Simpson remained one of the most recognizable athletes in America through his appearances in films such as *The Naked Gun*, as a sideline reporter for NBC, and most notably, running through airports as the pitchman for Hertz. On June 12, 1994, O.J.'s estranged wife, Nicole Brown Simpson, and her friend Ronald Goldman were brutally murdered in front of Brown Simpson's home. On June 17, the day of Game 5, Simpson was charged with the murders and agreed to turn himself in to the authorities that morning. Then he disappeared.[38]

Los Angeles District Attorney Gil Garcetti announced Simpson was a fugitive from justice. The Juice was loose. A manhunt was underway. That afternoon, Simpson's friend and attorney, Robert Kardashian, read what sounded like a suicide note from Simpson on television.[39]

A few hours later, during the second quarter of Game 5, O.J. was found cruising down the 405 Freeway in Los Angeles in the back seat of his long-time friend Al Cowlings' white Ford Bronco. Cowlings, who was at the wheel, informed the Los Angeles Police Department that Simpson had a gun to his own head. The LAPD followed Simpson with a convoy of vehicles, while every major news network scrambled to send a helicopter to the scene. The entire nation tuned in to witness the shocking events.[40]

NBC had a difficult decision to make about whether to cover the chase or stick with the game. It was Game 5 of the NBA Finals, not a rerun of *Mad About You*. Commissioner Stern was at the game sitting next to Dick Ebersol, the chairman of NBC Sports, in the fourth or fifth row across from the Knicks bench. Stern yelled, "Don't do it!" as Ebersol spoke on the phone with news executives about whether they should cover the chase.[41]

Ultimately, NBC could not ignore the biggest news story in years, and the network switched to coverage of O.J. with 1:45 left in the first half. The television audience missed a scuffle in the final minute of the half between Hakeem and Mason after Olajuwon elbowed Mason in the jaw during a move to the basket.[42]

Knicks guard Corey Gaines remembers him and his teammates wondering what was going on with the crowd. "You could tell there was a buzz about something else."[43] Prior to the days of cell phones, many spectators left their seats to find a television. According to Starks, the Knicks learned of the chase in the locker room at halftime.[44]

Kenny Smith caught a peek of the chase on a television at the scorer's table and filled in his Rockets teammates in the huddle. An incredulous Tomjanovich asked his players, "What are you doing? We're in the middle of the NBA Finals!" Then, he drew up a play. As the players walked out of the huddle, Tomjanovich grabbed Smith and asked, "Is he really on the run?"[45]

The broadcast was bizarre, as NBC shifted back and forth from the game to the chase. Marv Albert and Matt Guokas were announcing the game, and Bob Costas acted as an intermediary in the studio, transitioning from Albert and Guokas to Tom Brokaw on the news desk. There were periods when NBC went to a split screen between the two events.[46]

The Simpson saga was particularly difficult for Albert, Costas, and Ahmad Rashad, NBC's sideline reporter. O.J., Marv, and Costas worked football games together for NBC. O.J. was the best man at Rashad's wedding and mentioned his former Bills teammate in his apparent suicide note. NBC was using two sideline reporters that night with Rashad and Hannah Storm, and Ebersol told Rashad to go home when news of the chase broke.[47]

The game was tied at 61 heading into the fourth quarter before the Knicks pulled away in the final few minutes for a 91–84 victory. Knicks fans serenaded their heroes with cheers of "one more" and "Knicks in six." Ewing delivered his finest performance of the series with 25 points on 11-of-21 shooting, 12 rebounds, and eight blocked shots. Mason contributed 17 points and nine rebounds, while helping force Olajuwon into eight turnovers. Harp dropped 14 points and seven assists, while continuing to frustrate Smith on the other end of the floor. Game 5 had a 7.8 television rating due to the chase, the lowest of any Finals game that decade.[48]

The night after Game 5, Rockets swingman Mario Elie smelled fish from his hotel room. He searched for the source and found Hakeem in all-white prayer garb cooking fish in his room with some friends. Hakeem noticed Elie looked concerned and asked his teammate what was wrong. Elie was distraught the Rockets were down 3–2. Olajuwon calmly reminded Elie they were going home for Games 6 and 7, and everything would be okay. That settled Elie down. If Hakeem was that confident, there was no reason to worry.[49]

10

Starks Reality

"I was at the finish line before I ran the race."[1]—John Starks

New York flew back to Houston with two opportunities to win the championship, though Riley stressed to his team the importance of wrapping up the series in six. After all, the home team had won the previous 19 Game 7s.[2]

New York jumped out to an early 15–8 lead, but the Rockets leveled the game and eventually took a three-point lead heading into the fourth quarter. Midway through the final period, it looked as if the game was slipping away from the Knicks. Ewing was ice cold, and the team collectively was struggling to put the ball in the basket.

Then Starks caught fire. The shooting guard posted 16 points in the fourth quarter, including 15 in the final 9:11. It was quite a performance from Starks, who did not admit at the time that his surgically repaired knee was far from 100 percent.[3]

Kenny Smith knocked down a three-pointer to put the Rockets up 84–77 with 3:17 left. Starks responded with a three, then a Mason jumper from the baseline with 32 seconds remaining pulled the Knicks within two. Harper forced Smith into a difficult shot at the end of the shot clock on the other end, and Mason hauled in the rebound with 7.6 ticks remaining.

New York called timeout. A two-pointer would send the game to overtime and a three would win the championship.

Riley called a play named "Floppy Up." Oakley was to inbound the ball to Starks, while Ewing would set a high screen, giving Starks three options: drive, shoot, or pass to Patrick who would be rolling to the basket. It was the same play that ended in a Ewing dunk in Game 7 of the Pacers series.[4]

Oakley inbounded the ball to Starks, and Horry fouled him, so the Knicks started again with 5.5 seconds on the clock. Once again, Starks received the inbounds pass and Ewing set a screen on Maxwell. Starks took two dribbles toward the left corner and let it fly. He was certain it was going in.[5]

Tomjanovich told his team to switch on any picks and Olajuwon decided he was not going to allow the hot Starks to get a shot off.[6] Hakeem slipped a bit, but was able to recover and lunged at Starks' shot. He got just enough of his fingertip on the ball to force it to drop short of the hoop. Starks was shocked Olajuwon reached him in time. David Robinson was the only other center who might have been able to cover that much ground so quickly.[7] It was a career-defining moment for one of the greatest players to ever play the game.[8]

On replay, Ewing appeared to be open, though relatively far from the basket, a couple of steps left of the elbow. Starks earned the right to take that shot. He scored 16 of the Knicks' last 22 points, including 3-of-3 on three-pointers, and appeared to have an open look.

In a cruel twist of fate, years later, Patrick was an assistant coach for the Rockets under Jeff Van Gundy, and the Rockets had a picture of Olajuwon blocking that shot hanging in the players' lounge. He had to view the photograph of himself wide open every day. All those years later, Patrick called Starks and yelled at him for not passing him the ball.[9]

Starks did not talk to anybody about his potential championship-winning shot. That included skipping the mandatory media session prior to Game 7, which resulted in a $10,000 fine. In retrospect, his silence was an ominous sign. Starks never put Game 6 behind him and thus was not mentally prepared for the biggest game of his life.[10]

When Checketts entered the Knicks locker room after Game 6, Riley turned his back and would not speak to his boss. Both men knew the Knicks had likely blown their best opportunity to win a championship.[11]

Riley spent the afternoon of Game 7 hanging out in his hotel room at the Ritz Carlton with his friend Dick Butera. At about 4, the two men headed for the arena. As they were waiting for the hotel elevator, Riley said to Butera, "Well, buddy, I know three guys that are gonna show up tonight." Butera asked, "Who?" Riley replied, "You, me, and John." The John he was referring to was Starks.[12] The shooting guard was Riley's most fearless player and was having a great series.

Despite Riley's belief that the Knicks' best chance to win the series was in Game 6, the players' confidence was as high as it had been all season. Prior to the game, Harper saw the champagne being wheeled into the Summit. He thought it was an omen that he and his teammates would be sipping and spraying that champagne a few hours later. Harp would have bet his life the Knicks would win the series before it began and nothing in the first six games changed his opinion.[13] Riley's final motivational tactic was to show his team a tape of a championship parade before they took the floor.[14]

New York trailed Houston by three points heading into the fourth quarter of Game 7. Harper was the only Knick with the knack offensively. Ewing's shot was off, and Starks had missed 7-of-8 attempts through three quarters. Undeterred, the shooting guard came out firing in the fourth. He had scored double digits in the fourth quarters of Games 4, 5, and 6 and thought he needed to carry the Knicks offensively once again. Like any shooter, he believed he was one basket away from catching fire.[15]

John Starks attempted what would have been a championship-winning three-point shot in the closing seconds of Game 6 of the 1994 NBA Finals. Hakeem Olajuwon got just enough of his fingers on the shot to make it drop short, sending the series to Game 7 (AP Photo/Pat Sullivan).

What happened next was one of the most infamous performances in Finals history. Starks continued launching from long range, and his shots kept clanking off the rim. Herb Williams encouraged Starks to drive the ball to the basket to try to score easy buckets or establish a rhythm at the foul line, but Starks continued to bomb away.[16] Riley had Rolando Blackman and Hubert Davis available off the bench, but he stuck with Starks.

"Feast or Famine" shot the Knicks out of the game. He finished the night 2-of-18 from the field, including 0-of-11 from behind the arc. He connected on just 1-of-10 shots in the fourth quarter.[17]

The Rockets won, 80–74, behind 25 points, 10 rebounds, and seven assists from Olajuwon, who held Ewing to 17 points on 7-for-17 shooting. Maxwell added 21 for Houston. Harper was the Knicks' leading scorer with 23. New York shot a dismal 39.7 percent for the game.

Olajuwon was named Finals MVP, staking his claim as the greatest center in the game. He outscored Ewing in all seven games, averaging 26.9 points on 50.0 percent shooting, compared to Patrick's 18.9 points on 36.3 percent shooting. The Knicks center had superior rebounding numbers 12.4 to 9.1 per game and blocked a few more shots than Hakeem, a Finals record 32. However, the gap in assists in Olajuwon's favor, 4.1 to 1.7 per game, may have been the most telling statistic, as the Dream was more effective at creating open shots for his teammates.

The one thing many members of the Knicks organization recall about the locker room after Game 7 was the silence. Curtis Bunn, who covered the Knicks for the *Daily News*, said it felt like a funeral.[18]

Starks was driven to tears and had to be pulled out of the shower after 45 minutes.[19] "I never felt as empty after a game as I did after Game 7," he said.[20] The lasting image for some of those who were there was of Starks staring angrily off into the distance with tears in his eyes. David Steele, who covered the Knicks for *Newsday*, recalls, "I think a lot of us wondered, 'Would he ever recover from that?'"[21]

The locker rooms in the Summit were so close together that Harper and his teammates could hear the Rockets celebrating with bottles of champagne he believed were destined for the Knicks. He felt like he couldn't move. "Emptiness" was how he described the feeling.[22]

Eventually, Riley sat with his point guard to console him, and the two cried together.[23] Harper, who might have been Finals MVP if the Knicks had pulled out the series, blames himself to some extent for Starks' off-target bombing. As the point guard, he could have directed the ball away from the cold shooter or instructed Starks to pass the ball.[24] However, Harper was still new to the team and he and Starks had just recently grown comfortable playing together. "I don't know what it was earlier in the year, but we didn't really click," Harper said.[25] The point guard may not have felt comfortable taking on a leadership role with his new team yet, particularly in relation to Starks.

Some of those shots Starks hoisted were plays called for Ewing. Riley's players had the freedom to break off a play as long they stuck to one of their strengths. Rivers noted a year earlier, "John Starks is the biggest play-breaker of all time, but Riley lets him try things because John makes things happen for us."[26]

Ewing should have called Starks aside and said, "Get me the damn ball!" It was Patrick's team and his legacy on the line. But that was not his personality.

Riley said after the game that he loved Starks "for his fighting nature" and did not sound like he regretted leaving his streaky shooting guard in the game.[27] The coach was more disturbed about the ending of Game 6.

"That was the game," Riley said the following year. "That was our chance to win the championship."[28]

Riley recalled, "I set up a play for him [Starks] and Patrick. It was the same play that got us to the Finals. It had finished then with a Ewing dunk. But this one ended with Starks hoisting a long jumper that was deflected by Hakeem Olajuwon. Ewing was waiting and open under the basket. John had the ultimate responsibility to make the ultimate play," said Riley. "And in that case, the play was to make the pass to Patrick."[29]

Riley addressed that play in a letter he wrote to Starks. "It was the ultimate responsibility in the ultimate game, and obviously I did it for a reason: I felt he could do it. I told him in the letter that I didn't care about him going 0-for-11 ... I told him I wanted him to think about that one play, and the effect it had on his teammates and that if I'm ever going to give you that responsibility again, you have to earn it. That's earned, the right to win games."[30]

Since '94, Riley has delivered mixed messages about leaving Starks in Game 7. In September 1995, he scoffed at the idea of pulling his shooting guard. "People said I should have taken him out of the seventh game when he was shooting like that. Bull----. If it wasn't for John, we wouldn't have gotten to Game 6," said Riley. "I'm not taking him out then. What the f—do you think I'm gonna do? I'm not going away from my guy. John is the player I put more faith in than probably any player I've ever coached, and I did it for the right reasons."[31]

In 2006, while coaching the Heat in the Finals, Riley expressed the opposite point of view, referring to his decision to leave Starks in as the "biggest mistake I ever made." He added, "That's why we brought Rolando there. Immediately afterward, I knew. If we had played the two of them, but especially

Ro, we would have won the championship." (The other person Riley was referring to was Rivers.)[32] Riley later expressed similar sentiment to Checketts,
stating that he "cost us all a ring."[33]

However, the coach recently conceded to columnist Harvey Araton that
he could not have pulled his most fearless player, Starks, in Game 7 of the Finals.[34] Starks was his guy, the player who reminded him most of himself, and
had been so integral to the team's success. "To this day, I believe in John, believe that he'd make two in a row and we'd win," Riley said over 20 years later.[35]

Grunfeld believes Riley should have pulled Starks, though he under-
stands why he did not. "Riley said, 'Let's dance with the girl we brought to the
dance,'" said Grunfeld.[36] Oakley is the one player who has openly criticized
Riley for leaving Blackman on the bench. "I think it hurt us not playing him
[Blackman]. He's a veteran with over 20,000 points (actually 17,623). Give
him a shot. But he [Riley] coached his way."[37]

Riley made the right decision. Perhaps, he deserves blame for not working Blackman into the rotation earlier in the postseason. By Game 7 of the
Finals, neither Blackman, who was nearing the end of his career and had not
played all series, nor Davis, who received minimal playing time in the Finals,
was a realistic option.

Rivers would have been a solid replacement for Starks, had he been
healthy. But even if Rivers' knee had fully healed, it would have taken him
a while to work off the rust from not playing for half a year. It's a stretch to
believe he could have made an impact in the Finals.

Starks had nightmares about Game 7 that summer.[38] He returned to
Tulsa, where family, friends, and "a lot of prayer" helped him deal with the
devastation. He also began playing golf to take his mind off basketball.[39]
Starks still thinks about that game often but does not remember specific details. "That game, I really, truly just blocked out," he said.[40]

He believes Game 7 might have turned out differently for himself and
the Knicks if the team had engaged in an entertaining activity, rather than
staying in Houston between Games 6 and 7. Game 6 fell on a Sunday. Riley
considered taking the team to New York after the game, but decided against
it.[41] The players hung around their hotel rooms until Wednesday night. Starks
had plenty of time to think and was admittedly too revved up when Game
7 tipped off.[42] "I wasn't relaxed. When I'm not relaxed for a game, that's not
good."[43]

He also regrets not having an opportunity to redeem himself. Dennis
Johnson of the SuperSonics missed all 14 of his shots in Game 7 of the 1978
Finals against the Washington Bullets, and the Sonics lost the game. The fol-
lowing season, Johnson was named Finals MVP as his Sonics avenged the

devastating loss, defeating the same Bullets to secure the championship.[44] Starks never had a second opportunity.

Blackman was devastated he was not given the opportunity to help his team. He hit countless big shots during his career and prided himself on delivering under pressure. Despite dropping out of the rotation, he kept himself in immaculate shape and was always prepared in case his number was called.[45] Ro wishes he or Hubert could have at least given Starks a breather for two or three minutes to clear his head. He decided during a 40-minute postgame shower that his NBA career was over. Blackman and Riley have never discussed the coach's decision to leave him on the bench.[46]

Davis was also disappointed he was not called upon when Starks was struggling. He went from starting at the beginning of the playoffs to logging minimal playing time in the Finals. The young shooting guard believes he had been playing tentatively, afraid to make a mistake, which affected his performance on the court, as well as Riley's confidence in him.[47] The moment was too big for him.

After the Knicks locker room cleared out, Riley took a car back to the hotel with Van Gundy and Butera. The three men sidled up to the bar, and a dazed Riley ordered a vodka with Coke. The bartender asked the coach if he was sure because they typically didn't make vodka and Cokes. "He [Riley] was in a trance after that game," Butera said. Riley, Van Gundy, and Butera sat at the bar for a long time, mostly in silence, except for when they expressed their disbelief at Starks' shooting.[48]

Many NBA fans thought the 1994 Finals were boring. No team scored more than 93 points in a game, and television ratings plummeted 30 percent from the previous year.[49] The latter was due in large part to Jordan's absence and the O.J. chase that captivated the nation's attention.

The following summer, the NBA made significant rule changes designed to improve the flow of the game and increase scoring. Rod Thorn, then the NBA's Executive Vice President of Basketball Operations, notes, "There was so much contact occurring that it was impossible, virtually impossible, for players to move. Strength was overtaking skill."[50]

Hand-checking was eliminated from one end of the court to the opposite foul line, and post defenders were no longer allowed to lock their elbows when fighting for position. The league also moved the three-point line in from 22 feet in the corners and 23 feet and nine inches at the top of the key to 22 feet all around.[51] Rivers refers to these as "the anti–Knick rules."[52]

11

The Hangover

"We were a championship team that didn't win it."[1]—Hubert Davis

When the Knicks exited the locker room at the Summit following their devastating Game 7 defeat, the words "1995 = The Knicks' Year!" remained on the chalkboard in the visitors' locker room.[2] It was not clear who wrote those words, though it seemed like one of Riley's messages.

Starks' horrific Game 7 performance hammered home the Knicks' need for a consistent second scorer, but New York lacked the cap space or tradable assets to acquire such a player. They did have two first-round draft picks to work with, their own at 24 and the 26th pick, which they acquired from the Hawks in 1991.

The Knicks used the 24th pick to select Monty Williams, a 6–8 forward out of Notre Dame University. Williams was a versatile scorer who averaged 22.4 points per game the previous season after sitting out two years with a heart ailment. The forward had been cleared by doctors, and the Knicks believed he was worth the risk at that point in the draft.[3]

New York used the 26th pick on a point guard from Thomasville, Georgia, named Charlie Ward. Ward was best known for winning the 1993 Heisman Trophy and national championship as the quarterback of the Florida State Seminoles. He was one of those remarkable athletes who excelled at every sport in which he competed, from tennis to swimming to football.

Ward was the first Heisman winner not to be drafted by the NFL because he refused to commit to football. He wanted to wait until he knew what his options were before deciding between football and basketball.[4] The Kansas City Chiefs contacted him during the fifth round of the NFL draft and asked for a guarantee he would play football. He declined.[5]

Ward likely would have been selected in the third round or earlier had he committed to football. Super Bowl-winning coach Tony Dungy, then the defensive coordinator of the Minnesota Vikings, was one of many coaches who saw potential in the young quarterback and tried to convince Vikings coach Dennis Green to draft Ward. Green did not want to waste a pick on a player who might not play football. Dungy recently said of Ward, "He could have been Russell Wilson 20 years before Russell Wilson."[6]

While the Jets and Giants shuffled through an array of subpar quarterbacks during the mid- to late '90s, there was a popular refrain that Charlie Ward was the best quarterback in New York.

The addition of Ward gave the Knicks four point guards. Harper was entrenched as the starter, and Ward was to be groomed for the future. He had a lot to learn having never played a full season of college basketball. That left the backup role to Anthony or Rivers. Anthony was a very good defender, but still played erratically with the ball. Conversely, Rivers brought a steady presence to the position. The question was: How much did he have left in the tank at 33 after major knee surgery?

After receiving minimal playing time during the first month of the season, Rivers stormed into Riley's office and asked to be released so he could play with another team. The ensuing argument was so heated that Knicks staffers were prepared to bust down the door to stop a potential brawl. When the player and coach finally calmed down, Riley informed Rivers he was stubborn enough to make a great coach one day.[7] The Knicks tried to trade Rivers, but they couldn't find any takers. He was released on December 16 and signed with the Spurs 10 days later.[8]

The Knicks said all of the right things about moving on from their heartbreaking loss in the Finals, but they experienced a Finals hangover early in the '94–'95 season. New York dropped to 12–12 on Christmas day after losing a close game to the Bulls.

Starks, who could be heard uttering, "I got unfinished business" throughout training camp, seemed to be haunted by his disastrous Game 7.[9] His frustration boiled over during a December 9 loss to the Hawks. Mired in a terrible shooting slump, he sat at the end of the bench in the fourth quarter with a towel over his head and sobbed.[10] Harper admitted he had never seen such a display.[11]

The Knicks trailed Atlanta by three with 39 seconds left. Oakley, who was inbounding the ball, refused to pass it to an open Starks who was in position to take a potentially game-tying three-pointer. Oak claimed after the game he did not see Starks, but it appeared the co-captain was sending a message to Starks: "Stop shooting!" It was six months too late.[12]

After the Hawks game, Starks suggested he should be removed from the starting lineup. Riley took it a step further and benched Starks the following game.[13] Starks was not over Game 7. He poured his angst into his craft, working harder on his game than ever before, but that was not enough. He had to face the demon.[14]

Starks typically watched a tape of every game he played later that night before going to sleep, but he never watched Game 7.[15] After the Hawks game, he viewed it for the first time. It was cathartic. He was finally able to move on.[16]

Christmas Day was a turning point for the blue and orange. Starks began knocking down shots again, and the Knicks won 14 of their next 15 games without Oakley, who underwent surgery on December 27 to fix a dislocated toe on his right foot. The injury ended his streak of 268 consecutive games played. His teammates were so accustomed to seeing Oak on the floor that Harper assumed the big bruiser was kidding when he said he couldn't play.[17]

During a March victory over the Nuggets, Riley and Mason butted heads once again. They argued in front of the Knicks bench about whether Mason should have double-teamed the post on a recent possession. Mase sat down at the end of the bench, then stormed off to the locker room upon Riley's suggestion, knocking down a stanchion on the way. Smith, who was not playing due to injury, followed Mase in an attempt to calm him down. Moments later, Mason returned to the bench, but Riley did not play him for the remaining 20 minutes of the game.[18]

Mason was suspended for "at least five days" for "conduct detrimental to the team and for repeated violations regarding his conduct as a professional on and off the court," announced Grunfeld. Mase routinely answered Riley back, glared at his coach, or looked away when Riley talked to him. Riley, in turn, rode Mason hard because he knew if Mase was angry, he would only work harder.[19]

Mason's agent, Don Cronson, believes Mason and Riley clashed so frequently because they had very similar personalities. "Anthony Mason, in many ways, was Pat Riley," Cronson said. Both were blunt, hardheaded, and fierce competitors. Every so often, Riley had to remind Mason who was in charge.[20]

Mason's clashes with Riley were not personal. According to Scott Fiedler, who was like a brother to Mason, "Anthony loved Pat." He appreciated Riley for giving him a shot in the NBA.[21]

The feeling was mutual. Riley would later say, "I knew Mase and Mase knew me. We had respect for each other. Whatever crazy way it manifested itself, believe me, we respected each other."[22]

Mase could also be combative with opponents, officials, other coaches, teammates, and the media. Mase and Starks believed they could not back down from anybody because of their backgrounds and the paths they took to the league. Mase, in particular, did not like to be held back, reprimanded, or challenged in any way. When a reporter asked him about his lack of offensive production after a game, the defiant forward shot back in his gravelly voice, "What is offense? I score three points, my man scores two, that's offense."[23]

"For a while, Mason was impossible to please," according to announcer Mike Breen. "He was never happy."[24] Mase was often dissatisfied with his role, minutes, shots, or who he was guarding. If he scored 25 points and grabbed 14 boards in 42 minutes, he would be angry that he did not play all 48. More than once, he received a technical foul after making a basket because he complained about not receiving a foul call.[25]

Oakley, along with Starks, was Mase's closest friend on the team. "We were like peanut butter and jelly," Oak said. That did not stop the two forwards from frequently tussling during practice.[26] Like Oak, Mase delivered his share of hard fouls and was feared by those around the game.

Riley ran conditioning tests on the first day of training camp during

which players had to run sprints called 17s in a specific amount of time. If they did not meet the stated goal, they had to come in early the next morning before practice and do the 17s over until they achieved the requisite time. Assistant coach Salmi was monitoring Mason's line and determined Mason missed the mark by about two seconds.[27]

Mason was furious. For the rest of practice, he kept coming up behind Salmi and saying things like "Fuck you. You know I made it." Salmi was terrified Mason might come after him. He changed rooms in his hotel that night so the forward could not find him.[28]

Anthony Mason played basketball around the world before receiving his break in the NBA with the Knicks. He and Pat Riley clashed at times, but Mason always appreciated Riley for giving him a shot in the league (AP Photo/Ron Frehm).

Mase's irascible demeanor was at least in part a product of his ultra-competitiveness. Rivers claims Mason was one of the two or three most competitive players he ever played alongside, comparing the brawny forward's pugnacity to that of Michael Jordan.[29] Mase was once expelled from the Wheelchair Classic, a charity game held at MSG to benefit disabled people, for brawling with J.R. Reid.[30]

There was a softer side to Mason that the public did not see. Mase was a mama's boy, in the best sense of the word, regularly doting on his mother, Mary.[31] Right before player introductions prior to one of Mason's first games with the Knicks, he handed ball boy Steve Masiello a piece of paper with a number on it. He told Masiello to call his mother and tell her he loved her and wished she were at the game.[32] Mase insisted on driving his mother home to White Plains after every game she attended, then often drove back to the city to go out with his friends.[33]

Mase was also very close with his high school coach, Ken Fiedler, whom he called "dad," and Fiedler's sons, Scott and former NFL quarterback Jay, whom he introduced as his brothers.[34] He treated everybody from the trainer to the ushers at MSG with kindness and enjoyed hanging out with the ball boys, often playing one-on-one with them after practice.[35]

Mase worked a one-week basketball camp with Scott Fiedler every summer, where he stayed in a cabin like the campers and did everything from officiating to playing the kids one-on-one. He often bought new basketballs for the camp and reimbursed the winner of a free-throw contest the cost of tuition. The camp included an annual game between the counselors and campers, which Fiedler had to cancel because Mase was too rough with the kids.[36]

Checketts recalled that Mason was great with kids and the first Knick to volunteer for charitable team events at hospitals and schools. He typically found the child who was standing alone in the corner and befriended him.[37] On one occasion, Mason spent four or five hours with children in the cancer ward at Mount Sinai Hospital in New York before exiting the hospital barefoot because he autographed his sneakers and gave them to a child.[38]

The Orlando Magic were a new juggernaut in the Atlantic Division. Many prognosticators believed Shaquille O'Neal and company were still a year or two away from being serious title contenders, but the emergence of Anfernee "Penny" Hardaway and the addition of Horace Grant catapulted the Magic to elite status. In just his second season, Penny averaged 20.9 points and 7.2 assists per game, while shooting 51 percent from the field. He was named to the All-NBA First Team. Orlando opened the season 32–7 and did not look back.

As if the Magic and Pacers were not enough to worry about, New York's old nemesis, Michael Jordan, resurfaced on March 19, 1995. Baseball players were on strike, and Michael did not exactly tear up Double-A pitching with his .202 batting average. Reports circulated that he had been practicing with the Bulls, and he made his return official with a two-word press release: "I'm back."[39] Sporting a new number, 45, MJ turned in 19 points, six rebounds, and six assists in his first game back against the Pacers after 17 months away from the game. He scored 27, 21, and 32 points over his next three contests, respectively.

In his next game, on March 27, Jordan erupted for 55 points against the Knicks at the Garden. Perhaps it was the sight of his old rivals or the bright lights of Broadway, or maybe he was beginning to round into shape with four games under his belt.

The Knicks threw Starks, Harper, Anthony, and Bonner at him and contested nearly all of his shots. It didn't matter. MJ could not be stopped. He hit turnarounds, fadeaways, and leaners. He connected from the elbows and behind the arc.[40]

Then, with the game tied at 111 in the closing seconds and everybody in the arena thinking he was going to take the winning shot, Jordan delivered a bullet pass to Bill Wennington for the game-winning dunk. "Michael and I combined for 57 points," joked Wennington.[41] Van Gundy believes Jordan's performance against the best defense in the league so early in his comeback was "truly the most remarkable game I've seen anybody play."[42]

MJ was back, and New York's road to the Finals became that much more difficult. The Knicks lost to Chicago again on April 15. This time, Pippen played the role of hero, pouring in 29 points to go with eight rebounds, five assists, and seven steals. The Knicks finished the year with 55 wins, two fewer than Orlando.

New York's opponent in the first round was Cleveland. The Cavaliers compiled a 43–39 record and finished fourth in the Central Division. Their stingy defense, which surrendered a league-low 89.8 points per game, made them a formidable foe. New York ranked second with 95.1 allowed per game. The Cavs offense was pick-and-roll heavy, designed to free up point guard Mark Price to pull the trigger on his deadly jump shot or drive and create shots for his teammates. The teams split the season series, 2–2, with each team taking both games on the other's home floor.

The Knicks jumped out of the gate fast in Game 1 and did not look back, securing a 103–79 victory. New York shot a blistering 63 percent from the field, as Ewing led the way with 21 points. Defensively, they smothered Price by blitzing him on pick-and-rolls. Harper and company held the sharpshooter to just six points on 1-of-6 shooting and the Cavs to below 40 percent as a team.[43]

The Knicks followed the win with a lackluster Game 2 performance. Chris Mills led the Cavs with 21 points, and Price added 15 points and seven assists. The Cavs evened the series with a 90–84 win, thus stealing home-court advantage, at least for the time being.

Game 3 at Gund Arena in Cleveland went down to the wire. The Knicks were up 83–81 in the closing seconds. Danny Ferry set a pick for Price, and Mason, who was covering Ferry, yelled for Harper to switch, but Harper didn't hear him. Both men stuck with Price, leaving Ferry wide open. Fortunately for the Knicks, Ferry missed a 25-foot three at the buzzer.[44] New York then finished off the Cavs in Game 4, 93–80. Harper paced the Knicks with 30 points, including a Knicks playoff record seven three-pointers.[45]

Next up for the Knicks was a rematch with the Pacers, who were outspoken about wanting to play the Knicks after sweeping the Hawks in the first round. They had revenge on their minds.[46] New York had disposed of Indiana in each of the previous two postseasons, but the Pacers were an improved team with the addition of former Knicks guard Mark Jackson.[47]

Indiana won 52 games in 1994–95 and allowed the league's fourth fewest points per game at 95.5. New York won three of the four regular-season matchups and had home-court advantage.

It was a devastating start to the series for the Knicks, who lost Game 1 in the closing seconds on an improbable ending. New York led 105–99 with 18.7 seconds to go. Believing the game was over, Indiana's general manager, Donnie Walsh, turned off the television in his suite at the Garden and made his way to the locker room.[48] Then the Knicks unraveled.

Indiana inbounded the ball to Miller, who hit a quick turnaround three. Harper, who usually inbounded for the Knicks, was ejected in the third quarter. Mason inbounded instead. He could not find an open player, and the Knicks were out of timeouts. Fearing a five-second violation, Mase lofted the ball toward Anthony, who fell to the floor with a little help from Miller. Miller caught the ball and took one dribble behind the arc before nailing another three. Tie game.[49] Reggie admitted years later during his Hall of Fame speech that he pushed Anthony on the play.[50]

The Knicks and the MSG crowd were stunned. Greg Anthony said, "I had never heard the Garden that quiet. We've had shootarounds at the Garden when there was no one there but the janitors, and it wasn't that quiet."[51]

The game was tied with 13.4 seconds left. Sam Mitchell fouled Starks, whose mind was on the blown lead. "We watched John's eyes," Jackson said. "And he wanted no parts of those foul shots." Starks missed both.[52]

Reggie Miller (center) tormented the Knicks and their fans throughout the 1990s. He called the Knicks chokers after he scored eight points in nine seconds to steal Game 1 of the 1995 Knicks-Pacers playoff series (REUTERS/Reuters Photographer—stock.adobe.com).

Ewing secured the rebound and missed a jumper from eight feet. Then, Mason inexplicably fouled Miller by going over his back with 7.5 seconds left. Miller drained both free throws. Anthony brought the ball up the court but fell down when he tried to make a move, losing the ball on the final possession.[53]

Miller yelled "choke artists" as he ran out of the tunnel and said during a postgame interview that Mason and Starks choked. Van Gundy stated in the ESPN film *Winning Time*, "That sequence was the biggest meltdown that I can remember ever seeing in the NBA."[54]

Game 1 was played on a Sunday afternoon. Smits recalls the streets of Manhattan were eerily quiet in the hours after the game. It was as if the entire city was in shock.[55]

The Knicks were reeling, though Mason received some personal satisfaction when he was named NBA Sixth Man of the Year.[56] Mase averaged 9.9 points on upward of 56 percent shooting and grabbed 8.4 rebounds per game for the Knicks during the '94–'95 season. The recognition meant a great deal to the forward who felt he should be starting and had been so instrumental to the team's success over the past four seasons.

However, the big story in the days between Games 1 and 2 was Reggie's comments about the Knicks being chokers. Larry Brown was not happy about his star's remarks. He felt they took the focus off of how great the Pacers had played and their amazing comeback.[57]

Game 2 became a must-win for the Knicks, who could not afford to lose the first two games at home. They played like it. The crowd harassed Miller with chants of "Reggie sucks" and "Cheryl." New York started the second half on a 25–4 run and proceeded to rout the Pacers, 96–77. Miller was held to just 10 points, and the Pacers turned the ball over 33 times. Harper led the Knicks with 24 points and eight assists.[58]

Ewing was noticeably struggling through a strained left calf muscle, so the Pacers went right at him.[59] He began wearing a protective stocking in Game 2. The Big Fella only scored 15 points that game after being outscored by Smits, 34–11, in Game 1.[60]

The teams traveled to Indiana for Game 3 with the series tied at one. New York led by 10 points with less than five minutes to go, but Indiana hung around. The Knicks were up 87–81 when Ewing fouled out on an illegal screen with 3:30 remaining. Smits took advantage of Ewing's absence by connecting on a couple big buckets down the stretch. With the game tied at 88, Reggie missed a potential game-winning, step-back three at the buzzer.[61]

The Knicks were unable to protect the rim in overtime without Ewing and Smith, who also fouled out. Derrick McKey blocked Oakley's three-point attempt at the buzzer, and the Pacers escaped with a 97–95 win. Reggie delivered 26 points and 11 rebounds, and Smits outscored Ewing again, this time 21–11.[62]

New York lost again in Game 4, putting themselves in a 3–1 hole. It was a one-point game at halftime. Then, the Pacers blew it open in the second half, outscoring the Knicks 34–17 in the third quarter. Sam Mitchell was an unlikely hero, contributing 11 points while filling in for Dale Davis, who dislocated his shoulder in the first half. The Pacers outrebounded the Knicks, 43–33, despite playing most of the game without Davis, their best rebounder. Smits paced Indiana once again with 25 points and 11 rebounds.[63]

The odds were stacked against the Knicks. Only four teams in NBA history had overcome a 3–1 deficit, and it had not happened since 1981 when the Celtics defeated the 76ers in the Eastern Conference Finals.[64] Undaunted, Starks told the press, "We will win this series."[65]

Prominent athletes use aliases on the road when they check into hotels so people do not bother them. Some use a rotation of a few aliases, which they guard closely, lest they be woken up in the middle of the night by a crazed fan of the local team. Reggie's alias was Sherlock Holmes.[66]

The day before Game 5, Miller received a phone call early in the morning telling him he was a great player. Then he went to morning shootaround. When he returned to his room, he had about 25 messages saying things like "You suck" and "The Knicks are going to beat your ass." One of the local radio stations had broadcast his alias.[67]

The next day, the Knicks and Pacers faced off in Game 5. New York started with a sense of urgency that appeared to be lacking in Game 4. The Knicks were up 94–87 with 53 seconds remaining, then the Pacers scored the next eight points. Reggie hit a three to cut the deficit to two, and Byron Scott hit a deep three to give Indiana the lead with 5.9 seconds on the clock. New York appeared to be on its way to another catastrophic loss.[68]

This time, the Knicks had a timeout remaining, and Riley drew up a play. New York passed the ball to Starks, who sent it over to Ewing. The big man hit a running seven-footer with 1.8 seconds left to give the Knicks a 96–95 lead.[69]

The Pacers had one final chance. They inbounded the ball to Reggie, who came off a double screen, but his 30-foot shot just missed. The Knicks remained alive to fight another day. When they landed in Indianapolis for Game 6, Riley brought his team directly to a movie theater to see *Die Hard with a Vengeance*, sending the message that they too would not go down easily.[70]

The Indiana media asked the Pacers if they felt a sense of déjà vu because they were in the same position as the previous season, up 3–2 on the Knicks and heading back to Indiana. Brown's club looked tight in Game 6, and the Knicks came away with the 92–82 victory. Ewing appeared healthier than in the previous games and scored 25 points while grabbing 11 rebounds. Reggie shot just 4-of-13 from the field, and Dale Davis looked uncomfortable wearing a harness on his injured shoulder.[71]

The odds seemed to shift in the Knicks' favor, as they headed back to New York for Game 7. New York had the momentum, and no road team had won a Game 7 since 1982. Smits recalls: "I'm thinking 'Wow. The same thing is happening over again. We're gonna lose.'"[72]

The Pacers controlled Game 7 through three quarters, taking a 74–59 lead late in the third. Then the Knicks clawed their way back with the help of some timely threes by Starks and Harper. Ewing put the Knicks ahead 84–83 with 6:53 remaining. Reggie, who attempted only one of his 18 shots in the fourth quarter, looked completely gassed.[73]

Indiana regained the lead and led 97–92 when Starks hit a three from the corner to cut the deficit to two with 32.3 seconds left in the game. New York stopped Indiana on the following possession and got the ball back with five seconds left.[74]

Harper inbounded the ball from midcourt to Ewing on the left side of the floor near the top of the key. The center drove right and turned the corner on Antonio Davis. Patrick had a clear path to the hoop, but he was unable to elevate and dunk the ball due to his sore calf. He tried an uncontested finger roll from a few feet away. The ball hit the back of the rim and bounced out.[75]

Mark Boyle, the voice of the Pacers, jubilantly exclaimed, "Ring the bell! Ding-dong, the witch is dead!" The Pacers had finally slayed the Knicks. The Knicks and the Garden crowd were dumbfounded. After the game, Harper reflected on the devastating beginning and end to the series and concluded, "God didn't want us to win this series."[76]

The season was over, and there was a sense that the Knicks' run may have been as well. The team as constructed could not win a championship. Changes would have to be made. Smith later said of Ewing's miss, "That shot put the lid on the basket for all of our careers moving forward."[77]

Riley stated after the game that dissension in the locker room and lack of chemistry caused the Knicks' demise, which had become a convenient fallback explanation of his when things did not work out. He called the 1994–95 campaign his most difficult season in coaching.[78]

12

Riley's Exit

"The reason I came to New York was Dave Checketts. But he's also the reason I left."[1]—Pat Riley

New York was never home for Riley, not like Los Angeles was. Pat, and his wife, Chris, had made lifelong friends in L.A. They envisioned retiring to their house in Malibu if Pat could ever pry himself away from the game. After losses, Riley went straight home instead of socializing with friends, as he did in L.A.[2] He had grown tired of the constant media criticism and later admitted to journalist Mark Kriegel that he "was miserable in New York."[3]

Riles also knew he had maxed out the potential of the Knicks' determined, but flawed, roster. Ewing was about to turn 33 and would undergo a fourth surgery on his right knee during the offseason. Oak was 31, and Harper would turn 34 the following season. The team did not have much roster flexibility to improve the talent level. There was no second superstar to pair with the big man on the horizon.

Moreover, not only were the Knicks eliminated by the Pacers, but they also had to worry about the ascendant Magic and the Bulls with the return of Jordan. It may have been the perfect time for Riley to walk away.

There was a contingent within the Knicks front office that would not have been sad to see Riley go. The Knicks needed to incorporate younger players into the rotation and at least consider the possibility of trading Ewing and starting over. Riley may not have had the patience for that. Checketts said of Riley, "You've never heard any of his players say, 'He's a teacher.'"[4]

The coach still had one year remaining on his five-year deal, which expired at the end of the 1995–96 season. Even so, as early as March, there were rumors that he could leave New York following the season because he had not signed an extension. Checketts and Riley had been negotiating for the better part of a year, with the trust between the two eroding with each discussion.[5] Word leaked that New York had offered Riley a new deal worth $3 million per year, though according to Checketts, the number was closer to $5 million per year for three years.[6] Riley balked, making it clear he was interested in not only money, but control of basketball operations.

In August 1994, Viacom Inc., which took over Paramount earlier in the year, agreed to sell Madison Square Garden, the Knicks, the Rangers, and MSG Network to ITT and Cablevision for $1.08 billion.[7] ITT purchased 87 percent of the assets, and Cablevision bought the remaining 13 percent, though Cablevision reserved the right to purchase up to 50 percent of the properties at any time.[8]

Riley was concerned the ownership change could create instability within the franchise.[9] He preferred the Jerry Buss model of ownership he had with the Lakers in which there was one individual owner with whom he could establish a relationship. Riley claims Checketts assured him he would be released from the final year of his contract if he kept quiet about his concerns pending sale of the team, which was not completed until March '95.[10]

Viacom fired Bob Gutkowski as president of the Garden in August '94, upon Cablevision's request, and replaced him with Checketts on an interim basis.[11] Riley wanted an ownership share of the Knicks and to replace Checketts as team president. Checketts informed Riley that ownership was not a possibility, so the coach requested a meeting with Rand Araskog, the CEO of ITT.[12]

After a few minutes of small talk with Araskog, Riley reached for his briefcase. Araskog, who knew what was coming, said, "Pat, don't do it. Leave your briefcase alone." The CEO confirmed ownership was not an option. He believed it would have been difficult to navigate the terms between himself, Charles Dolan of Cablevision, and each's corporation.[13]

"We could have done it, but it wouldn't have sat well with many people, and I think the board would have fired me," said Araskog. Half an hour after his meeting with Riley, Araskog received a call from Checketts, at which point he reported, "Dave, I'm sorry, but I guess we're going to lose him."[14]

Grunfeld threatened to quit if Riley were made president over him.[15] Checketts claims he made it clear to Riley he could have the position of president anyway, believing Riley was more important to the organization than Grunfeld.[16] However, there is evidence to the contrary.

Checketts entered Gutkowski's office after he received the news that his boss had been fired and told Gutkowski it was a terrible day for him (Checketts). Gutkowski asked why, noting that Checketts was being named interim president of MSG. Checketts said the Knicks were going to lose Riley because the coach was going to want to replace him as president of the team "and I can never let him run *my* club."[17] Checketts also told journalist Peter Vecsey there was "no fucking way" he was going to give Riley the power he was seeking.[18]

Checketts' ego affected his decision-making. Riley was one of the rare figures who could change the course and culture of an NBA franchise. He was the most important person in the Knicks organization, and Checketts should have done everything in his power to keep him. Riley was not going to receive ownership, but the title of president may have been enough to keep him.[19]

Not long after the season, Riley's agent informed Checketts the relationship between Riley and Checketts was no longer working. He suggested Checketts and Riley meet and figure out how to part ways. Checketts was defiant, noting Riley had one year left on his contract. He drove to Riley's house in Greenwich, Connecticut, and the two had a long talk. Riley listed several concerns, none of which seemed serious to Checketts, which made Checketts suspect Riley was negotiating with another team. Riley reiterated that he was done coaching the Knicks.[20]

On June 15, Riley faxed in his resignation before leaving for a vacation in Greece. A case of "he said, he said" ensued. Riley issued a statement through a public relations firm, claiming philosophical differences with management and their refusal to give him more control over the team led to his decision. According to Riley, Checketts told him he could be released from his contract as soon as the sale of the team went through. The coach also later claimed he had verbally resigned on June 1, two weeks before the fax.[21]

Upon receiving the fax, Checketts immediately called a press conference. He contradicted Riley's claim that he agreed to release the coach from his contract. He also stated Riley already had veto power over all personnel moves and final say on all disciplinary matters.[22]

Riley and Grunfeld had a strong working relationship.[23] The GM looked to improve the roster, while Riley focused on the players who were there. If Grunfeld discovered a move he thought could benefit the team, he discussed it with his coach. Riley did not exactly have "veto power," though it is highly unlikely Grunfeld would have made a move Riley strongly opposed.[24]

The New York media crushed Riley, due in large part to the way he exited, with headlines like "Gutless" and "The Quitter Within."[25] It looked like he quit and ran out of town. Pat's absence also allowed Checketts to control the narrative.

Ewing was shocked by the news and disappointed he had to hear about it on television rather than from Riley himself.[26] Assistant coach Jeff Van Gundy did not see it coming either.[27] Other Knicks were not caught as off-guard. Starks notes that Riley took the losses as hard as the players, and it had been a grueling four years. It was a business decision, and there had been rumors about his departure for months.[28]

Riley cracked the whip harder in his final season in New York. "I began to push hard, real hard, on the players," Riley said, a few months after his departure. "It was time. It was time for them to take true responsibility for wanting to win a title." The coach called his players cream puffs and unprofessional. He punched a hole in a blackboard during an uninspiring performance against the Pistons.[29]

Riley's players held him in high esteem, but they were not necessarily sad to see him go. "I don't think anybody was upset about his decision as far as players because it kind of ran its course a little bit," Starks reflected years later. After Riley pushed the team so hard for four years, Starks believed it was time for a new voice in the locker room.[30]

Oak was the one Knick to publicly criticize Riley. "He [Riley] had some guys on the team brainwashed," Oak said months later. "The only guys who were upset when he left were the ones carrying his bags." He believed Riley did not hold the "main guys" accountable for their mistakes, likely a reference to Ewing and Starks.[31]

The Knicks had a fantastic four-year run under Riley. New York posted a record of 223–105, won two Atlantic Division titles, advanced to two Eastern Conference Finals, and came within a game of a championship, all with just one star player on the roster. Tomjanovich said in his autobiography, "The true measure of a coach is if he can win with different personnel and with different styles."[32] Riley proved he could do that in New York.

A few days after Riley's resignation, Dave Wohl, executive vice president of the Heat, confirmed he was interested in hiring Riley but stated he had neither spoken to Riley nor the Knicks. The Heat were required to receive permission from the Knicks before contacting Riley because he was still under contract.[33]

A week later, Heat owner Micky Arison stated during a radio interview: "We will go to great lengths to get Pat here if given the opportunity to negotiate with him." Wohl and Arison's remarks prompted the Knicks to file tampering charges against the Heat for tortious interference with the contract between Riley and the Knicks.[34]

The Knicks believed the Heat had been courting Riley as early as February when Arison purchased the majority share of the team, then dismissed Kevin Loughery and named Alvin Gentry the interim coach.[35] Arison had asked Wohl for potential replacements for Loughery at that time, and Wohl put Riley atop the list.[36] He told Arison the coach had likely taken the Knicks as far as they could go, and there were rumors he was unhappy in New York.[37] Arison wooed his target by indicating the Heat were looking for a coach "like Pat Riley," but there is no evidence he actually spoke to Pat.[38]

Checketts spearheaded the case with an arsenal of Garden attorneys at his disposal. Araskog was not interested. "My own personal attitude was if a guy wants to go somewhere, it isn't going to do much good to try to keep him, number one, cause he's not gonna want to stay," the CEO said. "And unless someone does something too egregious, I wasn't too excited about it."[39]

The Knicks and Heat were scheduled to state their cases on tampering before David Stern on August 4. On the morning of the hearing, Checketts received a phone call from the owner of the Carnegie Deli, a big Knicks fan named Freddie Klein. Checketts frequented the famous deli, and the two had become friends.[40]

Klein said Raanan Katz, a minority owner of the Miami Heat, asked him to deliver a message. Katz told Klein to ask Checketts if he remembered 1972 in Munich, a reference to the kidnapping and killing of 11 members of the Israeli Olympic team by the Palestinian terrorist group Black September. Checketts said, "Of course, I remember." Katz, who was born in Israel and served in the Israeli army, suggested he knew people like the Israeli commandos who retaliated for the Munich attack, and Checketts better watch out for himself and his family.[41]

Checketts reported the incident to Stern, who arranged for security outside of Checketts' house. The NBA investigated the incident. Katz admitted sending the message, but said he only meant that if Checketts messed with the Heat they would mess with him back.[42]

At the arbitration hearing, New York presented a memorandum from Riley to Arison dated June 5, 10 days before Riley resigned, which included his contract demands. One of them was 20 percent ownership of the team. It began, "All discussions are to be in strict confidence. We will publicly deny any discussion and any public release will kill the deal."[43]

The coach who wrote about how "The Disease of Me" could undermine a team was negotiating with one team while coaching another. At the end of the hearing, Stern pushed both sides to reach an agreement, warning, "You don't want me to decide this."[44]

Other evidence presented at the hearing included telephone records and correspondence provided by Arison between the Heat and Dick Butera, a friend of Riley's who was acting on his behalf.[45] Butera and Arison spoke for the first time in February, and members of the Heat organization indicated that Riley's name was discussed, though Butera claims the conversations were solely about his interest in purchasing the team.[46]

According to Butera, he did not talk to Arison about Riley until after the season was over. Riley called him from the team bus after the Knicks lost to the Pacers and asked Butera if he was still friendly with Arison. Butera said he was, and Riley replied, "Well, I'm done. I'm finished with the Knicks. Get me a deal."[47]

Butera encouraged Riley to think it over and the two talked again a few days later, at which point Riley said, "Checketts has lied to me for the last time. I don't want to deal with this organization."[48]

Butera, who was not an agent, was not sure where to begin. He informed Arison Riley wanted $50 million over 10 years, which included an ownership share in the team. Arison responded, "Why did you bother calling me? This is a joke." But he did not end the discussions.[49]

Butera was not concerned about negotiating with Arison because he believed Checketts had released Riley from his contract. "The only problem with the release was that it was verbal, not in writing," Butera said years later.[50]

Checketts disagrees with Butera's version of events. "I will never forget that they were exchanging offers during the 1995 playoffs against Indiana. [Riley] lost his focus, and we lost the series," Checketts said.[51]

Russ Granik, who was deputy commissioner at the time, participated in the arbitration hearing. He recalled, "Miami had tampered with Pat when he was still under contract with the Knicks." Granik continued: "I don't remember anything [else] quite like that."[52]

According to Checketts, Stern called him and Araskog a few days after the hearing and informed them they won the case. He said the Knicks could have Riley banned from coaching for the 1995–96 season or seek compensation from Miami, though he reiterated his desire for a settlement.[53] The Knicks pushed for $3 million and an unconditional draft pick. On the night of September 1, hours before Stern was set to announce his decision, the two teams struck a deal. They settled for a conditional first-round pick in the 1996 draft (top-five protected) and $1 million.[54]

That same night, Miami announced it reached a deal with Riley. Months earlier, Butera had two or three meetings with Arison, then Riley and Arison "basically shook hands on the phone." The Heat gave Riley $40 million, 10 percent ownership of the team, and control over personnel decision-making.[55] It was a deal the Knicks never would have matched. For his efforts, Butera received a Heat track suit in the wrong size from Riley.[56] Meanwhile, Grunfeld filled Checketts' old job as president of the team.

Checketts and Riley continued to exchange barbs after Riley signed with Miami. Riley said, "I got tired of being used, manipulated, promised, ignored, threatened and eventually, I got tired of somebody not living up to his word. [Checketts] went from being my ally to my adversary." Checketts reflected the sentiment of many Knicks fans when he said Riley was "motivated by his own selfishness [and], turned his back on the New York Knicks team, the organization, and the fans of New York."[57] Both men carried their share of blame. They would not speak to each other for many years.

Riley's relationship with New York would change dramatically, but it was far from over. Over the next several years, his Heat would develop one of the league's most intense rivalries with his former team.

13

The Nellie Experience

"It may be as simple a situation as I was the wrong guy for the job."[1]—Don Nelson

Checketts and Grunfeld wanted an experienced coach to replace Riley. The Knicks were built to contend immediately, and there was no time for a young coach to learn on the job.[2] New York's first target was Chuck Daly, who checked all the boxes. From his days with the Pistons, he had a championship pedigree and the cachet that came with it. He coached Ewing in the 1992 Olympics and had the charisma to handle the New York media. Perhaps, most importantly, Daly was available. After a stint with the Nets, he was working as an analyst for Turner Broadcasting.[3]

New York offered Daly the job with the caveat that he would have to bring in an assistant coach to groom as his eventual replacement. Daly was 64 years old, and management did not want to conduct another coaching search in two or three years.[4] The coach was intrigued by a Knicks roster that reminded him of his Pistons teams. Ultimately, he did not want to put himself through the grueling schedule of coaching any longer and passed on the opportunity.[5]

Checketts and Grunfeld turned their sights toward two out-of-work, veteran coaches, Don Nelson and former Celtics coach Chris Ford.[6] Nelson, who coached Grunfeld in Milwaukee, emerged as the frontrunner. In fact, Checketts had approached Nelson at an NBA draft workout in May and said he would like to talk to him if things didn't work out with Riley.[7] A couple of days after Riley resigned, Nelson called Grunfeld to express his interest in the job.[8]

The whimsical Nelson was the mad scientist of the NBA, known for trotting out unique lineups and experimenting with unusual offenses in order to take opponents out of their game plan and create favorable matchups. During his first stint as coach of the Warriors, he encouraged 7-foot-6 center Manute Bol to launch three-pointers, at a time when big men did not dare fire away from behind the arc.

Nelson won five championships as a reserve forward on the great Celtics teams of the 1960s and '70s. His shining moment occurred in Game 7 of the '69 Finals when he connected on a foul-line jumper to help seal the championship. As a coach, he had done everything but win a championship. Nellie compiled 817 victories while manning the sidelines for 11 years with Milwaukee, followed by six and a half seasons with the Warriors. His teams won at least 50 games nine times, and he was named Coach of the Year on three occasions. In 1994, he coached "Dream Team II" to the FIBA championship.[9]

The one blemish on Nellie's resume was the end of his tenure in Golden State. Nellie believed in breaking rookies down, then building them back up. Accordingly, he was very hard on the first pick of the 1993 draft, Chris Webber, during his rookie season. Webber felt Nelson's criticism crossed the line and verbally fired back. He also did not like playing center in Nellie's small-ball lineups.[10]

The former University of Michigan star went on to win NBA Rookie of the Year, then months later sat out the beginning of the 1994–95 season and demanded a trade. The Warriors complied, sending him to the Bullets to play with his "Fab Five" teammate Juwan Howard, in exchange for Tom Gugliotta and three first-round draft picks.[11]

The Golden State players were disgruntled by the Webber affair, particularly shooting guard Latrell Sprewell, who was very close with Webber. Nellie lost the locker room and then his job when the Warriors started the 1994–95 season 14–31.[12]

However, Nelson's conflict with Webber appeared to be an anomaly. He'd built a reputation over many years as a players' coach and his contrast with the overbearing Riley was viewed by some within the Knicks organization as a welcome change of pace for a disciplined, veteran team.

Casual in style and demeanor, Nellie often donned a mock turtleneck and sport jacket on the sideline to go with his ruffled blondish-white hair. He was laid-back and outgoing, somebody with whom the players and media could joke around. He liked to have a few beers with lunch, on the team bus, or in the locker room after games.[13]

After one preseason shootaround, Mason did his best Nellie impression for his teammates, sauntering across the court with Nellie's trademark dazed look on his face. Ewing tossed Mase a basketball, which Mase put under his shirt to complete the image. All of his teammates were hysterical. Such a scene never would have occurred under Riley.[14]

It was not unusual for Nellie to design a play on a napkin in a restaurant, then crumple it up and stuff it in his pocket.[15] He did not even use a playbook. Instead, the coach handed out notebooks to his players and expected them to take notes on X's and O's and draw diagrams as he lectured at the chalkboard. He gave the players written quizzes on the material and fined them $10 for each wrong answer.[16]

In July '95, Nelson signed a three-year deal with the Knicks for just shy of $6 million. Assistant coaches Bob Salmi, Jeff Van Gundy, and Jeff Nix remained with the team. Nelson also added former Rockets coach Don Chaney to the staff. The first time Nellie met Van Gundy, who had been Riley's top assistant and one of the premier up-and-coming coaches in the league, he looked at him quizzically and stated, "I don't think I've ever seen you before."

The one significant personnel change the Knicks made for the 1995–96 season came at the backup point guard position. Greg Anthony was one of three players New York left unprotected for the expansion draft held by the NBA's newest teams, the Vancouver Grizzlies and Toronto Raptors. The Grizzlies selected the guard with the second overall pick after the Raptors chose Chicago's B.J. Armstrong.[17] In response, New York signed veteran point guard Gary Grant to compete with Ward for minutes backing up Harper.[18]

The Knicks also re-signed Mason, who was an unrestricted free agent, to a six-year, $25 million contract. Despite Mason's confrontational demeanor, he was too valuable to let go.[19] Surprisingly, Riley phoned Mason's agent and expressed interest in the combative forward, but Mase was intent on remaining in New York.[20]

Nelson, who had a well-deserved reputation for thinking outside the box, had big plans for Mason, whom he declared the Knicks' best young player and the future of the team.[21] Mason replaced Smith in the starting lineup and operated as a point forward with the offense running through him at times. Nellie had success using Paul Pressey in Milwaukee and Billy Owens with the Warriors in that role.[22]

In the fall of 1995, Mase had "one-handed" shaved into his scalp, in honor of his new free-throw shooting style.[23] He previously displayed one of the ugliest foul-shooting forms in the league, which caused numerous lane violations because he hesitated before releasing the ball. During the summer of '95, Mase began shooting foul shots with just his left hand, his right hand lingering a few inches away from the ball. His shooting from the charity stripe improved from 64 percent the previous season to 72 percent.

Nellie did not want to mess with the Knicks' defense, which had been the hallmark of their success under Riley. Offense was a different story. He desired to inject pace and ingenuity into a Knicks attack that had been slow and predictable, believing they had advanced as far as they could by primarily dumping the ball into Patrick.[24] The coach wanted the Knicks to play what had become known as "Nellie Ball," with small lineups that pushed the tempo to create mismatches, a strategy he credited to his coach with the Celtics, Red Auerbach.[25]

Ewing, creaky knees and all, was wary of playing at a quicker pace.[26] When he and Nellie sat down together for the first time, Nellie told Patrick he wanted him to become a better passer. Ewing, who had grown accustomed to being praised by the coaching staff, thought he was already a very good passer and did not take kindly to the coach's suggestion.[27]

Nelson believed in being direct with players. The first time he spoke to Davis, he told the shooting guard if he wanted to see the court, he had to expand his game beyond shooting. The coach could also be stern when necessary. Sarunas Marciulionis, who played five seasons for Nellie in Golden State, referred to him as a "dictator type."

The free-wheeling Nelson eased up on the Knicks due to the age of their key players. There were no more two-a-days during training camp and practices ran closer to one hour than Riley's marathons. Nellie did not realize his veterans wanted to be pushed.[28] Starks noted derisively in his book, *My Life*, "If Riley's practices were wars, Nelson's were tea parties."[29] Whereas Riley spent much of the day at the practice facility poring over film, Nelson often bolted for the golf course as soon as practice ended.[30]

With their revamped offense, the Knicks jumped out to a 17–6 record by the time Riley and the Heat came to town on December 19. Riley would later refer to the time from when he resigned until his first trip back to the Garden as "one of the worst times of my life publicly, as far as getting criticized and being called names and being called out and probably I deserved all of that." The coach received death threats, and the criticism irritated him.[31] Riley even challenged columnist Peter Vecsey, who had been very critical about the way he left New York, to a fight outside of the Heat locker room at Orlando Arena.[32]

The Garden faithful voiced their displeasure the minute Riles exited the tunnel. Years later, the coach recalled seeing a kid about 10 years old sitting in the front row holding a sign that said, "Riley, you suck."[33] Another prominently displayed sign read, "Benedict Riley."[34] The typically reserved coach was visibly unnerved by the atmosphere. He began blowing kisses to the crowd and mouthed, "I love you." Then he went to center court and waved for the fans to bring it on.[35]

The Knicks had no hard feelings toward their former coach. Starks felt Riley deserved a standing ovation for resurrecting the franchise. Before tipoff, Ewing gave Riles a hug. Harper and Starks followed.[36]

Throughout the game, Riley was serenaded with chants of "Riley sucks." With the Knicks comfortably ahead in the second half, the crowd taunted their once beloved former coach with chants of "Ri-ley." Miami played the game shorthanded with Alonzo Mourning, Kevin Willis, and Billy Owens out with injury, and the Knicks gained an 89–70 victory.[37]

"What I felt versus what they felt was entirely different," Riley said afterward. "I spent four years here, and I think that they know what I put into this, and we were very successful. I always thought the fans of New York—I think they're the very best."[38]

Nelson's unconventional moves were successful early on. He experimented with a big lineup, playing Ewing, Oakley, Mason, and Smith together with Harper in the fourth quarter of a New York victory over Houston in November.[39] On other occasions, he turned to small ball, playing four guards along with Ewing or Mason.

Despite the team's success, the players began bickering in December. Ewing complained he was not receiving enough touches. Mason, who was taking those touches, argued his teammates should put the team first and stop worrying about themselves. Oak jumped into the fray by telling everybody to shut up and play.[40]

There was a history of tension between Ewing and Mase. The two exchanged words on several occasions in practice and had to be separated by teammates on the team plane when a friendly argument turned heated during the preseason.[41] The squabbling was noteworthy because it was done in public. Riley had not tolerated his players airing the team's dirty laundry, whereas Nelson believed they were professionals who were entitled to speak freely to the media.[42]

The Knicks hit the skids in January, losing

Pat Riley was vilified in New York upon his return to the Garden on December 19, 1995, as the coach of the Miami Heat. Knicks fans and the media took offense to Riley's decision to resign by fax, then skip town (AP Photo/Mark Lennihan).

six of nine. Nelson broached the subject of trading Ewing with management because he thought New York had a legitimate shot at landing Shaquille O'Neal. Nellie had developed a relationship with Shaq while coaching the World Championships in 1994 and was confident Shaq was going to leave Orlando as a free agent that summer. The coach expected "The Diesel" to choose between the Knicks and Lakers and believed if the Knicks offered Ewing, the Magic would deal Shaq rather than risk losing him for nothing.[43]

Nellie's idea was rejected. Dealing Ewing for Shaq would have been a no-brainer. Shaq was the more dominant player and 10 years younger. But Checketts did not believe the Knicks could acquire Shaq and was unwilling to risk word leaking to Ewing that they were shopping him.[44] Still, Ewing caught wind of Nellie's suggestion, signaling the end of their relationship.

Ewing's agent, David Falk, complained to management about Nelson on two occasions.[45] Oakley also had concerns about Nelson's coaching style. He felt the Knicks were not practicing hard enough and spoke to Nellie several times about being more assertive with the team. Oak also blamed his teammates for their lack of effort.[46]

Nellie began his Knicks tenure on shaky ground with Starks, and the rift between them increased as the season progressed. The conflict dated back to '88–'89, when Starks played for Nelson in Golden State. Starks believes it began as a clash of personalities. He was a young hotshot, trying to make it in the league, and Nellie was an old-school coach. Starks warned Knicks management against hiring Nellie when he was interviewing for the job. He pointed out that Nelson preferred big men who could face the basket and did not know how to utilize a back-to-the-basket center like Ewing.[47]

Nelson lost Starks completely when he benched the fan favorite during the team's losing streak, then justified the decision by publicly stating Davis was the better player. "Everybody thought he'd be a good coach, but sometimes nightmares happen," Starks responded.[48] Nelson pushed for the Knicks to trade Starks for Vinny Del Negro before the trade deadline, but Grunfeld killed the idea.[49]

One night at a bar at the Ritz Carlton in Marina del Rey, California, Nelson told two reporters a story about Starks. "We were getting onto the team bus," Nelson said, "and a guy ran up to Starks and said, 'John I'm a big fan. Will you please sign this?'" Starks, who signed for anybody at any time, said, "Sure." The guy then asked, "Can you make it out to my brother, Marc? It's Marc with a C." Starks signed it to "Cark."[50]

The story has since become part of Knicks lore, though Nelson's retelling of it represented a mean-spirited attempt to make Starks look stupid.[51] John was popular in the locker room. His teammates liked to poke fun at him the way that brothers joke with one another. They could give their little brother a hard time, but nobody else could. Chris Childs, who played with Starks for two seasons, loves telling the story about when he, Starks, Oakley, and Ewing went to dinner at Ruth's Chris Steakhouse. Starks ordered lobster for dinner and requested for it to be "falling off the bone."[52]

Starks' teammates had the ultimate respect for his competitiveness. Davis calls Starks and Harper "the toughest people I have ever been around."[53] Starks did not back down from anybody, verbally or physically, including Oakley and Mason at practice.

Once Nelson lost Ewing and Starks, he lost most of the team. The collective effort on the court waned noticeably. Nellie did not make much of an attempt to win his players back, either. It appeared to some opposing coaches that he had given up.[54] Mike Wise of the *New York Times* and a few of the other beat writers believe Nellie was actually trying to get fired by that point.[55]

Still, the Knicks were 30–16 when Oakley fractured his thumb on February 16. Then they went into freefall. New York lost eight of 11 games, including an 0–4 West Coast trip, which culminated in a 17-point drubbing at the hands of the lowly Clippers.[56] Two days later, Nelson was fired. His record for the season was 35–24.[57]

Grunfeld cited numerous losses to bad teams and the players' lack of effort as the reasons for Nelson's dismissal. The general manager noted months later, "We pride ourselves on defense and rebounding. Those are our strengths. We got away from that and lost our identity and our work ethic."[58]

Nelson believes he was fired because Ewing found out the coach wanted to trade him.[59] Nellie hailed from an era when coaches prevailed in conflicts with players, but it had since become a players' league.

Grunfeld was right to fire

Don Nelson lasted just 59 games after replacing Pat Riley as coach of the Knicks. Conflicts with Patrick Ewing and John Starks were at the heart of his downfall (REUTERS/Jeff MitchellJM).

Nelson when he did, rather than waiting until the end of the season. The relationship between coach and players was not going to improve. The Knicks were flush with cap space and needed to stabilize the franchise in order to attract free agents.

The players deserve some of the blame for their struggles under Nelson. They'd grown accustomed to playing a certain way and were reluctant to change. Nellie never had a shot in New York. However, he did a poor job of communicating with his players and ultimately failed to maximize their potential as a team.

"It's really strange," Nelson said. "I thought change would be good for this team, but, looking back, it was a bad fit. I'm kind of a creative coach, and this is an uncreative team."[60] Nellie fired a couple of parting shots on his way out, stating he did not think Ewing could be the best player on a contender any longer and reiterating his stance that Davis was better than Starks.[61]

Nelson resurrected his career in Dallas, where he developed Dirk Nowitzki and Steve Nash into All-Stars. He built the Mavs into contenders before retiring as the all-time leader in coaching victories after another stint as the head man in Golden State.

14

Van Gundy Takes the Whistle

"He's the little man we should have taken care of a while ago."[1]—Charles Oakley on Jeff Van Gundy's contract being guaranteed

Pat Riley planted the seed of being a head coach in Jeff Van Gundy's head. After Van Gundy's first season under Riley, Riley gave him a performance review of his strengths, weaknesses, and areas that needed improvement, like one would receive in a corporate job. Then, Riley asked Van Gundy if he could see himself as a head coach. Van Gundy admitted he had never thought about it. Riley told him that all players care about is whether their coach is competent, sincere, reliable, and trustworthy, with competence being most important. If you are those four things, he told him, NBA players will allow you to coach them.[2] Four years later, in March 1996, Van Gundy was about to find out if he fit the bill.

Grunfeld knocked on Van Gundy's hotel door at the Ritz Carlton in Philadelphia and informed him he was the new head coach of the Knicks.[3] At 34 years old, he was the youngest head coach in the league. Van Gundy summoned beat writers Mike Wise, Frank Isola, and Thomas Hill to his room and shared the news. He could not help but reflect on his father, Bill, a great coach in his own right, who bounced from one small college to another. Now, Jeff was the head coach of one of the NBA's marquee franchises.[4]

Next, Van Gundy informed the players and coaches, who were all surprised by the news. Assistant coach Bob Salmi said Van Gundy looked shocked himself.[5] The coach was both caught off-guard by Nelson's dismissal and surprised management chose him over former Coach of the Year Don Chaney.[6]

On the surface, Van Gundy was the polar opposite of his mentor. The *New York Post* ran a tale of the tape, comparing Riley and Van Gundy in everything from hairstyle to clothes, which brought Jeff's wife, Kim, to tears.[7] If Riley resembled a Wall Street banker with slicked back hair and $2,000 suits, Van Gundy looked like an accountant with a bad comb-over and bags under his eyes. Riley was tall and handsome. Van Gundy was short and disheveled. Riley received limousine service to the games. Van Gundy preferred to drive his Honda Civic.[8]

Van Gundy played up his everyman image, which made him relatable to fans. He showed off his $8 watch and referred to his ordinary clothes as "Van Gundy wear."[9] When asked what his favorite restaurant was, the coach replied, "the McDonald's drive-thru."

Van Gundy also benefited from the ill-fated Nelson era. Instead of receiving the job when Riley resigned and enduring the pressure that would have come with replacing a legend, he represented a return to normalcy at the Garden.

Below the surface, however, Van Gundy was very similar to Riley as a fellow fiery competitor and tireless worker with a brilliant basketball mind. "Jeff and I equate losing with dying," Riley once said proudly.[10] It was not unusual for Van Gundy to flip the desk in his office after a tough loss.[11]

The coach was detail-oriented and obsessive about basketball. "You can not beat him into the office in the morning," assistant coach Brendan Malone said of his boss. "He's in there before 7 a.m., and he stays until after 7. He's an office guy." Van Gundy kept a pillow and blanket at the practice facility so he could fall asleep there after road games.[12]

Don Chaney said that on the road, "very seldom do you see him [Van Gundy] outside. He's always in his room, watching tapes. All the time. He watches more tape than any coach in the NBA, and he probably sees less daylight than any coach in the NBA. Everything is in his room. He eats in the room. He works in the room and sleeps in the room."

Van Gundy once rammed his car into his garage door without opening it first because his mind was focused on stopping the Pistons' Grant Hill.[13] "I personally would like to see him get involved in another hobby to take him away from basketball," Chaney said. "Sometimes this business gets very stressful and you need an outlet, and I don't think he has one."[14]

Jeff grew up in a coaching family. His dad, Bill, coached at several colleges. At a young age, Jeff and his brother, Stan, tagged along with Bill to practices, on recruiting trips, and scouting trips, during which they began producing their own scouting reports.

Van Gundy graduated from Brockport High School in New York, standing 5–9 and weighing 150 pounds. He began his college career at Yale University but transferred to Menlo Junior College in Menlo Park, California, after he was cut from the basketball team. That was how much he loved the game. "I thought he was nuts," said his wife, who was his girlfriend at the time. "But

I did know that he needed to play." Van Gundy attended four colleges over five years, playing one season for his father at SUNY Brockport, before finishing up at Nazareth College.[15]

Jeff was a student of the game who would acquire knowledge from any source available. In the early '90s, before the internet, the back pages of basketball magazines, such as *Basketball Digest*, contained advertisements for homemade basketball coaching videos. Anybody could make and sell a video. Van Gundy ordered all of them in the hopes of gleaning some piece of information or strategy he could use.[16]

Jeff also sought the knowledge of other coaches, including those in different sports. Early in his tenure as head coach of the Knicks, he struck up a friendship with legendary football coach Bill Parcells. Parcells was coaching the Jets at the time and invited Van Gundy to practice. Keyshawn Johnson, the Jets' star receiver, approached the two coaches. It was his second season, not long after the release of his book *Just Give Me the Damn Ball*.[17]

With Keyshawn standing there, Parcells asked Van Gundy, "Hey, Jeff. Do you like restaurants?" Van Gundy said, "Yes." Parcells replied, "If you want to know about restaurants, Keyshawn's your guy. Do you like clothes?" Van Gundy self-mockingly asked, "Have you ever seen me dress?" Parcells said, "Well, if you ever change your mind, Keyshawn is your guy." Then the Jets coach asked Van Gundy, "Do you like winning?" Van Gundy replied, "Of course, Coach. I like to win." Parcells responded, "Well, then do not talk to Keyshawn Johnson. He does not know one thing about what it takes to win."[18]

By watching Parcells interact with his players, Van Gundy learned the importance of bluntness and humor when dealing with professional athletes over a long season.[19] However, Jeff's lighter side, to which NBA fans have grown accustomed from his years as a national color commentator, was rarely on display as a coach. Riley's protégé was stern with his players, and as Mike Breen put it, "looked like he was making a hostage tape during press conferences."[20] Marcus Camby, who played three-plus seasons for Van Gundy, says he never saw the coach smirk or smile.[21]

On the rare occasion Van Gundy did joke, it was self-deprecating. He told his center, Chris Dudley, who attended Yale, that he, too, went to Yale for one year, then transferred to junior college because "the coach sucked" and he did not make the team. Then, he left junior college because "the coach sucked" and he was not receiving enough playing time. Eventually, he played for his father and still did not receive many minutes. That was when he realized that he sucked.[22]

Van Gundy's only head coaching job prior to the Knicks was for McQuaid Jesuit High School in Rochester, New York, right out of college. He was there for one season, and as he recalls, his record was about .500. Stu Jackson, then an associate head coach under Rick Pitino at Providence College, met Van Gundy when he recruited one of his players. Jackson convinced Pitino to interview Van Gundy for the position of graduate assistant. At the end of the interview, Pitino said, "Well, congratulations, *Jim*. You've got the job."[23]

After Providence, Van Gundy worked as an assistant coach at Rutgers University. Later, in the summer of '89, Jackson, then the head coach of the Knicks, offered Van Gundy a job as an assistant coach on his staff. Van Gundy would ultimately serve in that role under Jackson, John MacLeod, Riley, and Nelson.[24] He was briefly bumped up to the front office before Riley arrived, but Riley had heard great things about him and wanted him on the bench.[25]

Days before Van Gundy was elevated to head coach, there was an incident at Knicks practice involving Starks and Thomas Hill of the *New York Post*. Hill had contacted the shooting guard's mother, grandmother, and sisters to inquire about Starks' thoughts on playing for Nelson. Starks deemed the inquiries an invasion of his privacy and was furious. He was working out with Van Gundy when Hill entered the practice facility the following day and Van Gundy started firing off expletives at Hill. Starks then charged Hill, screaming at the reporter until he was pulled away.[26]

Van Gundy's actions were unprofessional, though, with them, he demonstrated he had his players' backs. When asked if the incident could hurt Van Gundy's career in New York, Checketts replied, "Just the opposite." He added, "We didn't know Jeff had that in him. If he plays his cards right, he might be able to someday land a good college coaching job somewhere."[27]

Van Gundy and Starks were close. The coach made a trip to Tulsa every summer to work with Starks on his game. Ewing, Oakley, and Starks had developed relationships with Van Gundy over several years. They trusted him and were content to play for him.[28]

Upon taking the head job, Van Gundy had to absorb a lot of information quickly. The team had a game that night against the 76ers. The coach decided to bring back the discipline and style of play that proved successful under Riley. New York was going to outwork other teams, rely on its defense, and play through Ewing in the post. Riley called Van Gundy that afternoon to congratulate him on his new job.[29]

Instead of conducting a customary shootaround, Van Gundy held a full practice on the day of the 76ers game. Perhaps, shocked by the day's events, the team turned in another listless performance in Philadelphia, falling to the 76ers, the worst team in the league.[30]

Next up for Van Gundy and the Knicks was a nationally televised matchup against the vaunted Bulls at MSG. Jordan was in peak form during his first full season back, and the Bulls had added Dennis Rodman. They came into MSG with a record of 54–6 on their way to a record-breaking 72–10 season. There was little reason to believe the struggling Knicks would pose a threat.[31]

The day before the Bulls game, Van Gundy put the Knicks through a grueling three-hour practice. Harper told the media it was the team's best practice of the season and they were going to beat the Bulls. Van Gundy was so overcome with emotion by the recent turn of events that he sat down in his office hours before the Bulls game and wept.[32]

The previous day's practice carried over to the game. The Knicks defense suffocated Chicago's attack. Meanwhile, they were hot from outside, particularly Harper who finished with 23 points and six assists. New York routed Chicago, 104–72. After the game, Van Gundy ran off the court, pumping his fist in the air.[33]

Grunfeld was quick to point out Van Gundy was not an interim coach. Still, the Knicks didn't provide their new coach any job security. The two sides agreed to a deal in which Van Gundy would be paid about $1 million a year through the 1997–98 season, but the contract was not guaranteed and the Knicks had the option to decline it up until July 1.[34] Checketts viewed Van Gundy as nothing more than a stop gap and intended to replace him at the end of the season with a big-name candidate.[35]

One such potential successor was Phil Jackson, who, in the last year of his contract, had yet to reach an agreement on a new deal with Chicago. As soon as Van Gundy took over, speculation began that Phil would return to the team he played for, replacing the young coach at season's end. Jackson fanned the flames by saying of course he would consider coaching the Knicks if negotiations with the Bulls didn't work out.[36]

Van Gundy was furious Jackson was campaigning for a job that was already filled. He viewed it as a violation of the code of etiquette between coaches. A few weeks later, he fired back at the Zen Master through the media. "People who weren't raised as coaches react in different ways. They speculate and use it for bargaining position and stuff like that. People in the coaching profession raised by coaches react in predictable fashion. They know proper protocol."[37]

It was the start of a bitter feud between Jackson and Van Gundy. Jackson subsequently referred to Van Gundy as "Jeff Van Gumby," and Van Gundy took aim at Jackson's affinity for Native American philosophy and his Triangle offense by derisively dubbing him "Big Chief Triangle."[38]

Riley argued that Van Gundy should not have to audition for his job. He noted Van Gundy was a great coach in a league short on them, adding that

Jeff had been coaching the Knicks for seven years. Management knew what they had in him, Riley suggested, and should lock him up to a long-term deal.[39]

Ewing publicly threw his support behind Van Gundy, as did Oakley.[40] The players respected how hard Van Gundy worked to prepare them to win. The bags under his eyes were a badge of honor, a testament to the sleepless nights he spent watching film. The players took comfort in knowing that no matter how early they showed up to the gym, their coach would already be there.[41]

New York finished the season with a 13–10 record under Van Gundy, playing much of the stretch without Oakley, who fractured a bone below his right eye after returning from his thumb injury.[42] The team's record for the season was 47–35, good enough to earn the fifth seed and a matchup with the Cavaliers in the first round.

Cleveland lacked the talent of previous seasons. Chronic back problems forced Brad Daugherty into early retirement, and the Cavs traded Mark Price to the Bullets prior to the '95–'96 season. Still, Mike Fratello's team boasted the stingiest defense in the league, surrendering a mere 88.5 points per game, and Price's replacement, Terrell Brandon, had blossomed into an All-Star.[43]

One person who liked the Cavs' chances heading into the series was Checketts. The Knicks' president expressed his belief over lunch with beat writer Mike Wise that the Knicks would lose in the first round. Wise questioned what would happen to Van Gundy, and Checketts dismissively suggested Jeff would end up coaching a Division I college program or serving as an assistant coach elsewhere.[44]

New York put forth a masterful Game 1 performance. They connected on 17-of-22 three-pointers and stifled Cleveland's attack, sparking a 20–0 fourth-quarter run. Oakley scored 17 points in the first three quarters while playing with a mask on his face to protect his eye. New York won, 106–83.[45]

Games 2 and 3 were closer, though the Knicks defense prevailed, resulting in a 3–0 sweep. Van Gundy's team made the most of its offensive opportunities, shooting 50 percent from the field and a blistering 59 percent from beyond the arc for the series. On the other end of the floor, the Knicks held the Cavs to just 42 percent shooting and 25 percent from downtown. Five Knicks averaged in double-figures, led by Starks at nearly 20 per game, compared to just two Cavs, Brandon and Dan Majerle. Riley's Knicks had never swept an opponent in the playoffs.

Next up for the Knicks were the Bulls. New York began the series as heavy underdogs against the team in red and white. Jordan scored 44 in a Bulls Game 1 victory. New York hung tight with MJ and company in Game 2, but once again fell short, 91–80.

The Knicks' chances looked bleak, but they were fierce competitors. Mason showed up for Game 3 with a new message carved into his scalp, "We've got faith." There was a comical moment in the fourth quarter when referee Hue Hollins inadvertently smacked Van Gundy in the face while signaling a foul call. The first-year head coach reached for his face while crumbling to the ground, but was able to stay in the game.[46] The Knicks staved off 46 points by Jordan and a furious Bulls comeback in the final minute and a half, to hold on for the 102–99 win. Ewing, Mason, and Oakley all recorded double-doubles, and Starks poured in 30 points.[47]

The Knicks fought valiantly in Game 4, overcoming a 10-point deficit midway through the fourth quarter to take a 91–88 lead with a minute and a half remaining. Unfortunately, they could not close out the game. Chicago grabbed a one-point lead on a Wennington jumper before Ewing missed a difficult fall-away from the baseline with 19.6 seconds on the clock. The final score read 94–91, Chicago. The difference in the game was second-chance opportunities. The Bulls grabbed 23 offensive rebounds, compared to four by the Knicks.[48]

The Bulls closed out the series at home in Game 5. They then avenged the previous season's loss to Orlando by sweeping Shaq and Penny in the conference finals before capping off their sensational season by defeating the SuperSonics in the Finals for their fourth championship.

One week after the Knicks were eliminated, management guaranteed Van Gundy's two-year contract for $2 million. The sweep of the Cavs, along with the support of his two captains, were enough to make his case.[49] Days earlier, Ewing reiterated his desire for Van Gundy to remain the coach. He even sidestepped a question about whether he would request a trade if Van Gundy were not retained.[50]

15

The Summer of '96

"We hit the jackpot!"[1]—Ernie Grunfeld

Nineteen ninety-six was a crucial summer for the Knicks and the NBA. The Knicks were flush with nearly $10 million in salary cap space in anticipation of a free-agent class that included Michael Jordan, Shaquille O'Neal, Alonzo Mourning, Reggie Miller, Gary Payton, Tim Hardaway, Dikembe Mutombo, Juwan Howard, Allan Houston, Latrell Sprewell, and Kenny Anderson.[2] Big-name talent such as Charles Barkley and Larry Johnson was on the trading block too. New York also had three first-round picks in what turned out to be a historic 1996 draft.

New York's core of Ewing, Mason, Oakley, Starks, and Harper had run its course. Ewing, Oak, and Harp were now in their mid–30s. New York needed to add young, offensive firepower to win a championship. That summer, Grunfeld utilized free agency, the draft, and the trade market to revamp the roster.

The 76ers selected Allen Iverson out of Georgetown with the first pick in the draft. Marcus Camby, Shareef Abdur-Rahim, Stephon Marbury and, Ray Allen rounded out the top five. Iverson was one of three future MVPs drafted that night, along with Kobe Bryant, who was selected by the Hornets at No. 13 before being traded to the Lakers, and Steve Nash, who was chosen by the Suns 15th overall. Seven other selected players would become All-Stars, along with one undrafted player, Ben Wallace.[3]

New York had the 18th, 19th, and 21st picks. Grunfeld worked the phones in an attempt to flip the 19th and 21st picks for one in the 10 to 15 range, but the Knicks ended up standing pat. They selected three forwards, John Wallace from Syracuse University, Walter McCarty from the University of Kentucky, and Dontae' Jones out of Mississippi State.[4]

Wallace was the most intriguing of the three prospects. The 6-foot-8 forward had been projected to be selected significantly earlier. He averaged 22.2 points, 8.7 rebounds, and 1.7 blocks during his senior season, while shooting over 50 percent from the field for his college career. His stock skyrocketed after he carried the Orangemen to the 1996 National Championship game, where they fell short against the heavily favored Kentucky Wildcats.[5]

Wallace dropped in the draft because of questions about his character. He had an argument with Bill Fitch and Elgin Baylor, the coach and general manager of the Clippers, respectively, during the pre-draft interview process.[6] He was also rumored to be out of shape. In addition, executives were concerned about his close relationship with fellow Syracuse product and chronic malcontent Derrick Coleman.[7]

The pro–Knicks crowd at Continental Airlines Arena in New Jersey was not concerned. Chants of "We want Wallace" echoed throughout the arena when the Knicks were on the clock. The forward was disappointed he fell to 18, but the excitement of being drafted by his childhood team and a lucrative sneaker deal made up for it.[8]

After the draft, Grunfeld turned his attention to free agency. New York had made two trades prior to the 1996 trade deadline, which gave the franchise close to $10 million in cap space for the summer. First, Grunfeld shed Charles Smith's contract by sending the veteran to the Spurs, along with Monty Williams, in exchange for Brad Lohaus, J.R. Reid, and a first-round draft pick.[9]

Then, he traded Herb Williams and Doug Christie to Toronto for Willie Anderson and Victor Alexander. Alexander and Anderson were in the final year of their contracts, whereas Christie had two more years remaining and Williams one. The Raptors released Williams a few days later, and the backup center re-signed with the Knicks.[10]

The Knicks' primary focus in free agency was at shooting guard, and many assumed their longtime tormentor, Reggie Miller, would be their first choice. Miller, for his part, had been sweet-talking the Knicks through the media. When asked whether his free-agent status could lead him to one particular team, he replied, "I think it would have to be New York." Miller continued, "Just the fact that it's New York, with its history, the building, the players. Plus, I like the rivalry they have with the Bulls, them never being able to get past them. You wonder if they had a different mix, if they could. That if they had a real shooting two-guard, if they could." It was a blatant swipe at Starks.[11]

Free agency began on July 14. Grunfeld's first move was a trade, sending Mason and Lohaus to the Hornets for two-time All-Star Larry Johnson. In doing so, the Knicks took on the remaining nine years and $71 million of Johnson's contract, and were forced to pay an additional $5 million as part of a 15 percent trade bonus included in the deal.[12]

Johnson grew up in the Dixon Circle Projects of South Dallas, where plenty of kids from the neighborhood succumbed to the crack epidemic. When Larry was in third grade, he and his friends waited outside the local convenience store for kids to go inside, then stole their bikes. His mother, Dortha, noticed all of the new bikes in her home and threatened to throw Larry out of the house. When a big bus pulled up in front of the projects, Johnson thought he was being taken away, but it belonged to the Dallas Police Athletic League and transported kids to a gym where they learned to box. Boxing was Larry's introduction to sports, which stabilized his life and kept him out of trouble.[13]

Larry never drank or did drugs. The gangbangers and drug dealers told him to stay away from all of that. They could see the man-child who had sprouted to 6–2 and 190 pounds by seventh grade had a gift that would enable him to escape the drugs, violence, and poverty.[14]

You had to be tough to play basketball in the Dixon Circle Projects. "Everybody fights," said Johnson of his neighborhood games. "You'd have a fight a week. If you played Monday through Saturday and didn't have a fight, you knew you had to be ready for Sunday because you'd surely have a fight. Myself, I liked to get my fight over on Monday or Tuesday and not worry for the rest of the week."[15] LJ proclaimed on NBA Inside Stuff during his rookie season, "Ain't nobody tougher than me … maybe better, but not tougher."[16]

Johnson committed to play ball at nearby Southern Methodist University but spent his first two years at Odessa College in Texas instead due to controversy surrounding his SAT scores. Then, he transferred to UNLV for his final two collegiate seasons, where he played for coach Jerry Tarkanian. Johnson had difficulty adjusting to Division I basketball and wondered during the first month if he could make it at that level. It was coach Tark who encouraged him to keep striving, keep pushing.[17]

LJ was named First Team All-American in each of his two seasons at UNLV. He led a Runnin' Rebels team, which included Greg Anthony, Stacey Augmon, and Anderson Hunt to a national championship in 1990 and was named John Wooden College Player of the Year and Naismith College Player of the Year in 1991.[18] The Hornets selected him with the first pick in the 1991 draft. Due to his massive success at UNLV, he entered the NBA as a national star.

The 6–6 Johnson was short for a power forward, though his chiseled physique, tremendous strength, and explosive leaping ability made up for his lack of height. His game resembled that of a young Charles Barkley. LJ threw down monster dunks, then flexed his muscles and screamed at the camera.

LJ expected to sign an endorsement deal with Nike. UNLV was a Nike school, and Johnson had known Nike's marketing guru, Sonny Vaccaro, for a few years. Nike had inked Anthony and Augmon, but Vaccaro was dodging LJ's phone calls. Finally, Vaccaro told LJ, "They didn't want to sign you because they don't think you'll be a good pro." Converse swooped in and gave Johnson his own shoe deal, which was rare in the early 1990s, beginning a memorable advertising campaign featuring Johnson playing the role of his own grandmother named "Grandmama."[19]

Converse initially told Johnson he would be doing a commercial with Larry Bird and Magic Johnson. The concept was that Magic and Bird would be surgeons attempting to create the perfect basketball player, played by LJ under a sheet on the operating table. When they were done, they would argue over what to call him, with Bird saying his name should be Larry, and Magic arguing for Johnson. Eventually, they would settle on Larry Johnson.[20]

When LJ showed up to shoot the commercial, he was told Converse scrapped the idea because either Bird or Magic (they would not say which one) did not want to do it. Converse then told LJ he would be wearing a wig and dress instead.[21]

The premise of the first Grandmama commercial was that LJ's new sneakers were so light and quick that "even his grandma could whoop you in them." The ad campaign was a major hit. Grandmama even made a guest appearance on the popular television show *Family Matters.*[22]

Johnson made an immediate impact for the Hornets, averaging 19.2 points and 11.0 rebounds per game, and was named Rookie of the Year. He was even more impressive in his second season, contributing 22.1 points, 10.5 rebounds and 4.3 assists per game, while leading the league in minutes per contest. He was selected to his first All-Star team and named to the Second Team All-NBA.[23]

Charlotte drafted Alonzo Mourning with the second pick in 1992, giving them an imposing young duo up front. The ensuing season, they won 44 games and made the playoffs for the first time in the team's short history.

The summer of 1993 was a mixed bag for Johnson. The power forward herniated a disc in his back while playing in a charity game. Undeterred by the injury, the Hornets tore up Johnson's rookie contract and signed him to the richest deal in NBA history, a 12-year, $84 million contract. The contract sent shockwaves through NBA front offices.[24] A few months later, LJ tore a ligament along his spine and was out until March.[25]

The back injuries sapped LJ of his explosiveness. He was still incredibly strong and developed an effective repertoire of post moves, but Johnson had difficulty finishing around the basket against taller players and began drifting toward the perimeter. He was selected to his second All-Star game in 1995, while averaging 18.8 points, 7.2 rebounds, and a career-high 4.6 assists. The following season, his scoring average jumped back to 20.5. Most importantly, Johnson was healthy enough to play in 81 games in each of his last two seasons with the Hornets, while averaging about 40 minutes per affair.[26]

The Hornets traded Mourning to the Heat prior to the 1995–96 season and finished with a 41–41 record. They were a small market team, and Johnson's massive contract was becoming difficult for them to pay without advancing deep into the playoffs. They needed to unload his contract. The hard part was finding a taker.

The Knicks were still searching for a consistent second scorer, and management had tired of Mason's surly demeanor and off-the-court behavior. Checketts said the trade was part of an attempt to clean up the Knicks' image.[27] As Mason's agent, Don Cronson, put it, "The Knicks were always afraid of that 3 a.m. phone call."[28] Mason was accused of assault on two different occasions at China Club on Manhattan's Upper West Side, both in the previous year.[29]

The forward also sulked when Van Gundy reverted to running the offense through Ewing.[30] Van Gundy, who was consulted on the trade, felt Johnson was a better fit for the Knicks as they transitioned to more of a perimeter-oriented team.[31]

Mase did not want to be traded. He later called it the worst moment of his career. The forward speculated Ewing may have been responsible for his ticket out of town, though Patrick did not have the power to dictate roster moves.

Cronson tried to scuttle the deal, warning the Hornets that "they have not seen the definition of an unhappy camper unless they have seen an unhappy Anthony Mason."[32] For his part, Mason lashed out after the trade was done. "I'd been told I was part of the Knicks' foundation, then I was suddenly shipped out," the forward said. Mase also questioned the logic behind the deal: "I bring defense and passing," he argued. "What does Larry bring? Sure, he averaged six more points than me, but he took 600 more shots. I shot 56 percent from the floor. He shot 48."[33]

Mase's points were valid. He was the more versatile defender, and defense had been the Knicks' calling card since Riley's arrival. Mase was also coming off his best season, averaging what were then career highs in points (14.6), rebounds (9.3), and assists (4.4). He led the league in minutes played, while eclipsing the Knicks' record set by Walt Frazier in '70–'71 for most minutes logged in a season.

Pippen, who knew Mase's value as well as anybody, said New York was better with Mason and criticized Johnson. "He's garbage," Pip said of the Knicks' new forward. "He's been doing nothing but making money since he's been in the league." LJ fired back: "He's a bum. His only move is pass it to No. 23 [Jordan]."[34]

When it came to free-agency, the Knicks zeroed in on Allan Houston, not Miller, as their top target.[35] Age factored prominently into Grunfeld's thinking. He talked about the team's emphasis on forming a young core that could compete for a championship for many years to come.[36] Houston was 25. Miller, the team's second option, turned 31 that August.[37]

First, Checketts had to explore the possibility, no matter how unlikely, of landing Michael Jordan. Jordan was seeking a deal far in excess of the one-year, $18 million balloon payment the Knicks committed to Ewing. The Knicks only had around $10 million in cap space, while the Bulls could go over the cap to re-sign their own player under the "Bird exception."[38]

MJ's agent, David Falk, and Checketts developed a creative plan in which the Knicks would commit all of their cap space to Jordan and include a sponsorship deal with another ITT company, such as Sheraton, for an additional $15 million, totaling $25 million for one year.[39] Bulls owner Jerry Reinsdorf was outraged when he learned about the arrangement and complained to the NBA office. Typically, the league prohibits alternative forms of payment as a means of circumventing the salary cap. However, the league viewed Jordan's circumstances as unique because of his enormous commercial presence and was prepared to allow the deal. Reinsdorf threatened a lawsuit to stop the Knicks from signing Michael.[40]

The discussions between Falk and Reinsdorf heated up. Jordan insisted to Falk that there be no negotiating. He wanted Reinsdorf to throw out a number, which represented Michael's market value. Reinsdorf claims he proposed $45 million over two years, with additional incentives, and Falk countered with $30 million for one year.[41]

Falk argues he never stated a number, and it was Reinsdorf who came up with $30 million. The agent was scheduled to meet with the Knicks immediately after he concluded with Reinsdorf and informed the Bulls owner he had an hour to come up with a satisfactory number. In Reinsdorf's version of events, Falk gave him one hour to accept Falk's counteroffer of $30 million.[42] Either way, Reinsdorf and Falk agreed on $30 million for one year.

Would Michael have really left the Bulls? Falk is now dismissive of the plan, referring to the discussions as "casual, exploratory talks," and Rand Araskog, who would have had to approve such a deal, never even knew such conversations took place.[43] However, a couple of years later, Michael told author Roland Lazenby he would have left Chicago for New York. It was a matter of pride. He had been underpaid for a long time and wanted to know Reinsdorf appreciated his contributions to the franchise.[44]

Chicago was also never home to Michael. North Carolina was.[45] Jordan's brand and game would have flourished in New York, where he could have continued winning championships while playing alongside his friends Oakley and Ewing.

After completing the Mason deal, Grunfeld, Checketts, and Ed Tapscott, the Knicks' vice president of basketball operations, flew to Washington, D.C., to meet with Houston's agent, Bill Strickland, and Falk, who also represented Juwan Howard.[46] Howard did not fill an immediate need, but the 22-year-old was coming off a season in which he averaged 22.1 points and 8.1 rebounds per game for the Bullets.

The Knicks, Pistons, Heat, and Bullets made Howard an offer. New York's was for about $94 million over seven years and would have eaten up all of their cap space, leaving no room to sign another high-impact player.[47] Howard signed with Miami for seven years and $98 million.[48]

A couple of weeks later, the NBA voided Howard's contract because it violated the salary cap. The league said bonuses in P.J. Brown and Tim Hardaway's contracts left the Heat without enough money to sign Howard to those terms, and secondly, the Heat did not have enough cap space to sign Howard because they had already reached a deal with Mourning. (They could have signed Mourning after Howard by going over the cap to retain their own player.[49]) Howard ended up returning to the Bullets for $105 million over seven years.[50]

While the Knicks waited on a decision from Howard, Strickland and Grunfeld negotiated until 3 a.m. the next morning. Ewing accompanied them and Houston to New York, where the Knicks put on the full-court press. They drove Houston around in a limousine, showing him the houses of Luther Vandross and Diana Ross.[51] Houston, who never went through the recruitment process in college, was impressed by the pitch and appreciated that he was the Knicks' No. 1 target. Management sold him on the idea he could win a championship in New York.[52]

Houston initially wanted and expected to return to the Pistons. He liked their young nucleus of himself, Grant Hill, and Lindsey Hunter. He thought Miller would sign with New York and was hoping to use an offer from the Pacers as leverage with Detroit.[53] But the Pistons' offer of $30 million over seven years was underwhelming.[54] Houston was also insulted Hill did not reach out and try to convince him to stay.[55]

Five teams made Houston an offer: the Knicks, Pistons, Heat, Pacers, and Rockets. New York's was the highest at $56 million over seven years. After Grunfeld made the offer to Houston, he flew to Los Angeles to meet with Miller's agent, Arn Tellem. If Grunfeld did not hear from Strickland by the time he met with Tellem, he was going to pursue Miller. Strickland called Grunfeld that morning and said they had an agreement.[56]

Miller was in Indianapolis playing an exhibition game with the U.S. Olympic team when he received the news that Houston signed with the Knicks. According to Reggie, he immediately informed Grant Hill of the trade. "I ran out of my room yelling and started running down the hallway of the hotel, yelling, 'Your guy signed with the Knicks. He just screwed up my negotiations.'"[57] Hill was angry with Houston for not allowing the Pistons an opportunity to match the Knicks' offer. He and several of the Pistons skipped Houston's wedding that summer.[58]

Miller claims he never would have signed with the Knicks. His plan was to use New York as leverage to force the Pacers to increase their offer.[59]

Pacers GM Donnie Walsh had been worried about Miller bolting for New York. He set up a meeting with Tellem the same afternoon the Knicks were supposed to meet with him. That day, Walsh received a phone call informing him New York signed Houston and Chris Childs. He knew they did not have any money left for Miller. Tellem had lost his leverage.[60]

Two hours later, Tellem arrived at the meeting looking disheveled. He asked Walsh what was going on around the league, and Walsh told him about Houston and Childs. Tellem threw down his briefcase and started pleading with Walsh. "You gotta give him the money," said Tellem. Walsh assured him the Pacers would take care of Reggie, and they did. Just before the start of training camp, Indiana signed Reggie to a four-year, $36 million deal.[61]

After Grunfeld hung up with Strickland, he reached out to Steve Kauffman, the agent of point guard Chris Childs. Harper was a free agent and a few months shy of his 35th birthday. Accordingly, the Knicks were in search of a younger, quicker model.

Childs felt loyalty to the Nets, particularly general manager Willis Reed and coach Butch Beard, who gave him a shot in the NBA, but Beard had since been replaced by John Calipari. Childs met with the new coach, who assured him the Nets wanted him to return, though the point guard was skeptical because Calipari did not look him in the eye.[62]

Ultimately, the Nets' offer of $2.7 million per year was considerably less than he was offered elsewhere, and his decision came down to the Lakers or Knicks. He felt the Knicks' style of play best fit his personality, and the transition from New Jersey to New York would be an easy one. The point guard, who grew up a Walt Frazier fan, was excited to don the orange and blue. Grunfeld and Kauffman quickly worked out a deal for $23.6 million over six years.[63]

Childs was a tenacious defender, which pleased Van Gundy. He had a decent mid-range jumper and was the quickest Knicks point guard since Rod Strickland. The biggest question about his game was his decision-making, a crucial skill for a primary ball handler.

The addition of Houston and Childs rendered Harper and either Starks or Davis expendable. The Knicks traded Davis to the Raptors to free up additional cap space. In return, they received their own first-round pick in the 1997 draft. New York had originally traded the pick to the Mavericks in the '93 Harper deal, and the Mavs traded it to Toronto earlier that week.[64] Davis was shocked and devastated. He had talked to the Knicks' brass about an extension toward the end of the '95–'96 season and hoped to spend the rest of his career in New York.[65]

Harper was disappointed the Knicks let him go as a free agent. When they acquired him, management told him they would take care of him if he did his job. He felt he had. In addition to playing solid basketball, Harper taught Ward how to be a professional. The 34-year-old re-signed with the Mavs.[66]

New York used the cap space created by the Davis deal to sign veteran power forward Buck Williams.[67] At 36 years old, the former Trail Blazer was well past his prime, though still a serviceable backup who could give Oakley a break for 15 to 20 minutes per night. New York also brought back Herb Williams.

Elsewhere around the league, the Bulls kept their championship team intact. Jordan said he would only play for Jackson, so the Bulls inked the Zen Master to a one-year deal.[68] Jordan re-signed, as did Rodman.[69]

Lakers general manager Jerry West engineered a brilliant offseason, trading for Kobe and luring Shaq to L.A. The Magic entered free agency as the heavy favorites to retain the Diesel's services, possessing another young superstar in Penny Hardaway and Shaq's Bird rights.[70]

However, Shaq's relationship with the team and city rapidly deteriorated. Orlando made Shaq a low-ball offer of $54 million over four years, which was substantially less than the $20 million per year he was asking for and the $100-plus million deals Mourning and Howard signed. It was not until the Lakers created more cap space by discarding George Lynch and Anthony Peeler that the Magic grew concerned and upped their offer. Orlando's management further alienated Shaq by criticizing his defense and rebounding during the negotiations.[71]

Shaq's people put together a list of big-market teams with the financial ability to sign him. It featured the Knicks, Pistons, Heat, Hawks, and Lakers.[72] O'Neal's agent, Leonard Armato, informed Checketts that Shaq would sign with the Knicks if they traded Ewing. "Leonard was telling me in no uncertain terms that he wants to come to New York," Checketts said. "And I was just trying to figure out how I'd live with the headlines if I'd traded Patrick and hadn't signed Shaq. That's a career-ending move."[73] Checketts quietly made some phone calls to general managers he trusted to avoid news of the discussions leaking to the media, but the talks never became serious.[74]

The last straw for Shaq was a poll conducted by the *Orlando Sentinel*, which asked readers whether the big man was worth $115 million. Ninety percent of the 5,000 respondents said no. Never mind that this was when NBA salaries began to skyrocket and the voters likely would have voted no for any player. The temperamental Shaq was insulted. He signed a seven-year, $120 million contract with the Lakers.[75]

The Pacers fortified their squad for a run at the Bulls. In addition to re-signing Miller, Indiana locked up the Davis boys for seven more years. They also traded Mark Jackson, Ricky Pierce, and a first-round draft pick to the Nuggets for Jalen Rose, Reggie Williams, and a pick that turned into Erick Dampier.[76]

Riley's Heat also had a productive offseason even after losing out on Howard. Miami made Mourning the league's first $100 million player, signing him to a seven-year, $105 million contract. They also re-signed Hardaway for the bargain price of $17.7 million over four years and added former Nets power forward P.J. Brown on a seven-year deal.[77]

Barkley was traded to the Rockets, along with a second-round pick, for Sam Cassell, Robert Horry, Chucky Brown, and Mark Bryant. He, Olajuwon, and Drexler formed the league's new superteam. Mutombo bolted Denver for a five-year, $50 million deal with the Hawks, and Kenny Anderson inked a seven-year, $50 million contract with Portland.[78]

16

A Heated Rivalry

"Has there ever been a playoff basketball series this dis-
jointed, this aesthetically challenged, this turnover-infested,
this absolutely bone-ugly?"[1]—Michael Wilbon on the
Knicks-Heat series

Before the 1996–97 season, David Stern announced the 50 greatest players in NBA history as selected by a panel of former players, members of the
media, and team executives. It was part of a season-long celebration of the
50th anniversary of the league.[2] Ewing was among the players selected, along
with former Knicks Dave DeBusschere, Walt Frazier, Jerry Lucas, Earl Monroe, and Willis Reed. Forty-seven of the 50 players were in attendance for a
ceremony at the All-Star Game in Cleveland.[3]

The committee also chose the top 10 coaches and teams in league history. Former Knicks coach Red Holzman made the list, along with Phil Jackson, Pat Riley, and Don Nelson. The '69–'70 Knicks were named one of the
top 10 teams.[4]

The revamped Knicks opened the '96–'97 season with high expectations. During training camp, Checketts said, "I expect this team to be among
the top four teams in the league."[5] The Knicks added quickness at point guard
and two reliable scorers in Allan Houston and Larry Johnson. Jeff Van Gundy's team was two-deep at each position, but he faced no easy task in bringing
all of that talent together. The coach had to convince his players to subjugate
their egos and buy into his system. Johnson, in particular, had grown accustomed to being the No. 1 option in Charlotte.

Van Gundy's slogan for the season was "Twelve Men, One Goal."[6] That
goal was to win a championship, something he and his coaches discussed
often. Van Gundy had added veteran assistants Tom Thibodeau and Brendan
Malone to a staff that included Jeff Nix and Don Chaney. "The thing I enjoyed
probably most about just being part of that staff is you felt like you were going
to the best clinic in the world every day," recalls Thibodeau, who added: "Jeff
had worked for Pat Riley, Don Nelson, Pitino, John MacLeod, and his dad

was a great coach. You had Brendan Malone. He had been under Chuck Daly and Hubie Brown. You had Don Chaney, who'd been around the old Celtic teams with Red Auerbach and Bill Fitch. Jeff Nix had been under Riley, Don Nelson, and worked for Digger Phelps in college. You know I had worked for [Bill] Musselman and [Jerry] Tarkanian. Every day, you would talk about basketball and you'd share with each other, you know, how would Pat Riley handle this, or what would Chuck Daly do?"[7]

The team's coalescence on the court was complicated by an injury to Childs early in training camp. The point guard fractured his right fibula and missed the entire preseason as well as the first few weeks of the regular season.[8] The Knicks started slow at 9–6, and some of the New York papers were calling for Van Gundy's head. Then they took off, winning 38 of their next 48 games, despite Houston, Childs, and Johnson struggling to find their groove.

Starks believes the 1996–97 team was the best offensive team he played for in New York. Van Gundy played him and Houston together at times at the 2 and 3, which gave the Knicks more shooting and better spacing than in years past. Defenses were forced to choose between defending Ewing with single coverage or surrendering open three-pointers.[9] However, defense remained Van Gundy's first priority and the team's strength. The coach hammered that home by dedicating the entire first day of training camp to defensive drills.

New York being New York, the first couple of months of the season did not go without controversy. The Knicks hosted the lowly Clippers at the Garden on December 7 and jumped out to a 23-point lead. Then, Van Gundy's team lost focus and allowed the Clippers, in a span of five minutes, to finish the first half on a 21–0 run. Frustrated with their heroes, the Garden crowd rained down a chorus of boos. The Knicks fell behind by seven points in the fourth quarter before rallying to win the game, 89–80.[10]

After the game, an angry Ewing lashed out at the fans for booing the team. "If they're going to act the way they act, they might as well stay home. If they're going to support us, then support us. If you go other places, even when the team is still playing bad, the fans still support them. Here, they support you one minute, then if something goes wrong, they jump off the bandwagon. I'm just tired of it. It's been like that for 12 years, and I'm fed up with it." Ewing, who led the team with 28 points and 13 rebounds, had a valid point, though chastising the fans only expanded the chasm between him and them.[11]

The Knicks continued to measure themselves against the Bulls, while the Bulls were curious to see how the Knicks' restructured roster stacked up. The two teams met for the first time in Chicago on January 21, and Van Gundy set the tone by firing shots at Jordan. The Knicks coach accused MJ of softening up his opponents by befriending them off the court, then destroying them on it.[12]

"I admire him for it," Van Gundy said. "He uses everything he has to his advantage, whether psychological or physical. He cons them by inviting them to his movies. He cons them with the commercials. He pretends to enjoy guys, like them and befriend them. And all he wants to do is win."[13]

Jordan did not take kindly to Van Gundy's words. "That's a crock, and you can write that," Jordan said. Then, he lit up the Knicks for 51 points, including two big jumpers in the final minute to seal the 88–87 victory. After one pivotal basket, Jordan screamed, "Shut up, you little fuck," as he walked past Van Gundy.[14]

After the game, Jackson knocked the Knicks' style of play. Referring to the difference between the two teams, he noted, "Two styles, one of passing and cutting and shooting, and one of clutching and grabbing and holding."[15] Van Gundy had enough of Jackson's criticism. "I think it's very difficult to keep playing at a high level, and he has gotten them to do that over a long period of time," Van Gundy said. "But when I was an assistant, I didn't like how he degraded our team. Patrick Ewing, in particular, and Coach Riley. I think it was uncalled for."[16]

The Knicks had the following day off, and the players gave their coach a good ribbing for waving a red flag in front of the fiercest Bull.[17] Oakley and Childs did not find it funny and called their teammates soft for surrendering 51 points to Jordan. MJ and Pippen suggested the Knicks were not as tough as they used to be.[18] That touched a nerve for a team that lost two of its most rugged competitors in Mason and Harper and moved Starks to the bench. Van Gundy had been harping on them to play "nasty."

Nasty or not, the Knicks were playing solid basketball and having fun on and off the court. The tension of the Nelson era had disappeared, and all of the guys enjoyed hanging out together.

One night in Los Angeles, Van Gundy gave the team a rare day off after it defeated the Lakers. Every player on the team, except for Ward, who never went out, partied at the Century Club in L.A. after the game. Even Ewing, who enjoyed grabbing dinner with the guys, but was not much for the club scene, was in attendance. The Knicks took over the club, and the DJ played New York-themed music all night. Wallace remembers it as one of his favorite nights as a Knick.[19]

New York went into the All-Star break with a 34–14 record, two and a half games behind the Heat in the Atlantic Division. Van Gundy's team had revenge on their minds when they faced the Bulls on March 9 at MSG. Jordan scored 36 points, though the Knicks made him work harder for his shots.

Ewing swished a baseline jump shot with seven seconds remaining to give the Knicks the 97–93 win.[20]

The teams met for a third time on April 10, and the Bulls prevailed in another close contest, 105–103. Nine days later, they met again at the United Center in the final game of the season. The game remained tight throughout with clutch shots by both sides in the closing minutes, the biggest one coming from Starks, a three-pointer with 40 seconds left to give the Knicks a 103–99 lead. When Pippen airballed a three-point attempt in the final seconds, New York escaped with a 103–101 victory. Ewing led the way with 27 points.[21]

The victory provided a huge morale boost for the Knicks heading into the playoffs. It was a game the Bulls wanted badly. It would have given them 70 wins and tied the '85–'86 Celtics for the best ever home record at 40–1. The Knicks were the only team to beat the Bulls twice that season and proved they could win at the United Center.[22] They liked their chances of defeating the defending champions in the conference finals, but they had to get there first.

The Knicks finished the season 57–25, four games behind the Heat. A critical postseason loomed for the franchise. With Ewing's contract expiring, an early exit could spur him to bolt for greener pastures. Van Gundy had one year remaining on his deal, though he hadn't received a guarantee he would be back the following season. The Knicks committed a lot of money the previous summer. As a result, management may have had a quick hook for the fledgling coach.

Ewing tied his fate to Van Gundy's earlier in the season. When asked if he would leave as a free agent if Van Gundy were no longer the coach, Ewing replied, "Oh, definitely. Jeff's not here, I think I'm going to be in Miami or somewhere."[23]

The Knicks adopted the motto "Make 'em feel ya" for the playoffs as a reminder to play physical and aggressive on defense. Starks invented the slogan, and it was written on the team's warmups. The players also shaved their heads, with the exception of Ewing, Starks, and Buck Williams.[24]

The Knicks' first-round opponent was a Hornets team that had taken three of four from them during the regular season. The noteworthy matchup, of course, was Mason versus Johnson, the two forwards who were traded for each other. In addition to Mason, the Knicks had to worry about expert marksman Glen Rice, who scored 40 and 34 points, respectively, in the last two meetings between the teams.

The Knicks played their best team ball of the season against Charlotte, with Houston, Johnson, and Childs contributing the way Grunfeld envisioned when he acquired them. LJ and Houston led the Knicks to a 109–99 victory in Game 1 with 20 and 25 points, respectively. Starks, who was named

Sixth Man of the Year before the series began, chipped in 19 points and seven assists.

In Game 2, the Knicks withstood a barrage of jumpers from Rice, who ended up with 39 points, and prevailed, 100–93. Ewing shot a remarkable 15-of-21 for a team-high 30 points.

LJ knocked down a huge three-pointer with 44 seconds remaining in Game 3 to seal the sweep in his old arena. He was one of seven Knicks in double figures. New York shot a blistering 46 percent from behind the arc and 57 percent overall for the series. Johnson averaged a shade under 18 points and three rebounds, compared to 13 and 12 for Mason.[25]

Next up was a showdown with the Heat, replete with intriguing matchups. It began with the coaches: Riley versus Van Gundy, mentor versus protégé. There was tremendous respect between the two men. Van Gundy gave his daughter Mattie the middle name Riley after his old boss.[26]

Riley tried to poach Van Gundy from the Knicks when he bolted for the Heat, offering the young assistant more money. Checketts would not grant Riley any favors and refused to allow Van Gundy to go. He raised Van Gundy's salary to match what Riley had offered him. Based on Jeff's recommendation, Riley hired his older brother, Stan, the former coach of the Wisconsin Badgers.[27]

Two years after his departure from New York, Riley's imprint was still all over the Knicks franchise. Van Gundy coached the team in Riley's image, emphasizing defense and physical play, and used many of the same plays Riley implemented.[28] The "no layup rule" was still in effect, and practices were as intense as ever.[29]

For Van Gundy, seeing his brother on the opposing bench was more difficult than facing Riley.[30] Stan and Jeff were close and did not relish competing against each other with the stakes so high. "Those were never fun," said Stan. "For him [Jeff] as a head coach, there was a lot at stake and I wasn't rooting for him. And that was something I was not comfortable with."[31]

Another fascinating matchup was the battle of the big men, Ewing versus Mourning. Alonzo was a big fan of Ewing when Patrick was at Georgetown, and John Thompson used Patrick to recruit Alonzo, who ended up wearing Patrick's No. 33 for the Hoyas.[32]

Patrick and Zo became like brothers and fought like it on the court. Patrick returned to Georgetown every summer, where he engaged in spirited battles with Mourning and other former and current Hoyas. The two big men had dinner together when their teams met in the NBA, even in the playoffs, much to the chagrin of Riley. Patrick would be named godfather to two of Zo's children.[33] When Mourning needed a kidney transplant, Ewing offered his own and was a match. High blood pressure prevented him from being a donor.[34]

The two friends considered joining forces in the fall of '95. Zo was at a contractual impasse with Hornets owner George Shinn, who determined the best course of action was to trade the All-Star center. Alonzo's agent, David Falk, informed the Hornets Alonzo was interested in playing for Miami or New York.[35] Zo had leverage because he was going to be a free agent the following summer and could kill any potential deal by stating that he would not re-sign with a specific team.

Ewing and Mourning discussed the possibility of teaming up in New York. Ewing and Thompson, who was a mentor to both men, were concerned there would not be enough space for the two centers to operate down low. Mourning experienced that problem when he shared the court with Mutombo at Georgetown. Ewing ultimately advised Zo that playing for Riley would be the best way for him to develop his career.[36]

Grunfeld offered the Hornets Oakley and Mason for Mourning.[37] Instead, they opted for Miami's package of Glen Rice, Matt Geiger, Khalid Reeves, and a draft pick.[38]

Alonzo Mourning (left) and Patrick Ewing were like brothers and fought like it on the court over four consecutive playoff matchups between the Knicks and Heat (REUTERS/Reuters Photographer—stock.adobe.com).

The other Heat player the Knicks were concerned about was Tim Harda-way. The point guard possessed one of the most devastating moves in the game, a killer crossover, or "the UTEP Two-Step," as it was called in college. His ability to execute the crossover while moving toward the basket, rather than going side to side, like most players, was what made it so deadly.

Hardaway was a three-time All-Star during his first four seasons with the high-scoring Warriors teams known as "Run TMC," after their three stars, Hardaway, Mitch Richmond, and Chris Mullin. Then Hardaway missed the entire 1993–94 season with a torn ACL. He posted impressive numbers upon his return, though Golden State's new coach, Rick Adelman, replaced him in the starting lineup with B.J. Armstrong for the '95–'96 campaign. "I love B.J. Armstrong, but I knew he shouldn't be starting in front of me," Hardaway said.[39]

The Heat struggled during the '95–'96 season, putting Riley in jeopardy of not making the playoffs for the first time as a coach. During a game at Golden State, Hardaway gave Mourning a message to deliver to Riley: "If you get me, I guarantee you'll make the playoffs." Riley traded for Hardaway before the trade deadline, and the point guard delivered on his promise.[40]

The knee injury slowed him down, but he still possessed excellent han-dles and the upper-body strength to create space for his shot. He was also a deep threat with his knuckleball three-pointers. Hardaway returned to All-Star form during his first full season in Miami. Childs and Ward drew the assignment of trying to contain him. The battle between Childs and Harda-way, in particular, became quite chippy.

The animosity between the two teams began during a regular-season matchup in April when a scrum broke out after Zo elbowed Buck Williams in the head. Miami's players were outspoken about wanting to meet the Knicks in the playoffs.[41]

Van Gundy and Riley wished each other good luck over the phone at 6:30 on the morning of the first game, a game Mike Wise described as having "the esthetic appeal of cars being crushed at a junkyard." Both teams shot below 40 percent and committed an inordinate number of fouls. The Knicks were down at the half, but outscored the Heat 22–3 over the final 5:17 of the third quarter to gain a lead, which they never relinquished. New York came away with the 88–79 win. Houston's shooting stroke offered a beautiful sight in an otherwise ugly game. The shooting guard shot 5-of-7 from downtown and scored 23 of his game-high 27 points in the second half.[42]

Hardaway was blazing at the start of Game 2, scoring 25 of his 34 points in the first half. Jamal Mashburn put the finishing touches on Miami's 88–84 win by sinking a three from the left corner with 2.9 seconds to play. New York shot a lowly 38 percent from the floor, with Ewing connecting on just 6-of-20 attempts.[43]

Game 3 shifted to the Garden, where both teams continued to scratch and claw for every basket. The Knicks did not score a field goal in the final six minutes but still managed to come away victorious, 77–73. The score was tied at 73 with 2:42 left when Starks was fouled on a three-point attempt. He knocked down all three free throws to give the Knicks a 76–73 lead. As the closing seconds approached, the score remained fixed at 76–73. Hardaway lined up a potential game-tying three with 2.9 seconds left, but Ewing charged out of the paint and got a hand on the shot.[44]

The big man high-stepped around the court while pounding his chest as the crowd erupted. New York's defense was the difference, holding Miami to two field goals in the final six minutes. Childs kept Hardaway under wraps, with the Heat guard converting just 6-of-22 shots.[45]

Mike Lupica of the *Daily News* said of Game 4, "The Knicks did not just beat the Heat at the Garden. They tied Pat Riley's team to the back of a New York City taxicab and dragged it around the city for a while."[46] New York won easily by Knicks-Heat standards, 89–76, to take a 3–1 series lead.[47]

Many reporters were critical of the style of play in the Knicks-Heat series. The competition was extremely physical and neither team reached the 90-point mark through the first four games. The counterargument was that the two teams were competing with an intensity and physicality rarely matched in NBA history and the games were each closely contested.

The "Bad Boy" Pistons may have perfected that particular brand of basketball, but they never encountered a team with such a similar makeup and mindset. Stan Van Gundy compared the Knicks-Heat clashes to "an era in boxing where Marvin Hagler would get in the ring and just stand toe-to-toe with somebody and just keep throwing blows until somebody dropped."[48] Hardaway recalls the Knicks-Heat matchups as "the most exciting basketball I ever played."[49]

The Heat and Knicks took the unsightliness to another level in Game 5. Miami was firmly in control, up 12 with two minutes remaining, when Oakley knocked Hardaway to the floor with a hard screen. He then stepped over Hardaway's fallen body, which ticked off Mourning. Oak and Mourning shared some words as Mourning shoved Oak away. Oak received his second technical and was tossed from the game. Seconds later, Childs fouled Hardaway in the backcourt.[50]

As Hardaway sank his second free throw, Ward lowered his backside and aggressively boxed out Brown. Brown took exception, believing Ward was attempting to take out his knees. The 6-foot-10 forward picked up the 6–2 point guard and tossed him head over heels into the crowd along the baseline. John Wallace immediately grabbed Brown's upper body, as Ward went after his legs and the two tackled Brown into the stands.

Brown and Ward were among the two least likely players to start a fracas. During Miami's first-round series, Brown received the J. Walter Kennedy Citizenship Award for "outstanding service and dedication to the community." Although Ward was a former football player, he was extremely soft spoken and always had a bible in his hand. Van Gundy said of his point guard, "Charlie was a devout Christian, and during the game, he was going to try to cut your nuts off to win and then pray for you afterwards."[51]

The Ward-Brown incident occurred near the New York bench. Naturally, several Knicks left the bench and ran onto the court to break up the fight. Since the game had already been decided, some of the team's top players were among them. Houston and Johnson tried to separate the players. Starks entered the scrum, earned a technical foul, and was ejected. He gave the Miami crowd the finger on his way out. Ewing took a few steps onto the court, then stopped, and lingered near the Knicks bench. He never approached the brawl.[52]

Van Gundy blamed himself for attempting to break up the fight, rather than keeping his players on the bench. He does not recall if he and his staff practiced keeping players on the bench in the event of a fight, noting, "The result will tell you that even if we had, we didn't do it enough."[53]

The Heat remained on the bench. Stan Van Gundy believes, "Had it happened under our basket, we would have had the same problem, and they would have easily kept their guys on the bench."[54] Miami's players also would have had to run past their coaches to get on the court, as well as official Dick Bavetta, who was standing in front of their bench when the fight broke out.

Prior to the 1994–95 season, the NBA instituted a new rule, stating any player who comes off the bench during a fight will automatically be suspended for one game, even if his intention is to break up the fight. According to Rod Thorn, who was in charge of league disciplinary matters, the rule change stemmed in part from the Knicks' brawl with the Suns in '93.[55]

The Knicks knew there would be suspensions. The question was how many. Thorn announced the ruling the next day. Brown was suspended for two games, while Ward, Johnson, Houston, Starks, and Ewing each drew one-game suspensions.[56] The Knicks were particularly angry about Ewing, who merely wandered a few steps onto the court. He had no intent of joining the fracas. Van Gundy felt the league made an example out of Ewing and his suspension constituted "total mismanagement of the rules by the commissioner."[57]

According to Thorn, the league's position was "if you came out on the middle of the court, whether you were involved in the fight or not was irrelevant." He added, "If you're out there at the time, you're a suspect."[58]

There was merit to his argument. Some of the most infamous brawls in NBA history, such as Kermit Washington fracturing Rudy Tomjanovich's face and "The Malice at the Palace" escalated to include players who were lingering on the court or serving as peacemakers.

The Knicks were required to dress the league minimum, nine men, so with the exception of the principals in the fight, Ward and Brown, the order of suspensions was determined alphabetically by last name and split among the remaining games. Ward, Ewing, and Houston would sit out Game 6, and Johnson and Starks would be sidelined in the event of a Game 7. Knicks announcer Mike Breen pointed out, "If his name was Patrick Zewing, he would have played in Game 6," which was in New York.[59]

The National Basketball Players Association appealed in federal court for a temporary restraining order to allow the players to play in Game 6, but U.S. District Court Judge Jed S. Rakoff denied their plea. The players who came off the bench, he determined, had violated the letter of the rule.[60]

The Knicks dressed nine players and posted the message "nine men, one mission" on the Jumbotron at MSG before Game 6. Breen notes, "People always ask, 'What's the loudest you've ever heard Madison Square Garden?'" He said, "There's a lot of answers for that, whether it's the Larry Johnson four-point play or John Starks' dunk over the Bulls. But the loudest pregame I have ever heard was before that Game 6." Chants of "Riley sucks" echoed throughout the arena.[61]

New York held a 10-point advantage at the end of the first quarter and retained it for most of three quarters. Miami went on a 15–5 run in the fourth and broke the Knicks' back with a series of threes, two by Majerle and one by Mourning. Oakley scored 18 points and grabbed 12 boards in 46 minutes of action, and Childs dished out nine assists to go with 22 points, but it was not enough. The Heat won, 95–90, forcing a Game 7 in Miami.[62]

Ewing guaranteed victory before Game 7: "The only thing I've got to say is, 'See you in Chicago.'"[63] The big man did everything he could to back up his words, scoring 37 points and collecting 17 rebounds, but he didn't receive much support from his teammates. Through no fault of his own, once again, his guarantee went unfulfilled.

The Knicks desperately missed Johnson and Starks. Houston, who totaled 25 points, was the only other Knick to score in double digits. Hardaway led the way for the Heat with 38 points. Miami rode an 18–0 first-quarter run and a 15–1 run at the end of the third to a 101–90 victory.[64]

After the game, a devastated Van Gundy walked to Riley's office and congratulated his mentor. Wallace recalls Van Gundy sitting behind the team bus later that night, "drawing up these little pebbles in the ground. Just that distraught, and tuned into, like, 'All right, what plays would have worked better?' That's just the way he was wired."[65]

The Knicks were crushed. Once again, they believed it was their year. They had the talent, depth, and health. "That team would have won the championship that year," said Checketts.[66] Many of the Knicks agree with him. Van Gundy later said the '96–'97 squad was the best team he coached in New York. He would never forgive himself for failing to keep his players on the bench.[67]

17

Round Two

"They told me my career might be over. That's what the doctors said."[1]—Patrick Ewing

The Knicks returned the same cast of characters in 1997–98, with the exception of the longtime voice of the team, Marv Albert. Born Marvin Philip Aufrichtig, Albert wanted to be a sports announcer since he was a young child. He started recording himself calling games with a tape recorder in third grade. By the time he was in eighth grade, he had an imaginary radio station called WMPA (MPA being his initials) with interviews, commercials, and game coverage. He worked as a ball boy for the Knicks, then landed a job keeping statistics for legendary announcer Marty Glickman.[2]

After attending Syracuse University, Albert became "the voice of the Knicks" in 1967, first on radio and then television. He branched out to other sports, working everything from Super Bowls to Wimbledon. Beginning in 1990, his signature call of "Yes!" after a dramatic or important basket could be heard on *NBA on NBC* broadcasts, in addition to Knicks games.[3]

In September of '97, Albert pleaded guilty to a misdemeanor count of assault and battery, but not before enduring humiliating testimony from his accuser and another woman at trial. The two women claimed Albert bit them on the back and forced them to perform oral sex on him in hotel rooms. One woman claimed Albert was wearing women's undergarments during one of the incidents. NBC fired Albert, and he resigned from his job calling Knicks games for MSG Network.[4]

Albert later revitalized his career with the Knicks and the NBA, and his departure opened the door for a future voice of the league, Mike Breen, who moved from doing Knicks games on radio to television. The following season, Breen's old radio partner, Walt Frazier, joined him on the telecast. Together, the tandem developed into an iconic duo.

The other big news of the offseason was that Ewing and Van Gundy agreed to new contracts. Van Gundy received a three-year extension through the 1999–2000 season, which paid him about $2 million per year. The contract included a team option for a fourth year.[5] Ewing signed his name to a four-year contract worth $68 million and expressed his desire to retire as a Knick.[6]

Despite their new rivalry with the Heat, Ewing and his teammates remained obsessed with beating the Bulls. "I felt like we were going to beat them last year, but we didn't have the opportunity to prove it," Ewing said. "I still think we're going to beat them."[7]

Van Gundy posted an annual list of goals for the Knicks outside the locker room at their practice facility. It included items such as "Be the best defensive field goal team in the league." At the bottom of the list was the acronym "FJ," which stood for "fuck Jordan."[8]

New York's season took a disastrous turn on December 20, in a game in Milwaukee. With 24 seconds remaining in the first half, Ewing leaped to catch an errant alley-oop from Ward. Bucks center Andrew Lang pushed Ewing while he was in the air, causing the Knicks center to crash to the ground, landing awkwardly on his tailbone and right wrist. Ewing began writhing in pain. It was immediately apparent he was seriously injured.

The Knicks big man dislocated and tore ligaments in his right wrist, his shooting wrist. One of the bones nearly popped out of the skin. Team doctor Norman Scott said it was a very unusual injury, the kind you typically see in football. Ewing was declared out for the season and doctors told him the injury was career-threatening, but the defiant warrior vowed he'd be back for the playoffs, if not sooner.[9] With Ewing on the shelf, there was no guarantee the Knicks would make the playoffs. They had not even played very well with him, standing at 15–11.

Chris Dudley, whom the Knicks acquired from the Trail Blazers in a preseason trade, replaced Ewing in the starting lineup. Dudley was diabetic and had to prick himself with insulin at times on the bench. His teammates called him "Dr. Crash" because of his ferocious rebounding. He was a solid defensive center but did little on offense other than set screens. At the time, he was the worst free-throw shooter in league history, and his teammates teased him mercilessly about his herky-jerky foul-shooting motion.[10]

The Yale graduate filled in admirably for Ewing, before he too succumbed to the injury bug in late February, fracturing his right foot in a loss to the Warriors. That left Oak, who often gave up three or four inches and several pounds, to guard opposing centers.[11]

Not surprisingly, the Knicks struggled without Patrick, playing .500 ball. Houston picked up some of the slack offensively, raising his scoring average to 18.4 points per game, and LJ played more minutes at power forward. The one player from the 1996 summer spending spree who failed to meet expectations was Childs.

Chris took a circuitous path to the NBA. He was a fourth-generation alcoholic who began drinking in high school and upped his usage at Boise State University. First, it was beer. Then, cognac.[12]

Childs was projected to be selected in the late first or early second round, but his name was not called on draft night. He went out drinking until 3 a.m. the night before a pre-draft mini-camp, where he performed poorly and people could smell the alcohol sweating out of his pores. Teams were scared away.[13]

The Bakersfield, California, product spent the next five years with five different teams in the CBA, where his binge drinking increased. He never averaged more than 13 points and eight assists per game in his first four seasons and failed to draw interest from the NBA. It was not until he was criticized in a newspaper for his poor play during a playoff series that he decided to seek help.[14]

After the '92–'93 season, Childs checked into a substance abuse clinic in Houston run by John Lucas, the longtime NBA player and coach and a former drug addict himself. Childs left for Miami after 21 days in Houston to play for Lucas's United States Basketball League team, the Tropics, which consisted of former substance abusers. Chris suffered a relapse with the Tropics, and his teammates voted that he needed to return to rehab, so he enrolled at A Better Way in Miami. Childs had his last drink on June 26, 1993.[15]

Finally sober, he produced the best season of his career in '93–'94, averaging 17.6 points per game while leading the Quad City Thunder to the CBA championship and earning championship series MVP honors. That season, Maurice Cheeks, then an assistant coach with Quad City, contacted Nets general manager Willis Reed to tell him Childs belonged in the NBA.[16]

Reed scouted Childs and signed the 6–3 point guard to a contract. Childs blossomed in his second season in New Jersey, averaging seven assists and nearly 13 points per game. He was handed a starting spot after the Nets traded Kenny Anderson in January and responded by scoring 16 points per game for the rest of the season.[17]

Childs' teammates called him "Chili" because "I'm always smiling. I'm always chillin'. That's off the court. On the court, I'm all business."[18] His best friends on the team were LJ and Oak. They liked to play dominoes in the hotel during road trips. Childs also enjoyed golfing with Starks, Houston, and Herb Williams.[19]

During the '97 preseason, Van Gundy announced Childs had volunteered to give his starting spot to Ward. Ward's game was better-suited for the plodding starting five, whereas Childs was able to utilize his quickness to push the ball with the second unit. It appeared to be a very unselfish move.[20]

Van Gundy and Childs kept up the ruse long after they left New York. The point guard recently admitted it was Van Gundy's idea to move him to the bench. Losing his starting spot still bothers him to this day. Childs worked his butt off to become a starter and wanted the satisfaction of hearing his name announced in the starting lineup at MSG. It was Van Gundy's idea to claim he volunteered to give up his starting spot.[21]

Knicks fans and management expected a lot more than 6.3 points and 3.9 assists per game, even if he was coming off the bench. The Garden crowd turned on Childs in early January, booing him when he entered the game against the SuperSonics after he missed a potential game-winning shot the previous game against the Bulls.[22]

Childs and Ward developed a strong bond despite competing for playing time. Their lockers were next to each other at the practice facility and in the Garden. Neither was a star and they knew they both had to play well for the Knicks to accomplish their goals.[23]

Ward was quiet, though Childs, like most of the Knicks, held him in unusually high esteem for a young player. Winning the Heisman Trophy carried weight, though Ward's teammates were most impressed with his devotion to his faith. In an environment rife with opportunity, the point guard did not drink or womanize.[24] He also treated everybody from the locker room attendants to his teammates with respect.

Ward often chastised his teammates for their foul language and placed faith-based articles or prayers in their lockers.[25] There were times when his actions landed him in hot water. During the '98–'99 season, Ward circulated an article about football legend Reggie White calling for women to be banned from the locker room. Barbara Barker, who covered the team for *Newsday*, was furious, and the organization publicly disavowed Ward's remarks.[26]

A couple of years later, Eric Konigsberg, a freelance writer, who was writing a story about the Knicks for the *New York Times Sunday Magazine*, attended a Bible study meeting run by Ward in Houston's hotel room in Milwaukee. Ward, Houston, and Kurt Thomas were in attendance.[27]

The conversation moved to Konigsberg's religion, Judaism. Ward said, "Jews are stubborn, E., but tell me, why did they persecute Jesus? Because he knew something they didn't want to accept? They had his blood on their hands." Then, Houston quoted Matthew 26:67: "Then they spit in Jesus's face and hit him with their fists." Ward added, "There are Christians getting persecuted by Jews every day."[28]

Konigsberg included the quotes in his story, which became big news.

Ward delivered an apology of sorts, in which he defended his remarks, though a second apology appeared to be more sincere. The Anti-Defamation League issued a statement calling Ward and Houston's words anti–Semitic. Commissioner Stern, who was Jewish, weighed in, saying, "Ward would have been better off not to have uttered his uninformed and ill-founded statements." New York has a large Jewish population, and the Garden fans booed Ward every time he touched the ball during the team's next home game.[29]

During his rookie season, Ward arrived an hour before every practice to work on his skills with Van Gundy.[30] His game improved dramatically, and Van Gundy was rewarding him with a spot in the starting lineup.

Ward was steady, but far

Charlie Ward won the Heisman Trophy as a quarterback for Florida State University before becoming the starting point guard for the Knicks. Ward was also drafted by the Milwaukee Brewers and New York Yankees of Major League Baseball (Mitchell B. Reibel of Pro Shooter).

from spectacular. He took care of the ball, knew how to run an offense, and could knock down an open three. However, he was not the type of point guard who could consistently break down defenses and create shots for himself or others. Many wondered if the tandem of Childs and Ward was sufficient for the Knicks to win a championship.

Grunfeld looked for an upgrade. He inquired about the Raptors' Damon Stoudamire and offered the Trail Blazers Childs and Chris Mills, an offseason acquisition, for Kenny Anderson. Stoudamire and Anderson ended up traded for each other, and the Knicks held on to Childs.[31] The only deal New York made at the trade deadline was to acquire 37-year-old Terry Cummings from the 76ers in exchange for Herb Williams and Ronnie Grandison. Cummings filled in for the injured Buck Williams as the backup power forward.[32]

Philly released Herb, after which the 40-year-old rejoined the Knicks. It was the second time Williams was traded, then released by his new team, and re-signed by the Knicks. He had outlived his usefulness on the court, but was a crowd favorite at MSG and one of the most respected figures in the locker room.

Williams was a sensational storyteller who kept his teammates loose with his even-keeled demeanor. Wallace called him Confucius because he was wise about basketball and life in general. Herb taught Wallace how to invest his money and Ward how to be a professional.[33]

If a player was not sure where he was supposed to be on a given play, he could ask Herb, who knew each player's responsibilities at all times. "You know, when I was in high school, I used to get triple-teamed a lot, so my coach always used to make me know what everybody had to do on every possession on every play," said Williams.[34] Doug Christie, who played for the Knicks early in his career, always sat next to Herb on the bench, and the veteran dealt out little tips throughout the game.[35] He would remain with the franchise in different capacities for another 16 years.

New York finished the season 43–39 and wrapped up the No. 7 seed in the Eastern Conference. Their opponent in the first round of the playoffs was none other than the Heat. The bitterness between the two teams had elevated to the level of hatred. Prior to one of the games, P.J. Brown was still working on his post moves when the Knicks took the court for warmups. Oakley fired a ball the length of the court at Brown and yelled, "Get the fuck off the court!"[36]

The Knicks had lost eight of their last 11 games and entered the best-of-five series as heavy underdogs without Ewing. They played the part in Game 1, losing 94–79. The Heat took a 15-point lead midway through the first quarter and never looked back. Hardaway picked up where he left off the year before, scoring 34 points, including 6-of-9 shooting from three-point territory.

New York bounced back in Game 2 to even the series with a 96–86 victory. Starks, who had been in the midst of a slump, led the Knicks with 25 points. Johnson and Houston also topped the 20-point mark. Childs initiated the first controversy of the series in the closing minutes of the game. The point guard hit a three to hand the Knicks an eight-point lead with 1:52 remaining and followed it up with a throat-slitting motion as he made his way down the court.[37]

The Knicks relinquished home-court advantage as quickly as they had secured it. Miami's starting backcourt of Hardaway and Voshon Lenard combined for 55 points, and New York was overmatched in the paint down the stretch of Game 3. Heat guard Eric Murdock returned Childs' throat-slitting gesture in the final minutes of the game.[38] The Knicks fell, 91–85, and were on the brink of elimination heading into Game 4. That's when the fireworks erupted.

During a February 1 victory by the Knicks, Mourning forearmed LJ in the head, which Van Gundy believed was a "dirty play." Oak responded by elbowing Zo, and Chris Mills shoved the Heat center to the ground.[39]

The tension between Mourning and Johnson dated back to when they were teammates with the Hornets. LJ was drafted No 1. overall in 1991 and named Rookie of the Year. The following summer, Charlotte selected Mourning with the second pick. Zo had a huge rookie season himself. The Hornets appeared to have a bright future with two budding stars.

Not so fast. Soon after, Zo became jealous of Johnson's salary and status within the franchise. When the Hornets signed Johnson to the largest deal in league history in the fall of 1993, team owner George Shinn said, "He [Johnson]'s the leader of this team, and he will always be the leader of this team. And he will bring an NBA championship to Charlotte." That did not sit well with Mourning, who viewed himself as "the man."[40]

Mourning was also concerned about how Johnson's contract would affect his own financial situation. After Johnson signed his deal, Mourning yelled at Hornets coach Allan Bristow, "You paid him all this damn money, and now you won't pay me!" Unable to work out a new deal with Zo, Charlotte traded him to Miami.[41]

In Game 4, Hardaway badly missed a three-point heave with three seconds remaining and the Knicks up five. Mourning had set a screen on Johnson during the play, and Johnson was a little too aggressive boxing Zo out when the shot went up. After Hardaway's shot clanked off the backboard, Mourning threw a punch at Johnson, which missed. LJ retaliated.

The two exchanged a series of flailing punches with none hitting the mark. TNT's Doc Rivers summed it up best: "Fortunately for these guys, they are both awful fighters."[42] Johnson, who took boxing lessons as a kid, was teased by his teammates for "slap fighting."[43]

Members of both teams rushed to break up the fight, including Van Gundy. The coach was knocked down in the middle of the melee and ended up holding on desperately to Mourning's leg as Mourning tried to shake him off. Eventually, Oakley pulled Van Gundy to safety.

The video of Van Gundy dangling from Mourning's leg went viral and remains the most recognizable image of Van Gundy's career with the Knicks. The coach has no recollection of hanging from Zo's leg. He was dazed after being caught with a glancing blow from Johnson, had no idea what was happening, and believes he was trying to hold onto something as he fell toward the ground.[44] The Knicks watched the replay many times after the game and teased their coach mercilessly. Childs told Van Gundy he "looked like a jockey who fell off his horse."[45]

Mourning was an intense individual, fueled by rage on the court. Like Mason and Starks, he walked the fine line between channeling his emotions

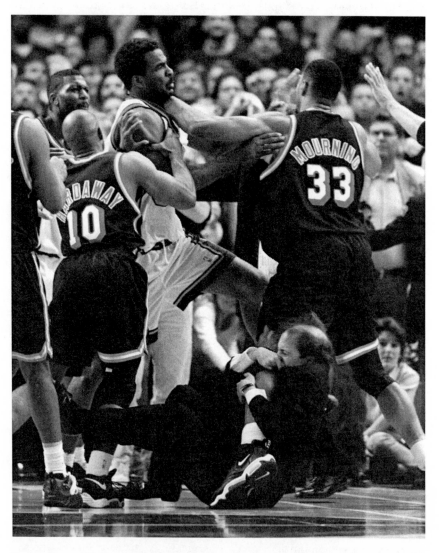

For the second season in a row, the Knicks-Heat playoff series was impacted by a brawl. Jeff Van Gundy hanging on to Alonzo Mourning's leg for dear life became the defining image of the coach's tenure in New York (Jeff Christensen of Reuters).

productively and losing control. Too often, he ended up in foul trouble or with a technical. Zo behaved well during the second half of the season, but he lost control on this night. Riley told his center, "You just blew the season," as he escorted him off the court.[46]

Prior to Game 5, Riley took a different tone. "The only thing I'm disappointed in is that Zo didn't connect when he tried to punch Larry Johnson in the face," the coach said. "I would have punched him too if he went after my injured face." (Mourning was playing without a mask for the first time since fracturing his cheekbone in March.)[47]

Riley had some choice words for his old protégé as well. He felt Van Gundy was out of control and should have held his own player back rather than grabbing onto Zo.[48] Proper etiquette is to hold back your own guy, and Van Gundy later recognized that. He was caught up in the heat of the moment.

Riley went a step further, calling Van Gundy a "cheap-shot" coach who incited violence. When asked about the comments in the context of his relationship with Van Gundy, Riley said, "This is coaching. This transcends friendship."[49]

Unlike the previous year, only one player left the bench, Chris Mills. Johnson and Mourning were both suspended for two games. Van Gundy argued that contrary to popular opinion, the Knicks suffered the bigger loss. Johnson outscored Mourning 20.8 to 19.3 points per game in the series, and New York desperately needed his post scoring without Ewing.[50] However, the loss of Mourning was particularly difficult for the Heat because they had dealt their talented backup center, Isaac Austin, to the Clippers in the middle of the season. Riley did not have an adequate replacement for Austin when Zo was suspended.

In the closing seconds of Game 2, some of the Heat players had told the Knicks the next time they came to Miami would be on vacation, the implication being that the Heat would wrap up the series in New York. In Miami Arena, the visiting team had to walk past the home team's locker room on its way to the court. Prior to Game 5, Oak opened the door to the Heat locker room and comically yelled, "We're baaaack."[51]

The Knicks looked like the hungrier team in Game 5, led by Oakley who played all 48 minutes. New York appeared to be in cruise control with a 69–48 lead in the third quarter, but Riley's team came storming back and cut the deficit to two midway through the fourth quarter. Then, the Knicks pulled away and won the game, 98–81. Oak scored 18 points and snatched 13 rebounds. Houston added 30 points.[52]

After the win, Van Gundy fired back at his mentor. "I have different values," Van Gundy said. "I was speaking to my wife about that today. I value family, friendship, and loyalty above job."[53] Commissioner Stern summoned Riley and Van Gundy to his office to reprimand them about the violence between the Knicks and Heat over the past two seasons.[54]

The Heat series was transformative for Van Gundy, who out-coached his mentor while coaxing a Knicks team without Ewing past a formidable Heat squad. "Coach Van Gundy can downplay it and be as humble as he wants, but he took a giant step today by beating Pat Riley," said the veteran Buck Williams, who scored 12 points and grabbed 14 rebounds in Johnson's absence. "Now he steps into his own personality as a coach. He's no longer in the shadows of Pat Riley."[55]

Next up for the Knicks was another old nemesis, the Pacers. Indiana's core of Miller, Jackson (Indiana re-acquired him from the Nuggets months after trading him), Smits, and the Davis boys remained, with the addition of future Hall of Famer Chris Mullin and an infusion of youth off the bench in Jalen Rose and Travis Best.

Larry Bird had also replaced Brown on the bench and won Coach of the Year in his first season on the job. Bird was much more laid-back than Brown. He believed the Pacers were professionals and did not need him to obsess over every detail of their job. He emphasized conditioning and free throws and delegated most of the coaching duties to Rick Carlisle and Dick Harter, who served as offensive and defensive coordinators, respectively. Smits joked, "The only time we heard Bird talk or say any coaching was in the playoffs when he had a microphone on his chest."[56]

Bird won three championships as a player with the Celtics and convinced the Pacers they were on the path to a title of their own. They won 58 games, second-most in the conference behind the Bulls. Miller believes it was the best team he played for during his tenure with the Pacers.[57]

Indiana snatched Game 1 behind 56 points from its bench, led by 18 each from Rose and Best. Ewing made his much-anticipated return in Game 2. The Knicks center was in the starting lineup and helped pull the Knicks within two with just under a minute left in the game, but the Pacers escaped with the 93–83 win. The Knicks required time to adjust to Ewing being back in the mix. They looked uncertain for much of the game offensively, and Ewing was noticeably winded. The big man played 27 minutes, during which he contributed 10 points and six rebounds.

The series shifted to the Garden for Game 3. Ewing looked sharper in his second game back, scoring a team-high 19 points and snaring seven rebounds. The Knicks trailed by two in the third quarter when they went on a 13–0 run sparked by Childs' defense on Jackson. New York captured its first game of the series, 83–76.[58]

The Knicks were buried in Game 4 by another legendary Miller performance. New York led by three in the waning seconds when Childs inexplicably left Reggie to help on Jackson. Reggie nailed a three-pointer from 26 feet to tie the game at 102 with 5.9 seconds remaining. Then, he scored seven points in overtime as the Pacers routed the Knicks in the extra period for a final score of 118–107. Miller finished with 38 for the game.[59]

The Knicks fought valiantly in Game 5, but were no match for the Pacers in Market Square Arena. Jackson posted a triple-double in the clinching game with 22 points, 14 rebounds and 13 assists, fueling one of the many what-ifs of the '90s Knicks. Would they have won a championship if they hadn't traded the elite passer?

Indiana lost to the Bulls in seven games in the conference finals, before Jordan and company defeated the Jazz in the Finals for the second year in a row to cap off their second three-peat of the '90s.

Once again, the Knicks were eliminated in the second round of the playoffs. This was New York. Expectations were high. Management did not care that Van Gundy's team was without their star player for much of the season and did not have time to find a rhythm once he returned. They expected more than second-round exits when they brought in Childs, Houston, and Johnson. Changes would be made.

18

Changes Abound

"Oakley has been a consistently tremendous ballplayer for New York who has contributed mightily night after night. Of course, I'd hate to wake up in the middle of the night and find him hovering over my bed with that look on his face, but on the court he's worth every cent they pay him."[1]
—Woody Allen

The 1998 offseason was transformative for the Knicks and the entire NBA. The owners and players had signed a six-year collective bargaining agreement in 1995, which contained a clause allowing the owners to opt out of the deal if players' salaries exceeded 51.8 percent of basketball-related income. Salaries had ballooned over the previous couple of years, with individual contracts topping $100 million, and players were receiving 57.0 percent of basketball-related income. There was a salary cap in place, but it contained numerous exceptions.[2]

On March 23, 1998, the owners voted to reopen the collective bargaining agreement. The two sides negotiated over the following months. But by July 1, when the 1995 deal was set to expire, the parties were unable to reach an agreement. The owners locked the players out. It was the first work stoppage in league history.[3]

During the lockout, teams were prohibited from negotiating with, signing, or trading players. Team workout facilities were closed, and teams could not conduct or facilitate any summer camps, exhibitions, practices, workouts, coaching sessions, or team meetings.[4]

The owners wanted to eliminate the "Larry Bird Exception," which allowed teams to exceed the salary cap to re-sign their own players. They were particularly disturbed by the six-year, $126 million contract the 21-year-old Kevin Garnett had recently signed with the Timberwolves and wanted to institute maximum salaries for players. They also wanted to create a sliding salary scale for rookies to protect themselves from committing outrageous amounts of money to unproven talent.[5]

The two sides were far apart in what became hostile negotiations. The league canceled the preseason, then began canceling games. On December 23, Commissioner Stern set January 7, as the date in which he would recommend canceling the season if a deal had not been made. After working through the night, the National Basketball Players Association (NBPA) and NBA reached a deal on January 6, but the players still had to vote on it. They all met at the General Motors building in Midtown Manhattan to discuss the agreement.[6]

Players had differing views about the proposed deal, and a lot of money was at stake. Emotions ran high, none higher than those of Oakley, who was due a balloon payment of $10 million that season. Oak entered the General Motors building and approached his longtime adversary, Charles Barkley, who extended his hand. Instead of shaking it, Oak chastised "Sir Charles" for talking about him, then smacked Barkley across the face. Billy Hunter, the executive director of the NBPA, was one of many witnesses. "He slapped the shit out of Charles. KA-POW!" Hunter said.[7]

Childs, who was also present, was not the least bit surprised. "I knew it was going to happen because I know Oak," he said. "He slapped a few people during my time in New York and Toronto. Several. I was there. I witnessed it." Barkley fled the room and was not seen again that day.[8]

Oakley and Barkley had an acrimonious relationship involving numerous on-court confrontations dating back to 1987.[9] Oak, who knows how to hold a grudge, simmered with resentment. In December, during the lockout, Barkley was at a charity game with many players and opined that if the best thing you can say about Oakley is he plays hard, he is not much of a player. Barkley's comment got back to Oakley, who vowed to slap Barkley when he saw him.[10]

The incident commenced the slapping portion of Oak's career. He slapped Tyrone Hill of the 76ers in the face during warmups before a preseason game in 2000, over $54,000 Hill owed him from a dice game.[11] (Yes, the same Hill he knocked out over a gambling debt a few years earlier.)

Later in the season, Oak fired a ball at Hill's head and ordered him to get off the court when it was time for the 76ers' shootaround to end and his team's to begin. With both teams watching, the 6–10, 250-pound Hill lowered his head and meekly walked off the court.[12] Oak said years later of the incident, "Nothing personal. When you beat your kids, you love them still."[13] That same year, in between morning shootarounds, he slapped the Clippers' Jeff McInnis over a woman.[14]

After the "slap heard 'round the basketball world," the players voted to approve the proposed collective bargaining agreement (CBA). Most basketball insiders believed the owners won the deal, which set maximum salaries for players, ranging from $9 million to $14 million per year, depending on how long a player had been in the league. The CBA also introduced a rookie pay scale, limiting how much players could earn on their first contract.[15]

However, the players prevented the implementation of a "hard" salary cap. Several exceptions remained, which allowed teams to spend over the cap, including the Bird exception. The players also received a $15,000 increase on minimum salaries.[16]

Due to the late start, the season was shortened to 50 games. Coaches often refer to an NBA season as a marathon, but the 1999 campaign was decidedly a sprint. Training camp opened on January 21, and games began on February 5. It was a grueling schedule with several back-to-back-to-back games and in some cases, four games in five nights. Plenty of players let themselves go physically, believing the season would be canceled, and had little time to work back into shape.

The limited preseason was particularly problematic for a Knicks team that traded away two of its pillars and had a number of new faces in the locker room. Days before the lockout began, Grunfeld shocked the fan base by trading Oakley to the Raptors for Marcus Camby. The Knicks fell victim to the athleticism of Indiana's frontline in the '98 playoffs, and Grunfeld felt Oak, in particular, was outplayed by Dale Davis. Oak was 34, and Grunfeld wanted to make the team younger and more athletic.[17]

Grunfeld discussed the deal with Van Gundy before pulling the trigger, and the coach claims the only thing he disagreed with was the "procedure of the Camby trade," but refuses to elaborate.[18] Van Gundy was not on board with the trade and it became a point of contention between him and Grunfeld. "All of us were wondering why we ever made that trade," Brendan Malone said of the coaching staff.[19] Ultimately, it was incumbent on Ernie as the GM to acquire players who were palatable to his coach.

Ewing was also not pleased the Knicks traded the teammate who had his back for 10 years. Camby, who worked out at the same location as Patrick during the lockout, said Patrick never acknowledged his presence until it was time for camp.[20]

Checketts and Grunfeld, like the players and coaches, understood what Oak meant to the team on and off the court. Years later, Van Gundy said of Oakley, "This is a man who never took a shortcut, never took a day off, never expected anything, earned everything." Oak left the Knicks as the NBA's all-time leader in flagrant fouls with 30.[21]

Grunfeld made the right move for the future of the franchise. Camby was more athletic and 10 years younger than Oakley. It is understandable that

Van Gundy, whose job was always on the line in New York, did not want to part with one of his most dependable players. Oakley knew the coach's system and could help the Knicks win immediately. Conversely, Camby was an unproven commodity who had not reached his prime.

Oak was shocked and angered by the trade. At his exit interview, Grunfeld addressed his role with the team going forward, then traded him soon after. Oakley believes Grunfeld knew he intended to trade him when they met. When Grunfeld tried to talk to Oak the day after the trade, the forward uttered, "Get the fuck out of my face."[22]

Camby hailed from one of the roughest neighborhoods of Hartford, Connecticut, where the game was as much about avoiding drugs and gangs as putting the ball in the basket. But you would never know it. Marcus was friendly and soft-spoken with an infectious laugh.[23] His father was not around much when he was a kid, so his mother played both parental roles.[24]

Money was tight in the Camby household. They didn't own a car, and Marcus was forced to wear ill-fitting clothes during his frequent growth spurts, which led to teasing from his peers. Fishing, a hobby he resumed during his NBA career, and the basketball court were his means of escape.[25]

Camby led Hartford Public High School to a 27–0 record and the No. 1 ranking in the state during his senior season as arguably the most sought-after New England prospect since Ewing.[26] The big man proceeded to a stellar career at the University of Massachusetts. There, he won the John R. Wooden Award and the Naismith College Player of the Year Award while leading the Minutemen to the Final Four in his junior season.[27]

Camby declared for the NBA after his junior year and was selected second overall by the Raptors in the stacked 1996 draft. Two years later, he had a reputation as an injury-prone underachiever. There were also questions about his character after details surfaced about gifts he received from an agent while at UMass in violation of NCAA rules, which included money, jewelry, rental cars, and prostitutes. Such activity was rampant on athletic campuses. The true indication of Marcus' character was that he accepted full responsibility for his actions and voluntarily repaid UMass the $150,000 in television revenue it was required to forfeit.[28]

Toronto feared Camby would leave as a free agent in the summer of '99 and did not want to be left empty-handed, so it made the deal for Oakley. Grunfeld envisioned Camby as the big man of the future, a long, agile athlete who could block shots and run the floor.[29] Whereas Oak was built like a tree trunk, the 6–11 Camby resembled a stick figure. His tremendous wingspan and superb athleticism allowed him to make plays in the air that Oak could only dream of. Camby led the league with 3.7 blocks per game in '97–'98. The glaring weakness in his game was his shot, which he released awkwardly from above his head.

After the lockout, management contemplated a move far more controversial than the Oakley trade. On December 1, 1997, Latrell Sprewell of the Warriors strangled his coach, P.J. Carlesimo, at practice. Pictures of the bruises on Carlesimo's neck depicted a gruesome scene.[30]

Sprewell was initially suspended by the league for a year, though an arbitrator reduced it to the remainder of the '97–'98 season, which totaled 68 games. Now that Sprewell's suspension was over, the Warriors were desperate to trade the three-time All-Star.[31]

Carlesimo and Sprewell had butted heads since training camp in 1997, Carlesimo's first year on the job. Sprewell often failed to put forth his best effort in practice and talked back to Carlesimo when criticized for his actions. Three days before the choking incident, Spree was fined for missing a team flight.[32]

On the day of the attack, Carlesimo encouraged Sprewell to "put a little mustard on those passes," to which Sprewell replied, "I don't want to hear it today." Carlesimo approached Sprewell despite the player's warnings. "Don't come up on me, don't come up on me," Spree said. When the coach continued walking toward him, Sprewell grabbed him by the throat and choked him for 10 to 15 seconds before his teammates pulled him off. Fifteen minutes later, Spree returned to the court, screamed, "I'm going to fuck you up," and punched Carlesimo.[33]

It was not the first violent outburst of Spree's career. During his rookie season, he engaged in a free-swinging brawl with his teammate, Byron Houston. On another occasion, he had an altercation with Jerome Kersey at practice, then waited for Kersey after practice and charged at him with a two-by-four.[34]

Yet, Spree had a good relationship with several of his teammates in Golden State. He and Webber were very close during Webber's lone season with the Warriors.[35] Latrell was also tight with Chris Gatling, and Tim Hardaway viewed his as a "great teammate, great person."[36]

There were people around the league who were not surprised Carlesimo was the victim of such an attack. The coach had a way of irritating players. Rod Strickland, who repeatedly clashed with Carlesimo when the two were in Portland, said, "When he [Carlesimo] signed with Golden State, I knew it was going to be a problem. I know how he tried to deal with players, and I didn't think that was going to work with Spree."[37] Even if such an attack was foreseeable, it was inexcusable.

Latrell was born in Milwaukee, where he lived with his mother and stepfather after his parents divorced. Latrell's father, Latoska, served jail time for stealing stereo equipment and clothing from Latrell's mother, Pamela, while trashing her apartment. Latrell's stepfather beat him.[38] "I just didn't like him whuppin' me," Spree said years later, having vowed he would never let anybody push him around again.[39]

When Latrell was seven, Pamela moved the family to Flint, Michigan, to live with Latoska's parents. Latoska eventually settled a couple of blocks away. Between his grandfather Chick's guidance and the money provided by Latoska, who was dealing marijuana, Latrell felt a sense of stability for the first time in his life. Then, Latoska went back to jail after police found a sawed-off shotgun in his trunk while he was out on bail from a drug bust. Latrell and his mother promptly returned to Milwaukee.[40]

Sprewell's basketball experience was limited to pick-up ball until he tried out for his high school team as a senior.[41] He attended Three Rivers Junior College in Poplar Bluff, Missouri, where he was recruited by the University of Alabama coach, Wimp Sanderson. Sprewell did not have the grades to play at Alabama, so Sanderson provided him with a room at the team's gym, Coleman Coliseum, while Spree enrolled at Shelton State Community College.[42]

Spree shared the room at the Coliseum—it was empty except for two beds—with a Bama team manager whom Sanderson assigned to look after him. The manager drove Latrell to and from class every day and used money from Sanderson to buy him food.[43] When Sprewell was not in class, he was putting up shots in the gym.[44]

Spree excelled in junior college and was admitted to Alabama for his junior season, where he was teammates with future NBA players Robert Horry and Jason Caffey. Sanderson was tough on Sprewell as he was with all of his players, but he never had a problem with the Milwaukee native. "Spree didn't hit me, but I was a damn good candidate," Sanderson likes to say. Sprewell worked hard, was highly coachable, and did not have any disciplinary problems at Alabama.[45]

Sanderson did not suspect Sprewell had an NBA future when he recruited him. The shooting guard did not play much his junior year. Then he worked out at Alabama over the summer, developing his ball-handling and shooting skills, and led the team in scoring his senior year.[46]

Spree was not sure if he would be drafted at all when the Warriors selected him with the 24th pick in 1992.[47] He was an All-Star in three of his first five seasons and named All-NBA First Team in 1993–94. Now, at the age of 28, his career was at a crossroads.

The Knicks, who were looking to add athleticism and offensive firepower to their lineup, could have greatly benefited from adding Sprewell. He was a tremendous talent in the prime of his career, who excelled in the open court and attacked the basket with reckless abandon. His trademark finish was a tomahawk dunk accompanied by a vicious scowl. He was also a tenacious defender.

Van Gundy thought trading for Spree was a no-brainer. He believed the shooting guard would be on his best behavior after the Carlesimo incident. The coach convinced Grunfeld and Tapscott the Knicks should trade for the troubled shooting guard, but Checketts was hesitant.[48]

Toward the end of the lockout, Checketts heard that New York's rivals, Indiana and Miami, were interested in Spree. At that point, he called deputy commissioner Russ Granik and asked if the Knicks could have permission to meet with Sprewell. Granik agreed, as long as it remained confidential.[49]

Van Gundy, Tapscott, Grunfeld, and Checketts met Sprewell at his home in Milwaukee. Spree answered the door in a tank top and red gym shorts and looked the Knicks brass in the eye, which Van Gundy interpreted as Sprewell being genuine with them. The group talked about basketball philosophy and how Spree would fit with the team. The Knicks' contingent found Latrell to be articulate, honest, and easy to talk to.[50]

There was one episode in particular that bothered Checketts. In 1994, Sprewell's pit bull bit his four-year-old daughter's ear off. When asked about it by a reporter, Spree dismissively said, "Stuff happens." Checketts, a father of six, was horrified by the response and asked Sprewell about it.[51]

Spree picked up a framed photo of his daughter and showed it to Checketts. He explained how upsetting the incident was for him, that he put the dog to sleep, and he only said "stuff happens" because he was tired of talking about the event and wanted his family to be left alone. Checketts was satisfied. The next day, he discussed the possibility of acquiring Sprewell with his family, and his sons helped him conclude everybody deserves a second chance.[52]

Tapscott also did extensive background checks on Sprewell. He spoke with Latrell's former teammates at Golden State, NBA security officials, and his high school coach, James Gordon.[53]

Sprewell had been interested in joining the Knicks for a few years. He was disappointed the team didn't pursue him as a free agent in 1996. Management had discussed it internally. At the end of the '95–'96 season, Grunfeld asked Starks whom he thought the Knicks should go after, Houston or Sprewell. Starks said Sprewell because of his toughness, though he thought Houston was a good choice too.[54] When the Knicks played the Warriors the next season, Spree pulled Ewing aside and told him to let management know how he felt.[55]

In order to acquire Sprewell, the Knicks had to surrender Starks. They were more willing to deal the streaky shooting guard than in years past. Starks had lost some of his athleticism and perhaps his focus. He infuriated some teammates, particularly LJ, by bringing his golf clubs to Indiana when the Knicks faced elimination in the playoffs the previous season.[56]

Still, John was a mainstay of the franchise who was loved by his teammates and fans. It was difficult to part with him months after Oakley left town. Checketts told Starks he would prefer not to include him in the deal, but the Warriors insisted. With Checketts' blessing, Starks called Golden State's GM, Garry St. Jean, and tried to convince St. Jean not to trade for him, but St. Jean coveted a big name in return for Sprewell.[57]

On January 21, the Knicks traded Starks, Terry Cummings, and Chris Mills for Sprewell. Starks cried when the trade went through.[58] Houston also wept when he heard the news. He later said of Starks, "He was the one person I know, more than anybody I ever played with, that would do whatever it took to win a game."[59] The departures of Oak and Starks left Ewing, Herb, and Ward as the only holdovers from the Riley era.

Sprewell was reinstated on January 21, after a meeting with David Stern. The following day, he held his first press conference as a Knick. It was the beginning of a prolonged attempt to restore his image. Spree wore non-prescription glasses and sweaters during the '99 season to look more proper. He began his press conference by apologizing to coach Carlesimo and the Warriors organization and thanked the fans, his family, and the Knicks "for giving me a second opportunity to come out and show you people the real Latrell."[60]

The "real Latrell" was very intelligent. Sammy Steinlight, a longtime public relations employee of the Knicks, described him as the kind of guy who "can

The Knicks took a risk in trading for Latrell Sprewell after he was suspended for choking his coach P.J. Carlesimo with the Golden State Warriors (REUTERS / Reuters Photographer—stock.adobe.com).

take a computer, disassemble it, and put it back together in front of you."[61] Spree had two passions away from the hardwood: technology and cars. He enjoyed assembling everything from computers to old stereos, and was knowledgeable about all of the latest technological developments. He also used computers to chat anonymously and play games online. Car games were his favorite.[62]

Latrell had been obsessed with automobiles since he worked on them in his grandfather's auto body shop as a young boy. He bought his first car, a 1992 Camaro Z-28, after he was drafted by the Warriors. By the late '90s, he owned about 10 cars, including a Lamborghini Diablo and a Mercedes SL600. He even opened his own online custom auto parts shop called Sprewell Racing, which specialized in rims and tires.[63]

Latrell also liked to play chess, which he learned from his father when he was 13. Over the next couple of seasons, chess became a frequent activity on the Knicks' team plane. Houston's father-in-law taught him how to play, and Johnson picked up the game in the summer of 2000, when he was looking for an activity that would not bother his back. The guys talked a lot of trash but never bet on chess the way they did with cards. Kurt Thomas, another Knicks addition prior to the '99 season, talked the most during chess, but rarely backed it up.[64]

New York took a lesser gamble by signing Thomas as a free agent. The power forward attended Texas Christian University, where he led the nation in scoring and rebounding in 1994–95, something that became a joke in the Knicks locker room. Thomas' teammates ribbed him for flaunting his credentials as a player and tough guy in order to justify his regular appeals for more playing time. He and Johnson, both of whom were from Dallas, would go back and forth about whether Thomas was from the toughest neighborhood in "Big D," as he claimed. The rugged forward played with a crazed look in his eyes and provided the physical presence the team lost in the Oakley trade, though according to Camby, Kurt was "soft as a teddy bear on the inside."[65]

The Heat selected Thomas with the 10th pick in 1995, and the Dallas native put forth an impressive rookie year. Then, he played just 23 games over the next two seasons for the Heat and Mavericks, due to two stress fractures in his right ankle. KT, as his teammates called him, offered an array of post moves as well as a dependable jump shot from 15 to 18 feet. He was also familiar with Van Gundy's system upon arrival after spending two seasons with Riley in Miami.[66]

The Knicks also signed forward Dennis Scott, a three-point marksman who played his first seven seasons with the Magic. He then split a campaign between Dallas and Phoenix before becoming a free agent. Grunfeld believed he could provide shooting off the bench. Scott's career in New York got off to a rocky start when the Garden faithful booed him for wearing Starks' No. 3 jersey.[67]

Another major change took place at the top of the organization. In March 1997, Cablevision bought out ITT, becoming the majority owner of the Knicks, Rangers, Madison Square Garden, and MSG Network. Charles Dolan founded Cablevision in the early 1970s and built it into a multi-billion-dollar corporation.[68]

His son, James, traveled a rocky path before riding his father's coattails to the top of the company ladder. The scion of Cablevision began his collegiate studies as a music major, then drifted through two colleges before landing at SUNY New Paltz, where he majored in Communications. James worked for the family business in various capacities but struggled through years of alcohol and drug abuse. In 1993, his father put him on a plane to the Hazelden Clinic in Center City, Minnesota, to get cleaned up. Two years later, Charles elevated his son to CEO of Cablevision. In 1999, James was named chairman of the Knicks and Rangers.[69]

Dolan's appointment began a cultural shift within the Knicks organization. James was known as a stubborn man who flew off the handle at the drop of a hat. He was obsessive about asserting control. Employees of the Knicks, Rangers, and MSG referred to his leadership as a "reign of terror" or "culture of paranoia." They were often more concerned with pleasing Dolan than excelling at their job.[70] James' controlling nature and bizarre decision-making would wreak havoc on the organization for years to come.

19

A Tumultuous Season

"It's a fishbowl existence, no doubt about it, and loyalties run kind of thin.... I think one of the biggest aspects of it is ego. You have an ego and then it's magnified by the fishbowl existence and then it collides with other egos. The Garden is packed full of jealousy—this team, that team, the network, his name was in the paper, my name's not in the paper.... There have always been behind-the-scenes machinations at Madison Square Garden, and I think there always will be. It's just kind of the sense of the building."[1]—Former president of Madison Square Garden Bob Gutkowski

On January 13, 1999, Michael Jordan retired from basketball for the second time. A few days later, the Bulls traded Pippen to the Rockets. Tim Floyd replaced Phil Jackson as coach, and Rodman signed with the Lakers. Chicago's dynasty was dead, opening the door for the Knicks, Pacers, or Heat to advance to the Finals.[2]

New York had to integrate six new players into Van Gundy's system with virtually no training camp. The guys participated in informal scrimmages at gyms around the New York City area during the lockout, but attendance was sporadic and the workouts were not a sufficient replacement for a grueling training camp.[3]

The Knicks began the season with a small starting lineup, playing Houston and Sprewell together with LJ at power forward, along with Ewing and Ward to round out the starting five. They lost their first two games to Orlando and Miami, then an MRI revealed a stress fracture in Sprewell's right heel. New York's other major acquisition, Camby, was glued to the bench, playing just 19 seconds against Orlando and five minutes in the Miami game.[4]

Due to Sprewell's injury, Van Gundy went to a more conventional lineup, starting Thomas at the 4 and moving Johnson to the 3. The adjustment freed up more minutes for Camby at power forward, though his playing time remained irregular. Van Gundy rode Camby hard beginning in training camp, when he called his work habits "unacceptable."[5] Camby was angry and confused by his lack of playing time, but he kept his head down and did his job.[6]

Years later, Van Gundy admitted he judged Camby too soon and it hurt their relationship for a while.[7] However, Camby, who went on to play 18 seasons in the league, says Van Gundy was his favorite coach to play for due to his knowledge of the game and focus on winning.[8]

To make matters worse for Marcus, he bore the burden of replacing the extremely popular Oakley. Oak received a rousing ovation upon his return to the Garden on February 16. Later, the crowd burst with enthusiasm when their hero landed in the seats behind the basket after diving for a loose ball. There was a humorous moment in the first quarter when Oak instinctively walked toward the Knicks bench during the first timeout.[9]

He finished the game with 11 points and seven rebounds, as Camby shined in limited action, hauling in 12 boards to go with 11 points in the Knicks' 95–85 victory. After the game, Ewing was asked if he spoke with Oak. "We chit-chatted for a minute," he said with a smile, "and then he tried to take my head off."[10]

With Oakley and Starks wearing different uniforms, there was a new dynamic in the locker room. The Knicks were a tight-knit team, though, like any squad, there were cliques. Spree, Camby, and Rick Brunson constituted one group. Thomas and journeyman Ben Davis hung out with them as well.[11]

The following season, Spree, Camby, and Brunson were joined by John Wallace, who re-signed with the team in the summer of '99. The foursome became known as "the jerks" because they enjoyed fooling around and acting like idiots. There was an ongoing debate over who was the biggest jerk, a title Wallace bestows on Brunson because "he was just an asshole." Most often, "the jerks" hung out in Sprewell's hotel room—because he signed a lucrative contract prior to the 1999–00 season—and the other three would order obscene amounts of room service they could never eat just to make Spree pay an exorbitant bill.[12]

Camby and Spree were particularly close, spending a great deal of time dropping beats in Spree's basement.[13] They played hours of Sony PlayStation and went through an original Nintendo phase, playing Tecmo Bowl in their hotel rooms late into the night with guard Erick Strickland.[14]

Ward, Houston, Herb, and Dudley formed a bible study group. Dudley recounted, "We would do chapel on the first night of a road trip. It wasn't the whole team, but it was five or six guys that would do it. I think that helped too with our core, just sharing that experience. Then guys would go out to eat or whatever."[15] The groups blended well under the leadership of tri-captains Ewing, LJ and Herb. Ewing and Herb were tight.[16]

There were a number of leaders on the team, though none more so than Johnson, who was the consummate teammate and the glue that held everybody together during a roller-coaster season. Brunson said, "To this day, the best teammate I've ever had at any level I've ever been a part of is Larry Johnson." LJ took the young point guard under his wing when he signed with New York. He taught Brunson how to dress and purchased a bunch of suits for him at Rochester Big and Tall.[17] Camby echoed Brunson's sentiment, adding LJ was somebody "who I really looked up to and tried to pattern myself after."[18]

LJ moved between different circles and had a strong rapport with the younger players. Prior to the season, he requested that Sprewell's locker be placed next to his so he could help the vexing swingman with his transition to New York. If LJ sensed something was bothering a teammate, he would invite him out to dinner to talk about it. He comforted Camby when the big man was frustrated by his lack of playing time and extolled Dudley for his defensive efforts.[19] Johnson's teammates also respected his unselfishness on the court. On a team loaded with scorers, he sacrificed his game the most.

Unfortunately, Johnson did not display the same maturity away from the game. In May 1998, LJ was one of the athletes featured in a *Sports Illustrated* cover story headlined "Where's Daddy?" about professional athletes fathering children out of wedlock. The article revealed LJ was supporting five children from four different women. Most disturbingly, one of the women Johnson impregnated, Laura Tate, alleged Johnson's former college teammate, Stacey Augmon, threatened to harm her if she did not have an abortion. LJ's promiscuity was not unique on the team. Sprewell fathered three children with three different women before he turned 21.[20]

Late in 1999, numerous Knicks were implicated in another sex-related scandal involving a strip club in Atlanta called the Gold Club. The club owner, Steve Kaplan, and several others were arrested on charges of using the club as a front for prostitution and money laundering for the Gambino crime family. Kaplan was ordering dancers to provide sexual favors to athletes, some of whom were Knicks.[21]

Kaplan informed manager Thomas "Ziggy" Sicignano that they needed to take care of celebrities in order to create buzz for the club.[22] Knowing Kaplan was a Knicks fan, Sicignano arranged for Starks and Greg Anthony to come to the club when New York was in Atlanta. Starks admitted through his attorney to having sex with Gold Club strippers before "re-dedicating his life to Christ." Sicignano also testified during the trial in 2001, that Kaplan sent Gold Club dancers to the Knicks' hotel in Charleston, South Carolina, during training camp in 1997.[23]

The biggest Knick ensnared in the Gold Club scandal was Ewing, who testified to receiving oral sex from strippers at the club on two occasions. Kaplan, who was in the room at the time, told Ewing the cost was "taken care of."[24] Oakley had his lofty bills at the club comped on a couple of occasions as well. Sicignano testified that other NBA players received sexual favors from strippers, including Reggie Miller, Dennis Rodman, and Dikembe Mutombo.

Ewing was one of the players who put on significant weight during the lockout. As president of the NBPA, he was constantly involved with negotiations during the fall of 1998 and had little time for basketball activities. He ballooned 15 to 20 pounds heavier than he had been at the start of the '97–'98 season.[25] Due to his broken wrist, Patrick had appeared in only four games over the past year. Those were troubling signs for a 36-year-old heading into a condensed season.

Once the labor negotiations ended, Ewing flew to Miami for a brief vacation with Mourning and worked out with many of the Heat players. "You could tell he was out of shape," said Heat guard Rex Walters. "He looked terrible. When it was game point, we couldn't even pass him the ball. We didn't think he'd make it through the season."[26]

On March 9, Ewing limped off the court 29 seconds into a Knicks loss to the Bucks with a sore left Achilles tendon. He was diagnosed with tendonitis and told it would take six weeks to properly heal. Patrick said, "I don't have six weeks," and returned to the lineup in a week and a half. The day after Ewing's injury, Grunfeld signed Camby to a six-year contract worth up to $48 million with incentives.[27]

A couple weeks later, Patrick joined an elite club, becoming the 12th player in NBA history to amass 20,000 points and 10,000 rebounds.[28] Then he demonstrated he still had something left in the tank, scoring 37 points and grabbing 15 rebounds in the Knicks' 94–93 victory over the Pacers at the Garden on March 30.[29]

The Knicks were maddeningly inconsistent over the first two months of the season, falling to 11–9 after a horrendous 76–63 loss to the lowly Bulls on March 12. The following day, Van Gundy released Dennis Scott, who showed up to camp out of shape and was shooting a dismal 30 percent.[30]

NBC reported Van Gundy could be fired if the Knicks lost their next game to the Hornets. New York beat Charlotte, 94–86, and the coach stayed afloat for the time being. Speculation about his job resurfaced after an embarrassing 106–82 loss in Charlotte on April 7.[31]

Johnson encouraged the Knicks to win for Van Gundy, and the team rallied around its beleaguered coach. Sure, they tuned him out at times, but they appreciated that he was all about the team.[32] Even with something as mundane as the Knicks' media guide, it was important to Van Gundy that the entire team or the logo be displayed on the cover, instead of an individual star or stars.[33]

The players also respected Van Gundy's attention to detail and the work he put into making them successful. During one game late in the season, Van Gundy called the play "Cross 4," which was designed for Johnson in the post. Sprewell complained that the Knicks ran Cross 4 all the time and never ran Cross 3 for him.[34]

The next day at practice, Van Gundy pulled out a sheet of paper, which documented all of the times the Knicks ran Cross 3 and Cross 4. He pointed out that Cross 4 had a much higher success rate. There was nothing for Sprewell to say. Van Gundy kept advanced statistics on every conceivable situation long before the word "analytics" was part of the NBA lexicon. The players were confident nobody could better prepare them to succeed than Van Gundy.[35]

When Parcells called Van Gundy for the first time, he asked the Knicks coach if they were on a secure line. Van Gundy had no idea what Parcells was talking about. Parcells replied, "If you don't think they're listening to what you're saying, you're an idiot. Now, go get a cell phone and call me back at this number."[36] Parcells' paranoia reinforced the narrative of team versus management Riley had preached and Van Gundy embraced.

Jeff had a framed sign in his office at the practice facility that said, "If you think they are all out to get you you're not paranoid—you're perceptive."[37] Not surprisingly, he assumed the rumors about him being fired originated with Grunfeld.[38]

Van Gundy's paranoia was warranted and a useful survival instinct in the shark tank that is the Garden. Mike Wise compared working at MSG to the mafia: "Some days you'd think you were coming in for a promotion and you were Joe Pesci. You'd wind up on the floor in your own blood. That's what working in Madison Square Garden was like. You just never know."[39]

Van Gundy was skilled at reading people and adept at working the press. As was Checketts, who was shrewd enough to survive three ownership changes. Grunfeld was not as inclined to play corporate politics and often came across as uncomfortable in front of the media.

Van Gundy and Grunfeld knew each other since they were both assistant coaches under Stu Jackson. Grunfeld was elevated to the front office during Jackson's second season, and there were rumors he played an instrumental role in Jackson's dismissal. Some members of the Knicks organization believed Van Gundy, whose relationship with Jackson dated back to their days at Providence, had been distrustful of Grunfeld ever since.[40]

Jeff and Ernie maintained a cordial working relationship during Van

Gundy's first few years as head coach, but they were not particularly close. Knicks management was headquartered in Manhattan and the team practiced upstate at SUNY Purchase, so the coach and GM did not interact on a daily basis as with other teams. When Grunfeld attended practices, Van Gundy did not go out of his way to make him feel comfortable, believing the facility was for coaches and players.[41]

Jeff Van Gundy replaced Don Nelson as head coach of the Knicks in March 1996. His players respected the hard work he put into his craft and took comfort in knowing that nobody could have them more prepared to face an opponent (Mitchell B. Reibel of Pro Shooter).

The Oakley trade lit the fuse between Van Gundy and Grunfeld. They began leaking information about each other to their own go-to guys in the media. The journalists even became ensnared in the feud and attacked each other in print.[42]

Grunfeld complained to Checketts, who was angry Van Gundy was "popping off to the press." He addressed the issue with the coach, and Van Gundy responded, "Are you telling me to shut the F up?" In so many words, Checketts said yes.[43]

The higher-ups at Cablevision were unhappy about the public rift and the results on the court. The Knicks had the highest payroll in the league and were sitting at .500 after an uninspired loss to the 76ers on April 19. Checketts met with Dolan and Cablevision vice chairman Marc Lustgarten, who handled the Garden and related properties for Dolan.[44]

Checketts argued it was not necessary for Van Gundy and Grunfeld to get along, pointing out that the Bulls' Phil Jackson and Jerry Krause "never spoke to each other for six championships." They just needed to keep their differences in house. Checketts proposed warning Van Gundy and Grunfeld to either stop undermining each other in public or they would both be fired. Dolan was not satisfied with that solution and wanted one of them gone.[45]

Checketts was reluctant to fire anybody. He believed the team needed time. The Knicks were integrating a lot of new pieces during a lockout-shortened season. Injuries to Sprewell and Ewing put them behind schedule.[46]

That night, Checketts received a call from Ewing. The center heard rumors about Van Gundy's job status and wanted Checketts to know the players supported their coach. It was the second time that season Ewing called Checketts in support of Van Gundy.

A couple of weeks earlier, Ewing responded to a question about a coaching change by saying Checketts assured him Van Gundy would be there for the entire season. The center added, "No, I don't want to play for another coach. I don't want to play for Phil Jackson. Phil Jackson can take his behind back to Chicago." Johnson and Houston also publicly backed their coach.[47]

Soon after talking to Ewing, Checketts heard from Lustgarten, who informed him, "Jimmy [Dolan] wants Ernie gone." Checketts asked why. Lustgarten replied, "I don't think he likes Nancy in Suite 200. Nancy Grunfeld [Ernie's wife] comes into Suite 200, and she's always bringing people, acting like she owns the place." (Suite 200 is a VIP hospitality suite where celebrities and executives can eat, drink and socialize.) Checketts asked in disbelief, "That's why you would fire him?"[48]

Checketts was the president of Madison Square Garden. Ultimately, the decision to fire Grunfeld was his. He considered the wishes of Dolan and the players and believed he had no choice.

Checketts and Grunfeld worked together for eight years and were close friends. They socialized with their wives and kids. "We were so close," said Checketts. "I couldn't bear to do it."[49]

On April 20, Checketts invited Grunfeld to dinner at Gregory's Restaurant in White Plains. The friends enjoyed a nice meal while discussing the state of the team. Then, as Ian O'Connor of the *Journal News* of Westchester put it, "In the middle of dessert, Grunfeld found out he was the main course." Over biscotti and fresh fruit, Dave fired Ernie, citing pressure from above.[50]

Grunfeld was shocked. The GM had not been concerned at all about his job.[51] He initially thought Checketts was kidding. Then he spent the next two hours trying to change Checketts' mind.[52]

Grunfeld assembled a team with a league-high $68.6 million payroll that appeared to have major flaws.[53] The Knicks were an awful rebounding team without Oakley, due in part to Camby's lack of playing time. Sprewell and Houston played the same position and had not figured out how to co-exist. Spree was unhappy coming off the bench, which he had been doing since returning from injury. He, Camby, and Childs thrived in a fast-paced

Dave Checketts (left) and Ernie Grunfeld became close friends while running the Knicks' front office throughout the 1990s. Then Dave fired Ernie over dinner in April 1999 (AP Photo/Marty Lederhandler).

offense, which was not conducive to the aging Ewing and his gimpy knees. And Grunfeld had not upgraded the point guard position.

However, firing Grunfeld at that time was impulsive and premature. He deserved more than 42 games in a season without a training camp for the team to come together.

Checketts took over the team and informed the players of the change the following day. Then, he invoked the memory of Red Holzman, the coach of the Knicks' two championship teams, who passed away before the start of the season. When Checketts joined the Knicks, he brought Holzman back as an advisor, and the two became good friends.[54]

The players wore a black patch on their jerseys in Holzman's honor. Checketts told them, "We ought to take it off there because frankly the effort that I've seen and the lack of togetherness, he [Holzman] would have been ashamed of."[55] After the meeting, Van Gundy half-jokingly told his coaching staff they were next to go.[56]

That morning, the *New York Post* ran a story in which Sprewell's agent, Robert Gist, ripped Van Gundy and Grunfeld for not starting Sprewell. Checketts told Spree he would be fined $25,000 for his agent's comments. It was a blip on what had been an encouragingly quiet few months for the embattled All-Star.[57]

Latrell had yet to find his groove on the court, due in part to injury, but was a fan favorite from the minute he put on the blue and orange uniform. The crowd chanted his name during New York's first preseason game, and his teammates spoke glowingly about his work ethic and presence in the locker room.

The apparel company AND 1 featured Sprewell in a commercial as an anti-hero. In the advertisement, Spree recited a monologue, while somebody braided his cornrows, with Jimi Hendrix's distorted version of the "Star Spangled Banner" playing in the background. It concluded with Spree saying, "People say I'm America's worst nightmare. I say I'm the American dream."[58]

Grunfeld was fired with eight games remaining. At the time, the Knicks were 21–21, had lost four in a row, and were tied for ninth in the conference. In their next game, Ewing sank a running jumper with 24.9 seconds left to seal the victory over a Hornets team that had won nine in a row.[59]

Two nights later, the Knicks pulled off their signature win of the season. Without Ewing, who was in and out of the lineup down the stretch of the season with Achilles tendonitis, they trailed the Heat by as many as 20 points in Miami—and 15 with seven minutes left. New York stormed back and tied the game on a Johnson three with 56.1 seconds remaining. Then, Camby threw down an emphatic dunk, was fouled, and converted the free throw to hand the Knicks a three-point lead. They held on for the 82–80 win.[60]

Camby, who was receiving more playing time in April, scored nine of his 15 points in the fourth quarter, and Thomas held Mourning to two points in the fourth. The Knicks celebrated as if they had won a playoff series.[61] They went on to win four of their final six games and secured the eighth seed with a 27–23 record.

20

A Friendly Bounce from Above

"My reaction was somebody just shot my dog right in front of me. That's how I felt. It was disbelief."[1]—Donnie Walsh on Larry Johnson's 4-point play

Allan Houston was born and raised in Louisville, Kentucky, where his mother, Alice, grew up two houses down from Muhammad Ali. The Champ returned to his old neighborhood after his first fight with Ken Norton. Allan's father, Wade, greeted the Champ at his car, at which point Ali, who had a broken jaw, asked Wade through a wired-shut mouth who he was and what he was doing in the neighborhood. Wade introduced himself as Alice Kean's husband. Ali replied, "You shouldn't have married her. That was my girlfriend growing up. You know you're not good-looking enough to be married to her."[2]

Ali started laughing, then made his way into the Houston home on what happened to be Allan's second birthday. Ali picked up and played with Allan and all of the other children in attendance. When Wade later became an assistant coach at the University of Louisville, Ali called recruits on his behalf.[3]

Allan was bowlegged and pigeon-toed as a toddler and had to wear corrective shoes with a bar between them to straighten out his legs and feet. Then he suffered through a separation of his growth plates, resulting in knee pain, which made it difficult to walk. He was confined to a wheelchair for a period of time.[4]

Once the lower limb problems were resolved, Allan could not sit still. He was so hyper that his parents enrolled him in sports to try to tire him out. From that point on, Allan grew up in gymnasiums. Wade coached high school basketball when Allan was young, and the boy took his first steps at one of Wade's practices. The son attended his father's games, where he would squirm away from his mother and make his way down to the players' bench.[5]

When Allan was five, his father was hired as an assistant coach under Denny Crum at Louisville. The younger Houston began attending Louisville summer basketball camps, where he learned Crum's UCLA offense and honed his skills playing one-on-one with his father.[6] Allan became a regular at Louisville practices and games and rode on the team bus after the Cardinals won the 1980 National Championship. Crum's players treated him like a little brother. "'Big Al's Used Cars' is what they used to call me," Allan said. "I had a lot of nicknames. I used to get pretty abused."[7]

When Houston was 13, he traveled with the team to a preseason tournament in Hawaii. Crum did not have enough healthy bodies to practice so he enlisted Allan's help. In the following years, Houston regularly balled with the Louisville players, as well as former Louisville Cardinals in the NBA who returned for the summer. He complemented his Louisville education playing pickup ball at Shawnee Park, where the game was fast and elbows sharp. "I wanted to experience an atmosphere where if you scored on somebody enough they were going to try to take your head off," Houston said.[8] Shawnee Park toughened him up.

Houston led Ballard High School to the Kentucky state championship in 1988. He initially committed to attend Louisville, but when the University of Tennessee hired Wade as the first African American head basketball coach in SEC history, Allan could not pass up the opportunity to play for his father.[9] During his four years in Knoxville, Allan surpassed Grunfeld as the school's all-time leading scorer.

In the 1993 draft, the Pistons selected point guard Lindsey Hunter and Houston with their two consecutive first-round picks at No. 10 and No. 11. Isiah Thomas and Joe Dumars were nearing the end of their careers, and Hunter and Houston were to be the backcourt of the future.[10] Houston averaged 8.5 points per game as a rookie, followed by 14.5 the next year. The shooting guard then had a breakout campaign in 1995–96, upping his scoring average to 19.7 points per game while shooting 42.7 percent from three-point range. In the summer of '96, he signed with the Knicks.

Allan was laid-back on and off the court and well-liked by his teammates. He formed a close bond with Ward based on their faith.[11] The sweet-shooting guard played like a coach's son with a poised demeanor and polished game. Sprewell called him "Easy" because he was so smooth on the court.[12]

In fact, Houston made the game look so easy that Knicks fans who were accustomed to the combustible Starks and later an enraged Sprewell questioned Houston's determination and toughness. His stoicism was interpreted as a lack of competitiveness.

That perception was compounded by Allan's well-known commitment to his faith. Religious athletes are often affixed the "soft" label because their values do not align with the archetype of the predatory superstar. Michael

Jordan's longtime teammate Will Perdue said, "Michael would throw his mother under a bus to win a game."[13] Surely, a God-fearing man like Houston would not do the same.

However, different personalities achieve optimal performance under different conditions. Perhaps, it was Allan's ability to keep the game in perspective and maintain balance in his life by devoting time and energy to his faith and family, which enabled him to thrive on the court.

Houston worked hard at his craft, loved to compete, and did not shy away from big moments. In each of his first four seasons in New York, his scoring average increased from the regular season to the playoffs. Still, to some, the coach's son appeared to lack the selfish streak that pushes elite scorers to take over games.

Allan Houston signed with the Knicks as a free agent in the summer of 1996. He had one of the sweetest jump shots in the game (Mitchell B. Reibel of Pro Shooter).

Allan's production was a bit disappointing during his first couple of seasons in New York, particularly the first year, when he averaged 14.8 points per game and sometimes found himself on the bench in the fourth quarter. By 1999, with Ewing ailing and Johnson's back failing him, the Knicks had become more perimeter-oriented with Houston and Sprewell as the first options. Houston delivered several momentous performances with the Knicks, though the signature moment of his career came in the 1999 playoffs.

At the start of the postseason, Las Vegas listed the Knicks at 25,000-to-1 odds to win the championship.[14] Their opponent in the first round was once again the No. 1-seeded Heat. It was not a typical 1–8 matchup. The Knicks were a very talented team that struggled to find its groove due to a new roster, the lockout, and injuries. They finished the season strong and would have climbed in the standings if it had been a regular 82-game campaign.

Plus, of course, these teams had history. There were no bro hugs before tipoff or chit-chatting during stoppages of play. The animosity even carried away from the court. If a Heat and Knick player crossed paths during the offseason at a pickup game or sponsorship event, they refused to acknowledge each other.[15]

The rivalry became so intense after the Ward-Brown and Johnson-Mourning fights that Miami hired extra security guards—one for each player—when the team traveled to New York and the players received a memo informing them they were not to leave their hotel without security. The Heat began changing hotels in New York City and even the lesser-known players were told to use aliases. Undercover police cars escorted the team bus to and from games and shootarounds.[16]

With the addition of Sprewell and Camby, the Knicks were more athletic than in previous seasons, though it remained to be seen how the new teammates would respond to a grueling playoff series. These Knicks were put together to compete for a championship. Management had already fired Grunfeld. If the Knicks did not beat the Heat, Van Gundy would almost certainly be out of a job as well.

The Knicks played well against the Heat during the regular season, particularly Ewing, who turned in a 24-point, 17-rebound performance in their first meeting and scored 31 points while grabbing 16 boards in the second. However, the Knicks lost both those games but won the two head-to-head games that Ewing missed with injury. This played into a growing narrative among a section of the media and fan base that the Knicks were better without their aging center.

Sprewell, Camby, and Childs played best in a fast-paced game, but Ewing had difficulty keeping up. When the Big Fella was in the game, New York reverted to its predictable, half-court offense. The issue was exacerbated by Ewing's ailing Achilles. The Garden crowd booed him during the regular season when they were not pleased with the offense.

In Miami, the Knicks ran the Heat off the court in Game 1, led by Houston and Sprewell, who finished with 22 points apiece. Mourning scored 27 for the Heat but did not receive much help. Voshon Lenard was the team's second-leading scorer with 11 points, as Hardaway shot just 4-of-19. The point guard had been nursing a bruised left knee ever since colliding with Grant Hill on February 26. He only missed one game but was clearly hobbled.[17]

The Heat responded with urgency in Game 2, particularly defensively, where they appeared to challenge every Knicks shot. Zo contributed 26 points and eight rebounds, while Ewing countered with 16 points and 15 boards despite struggling to move on his sore Achilles. Houston and Sprewell, who played so well in Game 1, had more turnovers than field goals, and the Knicks shot 39.1 percent from the field. Miami won, 83–73.[18]

New York routed the Heat at the Garden in Game 3, 97–73, putting the game away with a 32–2 run spanning the end of the second quarter and the beginning of the third. Miami shot 34 percent from the field and 17 percent from three-point range. In addition, the Knicks bench was too much for the Heat reserves. Sprewell led the charge with 20 points.[19]

The biggest ovation of the night went to the team's former shooting guard, John Starks, who watched from the walkway between the locker room and court. When the Garden showed his face on the Jumbotron, the crowd erupted. Starks was visibly moved by the fans' reaction. "It took everything I had to hold back the tears," he said.[20]

Childs and Johnson put an end to the postgame celebration in the locker room, reminding their teammates they still had business to take care of. The Knicks wanted to wrap up the best-of-five series in Game 4 to avoid returning to Miami for a Game 5.[21]

Van Gundy's team took control of Game 4 early and grabbed an 11-point lead midway through the third quarter. Then they collapsed offensively. They stopped moving the ball, demonstrated by Childs' zero assists in 20 minutes. Miami opened the fourth quarter on a 23–4 run, which included two deep threes from Hardaway. Mourning and sixth man Terry Porter paced the Heat with 16 points each in an 87–72 win.[22]

Miami carried its momentum from Game 4 into the start of Game 5, opening with a 21–8 burst. The Knicks cut the deficit to four at intermission, and, by the end of three quarters, the game was tied at 60. Miami led 77–74 with under a minute to play when Ewing, who was running on fumes, snatched a Sprewell miss and drew a foul on the putback attempt with 38 seconds left. He hit both foul shots, cutting the deficit to one. Spree stripped Hardaway on the ensuing possession, giving the Knicks a chance to win the game. With 4.5 seconds remaining, Porter knocked the ball away from Spree and out of bounds.[23]

The Knicks did not have a timeout, so they went with a set play called "Triangle Down." Two guys were stationed in the corners with two at the top of the key. Ewing set a screen near the foul line for Houston, who curled around it and received the ball at the top of the key. With Majerle guarded him tightly, he took two quick dribbles toward the hoop. Then, seeing Mourning under the basket, Houston pulled up for a one-handed leaner from the right elbow.[24]

The ball hit the front of the rim and then the backboard before appearing to hover above the cylinder for eternity. Van Gundy's job, Grunfeld's vision, and the future of the team hung up there with it. Finally, the ball fell through the hoop to give the Knicks a one-point lead with 0.8 seconds remaining.

The typically stoic Houston ran to the opposite baseline and emphatically pumped his fist. Before time expired, Porter launched a 30-foot prayer that landed short, giving the Knicks the series victory. It was the second time in NBA history that an eighth seed had defeated the first seed. Houston referred to the game-winning shot as a "friendly bounce from above."[25]

Riley marveled at Van Gundy for having a play up his sleeve for that crucial situation.[26] Van Gundy likes to say, "It's a make or miss league." He has no doubt he would have been fired if Houston's shot did not fall.[27]

The Knicks were celebrating on their way to the locker room, along with comedian Chris Rock, who was high-fiving every Knick he could find. That's when Ewing asked, "Where's Coach?" As soon as the buzzer sounded, Van Gundy darted toward referee Ed T. Rush and began screaming, "No fuckin' way. No fuckin' way."[28]

There were 0.8 seconds on the clock when Miami inbounded the ball, and Van Gundy rightly contended it was impossible for Porter to catch the ball, face up, dribble, and take a shot in that amount of time. An incredulous Checketts asked Van Gundy, "What are you doing? We won." Van Gundy replied, "Coaching for the next round."[29]

Houston hit the memorable shot, though the much-maligned Ewing was the star of the game. He outplayed Mourning for the first time in the series, scoring 22 points and collecting 11 boards. Childs said, "What he did moved me."[30] The Big Fella averaged nearly 15 points and a shade under 11 rebounds for the series. No other Knick grabbed as many as six rebounds per game.

Mourning, who averaged 21.6 points per game, didn't receive enough help. Brown ranked second on the team in scoring with a distant 10.2 points per contest. A gimpy Hardaway scored just nine points per game on worse than 27 percent shooting.

After the game, Checketts said he had not made up his mind about Van Gundy's future. There was much speculation the Knicks needed to at least defeat their next opponent, the Hawks, for the coach to save his job.[31]

Heat forward Mark Strickland believes Houston's shot had a lasting impact on the team. "That shot took a lot of air out of that team," he said. "I think after that shot it changed some of the closeness of the guys."[32]

Van Gundy did not talk to Riley after the 1998 series because Riley had attacked him in the press for the way he handled the Johnson-Mourning fight.[33] For that matter, Van Gundy no longer spoke to his brother, Stan, during the Knicks-Heat series. The two had an argument during the '97 series about the Ward-Brown fight and decided it was best not to talk to each other when their teams met in the playoffs.[34]

On the day of Game 1 of the Knicks' second-round series, Van Gundy received a Federal Express package from Riley addressed to "Coach Van Gundy" with the word "coach" underlined. It was the first time Riley addressed him as "Coach." Riley started the letter, "With rum and coke in hand," and went on to praise Van Gundy for his wonderful coaching job in the recently completed Knicks-Heat series. Van Gundy carried that letter around with him for a long time.[35]

Sprewell said, "After beating Miami, they were the No. 1 seed, we felt like we were the No. 1 seed, the team to beat."[36] Next up were the Hawks, led by another one of Ewing's Georgetown mentees, 7-foot-2 Dikembe Mutombo. Atlanta, coached by Lenny Wilkens, also boasted two marquee guards in Mookie Blaylock and Steve Smith. The Hawks, like the Knicks, survived an exhausting five-game series in the first round by outlasting the Pistons.

Everything pointed to their second-round matchup producing a slow-paced, low-scoring series. The Hawks played the kind of grind-it-out basketball that had been the Knicks' trademark. They surrendered the fewest points per game (83.4) and scored the second-fewest (86.3), operating at the league's second-slowest pace.

The Knicks ran an exhausted Hawks team out of the Georgia Dome in Game 1. Sprewell and Houston combined for 65 points in New York's 100–92 victory. The Hawks controlled the pace in Game 2, but the result was the same with the Knicks finishing ahead, 77–70. New York held Atlanta's starting backcourt to 9-of-36 shooting. For the winners, Sprewell scored 31 points for the second consecutive game, and Camby added 11 points and 13 rebounds off the bench.[37]

In the fourth quarter, Camby turned in the play of the night, a majestic, soaring dunk from just inside the foul line, over the outstretched arm of Mutombo. He capped it off by doing the Congolese center's signature finger wag in his face.[38]

The Knicks appeared in control as the series shifted to New York, but it would not be a Knick playoff series without drama. On the day of Game 3, Mike Wise reported that Checketts had secretly met with Phil Jackson in April. The two talked about the direction and personnel of the team. Doc Rivers and Dave Cowens contacted Checketts about a position within the organization. Checketts and Jackson denied the report. Van Gundy refused to comment.[39]

That night, the coach received a rousing ovation from the Garden crowd during introductions. During the game, Checketts released a statement through a spokesperson confirming that he reached out to Jackson through Bill Bradley to gauge his interest in working for the Knicks before Grunfeld was fired. However, he claimed there was no face-to-face meeting.[40]

Despite the distraction, the Knicks defeated the Hawks, 90–78, in Game 3. Five Knicks scored in double figures, and they limited the Hawks to 31 percent shooting. Ewing said after the game, "I'm not playing for Phil Jackson. There's no way. They can trade me if they get Phil."

Checketts finally came clean the following day, before Game 4. The president of the Garden admitted he met with Jackson and had lied about it. He said he reached out to the Zen Master when the team was 21–21 and the two met for a couple of hours.[41]

Checketts stated, "There were no offers exchanged. There was nothing that came out of the meeting, other than getting acquainted with a guy that I felt was a tremendous option for us, if in fact we continued the season the way it was going and didn't make the playoffs and we needed a new direction."[42] It would have been negligent of Checketts not to gauge Jackson's interest under the circumstances at the time.

Checketts had met with Van Gundy earlier in the day and apologized for lying about the meeting. The coach would not talk about their discussion. "He's the boss," Van Gundy said. "He can talk with whoever he wants to talk to."[43]

Game 4 tipped off hours after Checketts' press conference. New York was the deeper and fresher team. The Knicks led by 11 at the half and 24 late in the third quarter. Including a 79–66 Game 4 win, New York held Atlanta to 76.5 points per game on 31.6 percent shooting for the series.[44]

With a few minutes remaining in the fourth quarter and the game and series no longer in doubt, the entire Garden crowd chanted "Jeff Van Gun-dy." They continued for the final few minutes. Van Gundy almost broke down and reached for a Diet Coke to steady himself.[45] His wife, Kim, sobbed in the stands.[46] Van Gundy's players continued the chant after the game in the locker room. "What usually comes after that," Van Gundy shouted back, "is sucks!"[47]

New York's opponent in the conference finals was the No. 2-seeded Pacers. Despite New York's impressive wins over the Heat and Hawks, the Pacers were heavy favorites. They defeated the Knicks relatively easily in the playoffs the year before and had a significant size advantage, particularly with Ewing ailing. Still, the Knicks' run-and-gun second unit, headlined by Sprewell and Camby, posed a new challenge for Indiana.

Game 1 included 17 lead changes and came down to the final seconds. Ewing hit two big free throws to give the Knicks a 90–88 lead with 29.4 sec-

Knicks fans showed their support for Jeff Van Gundy prior to Game 4 of the Knicks-Hawks series in 1999 after word surfaced that Dave Checketts met with Phil Jackson about a role with the team (REUTERS/Reuters Photographer—stock.adobe.com).

onds remaining. The Pacers ran Reggie off a screen, but Houston shadowed him. Ewing then lunged at the sharpshooter, forcing his three-point attempt to graze the front of the rim with 13 seconds left. New York held on for the 93–90 win.[48]

Ewing scored six of his 16 points in the final two minutes as part of an 11–3 run to close the game, though his most critical contribution was his late defense on Miller. "He [Ewing] was jumping out on Reggie Miller on a sore Achilles that most wouldn't play on," said Van Gundy.[49]

New York trailed by as many as 14 in the third quarter of Game 2, but battled back to take a 78–72 lead with 8:25 remaining. Once again, the game remained in question until the final buzzer. With the scored tied at 86, the Pacers isolated Miller against Childs. Reggie drove left, pump-faked, leaned in, and drew the whistle. Childs did not appear to make any contact with the shooting guard. He and Van Gundy were outraged by the call. Miller calmly sank both free throws with 2.2 seconds left.[50]

The Knicks had one final opportunity. Former quarterback Charlie Ward heaved a pass the length of the floor. Ewing pushed off Antonio Davis, caught the ball, and launched a shot from about 14 feet. It clanged off the rim. Game over.[51]

Prior to the game, Ewing felt a tear in his injured left Achilles. Team doctor Norman Scott confirmed what Ewing already knew: he had played the entire game on a partially torn left Achilles tendon, just above the ankle. Ewing insisted he could play on it, but Scott warned him he would risk tearing it further. At age 36, a completely torn Achilles would have proven career-ending.[52]

A couple days before Game 3, Patrick called a team meeting. "I told them before practice started that I believe in them, and for them to go out there and get me my ring," Ewing said.[53] In losing Ewing, many prognosticators thought the Knicks' chances of defeating the Pacers had vanished. Camby was too frail to match up with the physical Davis boys, as the argument went. They were wrong.

Dudley filled Ewing's spot in the starting lineup for Game 3, though Camby came off the bench with boundless energy and started the second half, scoring 21 points, grabbing 11 rebounds, and snatching four steals. He used his quickness and length to go past, over, and around Dale and Antonio. Pacers coach Larry Bird said after the game, "Marcus Camby was the best player on the floor tonight."[54]

The score was tied at 69 at the start of the fourth quarter. Then, the Pacers went on an 18–6 run to take an 89–81 lead with 3:21 left. The Knicks responded with a 7–0 run of their own before Jackson hit two free throws to put the Pacers up by three with 11.8 seconds on the clock.

The Knicks called timeout, at which point Van Gundy drew up a play for Houston to come off a screen for a three-point shot. It was "Triangle Down," the same play that won Game 5 against Miami.[55] Sprewell cutting backdoor was the second option, but neither he nor Houston was open. Johnson, who was the third option, ran to the ball, and Ward threw it toward him. Jalen Rose tipped the inbounds pass, though Johnson was still able to grab it and square up from the left wing, about 25 feet from the basket.

LJ had worked hard to transform his game after injuring his back. Assistant coach Tom Thibodeau likened it to a pitcher adding a new pitch in the middle of his career. Johnson showed up two hours before every practice. First, he stretched for an hour, with a focus on loosening his back. Then, he worked out with Thibodeau for an hour. The routine included post moves and three-point shots. Finally, LJ concluded his workouts with a late-game scenario, often hoisting a three-pointer in what he pretended were the closing seconds of a tight game.[56]

Camby pulled LJ aside after the Knicks' timeout and told him the ball was going to him. Johnson had a feeling Camby was right because good NBA defenses typically eliminate the first two options. He told himself he was going to shoot if it ended up in his hands.[57]

In 1991, Johnson and his undefeated UNLV team trailed Duke by two with seconds remaining. Johnson had the ball on the right wing with a clean look at a three-point shot. He could have been the hero to send the Runnin' Rebels to their second consecutive championship game, but he hesitated. He ended up passing the ball to Anderson Hunt, who was forced to heave an off-balance shot from 30 feet, which came close but missed.[58]

LJ was distraught about not taking the open shot. A few days later, he changed his voice message to "Hi. This is Larry. I'm not home right now. And yes, I should've taken the last shot."[59]

LJ was not going to allow that to happen again. He dribbled twice to his left, pump-faked, then pulled up, and rose toward the basket with 5.7 seconds on the clock. "I blocked everything out," Johnson said. "That was the key. I was just in the moment. I had practiced that play and that shot over and over. I had envisioned getting the ball. I had envisioned taking that shot before I took it."[60]

Antonio Davis put his hand on Johnson's hip before LJ elevated for the shot. Noticing the contact, referee Jess Kersey blew his whistle. Marv Albert, who was back broadcasting games, was on the call. "It is good, and he was fouled!" he exclaimed. The crowd majestically rose as one. Ward, who won a national championship with Florida State, said it was the loudest crowd he had ever heard.[61]

Larry Johnson started flashing the "Big L" after big shots late in the 1999 season. Rick Brunson came up with the idea (REUTERS/Reuters Photographer—stock.adobe.com).

An elated Johnson ran to midcourt, where Childs grabbed LJ and reminded him he still needed to knock down the free throw.[62] John-

Larry Johnson's four-point play won Game 3 of the 1999 Eastern Conference Finals for the Knicks over the Pacers. Several members of the Knicks organization said it was the loudest they ever heard the Garden (REUTERS/Reuters Photographer—stock.adobe.com).

son calmly stepped to the line and connected on the foul shot. Jackson missed a runner at the buzzer, and the Knicks won.

The crowd chanted "Lar-ry, Lar-ry," and Johnson flashed what was becoming his signature pose, in which he bent his arms into the shape of an "L." Brunson came up with the idea in practice and started doing it on the sidelines during games. LJ did it for the first time, only jokingly, during a late regular-season game. From then on, every time he hit a big shot, he flashed the "L."[63]

At a later date, Kersey admitted to journalist Ric Bucher that he immediately knew he blew the call. He walked the 20 blocks from the Garden to his hotel after the game and did not sleep that night.[64]

Johnson went into his shooting motion after Davis touched him, and it was a light touch at that. If it was a foul, it was on the floor, and the shot should not have counted. The call still infuriates members of that Pacers team.

Indiana evened the series two nights later with a 90–78 win. For the game, Van Gundy inserted Sprewell into the starting lineup for the first time all postseason, but he was outplayed by the 35-year-old Chris Mullin. Off the bench, Rose proved to be a difficult cover too, scoring a game-high 19 points. Camby delivered another solid game with 18 points and 14 rebounds, but the Davis boys neutralized his output, combining for 26 points and 20 rebounds.[65]

It was now a best-of-three series, and Indiana had home-court advantage. The Pacers closed the first quarter of Game 5 on a 19–4 run to take a 28–14 lead. Then Spree and Camby brought the Knicks back, scoring 10 and nine points, respectively, in the second quarter to even the game at 42 at halftime. Finding his stroke after struggling through much of the series, Reggie dropped 30 points on Van Gundy's squad. Spree countered with 29 of his own.[66]

Once again, Camby proved to be the best player on the court. The 6–11 forward who flew to the ball on both ends of the floor compiled 21 points, 13 rebounds, and six blocks. Critically, his dunk with 5:55 remaining handed the Knicks an 81–80 lead, which they did not relinquish. Johnson helped the cause with back-to-back threes around the three-minute-mark. The Knicks won, 101–94.[67]

Game 6 took a dark turn for the Knicks midway through the second quarter. Pacers point guard Travis Best accidentally rolled into Johnson's legs, forcing LJ down in a heap as he screamed, "My knee, my knee." He had to be helped off the court and was taken to the hospital as the Garden crowd serenaded him with chants of "Lar-ry Johnson."[68] New York was already without Ewing. Now its emotional leader had gone down too. It was another obstacle to overcome in the most improbable of seasons.

After the intermission, Houston caught fire, hitting eight of his nine shots in the second half and finishing with 30 points for the game. Spree chipped in 20, and Camby was a force once again, scoring 15 points, grabbing nine rebounds, and blocking three shots while altering several others. Miller shot a dreadful 3-of-18, including 1-of-8 from downtown, and the Knicks won, 90–82.[69]

Childs flung the ball into the crowd when the final buzzer sounded. Van Gundy ran onto the court and hugged Houston, who was searching for his pregnant wife in the stands. Spree high-fived anybody he could find, as Childs hugged Spike Lee at midcourt. Then the Knicks huddled together and danced like a bunch of kids at a party. It was pandemonium at the Garden and on the nearby streets of Times Square.

Bird called Camby, who had to be consoled about his lack of playing by Johnson as recently as after Game 2 against the Pacers, the series MVP.[70] The big man averaged 18.8 points, 11.8 rebounds, and 3.3 blocked shots in the four games after Ewing's injury.

Van Gundy was the biggest winner in the Pacers series. Under the terms of his contract, he received a $500,000 bonus and the option year of his deal for 2000–01 was automatically picked up for $3.5 million.[71] Although Checketts refused to address Van Gundy's job until after the season, the coach finally seemed to be in the clear. It would have been a public rela-

Marcus Camby struggled to earn Jeff Van Gundy's respect after being traded to the Knicks for Charles Oakley. He went on to be an integral part of the team's Finals run in 1999 (REUTERS/Reuters Photographer—stock.adobe.com).

tions nightmare to fire the increasingly popular Van Gundy after he led the team to the Finals.

The Knicks' success also served as vindication for Grunfeld, who was fired before the team he assembled had a chance to show what it could do. In particular, he had to take pride in Camby's inspired play.

By virtue of advancing, the Knicks became the first—and remain the only—eighth seed to reach the Finals.

21

The Twin Towers

"He's better than I am. He handles the ball better than I do, he passes better than I do, and he shoots better than I do. He has great hands around the basket, he's a great rebounder, and I think his potential is sky-high."[1]—David Robinson on Tim Duncan before Duncan's rookie season

New York's opponent in the Finals would be the San Antonio Spurs. One of the four ABA teams to join the NBA in 1976, the Spurs were appearing in their first NBA Finals. Like the Knicks, they effectively weathered a rocky start to the season, which included just six wins of their first 14 games. Boos rained down on the home team at the Alamodome, and rumors swirled that the job of their coach and GM, Gregg Popovich, was in jeopardy.[2]

Then, San Antonio rattled off nine consecutive wins, which began a 31–5 finish that allowed the franchise to post a league-best 37–13 record. Due to the abbreviated nature of the lockout-altered season, New York and San Antonio did not meet in the regular season. The dominant Spurs came in with just one postseason loss, which was incurred in the first round against the Timberwolves. Then, they swept Shaq and the Lakers in the conference semifinals and the Trail Blazers in the conference finals.

Toppling San Antonio was going to be a tall task for the Knicks, especially considering how banged up they were. Still, the Spurs knew they were in for a fight. "The Knicks played harder than the three teams we played before," reflected Spurs forward Sean Elliott years later. "They were scrappy and they were tough and they got after it. We swept Portland and they had more talent. We swept the Lakers and they had more talent with Shaq and Kobe and Glen Rice. But the Knicks, they were like some junkyard dogs."[3]

The Spurs were led by two dominant 7-footers in David Robinson and Tim Duncan. Both were unassuming superstars who followed unconventional paths to the NBA.

Robinson did not play organized basketball until his senior season in high school and was a 6–7 small forward when he committed to the Naval

Academy. "We thought we were getting a Johnny Newman," said Robinson's coach at Navy, Paul Evans. Robinson grew to 6–9 before his plebe summer and added another three or four inches during his plebe year.[4] The Spurs selected "The Admiral" with the first pick in the 1987 draft, then had to wait two years for him to fulfill his obligations to the Navy before he could suit up on the hardwood.[5]

Robinson was an immediate star in the league, averaging 24 points, 12 rebounds, and nearly four blocks per game as a rookie. The accolades piled up over the next decade: Rookie of the Year, 1991–92 Defensive Player of the Year, 1992 Olympic Dream Team gold medalist, '93–'94 scoring leader, '94–'95 MVP, numerous All-Star appearances, and inclusion on the NBA's 50 Greatest Players of all time list. But like Ewing, he was overmatched by Olajuwon in the playoffs, and a championship ring eluded him.

Robinson became a born-again Christian during the '90–'91 season. As with Houston, there were people around the game who believed he was soft and lacked the requisite drive to win a championship, at least in part because of his religious devotion. Robinson was quiet and incredibly down to earth given his success. He always had a smile on his face, and did not curse.[6] Nike launched a massive "Mr. Robinson's Neighborhood" campaign, which played on his nice-guy image by portraying him as a friendly, sophisticated piano player, who transformed into a beast on the court.

The Admiral missed all but six games of the '96–'97 season due to foot and back injuries. The sustained absence ended up being the greatest break of his career. The Spurs tumbled in the standings without their star center and won the NBA lottery, giving them the first pick in the draft. Their prize was a soft-spoken 6-foot-11 post player from the U.S. Virgin Island of St. Croix named Tim Duncan.

Duncan's first love as a child was swimming. Like Robinson, he did not play organized ball until his teen years, when Hurricane Hugo destroyed the Olympic-size swimming pool near his home.[7] In an era in which top prospects routinely left school early, Duncan stayed at Wake Forest University for four years, where he mastered the fundamentals of the game. His footwork was flawless, and he could finish with either hand. Boasting tremendous range for a big man, he could also run the floor and possessed exquisite timing defensively.

"The Big Easy," as his teammate Mario Elie called him, won Rookie of the Year in 1997–98 and finished third in MVP voting in his second season. By the time the Spurs reached the Finals, most people in and around the game regarded him as the league's best player.[8]

Robinson had no intention of simply handing the team over to Duncan.

However, after working out with the youngster prior to his rookie season, Robinson realized the neophyte was already the superior player. In Duncan's second season, Robinson took a step back, effectively turning over the team to his young running mate.[9]

Popovich, who had been on the hot seat months earlier, was now being touted as one of the brightest minds in the game. He graduated from the Air Force Academy, where he led his team in scoring his senior season. He began coaching in the NBA in 1988 as an assistant on Larry Brown's Spurs staff. In '94, he was hired as the Spurs' general manager. Two years later, he named himself head coach on top of his GM duties.[10]

Pop believed in building a team based on character and sought out players who fit the description. It started with Duncan and Robinson, who allowed Pop to coach them and hold them accountable, and bled over to the rest of the roster. Pop's players appreciated that he did not only care about basketball. He was knowledgeable about many subjects, including politics and wine, and took an interest in his players' lives beyond the court, particularly the cultural backgrounds of his diverse team.[11]

San Antonio's starting point guard, Avery Johnson, was the model of perseverance. Undrafted out of Southern University after leading the nation in assists per game, he was cut by five teams, including the Spurs twice, before catching on with San Antonio.[12] The "Little General" played a huge part in the team's success that season.

During the lockout, the Spurs stuck together and worked out regularly, while most teams did so sporadically at best. The Spurs didn't simply hoist some shots and scrimmage. Johnson acted as coach and put the team through full practices. They practiced plays and conducted shooting and defensive drills.[13]

Another factor working in San Antonio's favor during the shortened season was its considerable roster continuity. Elie was the team's lone new rotation player.[14] The native New Yorker was a scrapper who played all over the world before finding a home in Houston, where he won two rings with the Rockets. Sean Elliott, the fifth starter, revealed after the series that he played the season with a serious kidney disease that required him to undergo a kidney transplant.[15]

The Spurs played through their two big men offensively, and Duncan and Robinson formed the backbone of a defense that held the league to under 85 points per game on 40.2 percent shooting (the lowest percentage since 1970–71). The Twin Towers combined for 4.9 blocked shots per game and controlled the defensive backboard.[16]

San Antonio's height was that much more daunting because of Ewing's absence. Houston said, "It was a feeling of David against Goliath."[17] Still, the Knicks liked their chances. They were underdogs throughout the playoffs. Why should the Finals be any different?

The series began in the Alamodome, which held 40,000 people. LJ was dealing with a sprained knee and was still listed as questionable a couple of hours before tipoff. He ended up playing with a bulky brace on his knee.[18] The Knicks jumped out to a 27–21 lead at the end of one, then scored just 10 points in the second quarter. The game was tight until the Spurs used a 13–4 stretch midway through the fourth quarter to take an 87–72 lead. The final score was 89–77.[19]

Duncan proved unstoppable, scoring 33 points and grabbing 16 rebounds. "People said he should have been the MVP and based on tonight, you'd have to agree," Sprewell said.[20] The Knicks were so desperate for big bodies when Camby landed in early foul trouble that Van Gundy dusted off 41-year-old Herb Williams at the end of the first half and played him together with Dudley.[21]

Tasked with trying to slow down Duncan for much of the game despite a sprained knee and notable size disadvantage, LJ was ineffective. Offensively, he tallied just five points in 21 minutes. Jaren Jackson provided the Spurs with a surprise boost off the bench, connecting on five three-pointers. Houston and Spree led the Knicks in the losing effort with 19 points each.[22]

The Knicks looked thoroughly overmatched again in Game 2. Robinson and Duncan combined for 41 points, 26 rebounds, and nine blocks, as San Antonio's defense stifled the Knicks' attack from start to finish. New York finished with 67 points, the lowest total in a Finals game during the shot-clock era, compared to San Antonio's 80. Forty-five of the 67 came from Sprewell and Houston.[23]

Even the baskets Spree and Houston connected on were difficult, contested shots, and they were unable to create scoring opportunities for their teammates. The Knicks dished just eight assists on the night. Through the first two games, New York shot 35 percent and had 17 shots blocked. The situation looked bleak. The Spurs had won 12 consecutive playoff games. Their fans were chanting "Sweep, sweep, sweep" at the end of Game 2.[24]

Van Gundy developed a new strategy for Game 3. He stationed the New York big men who were guarded by Duncan and Robinson by the three-point line in order to open driving lanes for Sprewell and Houston. The strategy worked.[25]

Houston and Sprewell attempted 22 foul shots, compared to 16 in Games 1 and 2 combined. Houston paced the Knicks with 34 points, and Spree scored 10 of his 24 in the fourth quarter.[26] Elliott, who played with Houston in Detroit, said of his former teammate, "Soft guys don't go out and score 30 points in the Finals."[27]

LJ delivered his best game of the series, scoring 16 points, while holding Duncan scoreless in the fourth quarter. Van Gundy also inserted Camby into the starting lineup in place of Dudley, though he fouled out in just 16 minutes. The Spurs didn't look as sharp on either end of the floor. They turned the ball over 20 times and allowed the Knicks to score 89 points. New York came out ahead, 89–81.[28]

No Knick was happier after the Game 3 win than Brunson. One of the benefits of playing in New York is that you are paid to wear a company's sneakers even if you are glued to the end of the bench. The Knicks' 12th man had a sneaker deal with Nike. As part of the contract, Brunson would receive an extra $25,000 if he appeared in the Finals, a significant sum for a player receiving the league minimum. The problem was that he had to actually play in a game for the clause to kick in and Brunson was not a part of Van Gundy's rotation. He wanted the money so badly that he considered telling Van Gundy about the clause after not playing in the first two games, but he thought better of it.[29]

Ward and Childs were both in foul trouble late in the second quarter of Game 3, so Van Gundy called Brunson's name with 3.2 seconds left in the half. He was at the scorer's table with his warmups off before the coach could finish the "R" in Rick. Those were the only 3.2 seconds he played all series, and it earned him $25,000.[30]

Johnson made headlines the day between Games 3 and 4 with controversial comments he made off the court. Earlier in the week, he was fined $25,000 for going on a profanity-laced tirade when two league officials asked him to stop shooting in order to participate in a mandatory media session. On this day, an ornery LJ said, "We've got a lot of rebellious slaves on this team. We don't have a lot of mainstream; we don't go with the mainstream. We're in a different stream on this team. We've got a lot of rebellious slaves. We don't go along with the masses."[31]

The comments appeared unprovoked, and it was not clear what exactly LJ was referring to. He may have been frustrated by the mounting pressure of trying to slow down Duncan on an injured knee.

NBC analyst Bill Walton, who had a history with LJ, added fuel to the fire by calling Johnson a "disgrace to the NBA" and a "sad human being" during Game 4. Johnson shot back at Walton and explained how a man making $84 million to play basketball could compare himself to a slave. "No one man can rise above the masses or the condition of his people. I am privileged and honored by the situation I'm in. No question, I have an excellent opportunity. And this is a beautiful country. Yeah, we've made beautiful strides, but what percentage of black people has made that stride when I go back to my neighborhood and see the same thing? I'm the only one who came out of my neighborhood. All of them dead, on drugs, selling drugs. Am I supposed to be honored and happy just by my success? Yes, I am. But I can't deny the fact of what's happened to us over years and years, and we're still at the bottom of the totem pole. I can't turn my head to that. That's my point."[32]

Duncan and Robinson dominated the Knicks again in Game 4, combining for 42 points, 35 rebounds, and seven blocked shots. They outrebounded the entire Knicks team, 35–34. The Spurs big men received plenty of assistance with all five of the San Antonio starters scoring at least 14 points. Spree and Houston combined for 46 points, but neither scored in the final 5:40. The Knicks managed to hang around until the final minute before losing, 96–89.[33]

Van Gundy said after the game, "Size does matter in this league, particularly in the playoffs. And their size beat our speed and quickness because not only did that affect us on the boards and in the post, but every penetration was a difficult, difficult shot because of their shot-blocking."[34]

New York faced a monumental task heading into Game 5. San Antonio had not lost consecutive games since February or three in a row all season. At the very least, the Knicks wanted to avoid losing the series on their home court. They provided great effort, particularly on defense, where they disrupted the Spurs' passing lanes. San Antonio led by two at the half, 40–38.[35]

With Sprewell intent on keeping the Knicks' season alive, the second half turned into a showdown between he and Duncan. During one stretch between the late third and early fourth quarter, they accounted for 28 of the 29 points scored. Spree dropped 14 points in the fourth and finished the game with 35. Duncan countered with 31.[36] New York did not have the size to stop him. Dudley, its best interior defender, had injured his right arm and was unable to extend it for the rest of the series, an ailment he tried to conceal from the Spurs.[37]

The two teams stayed close throughout the second half. Then, the Spurs clamped down defensively and held the Knicks scoreless for the final 3:12. The Knicks led 77–76 when Avery Johnson, who had been maligned for his poor shooting throughout his career, knocked down an open 18-foot shot along the baseline to hand the Spurs the lead with 47 seconds left. The score remained 78–77 for the next 45 seconds.

The Knicks had one last chance with 2.1 seconds left. After a timeout, Ward inbounded the ball to a cutting Sprewell, who caught it too far under the basket. In a microcosm of the series, he was immediately surrounded by a wall of defenders. Spree took a dribble away from the hoop before releasing

Jeff Van Gundy (left) congratulated Gregg Popovich after the Spurs defeated the Knicks in five games in the 1999 Finals. San Antonio's size was too much for the Knicks (REUTERS / Reuters Photographer—stock.adobe.com).

a contested fadeaway from the baseline. It fell short. The Spurs were NBA champions.

Duncan, who averaged 27 points and 14 rebounds per game, was voted Finals MVP. San Antonio held the Knicks to 39 percent shooting, including 20 percent from downtown. Sprewell and Houston averaged 26.0 and 21.6 points, respectively, but received little help. No other Knick averaged double figures.

The Knicks missed Ewing desperately against San Antonio, and he missed them. "Losing to Houston was tough," Ewing said, "but the one that hurts the most was losing to San Antonio and not being able to play."[38] He revealed years later that he went on the team bus when nobody was around and cried because he was unable to help his teammates.[39]

Ewing would have made the series more competitive. However, it is unlikely that even with a healthy Ewing the Knicks would have prevailed over the Spurs and their Twin Towers.

The big man was months shy of his 37th birthday, and his body was breaking down. He knew this may have been his last shot at a championship. His teammates were devastated they were not able to win a ring for him.[40]

The day before Game 5, Van Gundy announced that Checketts told him two or three weeks earlier he would be back for the following season. In July, he and the Knicks agreed to a two-year contract extension that was worth as much as $10 million with incentives and ran through the 2002–03 season.[41]

Less than a week after the Finals, the Knicks drafted a 7-foot-2 French center named Frédéric Weis. Weis was relatively unknown in the United States. He had been playing professionally in France at a time when few Europeans had succeeded in the NBA. Also, Weis had declined to work out for NBA teams prior to the draft.[42]

Meanwhile, Ron Artest, a New York City kid who played his collegiate ball in Jamaica, Queens, for St. John's University, was still available when the Knicks were on the clock. Knicks fans in attendance at the MCI Center in Washington, D.C., were furious their team passed on the local star for some unknown European guy.

Ed Tapscott had been serving as interim general manager since Grunfeld was fired in April and was responsible for the pick. He believed the Knicks needed a center for the future. Ewing was about to turn 37, had bad knees, and was recovering from a partially torn Achilles tendon. Tapscott knew Weis was a project, but one with an impressive offensive skill set and good rebounding ability. He reminded Tapscott of Zydrunas Ilgauskas, the center for the Cavaliers.[43]

Tapscott wanted everybody to be on the same page after the Van Gundy-Grunfeld rift and asked Van Gundy for his opinion on Weis. The coach told him he would rather leave the draft up to the scouts. They watched hours and hours of live games and film of the various prospects. Van Gundy did not have time to watch college basketball during the season, and the draft took place just a few days after the Finals. His opinion would have been uninformed.[44]

Checketts' son, Spencer, was a regional scout for the Knicks and was in the war room on draft night. According to Spencer, Tapscott said, "I'll never live down the fact that I passed on Zydrunas Ilgauskas," and used that as justification for choosing Weis.[45]

Three or four people in the room argued for Artest, to the point that they believed Tapscott was going to select the forward out of St. John's when he turned in the pick. Then he went rogue.[46] Knicks scout Scott McGuire said, "I was sick to my stomach because I loved Ron Artest."[47]

Interestingly, the Knicks might not have selected Artest even if Weis was not available. Artest skipped a pre-draft tryout with the Knicks, claiming he had a stomach ache. He was supposed to work out against Shawn Marion, who had severely outplayed him at a previous workout with another organization. Some members of the Knicks front office thought he was faking and began referring to it as the "Shawn Marion flu."[48]

Tim Shea, the Knicks' director of international scouting, was concerned it would be too much pressure for Artest to play in his hometown, and Tapscott preferred James Posey out of Xavier University.[49]

That summer, Weis arrived late for summer league due to commitments with the French National team. Van Gundy was less than impressed with the big man. He noted an out-of-shape Weis needed to work on his body.[50] For his part, Weis felt Van Gundy was unreasonably hard on him. After all, the Frenchman was still working his way back into shape after undergoing back surgery in April.[51]

DeMarco Johnson, the Knicks' second-round pick in 1998, was teammates with Weis that summer and could not believe the Knicks used a first-round pick on the center. "That guy wasn't an NBA player," Johnson said. "He had no skill set. He was just tall."[52]

Weis never wore a Knicks uniform again. Instead of signing a rookie contract, he returned to France. The following summer, he was the ignominious victim of a devastating dunk by Vince Carter during the 2000 Olympics in which Carter leaped over him. Weis played well during those Olympics as France won the silver medal. He was also a four-time All-Star in France, but will always be known on this side of the Atlantic Ocean for the Carter dunk. He chose not to play for the Knicks' summer league team in 2000 because he was out of shape after caring for his ill father. Then the Knicks lost interest in him.[53]

Tapscott was stunned to learn in August 1999 that he would not be the permanent general manager. He was a loyal, intelligent man with a law degree, coaching experience, and nine years with the organization. His close relationship with Grunfeld may have worked against him.[54]

Checketts says he passed over Tapscott because of the Weis pick. Scott Layden, whom Checketts hired as the new GM, told him most basketball people believed Weis would never play in the NBA. Checketts was in the crowd in Sydney for Carter's dunk and could not believe the team wasted a pick on Weis.[55]

Checketts knew Layden from his time in Utah. Layden had been with the Jazz since 1981 when he served as an assistant coach under his father, Frank.[56] He remained in that role under Jerry Sloan before moving to the front office in '88. Four years later, he was placed in charge of player personnel. Layden kept the Jazz in contention while their stars, John Stockton and Karl Malone, aged. Two of his best moves were trading for Jeff Hornacek in 1994 and drafting Bryon Russell with the 45th pick in '93.[57]

Layden resembled a bookworm with his glasses and short-cropped hair. Accustomed to operating in a small market, his reserved, bland personality left many wondering if he was an ideal fit for New York. A month after Checketts hired Layden, Steve Mills was named executive vice president of franchise operations to handle the business side of the team.[58]

22

End of an Era

"One of the most difficult things in sports is coaching a superstar in decline."—Jeff Van Gundy

The Knicks opened training camp in 1999 without Ewing. The tear in his Achilles had healed, but he was still experiencing pain from tendonitis in the region.[1] Ewing's absence sparked the growing debate over whether the Knicks were better off without him. Without the 11-time All-Star in the post, they were less predictable and their spacing improved, which opened driving lanes for Sprewell and the guards. Many fans felt he slowed the Knicks down, holding them back from playing their best basketball. To support their theory, they pointed to the team's success without him against the Pacers in the playoffs.[2]

Van Gundy was quick to defend the player who had stood up for him many times in the past. He noted the Knicks were 8–3 with Ewing in the 1999 playoffs and 4–5 without him and that they desperately missed his size and skill in the Finals.[3] Ewing was still capable of being a valuable contributor. The question was whether he was willing to take on a lesser role and cede control of the team to Sprewell and Houston.

Meanwhile, Sprewell's status with the team was unclear. New York's best performer during the Finals run was entering the last year of his contract, and the Knicks had to think twice about committing a tremendous sum of money to him given his troubled past. New York contacted the SuperSonics about trading Spree for Gary Payton over the summer. After the season began, he remained the most logical piece to be dealt in the team's ongoing pursuit of a point guard.[4]

Spree had not been involved in any major incidents since his arrival in New York, though he was fined on two occasions—once when his agent criticized the team, and a second time for $130,000 during training camp in 1999 for losing contact with the team and missing practices after a court appearance in California.[5]

The Knicks rolled the dice on the mercurial swingman, signing him to a five-year, $61.8 million contract.[6] Still, Van Gundy was not about to place all of his faith in Spree. He named Houston the third tri-captain, replacing the retired Herb Williams, along with LJ and Ewing.[7]

The Knicks experienced two homecomings early in the season. New York didn't play Golden State during the lockout season, so Sprewell made his first return to the scene of the crime on November 20, 1999. "I just want to go in there and crush them," he said. "There's bitterness, hatred, whatever you'd call it. It's there."[8]

Spree led the Knicks onto the court for pregame warmups, and the crowd at The Arena in Oakland showed no mercy for the former Warrior. The heckling came early and often, and Spree cursed back at the fans. The public address announcer saved Sprewell's name for last during player introductions to maximize the jeers.[9]

Spree was too amped up and struggled to find his rhythm, though with 5:30 left in the game, he drove past his man and threw down a monstrous one-handed jam. Then, he flexed his muscles and snarled at the Warriors bench as he shouted obscenities at the fans. Spree finished the game 6-of-17 for 14 points, and the Knicks won, 86–79. He was fined $10,000 by the NBA for cursing at fans.[10]

Starks' return to the Garden on December 7 could not have been more different. In the days before the game, Starks' former teammates reminisced about the shooting guard. Houston talked about how Starks embraced him when he signed with the team in 1996, even though he took Starks' starting position. Asked if he considered Starks one of his favorite teammates, Ewing responded, "He is my favorite teammate." He and John had grown extremely close over the years. Their families spent a great deal of time together.[11]

Mike Breen once said of Knicks fans, "If you show them you're willing to work and you show them you're willing to do anything to get you a victory, they'll love you for the rest of your life."[12] Starks is Exhibit A. The former Knick received a rousing ovation during player introductions. He stood at the foul line for a long time blowing kisses to the adoring crowd, at home yet looking out of place in a blue and yellow jersey. Starks finished the night with seven points on 3-of-12 shooting as Sprewell paced the Knicks to an 89–83 win.[13]

Ewing returned to the lineup against the 76ers on December 10, and Camby was relegated to the bench. The 11-9 Knicks were a different team than the one for which Patrick last played. New York had advanced to the Finals without him and forged a new identity in the process, built around Houston, Sprewell, and Camby.

Shots were harder to come by for No. 33. The old guard who looked to Ewing for leadership had moved on. His last close friend on the team, Herb, had retired. Ewing grew reclusive in the locker room.[14]

In early February, Van Gundy publicly called on Sprewell and Houston, not Ewing, to fill what he deemed a leadership void. "We need Allan and Latrell to step forward in that role," Van Gundy said. "Not to be anything other than what they are as far as personality, but really step forward, because your best players set the tone. I'm hopeful they'll feel comfortable enough as time goes on that they can assert more leadership."[15] Ewing was benched for the final 15 minutes of a three-point loss to the Cavs in early January for no apparent reason, and rumors surfaced that the Knicks discussed dealing their aging center to the Wizards for Juwan Howard.[16]

Still, the prideful Ewing carried on, battling on a nightly basis. When Camby went down with a knee injury in early February, the old warrior responded with vintage performances. He scored 25 points and grabbed 14 boards in a Knicks victory over the Heat.[17] A few weeks later, he dominated the 76ers to the tune of 21 points and 19 rebounds. Despite taking fewer shots in less playing time, Patrick still averaged 15.0 points and 9.7 rebounds for the season.

The Knicks overcame a slow start to finish the first half of the season at 29–18. Van Gundy coached the Eastern Conference All-Star team. That honor usually goes to the coach of the team with the best record in the conference, but Larry Bird coached the All-Stars the previous year. By rule, the coach of the team with the next best record received the nod. At the cutoff, the Knicks were tied with the Heat atop the Atlantic Division at 26–16. Since Riley coached the team a couple of years earlier, Van Gundy received the honor.[18]

Houston was the lone Knick to make the team.[19] He was also selected to represent the United States in the Olympics that summer. Knicks fans thought Sprewell deserved to be an All-Star, but NBA coaches belong to a tight fraternity. They were unlikely to vote for a player who choked one of their own two years earlier.

On April 2, Childs and Kobe Bryant were jostling for position in the paint during a Knicks-Lakers game in L.A. when Kobe threw an elbow around Childs' jaw. Afterward, Childs claimed it was the second time. He had already warned the Lakers superstar, he said. After sustaining the blow, the Knick point guard got in Kobe's face, and the two exchanged words.[20]

As play continued around them, Childs headbutted Kobe, connecting with his chin. Bryant responded with an elbow to Childs' face. Then Childs unloaded a one-two combination in the direction of Kobe's face. The blows fell short, and Kobe threw a couple of punches in retaliation, which did not land.[21]

Childs was deemed the instigator and suspended two games, while Bryant received a one-game ban. The Knicks point guard claims he could have knocked Kobe out if he stepped into his punches, but decided against it.[22] It was not the first time Childs stood up to one of the premier players in the league. During a Knicks-Bulls contest in December 1997, the point guard threw the ball at Michael Jordan after Jordan elbowed him in the side of the head.[23]

The Knicks finished the season 50–32, two games behind the Heat in the division. That was good enough for the No. 3 seed. Houston led the team in scoring, averaging 19.7 points per game.

New York's first-round playoff opponent would be the Raptors, who took the season series from the Knicks, 3–1. Toronto won the last three matchups by double digits, and Vince Carter averaged 33 points per game against the Knicks. Slowing him down would be the key to the series.

That is exactly what the Knicks did, sweeping the Raptors in three games. Sprewell was dynamite, and with the help of well-timed double teams, held Carter to 19.3 points per game on 30 percent shooting. The Raptors shot just 37 percent from the field. Game 2 in New York was the most intense of the three matchups as the Knicks overcame a 14-point fourth-quarter deficit to win by one on a Spree fadeaway with 7.9 seconds remaining.[24]

The most dramatic event of the series took place before Game 1, when Raptors coach Butch Carter filed a defamation lawsuit against Camby for $5 million. Days earlier, Camby called Carter a "liar," because the coach told him he was part of the team's future, then traded him soon after. The suit claimed Carter "has been damaged and suffered great pain and mental anguish, and has been held up to ridicule and contempt by his friends, acquaintances, and the public."[25] Players criticize former coaches all the time. It was a bizarre lawsuit.

Next up for the Knicks were the Heat. This marked the fourth year in a row Riley and Van Gundy's teams squared off in the playoffs. Stan Van Gundy opined that because the two teams were so similar and familiar with each other, "what those games came down to … it was toughness."[26] Even with Mason and Oakley no longer with the team, nobody was tougher than the Knicks. Thibodeau used to say, "We might be out-talented, but we were never outcompeted."[27]

Hardaway reiterated his feelings toward the Knicks prior to the series: "I hate them with all the hate that you can hate with. Can you hate more than that? If you can, I hate them more than that."[28]

The Heat took Game 1 in Miami. With the score tied at 83, Zo drove past Ewing—who was aching from back spasms the day before—for a layup with 41.8 seconds remaining. Then Zo sealed the game with a jumper with 5.6 seconds left. The Knicks did not connect on a field goal in the final five minutes. In a troubling development for the Heat, Hardaway sprained his left foot in the win.[29]

New York bounced back with an 82–76 victory in Game 2, despite shooting just 35 percent. Six Knicks finished in double figures, led by Ewing and Ward with 13 apiece. New York also held Mourning to 17 points on 5-of-18 shooting by doubling the big man whenever he touched the ball.[30]

The series shifted to New York for Game 3, a low-scoring affair even by these teams' standards. Miami won in overtime, 77–76, despite a combined 47 points from Houston and Sprewell. New York trailed by two when Ewing drained a 17-footer over an onrushing Mourning with 2.6 seconds remaining in regulation. The Garden exploded as Ewing held his follow-through while backpedaling down the court. Later, Ewing split a pair of free throws with 13.7 seconds left in overtime, putting the Knicks' lead at one, instead of two.[31]

On the ensuing possession, Heat backup point guard Anthony Carter launched a floater, which appeared to go over the backboard. It then hit the rim and bounced in with 2.2 seconds remaining for the win. Spree called Carter's prayer a "H-O-R-S-E" shot. Van Gundy went further, arguing it was illegal because the ball went over the backboard. Upon further review, the referees determined the replay was inconclusive. Therefore, the shot counted, and Miami went on to win despite shooting worse than 37 percent.[32]

New York bounced back in Game 4 to even the series with a 91–83 win. All five Knicks starters scored in double digits, led by Ward with 20 points. Hardaway continued to play ineffectively while laboring on his sprained foot. In retrospect, he believes he should have sat out and let his foot heal.[33]

Game 5 was back at American Airlines Arena, where the Heat locked down the Knicks on the way to an 87–81 victory. Houston was thrown off his game by the various defenders Riley sent his way and attempted just two shots in the second half. Majerle knocked down two long threes in the closing minute, then beat Sprewell off the dribble to set up a dagger three by Bruce Bowen. New York headed back home down 3–2 in the best-of-seven series.[34]

The somber mood on the plane ride back was alleviated by a comical incident at the end of the flight. Prior to 9/11, players and coaches parked their cars on the tarmac. The Knicks' chartered flight landed at Westchester County Airport, and as it taxied down the runway, a blast from the engine propulsion lifted Van Gundy's 1995 Honda Civic off the ground and sent it flying through the air. The car was totally destroyed, as were three others it landed on, including Houston's Mercedes. Van Gundy, who was still reeling from the loss to Miami, was furious, but his players found the scene to be hysterical, particularly after the fact.[35] It was the type of thing that could only happen to Jeff Van Gundy.

The Knicks played the first half of Game 6 as if they had already un-packed their golf clubs for summer. Ewing was the only Knick who showed up. New York trailed Miami by as many as 18 in the second quarter and was down by 15 at halftime. Then the soft-spoken Houston fired up the team with a speech at halftime.[36]

New York stormed back and tied the game in the closing minutes. Ewing, whose effort carried the Knicks down the stretch, stole a post entry pass intended for Mourning with 30.7 seconds left. Then Houston drove to the hoop and drew contact with 17.6 seconds remaining. He knocked down both free throws for the game's final two points and a Knicks 72–70 win. Houston finished with 21 points to go with Ewing's 15 points and 18 rebounds.[37]

For the fourth year in a row, a Knicks-Heat playoff series would culmi-nate in a decisive game, and for the third consecutive time, it would take place in Miami. Game 7 was close throughout. Hardaway, who played his best ball of the series, nailed a three-pointer to put the Heat up by 1 with 1:32 left. On the ensuing possession, LJ threw a pass to Ewing on the block. Mourning went for the steal and missed, giving Ewing a clear path to the basket. Beast slammed it in to give the Knicks an 83–82 lead.[38]

The Heat had one last chance with 12.4 seconds left. They inbounded the ball to Zo. LJ and Ewing quickly double-teamed him. Zo kicked it out to Mashburn, who passed on an open shot from the elbow and dished it to reserve forward Clarence Weatherspoon. After taking a couple of dribbles, Spoon launched a 12-foot jumper with Camby's hand in his face. The shot banged off the rim.[39]

Spree grabbed the rebound with 2.1 seconds remaining. Referee Bennett Salvatore blew his whistle, ruling that Sprewell stepped out of bounds, but the referees conferred and Dick Bavetta overruled him. It was Knicks ball.[40]

New York inbounded to Childs, who played exceptionally well down the stretch, and the point guard flung the ball into the air before he could be fouled. New York had eliminated the Heat in a winner-take-all game in Miami for the third year in a row. Ewing scored 20 points and grabbed 10 rebounds, while Zo finished with 29 and 13 in the losing effort.

The Heat were furious about Bavetta's call and complained bitterly after the game. Hardaway, who was also angry at Bavetta for overruling a fellow referee on another play—he called a jump ball between Ewing and Mourning instead of a foul on Ewing—called the referee "Knick Bavetta" in a postgame press conference.[41]

Riley often said, "There is winning and misery."[42] True to form, he was miserable after the game. The coach walked into his office, sat down at his desk, put his face in his hands, and proceeded to weep. Riley felt like he couldn't face his players after letting them down again. After waiting a long time for his coach to come out, Mourning entered Riley's office and the pupil became the coach.[43]

Zo said, "I know you're feeling a little bit low, Coach, but you gotta get up and do your fucking job." Riley knew Zo was right and addressed his team. "I almost quit that summer," Riley said. "I was broken."[44]

The Knicks headed to the Eastern Conference Finals, where they met the Pacers for the second straight year. Indiana wanted revenge after losing to the Ewing-less Knicks the year before. The Pacers returned essentially the same team minus Antonio Davis, whom they traded to the Raptors. Additionally, Jalen Rose replaced Chris Mullin in the starting lineup. Rose, who upped his scoring average from 11.1 to a team-high 18.2, was named the league's Most Improved Player.

Indiana took Game 1 at Market Square Arena, 102–88. The night belonged to a little-known forward named Austin Croshere. Croshere was the Pacers' first pick in the 1997 draft and idled on the bench during his first two seasons. A spot opened in Bird's rotation when Indiana traded Antonio Davis.

Croshere had a solid year for the Pacers, averaging 10.3 points and 6.4 rebounds, but he was not exactly at the top of the Knicks' scouting report. The forward caught fire from long range, connecting on 4-of-5 three-pointers and led the Pacers in scoring with 22 points. His hot hand carried the added benefit of pulling the shot-blocking Camby away from the basket.[45]

Six minutes into Game 2, Ewing came up hobbling. He sprained a tendon in his right foot and did not return. It felt like déjà vu. However, this time, the Knicks fell behind in the series, 2–0. New York led by six with eight minutes to go, but the Pacers chipped away at the lead by pounding the ball into Smits, who scored 10 fourth-quarter points in Ewing's absence.[46]

Sprewell, who was having what he called the worst playoff game of his career (he shot 3-of-14), still had an opportunity to tie the game on the Knicks' final possession. With New York trailing by two, Spree had the 6-foot Travis Best on him. He backed the point guard down to about 10 feet from the basket, then clanged a jumper off the rim. The Knicks fouled Dale Davis immediately. He missed both free throws, but grabbed his own rebound to seal the win.[47]

Game 3 at the Garden was a must-win game for the Knicks, and they played like it. Sprewell bounced back with 32 points, and Houston added 28. Playing without Ewing, New York held off a late Indiana charge led by Rose, who scored 22 points in the fourth quarter. Unfortunately, Camby sprained his knee in the 98–95 win, and an MRI revealed a fractured bone in Sprewell's left foot. Spree opted to continue playing, knowing he could do further damage to his foot.[48]

Despite the key injuries, the Knicks eked out a 91–89 win in Game 4 to even the series. Once again, Ewing did not play, though a gimpy Camby gave it a go. LJ was the leading man for the Knicks, hitting all five of his three-point attempts, including two critical ones in the fourth quarter, and finishing with 25 points. New York shot 10-of-14 from behind the arc.[49]

The Knicks looked like a different team with Ewing back in action for Game 5. They played well in the first quarter, outscoring the Pacers 32–17. Then, the offense stagnated, and they stopped attacking the basket like they did in Games 3 and 4. New York scored just eight points in the second quarter. Travis Best was a spark plug off the bench, scoring 24 points for Bird's team. Indiana won, 88–79, to bring the Knicks to the brink of elimination.[50]

The story after the game was whether the Knicks were better without Ewing. They played more freely and aggressively when he was not on the floor. The media noted the Knicks were 5–1 against the Pacers over the past two postseasons with Ewing sidelined and 1–4 when he played. New York talk radio heated up with angry Knicks fans venting their frustrations with the Big Fella.[51]

Ewing's counterpart, Smits, joined the chorus. Prior to Game 5, he said of Ewing, "Look at the percentage with or without him," adding, "I hope he comes back." Surprised by Smits' lack of respect for the future Hall of Famer, the Knicks came to their center's defense.[52]

However, even Sprewell, who routinely defended Ewing, admitted the Knicks appeared to play better against the Pacers without him: "If you look just at the numbers, the numbers definitely say we're better without him," Spree said. "We've won five and lost one without him. If you look at that, that's probably the case. That's what the numbers say."[53]

Sprewell's comments were an anomaly. Patrick's teammates typically defended him and claim to have never discussed internally whether they were better without him. The media created stories and fans had their opinions, but the guys in the locker room knew how valuable Ewing was. The Knicks may have posed a greater challenge to the Pacers with more speed on the court, but they were not a better team overall without Patrick.

Down 3–2, the Knicks remained confident. Ewing made another guarantee, telling anybody who would listen they were going to win the series. Childs backed him up, saying the Knicks would play their best game of the year in Game 6 and be back in Indiana for Game 7.[54]

Indiana and New York were tied in Game 6 heading into the fourth quarter when Reggie, who had been relatively quiet throughout the series, went off for 17 points in the final period. New York managed just 18 as a team. Reggie finished with a game-high 34. Spree had 32 on 26 shots, many of them ill-advised. Houston did a disappearing act after the first quarter, scoring just four points over the final three quarters. The Pacers won, 93–80, to eliminate the Knicks and advance to the Finals.[55]

Ewing turned in a respectable 18 points and 12 rebounds yet was still the subject of ridicule. The Knicks won the two games he missed with a sprained foot and lost the four in which he played (one of which was only for six minutes). They scored 83.2 points per game with him and 94.5 without him. Some of the vitriol spewed in Patrick's direction by the media and fans was unwarranted and cruel, particularly given how much he had done for the franchise.

There were other reasons why the Knicks lost to the Pacers after beating them the previous year. Camby was a relative nonfactor, averaging 3.3 points and 6.3 rebounds, compared to 14.3 and 10.7, respectively, in the '99 series. The Knicks were also out-rebounded in every game, through no fault of Ewing, the team's leading rebounder. Additionally, the Knicks were no longer Patrick's team. As the team's best player, Spree certainly deserved his share of criticism for its failure to reach the Finals.

As the Knicks' season came to an end, there was a sense the same group would not return the next year. They appeared to have maximized their potential, and Ewing and LJ, who battled plantar fasciitis during the Pacers series, were both breaking down.

In early July, Ewing's agent, David Falk, informed Checketts that Ewing wanted to be traded. Checketts told Falk he wanted to hear it from Patrick himself, so Ewing called Checketts and reiterated the request. Ewing first asked to be traded in January of that year, over dinner with Checketts at the 21 Club in Manhattan. It was about a month after he returned from his Achilles injury, and he was frustrated by his minutes and touches.[56]

Perhaps most importantly, Ewing felt like he didn't fit with the Knicks who had become more of a running team. With Oak, Starks, and Herb no longer there, Ewing had also become a loner in the locker room. "You know Patrick, he doesn't say much to us," Camby said during the 1999–00 season. "He doesn't talk to anyone."[57]

Brunson said, "I think you could tell he [Ewing] was unhappy with management, not with us or with Coach."[58] Other teammates had no idea anything was bothering Ewing. Wallace and Brunson took their children on vacation to Jamaica with Patrick after the '99–'00 season and the Big Fella was in a great mood.[59]

Checketts firmly denied Ewing's initial request, stating the Knicks needed him. He told Patrick if he still felt the same way after the season, he would reconsider. When Ewing broached the subject again in July, Checketts felt the Knicks owed it to Ewing to honor his wish.[60]

Patrick was tired of being blamed for the Knicks' failures and of hearing in recent years that the team was better off without him. He claimed there was grumbling in the locker room about him taking too many shots.[61] Falk singled out Sprewell as one of the players who complained.[62] Ewing also knew the team was going in another direction and did not "feel as wanted as I did before."[63]

Van Gundy believed Ewing was listening to the vocal minority. The people who criticized him on talk radio and held up derogatory signs at games did not represent the majority of Knicks fans. The coach believed Checketts should have denied Ewing's trade request.[64]

Falk discouraged Ewing from seeking a trade. He noted how few stars finish their careers with one team and believed Ewing could be jeopardizing valuable business opportunities in New York upon retirement if he were traded to another team.[65] Patrick did not heed his agent's advice.

Ewing had a no-trade clause so he was able to direct the process. He provided management a list of seven teams for whom he would be willing to waive his no-trade clause: the Magic, SuperSonics, Trail Blazers, Nets, Heat, Suns, and Raptors. Falk worked with Checketts to find a deal that benefited both parties. In late July, Ewing had a positive meeting with Sonics officials and their coach Paul Westphal, at which point his list dwindled down to one.[66]

The Sonics wanted to unload Vin Baker's bloated body and contract. Falk also roped the Lakers into the deal in order to relocate another client of his, Glen Rice, who wanted out of Los Angeles, where he had been feuding with Phil Jackson. The three teams included the Pistons in order to make a trade work and, on August 20, reached an agreement in principle on a deal. Then Detroit's general manager, Joe Dumars, backed out.[67]

When it was believed the trade was a done deal, the *New York Post* printed the headline "Good Riddance to That Menacing Scowl."[68] It was no way to treat a player who had carried the Knicks for 15 years. Childs was the only teammate who reached out to Ewing after the trade fell apart.[69]

Van Gundy flew to Washington, D.C., and tried to convince Ewing to stay with the team. He was unsuccessful.[70] The Knicks were in a tough spot because it would have been very difficult to bring Ewing back after he was so close to leaving.

On September 20, they finally traded Ewing to the Sonics as part of a four-team deal, in which the Suns replaced the Pistons from the original trade. New York received Rice and center Travis Knight from the Lakers, Luc Longley from the Suns, and a few other players to make the finances work, including Vernon Maxwell, Lazaro Borrell, and Vladimir Stepania. They also received from Seattle a first-round and two second-round picks, as well as the Lakers' 2001 first-round pick. The Knicks also sent Dudley and a 2001 first-round pick to Phoenix, and the Lakers received Horace Grant, Greg Foster, Emanual Davis, and Chuck Person from Seattle.[71]

Once again, Van Gundy flew to Washington to try to change Ewing's mind before the trade was finalized, but to no avail.[72] Van Gundy once said of the man he calls "the Mortgage,"[73] "I guarantee there was never a harder-working superstar or a more loyal star to his team, his teammates, and his coaches."[74] Not one Knicks player reached out to Ewing after the trade.[75]

Patrick departed as the franchise's all-time leader in points, rebounds, blocks, steals, field goals made, minutes, and games played. He is one of the three greatest Knicks of all time, along with Walt Frazier and Willis Reed. Reed has proclaimed Patrick to be the greatest player in franchise history, while Frazier gives the honor to Reed.[76]

Where Ewing ranks among the top three depends on how much one values longevity versus peak performance. He competed longer and contributed to more Knicks victories than Reed or Frazier, though Frazier and Reed at their best were superior to Ewing.

Reed won one regular-season and two Finals MVP awards. Ewing finished in the top five in MVP voting six times, though never higher than fourth. Frazier's finest hour occurred in the biggest game of his career, Game 7 of the 1970 NBA Finals, when he compiled 36 points, 19 assists, seven rebounds, and five steals. Ewing scored 17 points on 7-of-17 shooting in Game 7 of the 1994 Finals.

Ewing did not win championships like Frazier and Reed, though he never played with a Hall of Famer, while Frazier and Reed shared the court with many including each other. By the time the Knicks added the requisite talent around Ewing, his body began to break down.

It is also worth considering how different Ewing's legacy would be if Starks made his shot at the end of Game 6 of the 1994 Finals. Rather than being another name on the list of great players to never win a ring, Patrick would be remembered for carrying a team without a second star to a championship.

Ewing could have chased rings like many of today's stars, but the competitor in him yearned to defeat his rivals, not join them. Would winning a couple of titles with Jordan and the Bulls or Mourning and Hardaway in Miami have made him any more of a champion?

The Knicks were blown out at home, 101–72, on opening night of the 2000–01 season, their first game post–Patrick. Midway through the third quarter, chants of "Pat-rick Ew-ing" rained down from the Garden rafters.[77] Ewing, who was respected but never loved, was finally fully appreciated once he was gone.

Epilogue

The Ewing trade marked the beginning of a downward spiral for the Knicks that would last for decades. At the time, Patrick had one year and $18 million remaining on his contract. The Knicks should have let him play out his deal. Instead, they traded him for overpriced players who provided little value.

Management made another error the following summer by doling out an outrageous amount of cash to Houston. The shooting guard opted out of his contract and re-signed with the team for $100 million over six years, a tremendous sum of money for an athlete who nobody considered a franchise player.[1]

Checketts and Dolan mutually agreed to part ways during the 2001 off-season. Checketts was frustrated with Dolan's business decisions. He believed the owner was jealous of his success at the Garden and intentionally handed him so much responsibility that he would fail.[2]

The final straw was when Dolan refused to sign off on a deal Checketts spent weeks negotiating with George Steinbrenner and his partners, which would have kept the Yankees on MSG Network for 25 years. Checketts' biggest regret about his time with the Knicks is his inability to surround Ewing with enough talent to win a championship.[3]

Dolan was glad to see Checketts go. "I do think Jimmy [Dolan] just knew that I didn't like him, I didn't trust him, and it wasn't going to work," Checketts said.[4] Dolan also wanted a tighter grip on the organization.[5]

After failing his physical, Larry Johnson retired during training camp in 2001. His back could no longer hold up through the rigors of an NBA season.[6] Van Gundy said Johnson "was the embodiment of everything I believe in—hard work and playing at your best when the best was needed." The coach added, "I will miss him personally. I was as close to Larry as any player I have ever coached."[7]

Two months later, Van Gundy unexpectedly resigned 19 games into the season. The coach had been considering the move since the spring. He missed his daughter and was concerned about his diminished focus. He talked to Layden and a few coaches about it over the summer, and they encouraged him to stick with it and see if the focus came back. It never did.[8]

Van Gundy said, "The one thing I valued more than anything is that I gave our team my best. And when I didn't feel my focus was at its best, I didn't want to shortchange our team. That's why I made the most difficult decision professionally that I've had to make."[9]

The coach also felt the departures of Ewing and Johnson changed the fiber of the team, and it was time for the franchise to move in a new direction.[10] "Coaching in New York is like coaching in dog years," he said. "So I had been head coach 42 years."[11]

The 5-foot-9, Division III point guard who was not expected to survive more than a few months on the job, outlasted Checketts, Grunfeld, and Ewing before leaving on his own terms. He led the Knicks to the playoffs in each of his six full seasons as head coach, including a trip to the Finals.

The Knicks were 10–9 when Don Chaney replaced Van Gundy. They finished the season 30–52, ending their streak of 14 straight playoff appearances. In November 2002, their home sellout streak, which began in February 1993, ended at 433 games.[12]

In September 2008, Ewing and Riley were enshrined into the Naismith Memorial Basketball Hall of Fame, along with one of the men who stood between them and a championship, Hakeem Olajuwon. Van Gundy was in attendance, as both honorees recognized the impact he had on their careers. Ewing joked that the coach did not have bags under his eyes that evening.[13]

During his speech, Riley thanked Checketts profusely for bringing him to New York. Checketts was stunned. They had not spoken to each other since their acrimonious breakup.

After his speech, Riley approached his former boss and the two embraced. "I'm sorry," Riley said. "I want you to forgive me." "I'm sorry for my share in it too, Pat," Checketts responded, "and I want you to forgive me. It's over. It's all over."[14]

Checketts regrets firing Grunfeld the way he did. "The way Ernie handled it, I should have come in the next morning after dinner and told him to clean out his desk and fired him because I was being forced to," Checketts said.[15] Grunfeld landed the Bucks' GM job a few months later. After four years in Milwaukee, he joined the Wizards as president of basketball operations, a position he held for 16 years. He and Checketts are on friendly terms.[16]

Riley, Van Gundy, and Ewing all have regrets about the way they left the Knicks. "That was one of the biggest mistakes I've ever made in my life, the way I exited," Riley said. "I could have exited with more class." He later added, "The Knicks was a fiasco and it was my fault. I regret tortiously interfering to get myself out of the contract and get out of New York for whatever the reasons were."[17]

Reflecting on his time in New York, Riley said, "It's probably one of the biggest disappointments [I] had in my life, not being able to give them enough in Games 6 and 7 when we were in Houston, so Patrick could've gotten his first championship."[18] He recently said of the 1994 Finals, " Sometimes I'll think about it, and it torments me."[19]

Riley achieved greater success in Los Angeles and Miami, where he's won three more rings, though no team reflected his personality as much as New York. One can only imagine how the Knicks' fortunes might have differed over the past 25 years if they had retained him.

Van Gundy believes it was time for him to leave, but regrets doing so in the middle of the season. He said years later, "I know what quitting is. I did it. It's something I regret to this day. I live with it every day and I regret it. And I let my emotions come into it and I was just emotionally spent. I made a bad decision."[20]

Van Gundy, now a broadcaster for ESPN and ABC, references Houston's shot against the Heat in '99 at coaching clinics. He encourages his audience to picture the ball hitting the rim and bouncing up in the air. He then says, "Freeze the tape," and asks, "Good coach or bad coach?"[21] It is the perfect illustration of the role chance plays in the lives and legacies of players, coaches, and executives.

Ewing recently opened up about leaving New York. "If I had to do it over again," the Big Fella said, "I wouldn't have requested a trade." On his relationship with the fans, he observed, "I didn't know what I had in them, and they didn't know what they had in me."[22]

The Knicks retired Patrick's No. 33 on February 28, 2003, providing fans with an opportunity to open their hearts to the Big Fella. The lofty expectations, which clouded their perception of him, had finally been replaced with gratitude.

Patrick served as Jeff Van Gundy's assistant in Houston, then coached under Stan Van Gundy in Orlando. He is now the head coach at his alma mater, Georgetown University.

Riley never regained the status he once enjoyed in New York because of how he left and the subsequent rivalry with the Heat. Van Gundy, however, remains a Garden favorite,[23] and most of the players he and Riley coached are remembered with an adoration typically reserved for champions.

The major exception is Charles Smith, who never lived down the closing seconds of Game 5 of the 1993 conference finals, known to fans simply as "the Charles Smith Game." The sequence came to symbolize both Smith's disappointing tenure with the Knicks and New York's years of futility against Chicago. Smith is still occasionally harassed on the streets of New York by what he refers to as "Game 5 guys."[24]

In contrast, Starks, who shot his team out of the biggest Knicks game of the past half century, is adored at MSG, where he now works for the team in alumni relations. Spike Lee's forward to Starks' autobiography reflected a shared understanding among Knicks fans that Starks "got more out of what he had—and where he came from—than most human beings ever do."[25] It is a testament to John's mental toughness that he did not allow Game 7 of the Finals to define his career.

Starks is asked about "The Dunk" on a daily basis. A few years ago, Michael Jordan was sitting courtside at the Garden when they showed the play on the Jumbotron. Starks sidled up to MJ with a smirk on his face. Jordan shrugged, and the two laughed. Then, Michael asked why the play is shown every time he comes to the Garden. "I told him," said Starks, "'Then stop coming to The Garden.'"[26]

One former player who is not welcome at the Garden is Oakley. Oak was critical of Dolan and the Knicks while the team struggled in the 2000s and 2010s. That irritated Dolan, who snubbed Oakley in public and resisted third-party attempts to mend fences between them.[27]

During a Knicks game in February 2017, Dolan claimed Oakley was heckling him and sent security guards to escort Oak out of the Garden. Television cameras caught Oak shoving the security guards before several of them forcibly removed him from his seat. The Knicks legend was arrested for assault, a charge which was eventually dropped.[28] It was another black eye for the franchise, and Knicks fans were outraged.

New Yorkers shared an outpouring of grief when Anthony Mason passed away at the age of 48 in February 2015, following a heart attack. The tributes poured in through traditional and social media. None captured the former Knick as succinctly as journalist Mark Kriegel, who tweeted, "Anthony Mason was real New York: self-made, hard as hell, with a little crazy and a lot of great. Damn, he'll be missed."[29]

Riley attended the funeral and was standing over the casket when Mason's mother, Mary, entered the church in a wheelchair. They knew each other from Mason's time with the Knicks. The coach kneeled down on one knee and put his arm on Mrs. Mason's shoulder. They spoke like that for a while. When Riley stood up, tears were streaming down his cheeks. Then the coach delivered a moving eulogy for the player he went to battle with and against so many times.[30]

Some of Van Gundy's former players now work for the Knicks, including Allan Houston, whose career was derailed by a knee injury in the third year of his massive deal. The contract was deemed such a disaster that the owners and players agreed to the "Allan Houston Rule" in the summer of 2005, which allowed each team a one-time opportunity to escape luxury tax obligations for any contract on the books by releasing that player.[31]

Ironically, the Knicks did not use the "Allan Houston Rule" on Houston, opting instead to release forward Jerome Williams. Houston retired a few months later, in the fall of 2005, with two years left on his deal. He is now the team's assistant general manager.[32]

Sprewell's public makeover was short-lived. He returned to the All-Star Game in 2001, where he was teammates with Anthony Mason. It was Mase's first and only All-Star appearance, at age 34, as a member of Riley's Heat.

The Knicks suspended and fined Sprewell $250,000 on the first day of training camp in 2002, for failing to report that he broke his hand two weeks earlier.[33] The Knicks traded the temperamental guard to the Timberwolves a few months later.

During his Garden return, Sprewell repeatedly cursed at Dolan, who was sitting courtside, while taunting the Knicks bench on his way to 31 points in the Minnesota victory.[34] Spree and the Timberwolves advanced to the Western Conference Finals that season. Months later, with one year remaining on his contract, Latrell turned down a three-year, $21 million extension, claiming, "I've got my family to feed."[35] The quote is often cited as the epitome of athlete entitlement. Sprewell went unsigned the following summer and never played again. He is now nearly broke.[36]

Dolan reconciled with Sprewell the day after the Oakley incident. Spree and Larry Johnson sat next to the owner at the next game as part of a transparent public relations ploy. Knicks fans welcomed Spree back, but also chanted Oakley's name.

Latrell now makes appearances on the team's behalf. Johnson is also employed by the Knicks in business and basketball operations. Despite his record-breaking contract and lucrative endorsements deals, LJ filed for bankruptcy in 2015.[37]

Any remnants of the Knicks-Heat rivalry died with Riley's retirement in 2003,[38] and the animosity between the players of that era has all but disappeared. Ward and P.J. Brown have appeared at each other's charitable events.[39] LJ and Zo even stop and chat when they run into each other.[40]

Hardaway and Childs are the exceptions. "Me and him don't like each other," Hardaway said. "Right now, if we saw each other on the street, we fighting."[41] Childs replied, "Well, set it up." He added, "There's two guys that I have regrets that I didn't knock their front teeth out. He [Hardaway] was one, and Jordan was the other."[42]

The Knicks' fortunes took a drastic downturn following the Riley and Van Gundy eras. Over the 10 full seasons from when Riley came on board until Van Gundy left, the Knicks won 62.8 percent of their games. They went to the playoffs every year and advanced to the conference finals four times and the Finals twice.

Since Van Gundy's resignation in 2001, the Knicks have gone through 13 coaches, made the playoffs four times, and won just one playoff series. They've suffered the most losses in the NBA this century.

There will never be another team like the 1990s Knicks. The NBA legislated their style of play out of the game. The elimination of hand-checking and physical post play, along with additional rule changes in the late 1990s and early 2000s, led to a more open, fast-paced game. Basketball moved from the inside out with the proliferation of the three-point shot, and referees now call flagrant fouls for the slightest bit of excessive contact. "NBA basketball now is flag football compared to tackle football," said Van Gundy.[43] Scoring is up, but at a price. Gone are the days of brutal battles between heated rivals and the primal passion they evoked in players and fans.

Chapter Notes

Introduction

1. Waldman, Suzyn. Personal Interview. 26 Dec. 2019.
2. Barker, Barbara. Personal Interview. 20 Apr. 2018.
3. Rhoden, Bill. "Episode 75: Charles Oakley and Chris Herring." *Bill Rhoden on Sports.* soundcloud.com, 29 June 2016. https://soundcloud.com/user-876026376/episode-75-charles-oakley-and-chris-herring
4. Barron, David. "Van Gundy Remembers Rockets-Knicks 'Forgotten Finals.'" *Houston Chronicle.* 4 June 2014.
5. Van Gundy, Jeff. Personal Interview. 13 May 2019.

Prologue

1. Checketts, David. Personal Interview. 26 Feb. 2018.
2. *Ibid.*
3. Kay, Michael. "Patrick Ewing." *CenterStage.* YES Network, 1 July 2011. https://www.youtube.com/watch?v=VEF1TBFkcRM
4. D'Agostino, Dennis. *Garden Glory: An Oral History of the New York Knicks.* Triumph Books, 2003. Print.
5. Hahn, Alan. "Season 1, Episode 10." *Knicks Fix Podcast.* msgnetworks.com, 24 Jan. 2014. URL not available.
6. Checketts, David. Personal Interview. 26 Feb. 2018.
7. McCallum, Jack. "The Big Man Gets Bigger." *Sports Illustrated.* 22 Jan. 1990.
8. Falk, David. Personal Interview. 18 Aug. 2019.
9. Goldaper, Sam. "BASKETBALL; Rejected! Ewing Is Loser in Bid for Free Agency." *New York Times.* 30 July 1991.
10. *Ibid.*
11. *Ibid.*
12. Checketts, David. Personal Interview. 26 Feb. 2018.
13. Heisler, Mark. *The Lives of Riley.* Macmillan, 1994. Print.
14. Checketts, David. Personal Interview. 26 Feb. 2018.
15. D'Agostino, Dennis. *Garden Glory: An Oral History of the New York Knicks.* Triumph Books, 2003. Print.
16. Bianchi, Al. Personal Interview. 18 Oct. 2017.
17. Checketts, David. Personal Interview. 26 Feb. 2018.
18. *Ibid.*
19. *Ibid.*
20. *Ibid.*
21. *Ibid.*
22. *Ibid.*

Chapter 1

1. No author provided. "#NYK70 | 1985: Knicks Win Lottery, Pick Patrick Ewing." *NBA.com,* 25 Sept. 2016. https://www.nba.com/knicks/nyk70-1985-knicks-win-lottery-pick-patrick-ewing
2. McCallum, Jack. "The Year of Ewing." *Sports Illustrated.* 28 Oct. 1985; Wiley, Ralph. "The Master of the Key." *Sports Illustrated.* 7 Jan. 1985.
3. Ballard, Chris. "1 Patrick Ewing." *Sports Illustrated.* 5 May 2015.
4. *Ibid.*
5. Bondy, Filip. *Tip Off: How the 1984 NBA Draft Changed Basketball Forever.* Da Capo Press, 2007. Print.
6. Ballard, Chris. "1 Patrick Ewing." *Sports Illustrated.* 5 May 2015. The NBA switched to a weighted lottery in 1990.
7. Cirillo, John. Personal Interview. 20 Dec. 2019.

8. Hahn, Alan. "Season 1, Episode 10." *Knicks Fix Podcast*. msgnetworks.com, 24 Jan. 2014. URL not available.

9. Ballard, Chris. "1 Patrick Ewing." *Sports Illustrated*. 5 May 2015.

10. *Ibid*.

11. *Ibid*.

12. Ballard, Chris. "The Ewing Conspiracy." *Sports Illustrated*. 15 May 2015. https://www.si.com/longform/2015/1985/ewing/index.html.

13. Ballard, Chris. "1 Patrick Ewing." *Sports Illustrated*. 5 May 2015.

14. D'Agostino, Dennis. *Garden Glory: An Oral History of the New York Knicks*. Triumph Books, 2003. Print.

15. Araskog, Rand. Personal Interview. 2 Oct. 2019.

16. Ewing was injured during the six games that King played for New York during the 1986–87 season.

17. Hahn, Alan. *New York Knicks: The Complete Illustrated History*. MVP Books, 2012. Print. "Ewing and I talked about that together privately," King said. "If we had had the chance to play together, we would have won a title."

18. Pitino, Rick, and Reynolds, Bill. *Born to Coach: A Season with the New York Knicks*. NAL Books, 1988. Print.

19. *Ibid*.

20. D'Agostino, Dennis. *Garden Glory: An Oral History of the New York Knicks*. Triumph Books, 2003. Print.

21. Heisler, Mark. *The Lives of Riley*. Macmillan, 1994. Print.

22. D'Agostino, Dennis. *Garden Glory: An Oral History of the New York Knicks*. Triumph Books, 2003. Print.

23. Goldaper, Sam. "BASKETBALL; Ewing and Riley Get Together, Perhaps to Chat About Trade." *New York Times*. 21 Aug. 1991; Heisler, Mark. *The Lives of Riley*. Macmillan; 1994. Print. Wojnarowski, Adrian. "Patrick Ewing." *The Vertical Podcast with Woj*. sports.yahoo.com, 30 Mar. 2016. https://sports.yahoo.com/news/the-vertical-podcast-with-woj-patrick-ewing-140057572.html.

24. Hahn, Alan. "Season 1, Episode 10." *Knicks Fix Podcast*. msgnetworks.com, 24 Jan. 2014. URL not available.

25. Falk, David. *The Bald Truth: Secrets of Success from the Locker Room to the Boardroom*. Gallery Books, 2009. Print.

26. Harper, Zach. "*Patrick and Zo* Director Jon Weinbach." *Eye on Basketball Podcast*. CBSsports.com, 28 Apr. 2016. https://www.cbssports.com/nba/news/eye-on-basketball-podcast-patrick-zo-director-jon-weinbach/.

27. Harper, Derek. Personal Interview. 25 Jul. 2017.

28. McCallum, Jack. "The Big Man Gets Bigger." *Sports Illustrated*. 22 Jan. 1990.

29. Wallace, John. Personal Interview. 12 June 2019.

30. Justice, Richard. "Despite His Problems, Ewing Says That Life in the NBA Is Still Fun." *Washington Post*. 3 Nov. 1986.

31. *Ibid*.

32. Jarvis, Mike. Personal Interview. 15 Mar. 2019.

33. *Patrick and Zo*. Dir. Jon Weinbach. Perf. Patrick Ewing, Alonzo Mourning, Jeff Van Gundy and Michael Wilbon. *Sports Illustrated*, 2016. SI.com.

34. MacMullan, Jackie. "Life Has Tried, but Failed to Make Ewing Lose His Hidden Smile." *Boston Globe*, 2 May 2003.

35. Ryan, Adam. "Episode 82: Mike Jarvis." *In All Airness*. Inallairness.com, 30 Mar. 2018. http://inallairness.com/air082-mike-jarvis-legendary-high-school-and-ncaa-basketball-coach-podcast/.

36. Jarvis, Mike. Personal Interview. 15 Mar. 2019.

37. *Ibid*.

38. *Ibid*.

39. Wojnarowski, Adrian. "Patrick Ewing." *The Vertical Podcast with Woj*. sports.yahoo.com, 30 Mar. 2016. https://sports.yahoo.com/news/the-vertical-podcast-with-woj—patrick-ewing-140057572.html

40. O'Connor, Ian. "Patrick Ewing Has the Floor." *ESPN.com*, 1 Nov. 2017; Ryan, Adam. "Episode 82: Mike Jarvis." *In All Airness*. Inallairness.com, 30 Mar. 2018. http://inallairness.com/air082-mike-jarvis-legendary-high-school-and-ncaa-basketball-coach-podcast/.

41. Jarvis, Mike. Personal Interview. 15 Mar. 2019.

42. *Patrick and Zo*. Dir. Jon Weinbach. Perf. Patrick Ewing, Alonzo Mourning, Jeff Van Gundy and Michael Wilbon. *Sports Illustrated*, 2016. SI.com.

43. Jarvis, Mike. Personal Interview. 15 Mar. 2019.

44. *Patrick and Zo*. Dir. Jon Weinbach. Perf. Patrick Ewing, Alonzo Mourning, Jeff Van Gundy and Michael Wilbon. *Sports Illustrated*, 2016. SI.com.

45. Wojnarowski, Adrian. "Patrick Ewing." *The Vertical Podcast with Woj.* sports.yahoo.com, 30 Mar. 2016. https://sports.yahoo.com/news/the-vertical-podcast-with-woj—patrick-ewing-140057572.html

46. Thompson did not allow freshmen to speak to the media until their second semester, and Hoya players did not have their majors included in their biographies. During the NCAA tournament, when teams were being housed in hotels in the host city, the coach reserved rooms 30 minutes from downtown. He wanted to avoid distractions, including the media.

47. Stanton, Barry. Personal Interview. 13 Jan. 2020.

48. Araton, Harvey. Personal Interview. 13 Feb. 2018.

49. Johnson, Roy S. "Patrick Ewing and the Art of Defense." *New York Times.* 29 Sept. 1985.

50. Rivers, Glenn, and Brooks, Bruce. *Those Who Love the Game: Glenn "Doc" Rivers On Life in the NBA and Elsewhere.* Henry Holt & Co., 1994.

51. Wise, Mike. (@MikeWiseguy) "True story: Cavs cheerleader came up to me during '96 Knicks game. Said, 'Are you Mike Wise from The NY Times? OMG, I read everything you write.' I went to talk to her after game and she blew me off. I walked into locker room. Patrick Ewing looked up and smiled: 'April Fools.'" 1 Apr. 2019. 9:28 P.M. Tweet.

Chapter 2

1. Smith, Chris. "The Knicks Go for the Grand Slam." *New York Magazine.* 5 May 1993.

2. Gutkowski, Bob. Personal Interview. 9 Aug. 2019.

3. Heisler, Mark. *The Lives of Riley.* Macmillan, 1994. Print.

4. *Ibid.*

5. Le Batard, Dan. "Pat Riley." *The Art of Conversation with Dan Le Batard.* ESPN, 24 Feb. 2019. https://www.youtube.com/watch?v=Q3o1BS5_kFc

6. *Ibid.*

7. Heisler, Mark. *The Lives of Riley.* Macmillan, 1994. Print.

8. *Ibid.*

9. *Ibid.*

10. *Ibid.*

11. *Ibid.*

12. Riley trademarked the term "three-peat."

13. Heisler, Mark. *The Lives of Riley.* Macmillan, 1994. Print.

14. Le Batard, Dan. "Pat Riley." *The Dan Le Batard Show.* ESPN Radio, 7 Sept. 2015. http://www.espn.com/espnradio/play?id=13608705

15. Butera, Dick. Personal Interview. 27 Sept. 2019.

16. *Ibid.*; Le Batard, Dan. "Pat Riley." *The Art of Conversation with Dan Le Batard.* ESPN, 24 Feb. 2019. https://www.youtube.com/watch?v=Q3o1BS5_kFc

17. Heisler, Mark. *The Lives of Riley.* Macmillan, 1994. Print; Riley, Pat. *The Winner Within: A Life Plan for Team Players.* Berkley Books, 1993. Print.

18. D'Agostino, Dennis. *Garden Glory: An Oral History of the New York Knicks.* Triumph Books, 2003. Print; Wise, Mike, and Isola, Frank. *Just Ballin': The Chaotic Rise of the New York Knicks.* Simon & Schuster, 1999. Print.

19. Stanley, Alessandra. "Knicks Cheerleaders? Not Exactly." *New York Times.* 22 Sept. 1991.

20. Jaffe, Stanley. Personal Interview. 21 Aug. 2019.

21. D'Agostino, Dennis. *Garden Glory: An Oral History of the New York Knicks.* Triumph Books, 2003. Print.

22. O'Connor, Ian. "Losing Riley Doomed Knickbockers." *ESPN.com,* 25 June 2013.

23. D'Agostino, Dennis. *Garden Glory: An Oral History of the New York Knicks.* Triumph Books, 2003. Print.

24. Jaffe, Stanley. Personal Interview. 21 Aug. 2019.

25. Heisler, Mark. *The Lives of Riley.* Macmillan, 1994. Print.

26. Jaffe, Stanley. Personal Interview. 21 Aug. 2019.

27. D'Agostino, Dennis. *Garden Glory: An Oral History of the New York Knicks.* Triumph Books, 2003. Print.

28. Wise, Mike. "Former Player, Coach and GM Dave Wohl." *The Mike Wise Show.* purehoopsmedia.com, 2 Sept. 2019. https://purehoopsmedia.com/former-player-coach-and-gm-dave-wohl/

29. *Ibid.*

30. Heisler, Mark. *The Lives of Riley.* Macmillan, 1994. Print.

31. Rapaport, Michael. "Episode 260:

Doc Rivers." *I Am Rapaport Stereo Podcast.* Youtube.com, 13 Feb. 2017. https://www.youtube.com/watch?v=_VmfwLxZkKQ

32. Rose, Charlie. "Pat Riley." *Charlie Rose.* charlierose.com, 17 June 1993. https://charlierose.com/videos/26693

33. Finkel, Jon. *The Athlete: Greatness, Grace and the Unprecedented Life of Charlie Ward.* Archervision Inc., 2017. Print.

34. McCallum, Jack. *Golden Days: West's Lakers, Steph's Warriors, and the California Dreamers Who Reinvented Basketball.* Ballantine Books, 2017. Print.

35. Kalland, Robbie, and Rickman, Martin. "Episode 4: Greg Anthony." *The Dime Podcast.* Omny.fm, 18 Oct. 2017. https://omny.fm/shows/the-dime-podcast/episode-4-greg-anthony

36. Heisler, Mark. *The Lives of Riley.* Macmillan, 1994. Print.

37. Bunn, Curtis. Personal Interview. 16 Aug. 2019. Riley's banishment included broadcasters Marv Albert, who he had just worked with at NBC, and Knicks legend, Walt Frazier, who "took it as a slap in the face." Heisler, Mark. *The Lives of Riley.* Macmillan, 1994. Print.

38. Kalland, Robbie, and Rickman, Martin. "Episode 4: Greg Anthony." *The Dime Podcast.* Omny.fm, 18 Oct. 2017. https://omny.fm/shows/the-dime-podcast/episode-4-greg-anthony

39. Starks, John, with Markowitz, David. *My Life.* Sports Publishing LLC, 2004. Print; Heisler, Mark. *The Lives of Riley.* Macmillan, 1994. Print.

40. Gaines, Corey. Personal Interview. 23 July 2019.

41. Cleamons, Jim. Personal Interview. 4 Sept. 2019.

42. Heisler, Mark. *The Lives of Riley.* Macmillan, 1994. Print.

43. Smith, Chris. "Hoops Genius." *New York Magazine.* 27 Nov. 1995.

44. Steele, David. Personal Interview. 28 Aug. 2019.

45. Rubinstein, Barry. Personal Interview. 3 Sept. 2019.

46. Rapaport, Michael. "Episode 260: Doc Rivers." *I Am Rapaport Stereo Podcast.* Youtube.com, 13 Feb. 2017. https://www.youtube.com/watch?v=_VmfwLxZkKQ

47. Rivers, Glenn, and Brooks, Bruce. *Those Who Love the Game: Glenn "Doc" Rivers on Life in the NBA and Elsewhere.* Henry Holt & Co., 1994.

48. Marolachakis, Stefan, and Williams, Jesse. "Doc Rivers, President and Coach of the L.A. Clippers." *Open Run.* iheart.com, 18 Jan. 2017. https://www.iheart.com/podcast/8-open-run-28732052/episode/doc-rivers-president-and-coach-of-28732118/

49. Rapaport, Michael. "Episode 260: Doc Rivers." *I Am Rapaport Stereo Podcast.* Youtube.com, 13 Feb. 2017. https://www.youtube.com/watch?v=_VmfwLxZkKQ

50. Mannix, Chris. "Mike Breen." *The Crossover Podcast with Chris Mannix.* Sports.yahoo.com, 29 Nov. 2016. https://play.acast.com/s/theverticalpodcastwithchrismannix/espn-and-ny-knicks-broadcaster-mike-breen

51. Salmi, Bob. Personal Interview. 6 May 2019.

52. Marolachakis, Stefan, and Williams, Jesse. "Doc Rivers, President and Coach of the L.A. Clippers." *Open Run.* iheart.com, 18 Jan. 2017. https://www.iheart.com/podcast/8-open-run-28732052/episode/doc-rivers-president-and-coach-of-28732118/

53. Coslov, Noah, and Stanko, Adam. "Bob Salmi." *Catch and Shoot.* Art119.com, 6 Mar. 2019. https://art19.com/shows/catch-and-shoot/episodes/314dc7f9-3833-48b5-b5c4-4c49fac98663

54. Christie, Doug. Personal Interview. 13 June 2019. Christie went on to have a 14-year career with several teams. He was named to four NBA All-Defensive teams.

55. Coslov, Noah, and Stanko, Adam. "Bob Salmi." *Catch and Shoot.* Art119.com, 6 Mar. 2019. https://art19.com/shows/catch-and-shoot/episodes/314dc7f9-3833-48b5-b5c4-4c49fac98663

56. Harper, Derek. Personal Interview. 25 July 2017.

57. Gaines, Corey. Personal Interview. 23 July 2019.

58. Riley, Pat. *The Winner Within: A Life Plan for Team Players.* Berkley Books, 1993. Print.

59. Harper, Derek. Personal Interview. 25 July 2017.

60. Kriegel, Mark. "Escape from New York." *Esquire Magazine.* 1 Dec. 1995.

Chapter 3

1. Riley, Pat. *The Winner Within: A Life Plan for Team Players.* Berkley Books, 1993. Print.

2. Rose, Charlie. "Pat Riley." *Charlie Rose*. charlierose.com, 17 June 1993. https://charlierose.com/videos/26693

3. "The Garden's Defining Moments: Larry Johnson's 4-Point Play." *The Garden's Defining Moments*. 20 Mar. 2016. https://www.msgnetworks.com/shows/the-gardens-defining-moments/

4. No host provided. "Ep. 2.4: Exclusive Interview w/ Herb Williams, Assnt. Coach of NY Liberty & 18-Year NBA Veteran." Youtube.com, 15 Oct. 2019. https://www.youtube.com/watch?v=q3LK0vM_tOk&t=32s

5. Armstrong, B.J., and Newman, Eric. "Episode 3." *The Pure Hoops Podcast*. Art19.com, 1 Feb. 2019. https://art19.com/shows/the-pure-hoops-podcast

6. D'Agostino, Dennis. *Garden Glory: An Oral History of the New York Knicks*. Triumph Books, 2003. Print.

7. *Ibid.*

8. Bunn, Curtis. Personal Interview. 16 Aug. 2019.

9. *Ibid.*

10. Pooley, Eric. "High Anxiety: Will the Knicks Keep Flying in the Playoffs?" *New York Magazine*. 8 May 1989.

11. One of Wilkins' favorite drills was to practice shooting while sitting in a chair.

12. Payton, Gary. "O.G.'s Only." *theplayerstribune.com*, 21 Dec. 2017. https://www.theplayerstribune.com/en-us/articles/gary-payton-supersonics-oakland

13. McDaniel, Xavier. Personal Interview. 2 Feb. 2019.

14. Starks, John, with Markowitz, David. *My Life*. Sports Publishing LLC, 2004. Print.

15. *Ibid.*

16. Gschwandtner, LB. "The Pat Riley Formula for a Winning Team." *Sellingpower.com*, 2 Feb. 2010. https://www.sellingpower.com/2010/02/02/3528/the-pat-riley-formula-for-a-winning-team

17. *Ibid.*

18. *Ibid.*

19. *Ibid.*

20. Starks, John, with Markowitz, David. *My Life*. Sports Publishing LLC, 2004. Print.

21. Starks, John. Personal Interview. 10 July 2019; McCallum, Jack. "Hot Hand, Hot Head." *Sports Illustrated*. 15 May 1993.

22. Smith, Chris. "Hot Shot." *New York Magazine*. 12 Apr. 1993.

23. Starks, John, with Markowitz, David. *My Life*. Sports Publishing LLC, 2004. Print.

24. *Ibid.*

25. *Ibid.*

26. *Ibid.*

27. *Ibid.*

28. Masiello, Stephen. Personal Interview. 21 June 2019.

29. Starks, John, with Markowitz, David. *My Life*. Sports Publishing LLC, 2004. Print; Kriegel, Mark. "Riley Returns; Regrets Starks Passed On Pass." *New York Daily News*. 5 Sept. 1995.

30. Childs, Chris. Personal Interview. 12 July 2019.

31. Jacobson, Mark. "From the Archives: The Beloved Anthony Mason." *New York Magazine*. Feb. 2015. http://nymag.com/intelligencer/2015/02/the-beloved-anthony-mason.html

32. Fiedler, Scott. Personal Interview. 22 Mar. 2019.

33. Jacobson, Mark. "From the Archives: The Beloved Anthony Mason." *New York Magazine*. Feb. 2015. http://nymag.com/intelligencer/2015/02/the-beloved-anthony-mason.html

34. *Ibid.*

35. McCallum, Jack. "Arms And the Man." *Sports Illustrated*. 20 June 1994.

36. Jacobson, Mark. "From the Archives: The Beloved Anthony Mason." *New York Magazine*. Feb. 2015. http://nymag.com/intelligencer/2015/02/the-beloved-anthony-mason.html

37. Hahn, Alan. "Season 2, Episode 12." *Knicks Fix Podcast*. msgnetworks.com, 3 May 2015. URL not available.

38. Cronson, Don. Personal Interview. 6 Nov. 2017.

39. Jacobson, Mark. "From the Archives: The Beloved Anthony Mason." *New York Magazine*. Feb. 2015. http://nymag.com/intelligencer/2015/02/the-beloved-anthony-mason.html

40. Beastie Boys. "B-Boys Makin' with the Freak Frea.k" *Ill Communication*, Capitol Records, 18 May 1994. Beastie Boys. "Get it Together" *Ill Communication*, Capitol Records, 18 May 1994.

41. Starks, John. Personal Interview. 10 July 2019.

42. Christie, Doug. Personal Interview. 13 June 2019; Masiello, Stephen. Personal Interview. 21 June 2019.

43. Povtak, Tim. "Ex-UNLV Trio Wearing No. 2 in Salute to Tark." *Orlando Sentinel*. 3 Nov. 1991. No. 2 was Tark's college number.

44. Norwood, Robyn. "THE FINAL FOUR: Sen. Anthony a Pugnacious UNLV Leader: Rebels: A Republican, his forte is—as expected—defense." *Los Angeles Times*. 31 Mar. 1990.

45. Riley, Pat. *The Winner Within: A Life Plan for Team Players*. Berkley Books, 1993. Print.

46. *Ibid.*

47. Walsh, Bob. "Episode: Jeff Van Gundy." *The Dynamic Leadership Podcast*. 9 Feb. 2018 https://athleticdirectoru.com/audio/the-dynamic-leadership-podcast-jeff-van-gundy/

48. Walsh, Bob. "Episode: Jeff Van Gundy." *The Dynamic Leadership Podcast*. 9 Feb. 2018 https://athleticdirectoru.com/audio/the-dynamic-leadership-podcast-jeff-van-gundy/

49. Newman, Bruce. "Rough and Tough." *Sports Illustrated*. 11 May 1992.

50. *Ibid.*

Chapter 4

1. Wojnarowski, Adrian. "Patrick Ewing." *The Vertical Podcast with Woj*. sports.yahoo.com, 30 Mar. 2016. https://sports.yahoo.com/news/the-vertical-podcast-with-woj—patrick-ewing-140057572.html; McCallum, Jack. "Friends and Foes Together." *Sports Illustrated*. 31 May 1993.

2. McCallum, Jack. "Friends and Foes Together." *Sports Illustrated*. 31 May 1993; Norlander, Matt. "Patrick Ewing says KKK 'rally' partly why he didn't attend UNC." *CBSsports.com*, 13 June 2013. http://www.cbssports.com/collegebasketball/eye-on-college-basketball/22404746/patrick-ewing-says-kkk-rally-partly-why-he-didnt-attend-unc

3. McCallum, Jack. "Friends and Foes Together." *Sports Illustrated*. 31 May 1993.

4. Steiner, Brandon. "Episode 28: Patrick Ewing, David Falk, John Starks and Anthony Mason." *Unplugged with Brandon Steiner*. Brandonsteiner.com, 2012. https://www.brandonsteiner.com/blogs/unplugged/episode-028-patrick-ewing-david-falk-john-starks-anthony-mason; McCallum, Jack. "Friends and Foes Together." *Sports Illustrated*. 31 May 1993. After Ewing's freshman year, Thompson sat down with the family and told them Ewing's market value might already be $1 million per year.

Patrick's mother was adamant about him finishing his education. Wiley, Ralph. "The Master of the Key." *Sports Illustrated*. 7 Jan. 1985.

5. Wiley, Ralph. "The Centers of the Storm." *Sports Illustrated*. 24 Nov. 1986.

6. Cartwright was injured so frequently during his last few years in New York that Peter Vecsey of the *New York Post* started calling him "Medical Bill."

7. Smith, Sam. *The Jordan Rules: The Inside Story of a Turbulent Season with Michael Jordan and the Chicago Bulls*. Simon & Schuster, 1992. Print.

8. Oakley, Charles. Personal Interview. 8 May 2019.

9. Rhoden, William. "ON PRO BASKETBALL; Star Pick Is Oakley's Validation." *New York Times*. 14 Feb. 1994.

10. Robbins, Dave. Personal Interview. 29 Apr. 2019.

11. *Ibid.*

12. *Ibid.*

13. Smith, Sam. *The Jordan Rules: The Inside Story of a Turbulent Season with Michael Jordan and the Chicago Bulls*. Simon & Schuster, 1992. Print; Rapaport, Michael. '90s Hoops with Pippen and Oakley. *ThePlayersTribune.com*, 15 Nov. 2018. https://www.theplayerstribune.com/global/videos/90s-hoops-with-scottie-pippen-and-charles-oakley

14. Smith, Sam. *The Jordan Rules: The Inside Story of a Turbulent Season With Michael Jordan and the Chicago Bulls*. Simon & Schuster, 1992. Print.

15. *Ibid.*; Rhoden, Bill. "Episode 75: Charles Oakley and Chris Herring." *Bill Rhoden on Sports*. soundcloud.com, 29 June 2016. https://soundcloud.com/user-876026376/episode-75-charles-oakley-and-chris-herring

16. Smith, Sam. *The Jordan Rules: The Inside Story of a Turbulent Season with Michael Jordan and the Chicago Bulls*. Simon & Schuster, 1992. Print; Wise, Mike, and Isola, Frank. *Just Ballin': The Chaotic Rise of the New York Knicks*. Simon & Schuster, 1999. Print.

17. Smith, Sam. *The Jordan Rules: The Inside Story of a Turbulent Season with Michael Jordan and the Chicago Bulls*. Simon & Schuster, 1992.

18. Taylor, Phil. "Tower of Power." *Sports Illustrated*. 24 Jan. 2000.

19. Wise, Mike, and Isola, Frank. *Just*

Ballin': The Chaotic Rise of the New York Knicks. Simon & Schuster, 1999. Print; Mannix, Chris. "Mike Breen." *The Crossover Podcast with Chris Mannix*. Sports.yahoo.com, 29 Nov. 2016. https://play.acast.com/s/thevericalpodcastwithchrismannix/espn-and-ny-knicks-broadcaster-mike-breen

20. Brown, Clifton. "PRO BASKETBALL; Oakley, a Playoff Laureate With Elbows." *New York Times*. 21 May 1993.

21. Berkow, Ira. "NBA flagrantly needs to send message." *The Baltimore Sun*. 5 Jan. 1992. The definition of a flagrant foul and the resulting punishments have changed several times since 1980, including during Oakley's career. See NBA.com for rules history. https://web.archive.org/web/20110303213838/http://www.nba.com/analysis/rules_history.html

22. Salmi, Bob. Personal Interview. 6 May 2019; Kalland, Robbie, and Rickman, Martin. "Episode 4: Greg Anthony." *The Dime Podcast*. Omny.fm, 18 Oct. 2017. https://omny.fm/shows/the-dime-podcast/episode-4-greg-anthony

23. "Those teams were so tough. I think that's the one thing when you talk about the Knicks of the early 90s and late 80s, the teams I was around, they were just so tough. But the guys were just such sweethearts and good dudes." Masiello, Stephen. Personal Interview. 21 June 2019.

24. Christie, Doug. Personal Interview. 13 June 2019.

25. Wise, Mike, and Isola, Frank. *Just Ballin': The Chaotic Rise of the New York Knicks*. Simon & Schuster, 1999. Print; Barker, Barbara. Personal Interview. 20 Apr. 2018.

26. Waldman, Suzyn. Personal Interview. 26 Dec. 2019.

27. Brown, Clifton. "PRO BASKETBALL; Oakley, a Playoff Laureate With Elbows." *New York Times*. 21 May 1993; Brown, Clifton. "PRO BASKETBALL; Riley Says Oakley Is Solid as an Oak." *New York Times*. 10 Mar. 1993; McCallum, Jack. "Friends and Foes Together." *Sports Illustrated*. 31 May 1993.

28. Barker, Barbara. Personal Interview. 20 Apr. 2018.

29. Taylor, Phil. "Tower of Power." *Sports Illustrated*. 24 Jan. 2000.

30. Barker, Barbara. Personal Interview. 20 Apr. 2018; Wise, Mike, and Isola, Frank. *Just Ballin': The Chaotic Rise of the New York Knicks*. Simon & Schuster, 1999. Print.

31. Oakley, Charles. Personal Interview. 8 May 2019.

32. Hahn, Alan. "Season 1, Episode 16." *Knicks Fix Podcast*. Msgnetworks.com, 16 Mar. 14. URL not available; Barker, Barbara. Personal Interview. 20 Apr. 2018.

33. Wise, Mike. "PRO BASKETBALL; The Knicks' Family Man." *New York Times*. 22 Nov. 1995.

34. Barker, Barbara. "Charles Oakley: There's More to him than What You've Seen." *Newsday*. 15 Feb. 2017; Sandomir, Richard. "Dressed to Thrill, Inside the Closet of the Knicks' Charles Oakley." *New York Times*. 12 Mar. 1995.

35. Kimble, Bo. Personal Interview. 26 Sept. 2017.

36. Bonner, Anthony. Personal Interview. 26 Sept. 2017; Oakley, Charles. Personal Interview. 8 May 2019. Mason also hung out with some of the popular rappers of the day. The muscular forward served as a bodyguard at some of LL Cool J's parties in Queens.

37. Araton, Harvey. *When the Garden Was Eden: Clyde, The Captain, Dollar Bill, and the Glory Days of the New York Knicks*. HarperCollins, 2011. Print.

38. Jackson, Phil, and Rosen, Charley. *More Than a Game*. Seven Stories Press, 2001. Print.

39. Araton, Harvey. *When the Garden Was Eden: Clyde, The Captain, Dollar Bill, and the Glory Days of the New York Knicks*. HarperCollins, 2011. Print.

40. Ibid.

41. Ibid.; McCallum, Jack. *Golden Days: West's Lakers, Steph's Warriors, and the California Dreamers Who Reinvented Basketball*. Ballantine Books, 2017. Print.

42. Araton, Harvey. *When the Garden Was Eden: Clyde, The Captain, Dollar Bill, and the Glory Days of the New York Knicks*. HarperCollins, 2011. Print.

43. Kerber, Fred. "The Inside Story of Jackson, Pitino, and the Knicks." *New York Post*. 19 Mar. 2014.

44. Araton, Harvey. "BASKETBALL; Driving Force—Can the Bulls Be Stopped? Knicks May Have a Shot If They Get a Little Push." *New York Times*. 5 May 1992.

45. Wilkins, Gerald. Personal Interview. 24 June 2019. Wilkins later embraced the nickname "Jordan stopper," a moniker MJ poked fun at after torching Gerald, then a member of the Cavaliers, the following season.

46. Price, S.L. "Let's Get Physical." *Sports Illustrated*. 18 May 1992.

47. *Ibid.*

48. *Ibid.*

49. *Ibid.*

50. *Ibid.*

51. *Ibid.*

52. *Ibid.*

53. Starks, John, with Markowitz, David. *My Life*. Sports Publishing LLC, 2004. Print; Hersch, Hank. "Passing the Test." *Sports Illustrated*. 25 May 1992.

54. Beck, Howard. "Harvey Araton on GOAT Michael Jordan, Competitive Balance and the Lakers vs. the Knicks." *The Full 48 with Howard Beck*. Sticher.com. 2 Apr. 2019. https://www.stitcher.com/podcast/the-full-48/e/59810334?autoplay=true

55. Hersch, Hank. "Passing the Test." *Sports Illustrated*. 25 May 1992.

56. *Ibid.*

57. Heisler, Mark. *The Lives of Riley*. Macmillan, 1994. Print.

58. Riley, Pat. *The Winner Within: A Life Plan for Team Players*. Berkley Books, 1993. Print.

59. Malooley, Jack. "Aaaand Now … an Oral History of the Greatest Starting Lineup Introduction in Sports History." *theringer.com*, 13 Nov. 2018. https://www.theringer.com/nba/2018/11/13/18082986/oral-history-chicago-bulls-introduction-michael-jordan

60. *Ibid.*

61. Halberstam, David. *Playing for Keeps Michael Jordan and the World He Made*. Random House, 1999. Print.

62. Riley, Pat. *The Winner Within: A Life Plan for Team Players*. Berkley Books, 1993. Print.

63. After Game 7, Red Holzman came by the Bulls locker room to congratulate Phil and ended up gushing about what a great coach Riley was. Phil listened intently for some time, then Holzman looked into his eyes and said, "Phil, you're a good coach too." Smith, Sam. *The Jordan Rules: The Inside Story of a Turbulent Season With Michael Jordan and the Chicago Bulls*. Simon & Schuster, 1992. Print.

64. McCallum, Jack. *Dream Team: How Michael, Magic, Larry, Charles and the Greatest Team of All-Time Conquered the World and Changed the Game of Basketball Forever*. Ballantine Books, 2013. Print.

Chapter 5

1. Friend, Tom. "PRO BASKETBALL; Suns' Biggest Beef Is Over Anthony's 'Sucker Punch.'" *New York Times*. 25 May 1993.

2. Davis, Hubert. Personal Interview. 29 Sept. 2017.

3. Rose, Charlie. "Pat Riley." Charlie Rose. charlierose.com, 17 June 1993. https://charlierose.com/videos/26693

4. Doc Rivers said in his book *Those Who Love the Game* the 1992–93 Knicks were the first team he played for in which every player on the team stated that their goal for the season was to win a championship.

5. Araton, Harvey. "BASKETBALL; Knicks Go Shopping For Veteran Guard." *New York Times*. 18 June 1992.

6. McDaniel, Xavier. Personal Interview. 30 Oct. 2017.

7. Checketts, Dave. Personal Interview. 26 Feb. 2018.

8. Shouler, Kenneth. "To Fix the Knicks." *Cigar Aficionado*. Autumn 1996.

9. O'Connor, Ian. "Now It's Grunfeld's Team: Ernie Caps His Climb Up the Knicks Ladder." *New York Daily News*. 16 July 1996.

10. Shouler, Kenneth. "To Fix the Knicks." *Cigar Aficionado*. Autumn 1996.

11. Araton, Harvey. "BASKETBALL; Knicks Go Shopping For Veteran Guard." *New York Times*. 18 June 1992.

12. Brown, Clifton. "BASKETBALL; Watch This Space! Knicks Still Shopping." *New York Times*. 26 June 1992.

13. Brown, Clifton. "BASKETBALL; Knicks Get Shooting Lift In Deal For Blackman." *New York Times*. 25 June 1992.

14. Blackman's most recent all-star appearance was in 1990.

15. Ryan, Adam. "Episode 70: Rolando Blackman." *In All Airness*. Inallairness.com, 11 Apr. 2016. http://inallairness.com/air070-rolando-blackman-kansas-state-legend-four-time-nba-all-star-podcast/

16. Davis, Hubert. Personal Interview. 29 Sept. 2017.

17. Wilkins, Gerald. Personal Interview. 24 June 2019.

18. Brown, Clifton. "BASKETBALL; Watch This Space! Knicks Still Shopping." *New York Times*. 26 June 1992.

19. Brown, Clifton. "BASKETBALL; Hearing Today on Signing of Grant." *New York Times*. 14 July 1992.

20. Brown, Clifton. "Grant Is Hoping the Bullets Will Say Goodbye." *New York Times.* 17 July 1992.

21. Brown, Clifton. "BASKETBALL; Knicks Get Trade." *New York Times.* 23 Sept. 1992.

22. *Ibid.*

23. Araton, Harvey. "BASKETBALL; Knicks Lose McDaniel to the Celtics." *New York Times.* 11 Sept. 1992.

24. McDaniel, Xavier. Personal Interview. 30 Oct. 2017.

25. *Ibid.*; Falk, David. Personal Interview. 18 Aug. 2019.

26. McDaniel, Xavier. Personal Interview. 30 Oct. 2017.

27. Salmi, Bob. Personal Interview. 6 May 2019.

28. McDaniel, Xavier. Personal Interview. 2 Feb. 2019.

29. Brown, Clifton. "BASKETBALL; Knicks Get Trade." *New York Times.* 23 Sept. 1992.

30. Kimble, Bo. Personal Interview. 26 Sept. 2017.

31. Harvin, Al. "BASKETBALL; Knicks Fill in the Missing X By Getting Wolves' Campbell." *New York Times.* 15 Sept. 1992.

32. No author provided. "BASKETBALL; Knicks Start Exhibition Play." *New York Times.* 16 Oct. 1992.

33. Brown, Clifton. "BASKETBALL; Oakley Gets Physical To Make His Point." *New York Times.* 15 Oct. 1992.

34. Ryan, Adam. "Episode 70: Rolando Blackman." *In All Airness.* Inallairness.com, 11 Apr. 2016. http://inallairness.com/air070-rolando-blackman-kansas-state-legend-four-time-nba-all-star-podcast/

35. Araton, Harvey. "PRO BASKETBALL; Knicks' Slumping Smith Hits Double Figures in Frustration." *New York Times.* 2 Feb. 1993.

36. Ryan, Adam. "Episode 70: Rolando Blackman." *In All Airness.* Inallairness.com, 11 Apr. 2016. http://inallairness.com/air070-rolando-blackman-kansas-state-legend-four-time-nba-all-star-podcast/

37. Brown, Clifton. "PRO BASKETBALL; Harper Just Might Be Headed to Knicks." *New York Times.* 21 Dec. 1993.

38. Gutkowski, Bob. Personal Interview. 9 Aug. 2019.

39. Brown, Clifton. "BASKETBALL; Old Friend Gives Knicks a Nightmare." *New York Times.* 20 Nov. 1992.

40. *Ibid.*

41. Smith, Chris. "Go For the Grand Slam." *New York Magazine.* 31 May 1993.

42. Brown, Clifton. "BASKETBALL; No harm, No foul? Oakley Is Fined $10,000." *New York Times.* 1 Jan. 1993.

43. Freeman, Mike. "BASKETBALL; Broken Wrist Sidelines Anderson And Angers Nets." *New York Times.* 2 Mar. 1993.

44. Brown, Clifton. "PRO BASKETBALL; Starks and Mason Declare Peace." *New York Times.* 12 Oct. 1993.

45. Minas, Mick. *The Curse: The Colorful and Chaotic History of the L.A. Clippers.* 77 Publishing, 2016. Print.

46. Marolachakis, Stefan, and Williams, Jesse. "Doc Rivers, President and Coach of the L.A. Clippers." *Open Run.* iheart.com, 18 Jan. 2017. https://www.iheart.com/podcast/8-open-run-28732052/episode/doc-rivers-president-and-coach-of-28732118/

47. Minas, Mick. *The Curse: The Colorful and Chaotic History of the L.A. Clippers.* 77 Publishing, 2016. Print.

48. Rapaport, Michael. "Episode 260: Doc Rivers." *I Am Rapaport Stereo Podcast.* Youtube.com, 13 Feb. 2017. https://www.youtube.com/watch?v=_VmfwLxZkKQ

49. Anderson, Dave. "Sports of The Times; The Knicks' Real Loss: Poise." *New York Times.* 25 Mar. 1993.

50. *Ibid.*

51. Rivers, Glenn, and Brooks, Bruce. *Those Who Love the Game: Glenn "Doc" Rivers on Life in the NBA and Elsewhere.* Henry Holt & Co., 1994.

52. Smith, Chris. "The Knicks Go For the Grand Slam." *New York Magazine.* 5 May 1993.

53. Norwood, Robyn. "THE FINAL FOUR: Sen. Anthony a Pugnacious UNLV Leader: Rebels: A Republican, his forte is—as expected—defense." *Los Angeles Times.* 31 Mar. 1990.

54. Wilbon, Michael. "SCHOLAR-ATHLETE NCAA TELLS UNLV GUARD HE CAN'T MIND OWN BUSINESS." *Washington Post.* 28 Mar. 1991.

55. Norwood, Robyn. "THE FINAL FOUR: Sen. Anthony a Pugnacious UNLV Leader: Rebels: A Republican, his forte is—as expected—defense." *Los Angeles Times.* 31 Mar. 1990.

56. Salmi, Bob. Personal Interview. 6 May 2019.

57. *Ibid.*

Chapter 6

1. New York Knicks (@nyknicks) "'I didn't follow him in the CBA. I didn't know about him in college. But I know about him now.'—Michael Jordan on John Starks." 25 May 2018, 11:39 a.m. Tweet.

2. Utterback, Bill. "'Mr. Fluid' Fills Big East Void." *Chicago Tribune*. 27 Dec. 1985.

3. *Ibid.*

4. *Ibid.*

5. Smith believes his college coach, Paul Evans, first labeled him soft.

6. Brown, Clifton. "BASKETBALL; Smith Hopes Surgery Will End Knee Pain." *New York Times*. 10 Dec. 1993.

7. Geter, Lewis. Personal Interview. 23 July 2019.

8. Salmi, Bob. Personal Interview. 15 Aug. 2019.

9. Bunn, Curtis. Personal Interview. 15 Aug. 2019.

10. Wise, Mike. Personal Interview. 23 Feb. 2018.

11. Williams, Herb. Personal interview. 2 Sept. 2019.

12. Sin, Ben. "Checking in With Charles Smith." *New York Times Magazine*. 13 Dec. 2011.

13. No author provided. "PRO BASKET-BALL; Smith's Knee Acts Up Again." *New York Times*. 20 Mar. 1994.

14. Kriegel, Mark. "Riley Returns; Regrets Starks Passed On Pass." *New York Daily News*. 5 Sept. 1995.

15. *Winning Time: Reggie Miller vs. the New York Knicks*. Dir. Dan Klores. Perf. Reggie Miller, Cheryl Miller, Spike Lee, Patrick Ewing, and Donnie Walsh. ESPN Films, 2010. ESPN.

16. *Ibid.*

17. Marolachakis, Stefan, and Williams, Jesse. "Doc Rivers, President and Coach of the L.A. Clippers." *Open Run*. iheart.com, 18 Jan. 2017. https://www.iheart.com/podcast/8-open-run-28732052/episode/doc-rivers-president-and-coach-of-28732118/

18. Wise, Mike, and Isola, Frank. *Just Ballin': The Chaotic Rise of the New York Knicks*. Simon & Schuster, 1999. Print.

19. *Winning Time: Reggie Miller vs. the New York Knicks*. Dir. Dan Klores. Perf. Reggie Miller, Cheryl Miller, Spike Lee, Patrick Ewing, and Donnie Walsh. ESPN Films, 2010. ESPN.

20. Starks, John with Markowitz, David. *My Life*. Sports Publishing LLC, 2004. Print.

21. Perdue, Will. Personal Interview. 6 Aug. 2019.

22. Armstrong, B.J., and Newman, Eric. "Episode 3." *The Pure Hoops Podcast*. Art19.com, 1 Feb. 2019. https://art19.com/shows/the-pure-hoops-podcast

23. Heisler, Mark. *The Lives of Riley*. Macmillan, 1994. Print.

24. Starks, John with Markowitz, David. *My Life*. Sports Publishing LLC, 2004. Print.

25. Hahn, Alan. "Season 2, Episode 12." *Knicks Fix Podcast*. msgnetworks.com, 3 May 2015. URL not available Accessed 9 June 2016.

26. Starks, John with Markowitz, David. *My Life*. Sports Publishing LLC, 2004. Print.

27. Moran, Malcolm. "PRO BASKET-BALL; Pippen's Ejection Puts Bulls on the Spot." *New York Times*. 26 May 1993.

28. McCallum, Jack. "The Lips Were Zipped." *Sports Illustrated*. 7 June 1993.

29. Halberstam, David. *Playing for Keeps Michael Jordan and the World He Made*. Random House, 1999. Print.

30. Perdue, Will. Personal Interview. 6 Aug. 2019.

31. Moran, Malcolm. "PRO Basketball; Jordan Ran Up Golf Debts, Book Says." *New York Times*. 5 June 1993.

32. No author provided. "Bulls' Jordan Says Check Covered Gambling Losses." *New York Times*. 23 Oct. 1992.

33. Halberstam, David. *Playing for Keeps Michael Jordan and the World He Made*. Random House, 1999. Print.

34. McCallum, Jack. "The Lips Were Zipped." *Sports Illustrated*. 7 June 1993.

35. *Ibid.*

36. Coffey, Wayne. "Blocked Out Five Years After, Charles Smith Pursues New Goals." *New York Daily News*. 26 Apr. 1998.

37. Rivers, Glenn, and Brooks, Bruce. *Those Who Love the Game: Glenn "Doc" Rivers on Life in the NBA and Elsewhere*. Henry Holt & Co., 1994.

38. *Ibid.*

39. Williams, Herb. Personal Interview. 2 Sept. 2019.

40. *Ibid.*

41. Sin, Ben. "Checking in With Charles Smith." *New York Times Magazine*. 13 Dec. 2011.

42. Checketts, Spence. "Jeff Van Gundy (Part 1)." *Reality Check with Spence Check-*

etts. Realitycheckpod.com, 8 Nov. 2018. https://player.fm/series/reality-check-with-spence-checketts/jeff-van-gundy-part-1-on-coaching-against-michael-jordan-great-knicks-rivalries-and-his-relationship-with-david-stern

43. Cartwright, Bill. Personal Interview. 16 Apr. 2019.

44. McDaniel, Xavier. Personal Interview. 2 Feb. 2019.

45. Checketts, Spence. "Jeff Van Gundy (Part 1)." *Reality Check with Spence Checketts.* Realitycheckpod.com, 8 Nov. 2018. https://player.fm/series/reality-check-with-spence-checketts/jeff-van-gundy-part-1-on-coaching-against-michael-jordan-great-knicks-rivalries-and-his-relationship-with-david-stern

46. Rivers, Glenn, and Brooks, Bruce. *Those Who Love the Game: Glenn "Doc" Rivers On Life in the NBA and Elsewhere.* Henry Holt & Co., 1994.

Chapter 7

1. Wise, Mike. "Ewing, Vowing to Retire a Knick, Signs for 4 Years." *New York Times.* 3 July 1997.

2. Botte, Peter, and Red, Christian. "Michael Jordan's baseball foray: The inside story, 25 years later." *New York Post.* 16 Mar. 2019.

3. *Ibid.*

4. Both series went to seven games, making the defeats that much more devastating.

5. Brown, Clifton. "BASKETBALL; The Season, Is Over, But Oakley Battles On." *New York Times.* 8 June 1993.

6. *Ibid.* Oak threatened to sit out training camp the following season even though he still had four years left on his deal. He and the Knicks ultimately agreed to a one-year balloon payment of $10 million for the 1998–99 season.

7. No author provided. "PRO BASKETBALL; A Knick Fine For Oakley?" *New York Times.* 9 June 1993.

8. Oakley, Charles. Personal Interview. 8 May 2019.

9. Taylor, Phil. "Tower of Power." *Sports Illustrated.* 24 Jan. 2000.

10. Wallace, John. Personal Interview. 12 June 2019.

11. Brown, Clifton. "PRO BASKETBALL; As New Season Dawns, Riley Sounds an Alarm." *New York Times.* 9 Oct. 1993; D'Agostino, Dennis. *Garden Glory: An Oral History of the New York Knicks.* Triumph Books, 2003. Print.

12. No author provided. "PRO BASKETBALL; Smith's Knee Acts Up Again." *New York Times.* 20 Mar. 1994.

13. Taylor, Phil. "The NBA." *Sports Illustrated.* 17 Jan. 1994.

14. *Ibid.*

15. *Ibid.*

16. No author provided. "Thomas Tears Achilles, Retirement Imminent." *Deseret News.* 20 Apr. 1994.

17. Taylor, Phil. "The NBA." *Sports Illustrated.* 17 Jan. 1994.

18. Townsend, Brad. "Maverick forever: From humble beginnings to elite talent, Derek Harper's ride to the rafters had it all." *The Dallas Morning News.* 6 Jan. 2018.

19. Harper, Derek. Personal Interview. 25 July 2017.

20. No host provided. "Ep. 2.4: Exclusive Interview w/ Herb Williams, Assnt. Coach of NY Liberty & 18-Year NBA Veteran." Youtube.com. 15 Oct. 2019. https://www.youtube.com/watch?v=q3LK0vM_tOk&t=32s

21. Rivers and Harper were actually born on the same day, October 13, 1951.

22. Harper, Derek. Personal Interview. 25 July 2017.

23. *Ibid.*

24. Starks, John. Personal Interview. 10 July 2019.

25. Starks, John, with Markowitz, David. *My Life.* Sports Publishing LLC, 2004. Print.

26. Kriegel, Mark. "Riley Returns; Regrets Starks Passed On Pass." *New York Daily News.* 5 Sept. 1995.

27. Brown, Clifton. "BASKETBALL; It's Better Late Than Never, Oakley Joins All-Star Cast." *New York Times.* 9 Feb. 1994.

28. *Ibid.*

29. D'Agostino, Dennis. *Garden Glory: An Oral History of the New York Knicks.* Triumph Books, 2003. Print.

30. Saunders, Mike. Personal Interview. 2 Aug. 2017.

31. Jenkins, Lee. "The Hustle." *Sports Illustrated.* 15–22 May 2017. Such payments technically violated league rules, but that did not stop Riley.

32. Salmi, Bob. Personal Interview. 6 May 2019.

33. *Ibid.*

34. *Ibid.*

35. D'Agostino, Dennis. *Garden Glory: An Oral History of the New York Knicks.* Triumph Books, 2003. Print.

36. Starks, John, with Markowitz, David. *My Life.* Sports Publishing LLC, 2004. Print.

37. *Ibid.*

38. Heisler, Mark. *The Lives of Riley.* Macmillan, 1994. Print.

39. *Ibid.*

40. *Ibid.*

41. Cronson, Don. Personal Interview. 6 Nov. 2017.

42. Jacobson, Mark. "From the Archives: The Beloved Anthony Mason." *New York Magazine.* Feb. 2015. http://nymag.com/intelligencer/2015/02/the-beloved-anthony-mason.html

43. Checketts, Dave. Personal Interview. 26 Feb. 2019.

44. Lupica, Mike. "Ep. 54—Doc Rivers and Patrick Ewing." *The Mike Lupica Podcast.* Soundcloud.com, 1 June 2017. https://soundcloud.com/compass-media/the-mike-lupica-podcast-episode-54-doc-rivers-patrick-ewing

Chapter 8

1. Adande, J.A. "Hollins' call still resonates after 15 years." *ESPN.com*, 29 May 2009.

2. Hahn, Alan. "Episode 5." *Knicks Fix Podcast.* msgnetworks.com, 6 Dec. 2013. URL not available. Accessed 2 July 2016.

3. *Ibid.*

4. Brown, Clifton. "PRO BASKETBALL; Intensity and Poise Give Edge to Knicks." *New York Times.* 3 May 1994.

5. No author provided. "Sonics Draft Pippen—But Bulls Get Him." *Chicago Tribune.* 23 June 1987.

6. Johnson, Roy S. "Knicks Obtain Oldham." *New York Times.* 31 Oct. 1986.

7. Goldaper, Sam. "Knicks Trade Oldham for a Kings' Pick." *New York Times.* 16 Oct. 1987.

8. Goldaper, Sam. "Henderson Waived By Knicks." *New York Times.* 17 Nov. 1987.

9. Harvin, Al. "After Three Years, Bulls Finally Sign Kukoc." *New York Times.* 20 July 1993.

10. Taylor, Phil. "Deja Vu." *Sports Illustrated.* 23 May 1994.

11. *Ibid.*

12. *Ibid.*

13. *Ibid.*

14. *Ibid.*

15. *Ibid.* Cartwright said of the incident, "That for us was humorous ... JoJo English, that's great. It's not that JoJo English was a bad player because he wasn't. He was a very good teammate. But Harper was one of their leaders. Yeah, we didn't mind that."

16. *Ibid.*

17. *Ibid.*

18. Simmons, Bill. "B.S. Report: Horace Grant." *B.S. Report.* Grantland.com, 25 Feb. 2014. http://grantland.com/the-triangle/b-s-report-horace-grant/

19. McCallum, Jack. *Dream Team: How Michael, Magic, Larry, Charles and the Greatest Team of All-Time Conquered the World and Changed the Game of Basketball Forever.* Ballantine Books, 2013. Print.

20. *Ibid.*

21. Taylor, Phil. "Deja Vu." *Sports Illustrated.* 23 May 1994.

22. Araton, Harvey. *Crashing the Boards: How Basketball Won the World and Lost Its Soul at Home.* Simon & Schuster, 2005. Print; Cartwright, Bill. Personal Interview. 16 Apr. 2019.

23. Starks, John, with Markowitz, David. *My Life.* Sports Publishing LLC, 2004. Print.

24. *Ibid.*

25. *Ibid.*

26. *Ibid.*

27. Brown, Clifton. "PRO BASKETBALL; Knicks Get a Break and then Davis Does the Rest." *New York Times.* 19 May 1994.

28. Davis, Hubert. Personal Interview. 27 Sept. 2017.

29. Brown, Clifton. "PRO BASKETBALL; Knicks Get a Break and then Davis Does the Rest." *New York Times.* 19 May 1994.

30. Isaacson, Melissa. "Ref Admits That Pippen Foul Wasn't." *Chicago Tribune.* 13 Oct. 1994.

31. Araton, Harvey. "ON PRO BASKETBALL; All Right, Big Guy, Just Try to Get Back Up." *New York Times.* 21 May 1994.

32. *Ibid.*

33. Brown, Clifton. "PRO BASKETBALL; Knicks March On After Bulls Fall Down and Break Their Crown." *New York Times.* 23 May 1994.

34. *Ibid.*

35. *Winning Time: Reggie Miller vs. the New York Knicks.* Dir. Dan Klores. Perf. Reggie Miller, Cheryl Miller, Spike Lee, Pat-

rick Ewing, and Donnie Walsh. ESPN Films, 2010. ESPN.

36. Van Tryon, Matthew. "Reggie Miller was Hated when the Indiana Pacers Drafted Him." *Indystar.com.* 22 June 2017. https://www.indystar.com/story/sports/nba/pacers/2017/06/22/reggie-miller-hated-when-pacers-drafted-him-he-wasnt-steve-alford/420958001/

37. Smits, Rik. Personal Interview. 16 Apr. 2019.

38. No author provided. "Team-by-Team Look at the NBA for the 1993–94 Season." *Los Angeles Times.* 31 Oct. 1993.

39. Brown, Clifton. "PRO BASKETBALL; Ewing Grabs the Steering Wheel In Knicks' Title Drive." *New York Times.* 27 May 1994.

40. Miller, Reggie, with Wojciechowski, Gene. *I Love Being the Enemy.* Simon & Schuster, 1995. Print.

41. Brown, Clifton. "PRO BASKETBALL; One for Ewing, 68 for Knicks, and Life for Pacers." *New York Times.* 29 May 1994.

42. Bruton, Michael. "Trash-talking Pacers silence Knicks, 83–77." *Baltimore Sun.* 31 May 1994.

43. *Winning Time: Reggie Miller vs. the New York Knicks.* Dir. Dan Klores. Perf. Reggie Miller, Cheryl Miller, Spike Lee, Patrick Ewing, and Donnie Walsh. ESPN Films, 2010. ESPN.

44. Wise, Mike. "PRO BASKETBALL; Ewing Steps Into Garden's Center Ring." *New York Times.* 27 Feb. 2001.

45. Miller, Reggie, with Wojciechowski, Gene. *I Love Being the Enemy.* Simon & Schuster, 1995. Print.

46. *Winning Time: Reggie Miller vs. the New York Knicks.* Dir. Dan Klores. Perf. Reggie Miller, Cheryl Miller, Spike Lee, Patrick Ewing, and Donnie Walsh. ESPN Films, 2010. ESPN.

47. D'Agostino, Dennis. *Garden Glory: An Oral History of the New York Knicks.* Triumph Books, 2003. Print.

48. Donahue, Anthony. "Spike Lee Joins Anthony Donahue." *The Knicks Blog Radio: The Anthony Donahue Show.* podbay.fm, 1 Dec. 2010. http://podbay.fm/show/352611966/e/1291255200

49. Townsend, Brad. "Formidable step of title series requires Knicks to stay focused." *The Dallas Morning News.* 8 June 1994.

50. D'Agostino, Dennis. *Garden Glory: An Oral History of the New York Knicks.* Triumph Books, 2003. Print.

51. *Ibid.*

52. Berkow, Ira. *Autumns in the Garden: The Coach of Camelot and Other Knicks Stories.* Triumph Books, 2013. Print.

53. D'Agostino, Dennis. *Garden Glory: An Oral History of the New York Knicks.* Triumph Books, 2003. Print.

54. *Ibid.*

55. Araton, Harvey. "ON PRO BASKETBALL; The Big Guy Delivers With Finest Moment." *New York Times.* 6 June 1994.

Chapter 9

1. No author provided. "Forgotten Finals." *CBSsports.com*, 3 June 2014. https://www.cbssports.com/nba/feature/24559469/the-forgotten-finals

2. Olajuwon, Hakeem with Knobler, Peter. *Living the Dream: My Life and Basketball.* Little, Brown, 1996. Print.

3. *Ibid.*

4. Rapaport, Michael. "Episode 288: Sam Cassell." *I Am Rapaport Stereo Podcast.* Youtube.com, 25 July 2017. https://www.youtube.com/watch?v=WyzWmMFDMhw

5. Taylor, Phil. "Together Again." *Sports Illustrated.* 13 June 1994.

6. Olajuwon, Hakeem, with Knobler, Peter. *Living the Dream: My Life and Basketball.* Little, Brown, 1996. Print.

7. *Ibid.*

8. *Ibid.*

9. *Ibid.*

10. Rhoden, William. "Olajuwon Gets His Man: Ewing; When You Wish Upon a Star for the Finals, He May Show Up." *New York Times.* 7 June 1994.

11. Maxwell, Vernon. Personal Interview. 7 June 2019.

12. Rapaport, Michael. "Episode 288: Sam Cassell." *I Am Rapaport Stereo Podcast.* Youtube.com, 25 July 2017. youtube.com/watch?v=WyzWmMFDMhw

13. Marolachakis, Stefan, and Williams, Jesse. "Kenny 'The Jet' Smith at All-Star Weekend." *Open Run.* iheart.com, 22 Feb. 2017. https://www.iheart.com/podcast/8-open-run-28732052/episode/kenny-the-jet-smith-at-all-star-28732177/

14. Falkoff, Robert. *The Inside Story of the '93–'94 Houston Rockets' Championship Season.* Gulf Publishing Company, 1994. Print.

15. Feinstein, John. *The Punch: One*

Night, Two Lives, and the Fight That Changed Basketball Forever. Little, Brown, 2002. Print.

16. Falkoff, Robert. *The Inside Story of the '93–'94 Houston Rockets' Championship Season.* Gulf Publishing Company, 1994. Print.

17. Tomjanovich, Rudy. Personal Interview. 27 June 2019. There were no hard feelings between the two teams heading into the series. Oakley even attended Vernon Maxwell's party the night before one of the first two games.

18. Taylor, Phil. "East Meets Best." *Sports Illustrated.* 13 Dec. 1993.

19. Falkoff, Robert. *The Inside Story of the '93–'94 Houston Rockets' Championship Season.* Gulf Publishing Company, 1994. Print.

20. Ibid.

21. Brown, Clifton. "N.B.A. FINALS; Knicks Made Late Run, but Olajuwon Has the Head Start." *New York Times.* 9 June 1994.

22. Ibid.

23. Ibid.

24. Baker, Chris. "This Time, Derek Harper Didn't Have to Know Time." *Los Angeles Times.* 30 May 1988.

25. Heisler, Mark. *The Lives of Riley.* Macmillan, 1994. Print.

26. Rapaport, Michael. "Episode 288: Sam Cassell." *I Am Rapaport Stereo Podcast.* Youtube.com, 25 July 2017. https://www.youtube.com/watch?v=WyzWmMFDMhw

27. Fraler, Mike. "Episode 40—Tom Garrick." *Forgotten Mavs Podcast.* Player.fm, 15 Feb. 2019. https://player.fm/series/forgotten-maverick/episode-40-tom-garrick-1992

28. Taylor, Phil. "Arms and the Man." *Sports Illustrated.* 20 June 1994.

29. Tomjanovich, Rudy. Personal Interview. 27 June 2019.

30. Taylor, Phil. "Arms and the Man." *Sports Illustrated.* 20 June 1994.

31. D'Agostino, Dennis. *Garden Glory: An Oral History of the New York Knicks.* Triumph Books, 2003. Print.

32. Oakley grabbed nine offensive rebounds, compared to the Rockets' seven.

33. Araton, Harvey. "ON PRO BASKETBALL; For Game 4, Give Oakley a Passing Grade." *New York Times.* 16 June 1994.

34. Ibid.

35. Hahn, Alan. *New York Knicks: The Complete Illustrated History.* MVP Books, 2012. Print.

36. Ibid. The Knicks championship teams

of 1970 and 1973 did not receive a parade, which were typically reserved for baseball teams at that time.

37. *June 17, 1994.* Dir. Brett Morgan. Perf. Marv Albert, Rex Beaber and Chris Berman. ESPN Films, 2010. ESPN.

38. Ibid.

39. Ibid.

40. Ibid.

41. No author provided. "Forgotten Finals." *CBSsports.com*, 3 June 2014. https://www.cbssports.com/nba/feature/24559469/the-forgotten-finals

42. Ibid.

43. Gaines, Corey. Personal Interview. 23 July 2019.

44. Rome, Jim. "John Starks." *The Jim Rome Show.* CBS Sports Radio, 11 June 2014. URL not available.

45. Curtis, Charles. "Kenny Smith: Rockets Talked O.J. During '94 Finals." *USA Today,* 18 Oct. 2016. During Game 4 of the 2016 Finals, which Van Gundy covered as a broadcaster for ABC, he claimed Pat Riley told him that Al Cowlings ran into Riley at a car wash the summer after the chase. The driver of the white Ford Bronco informed the Knicks' coach that he was driving so slowly during the chase because Simpson wanted to hear the rest of the Knicks-Rockets game on the radio. It was a bizarre story, which neither Riley, Cowlings nor Simpson have confirmed or denied.

46. No author provided. "Forgotten Finals." *CBSsports.com*, 3 June 2014. https://www.cbssports.com/nba/feature/24559469/the-forgotten-finals

47. Ibid.

48. Ibid.

49. Elie, Mario. Personal Interview. 23 Apr. 2019.

Chapter 10

1. Skevich, Mark. "Knicks Legend John Starks talks about 'The Dunk' over Jordan, Knicks, Ewing, Steph Curry, Spike Lee." *Real Fans Real Talk.* Youtube.com, 21 May 2016. https://www.youtube.com/watch?v=psS4tAdaWhM

2. D'Agostino, Dennis. *Garden Glory: An Oral History of the New York Knicks.* Triumph Books, 2003. Print.

3. Starks, John. Personal Interview. 10 July 2019.

4. D'Agostino, Dennis. *Garden Glory: An Oral History of the New York Knicks*. Triumph Books, 2003. Print; Starks, John, with Markowitz, David. *My Life*. Sports Publishing LLC, 2004. Print.

5. Starks, John. Personal Interview. 10 July 2019.

6. Maxwell, Vernon. Personal Interview. 7 June 2019; No author provided. "Forgotten Finals." *CBSsports.com*, 3 June 2014. https://www.cbssports.com/nba/feature/24559469/the-forgotten-finals

7. Starks, John. Personal Interview. 10 July 2019.

8. Olajuwon believes the Knicks should have taken him out of the play by using somebody other than Ewing in the pick-and-roll.

9. Wojnarowski, Adrian. "Patrick Ewing." *The Vertical Podcast with Woj*. sports.yahoo.com, 30 Mar. 2016. https://sports.yahoo.com/news/the-vertical-podcast-with-woj—patrick-ewing-140057572.html

10. Starks, John, with Markowitz, David. *My Life*. Sports Publishing LLC, 2004. Print.

11. Checketts, Dave. Personal Interview. 26 Feb. 2018.

12. Butera, Dick. Personal Interview. 27 Aug. 2019.

13. Harper, Derek. Personal Interview. 25 July 2017.

14. Taylor, Phil. "'Hey, Call Anytime.'" *Sports Illustrated*. 4 July 1994.

15. Starks, John. Personal Interview. 10 July 2019; Heisler, Mark. *The Lives of Riley*. Macmillan, 1994. Print.

16. Williams, Herb. Personal Interview. 2 Sept. 2019.

17. D'Agostino, Dennis. *Garden Glory: An Oral History of the New York Knicks*. Triumph Books, 2003. Print.

18. Bunn, Curtis. Personal Interview. 16 Aug. 2019.

19. D'Agostino, Dennis. *Garden Glory: An Oral History of the New York Knicks*. Triumph Books, 2003. Print.

20. Starks, John. Personal Interview. 10 July 2019.

21. Steele, David. Personal Interview. 28 Aug. 29019.

22. Harper, Derek. Personal Interview. 25 July 2017.

23. D'Agostino, Dennis. *Garden Glory: An Oral History of the New York Knicks*. Triumph Books, 2003. Print.

24. Harper, Derek. Personal Interview. 25 July 2017.

25. Townsend, Brad. "Game 5 victory gives Knicks confidence to win in Houston." The Dallas Morning News. 18 June 1994.

26. Rivers, Glenn, and Brooks, Bruce. *Those Who Love the Game: Glenn "Doc" Rivers On Life in the NBA and Elsewhere*. Henry Holt & Co., 1994.

27. Heisler, Mark. *The Lives of Riley*. Macmillan, 1994. Print.

28. Kriegel, Mark. "Riley Returns; Regrets Starks Passed On Pass." *New York Daily News*. 5 Sept. 1995

29. *Ibid.*

30. *Ibid.*

31. *Ibid.*

32. Lawrence, Mitch. "Riley Knocks His Knick Moves." *New York Daily News*. 8 June 2006

33. Checketts, Dave. Personal Interview. 26 Feb. 2018.

34. Araton, Harvey. Personal Interview. 13 Feb. 2018.

35. Araton, Harvey. "Pat Riley firmly in Magic's corner: 'He's a prodigal son of the Lakers.'" Yahoosports.com, 6 Mar. 2017. https://sports.yahoo.com/news/pat-riley-firmly-in-magics-corner-hes-a-prodigal-son-of-the-lakers-143108623.html

36. Grunfeld, Ernie. Personal Interview. 3 Oct. 2019.

37. Oakley, Charles. Personal Interview. 8 May 2019.

38. Gervino, Tony. "Starks' Reality." *Slam Magazine*. 22 Sept. 2010.

39. Starks, John. Personal Interview. 10 July 2019.

40. Checketts, Spence. "John Starks." Reality Check with Spencer Checketts. realitycheckpod.com, 21 Feb. 2019. https://realitycheckpod.com

41. D'Agostino, Dennis. *Garden Glory: An Oral History of the New York Knicks*. Triumph Books, 2003. Print.

42. Starks, John. Personal Interview. 10 July 2019.

43. *Ibid.*

44. Starks, John, with Markowitz, David. *My Life*. Sports Publishing LLC., 2004. Print.

45. Ryan, Adam. "Episode 70: Rolando Blackman." In All Airness. Inallairness.com, 11 Apr. 2016. http://inallairness.com/air070-rolando-blackman-kansas-state-legend-four-time-nba-all-star-podcast/

46. Blackman, Rolando. Personal Interview. 6 Jan. 2018.

47. Davis, Hubert. Personal Interview. 29 Sept. 2017.

48. Butera, Dick. Personal Interview. 27 Aug. 2019.

49. No author provided. "Forgotten Finals." CBSsports.com, 3 June 2014. https://www.cbssports.com/nba/feature/24559469/the-forgotten-finals

50. Thorn, Rod. Personal Interview. 16 July 2019.

51. No author provided. "NBA Rule Changes for 1994–95 Season." *Washington Post.* 4 Nov. 1994.

52. Marolachakis, Stefan, and Williams, Jesse. "Doc Rivers, President and Coach of the L.A. Clippers." *Open Run.* iheart.com, 18 Jan. 2017. https://www.iheart.com/podcast/8-open-run-28732052/episode/doc-rivers-president-and-coach-of-28732118/

Chapter 11

1. Davis, Hubert. Personal Interview. 29 Sept. 2017.

2. Araton, Harvey. "N.B.A. FINALS: ON PRO BASKETBALL; Is the Writing on the Wall For These Knicks?" *New York Times.* 24 June 1994.

3. Rhoden, William. "BASKETBALL; A Surprise, A Heisman for Knicks." *New York Times.* 30 June 1994.

4. *Ibid.*

5. Patrick, Dan. "Charlie Ward." The Dan Patrick Show. Danpatrick.com, 16 Dec. 2013. http://www.danpatrick.com/2013/12/16/charlie-ward/ Ward was also drafted by the Milwaukee Brewers in 1993 and the New York Yankees in 1994, despite not playing baseball since high school.

6. *Ibid.*

7. O'Connor, Ian. "Rivers Still Pained by Finals Loss in '94. ESPN.com. 15 June 2010. Rivers fulfilled Riley's prediction and became an NBA head coach, winning a championship with the Celtics in 2008. He recently said of the trade that sent him to the Knicks, "That trade changed my life. If I didn't play for Pat Riley, I don't get into coaching."

8. Brown, Clifton. "PRO BASKETBALL; Starks Finds Range, Knicks Find Intensity." *New York Times.* 16 Dec. 1994.

9. Grandison, Ronnie. Personal Interview. 2 Apr. 2019.

10. Starks was shooting below 32 percent over his previous 10 games.

11. Araton, Harvey. "ON PRO BASKETBALL; 'Riley's Son' Is a Net in Knicks Clothing." *New York Times.* 12 Dec. 1994.

12. *Ibid.*

13. *Ibid.*

14. Starks, John. Personal Interview. 10 July 2019.

15. Acre, Mike. "Episode 25: John Starks: New York Knicks." *The G.O.A.T. Show.* youtube.com, 17 July 2018. https://www.youtube.com/watch?v=oQsRaZ3Edmw

16. Starks, John. Personal Interview. 10 July 2019.

17. Brown, Clifton. "PRO BASKETBALL; Starks Finds Range, Knicks Find Intensity." *New York Times.* 16 Dec. 1994; Brown, Clifton. "PRO BASKETBALL; Knicks Get Another Victory, But Have a Loss Too." *New York Times.* 29 Dec. 1994.

18. Brown, Clifton. "PRO BASKETBALL; The Knicks Meet the Enemy; It May be Themselves." *New York Times.* 15 Mar. 1995.

19. Araton, Harvey. "Sports of The Times; Another Rebellion at Fort Riley." *New York Times.* 16 Mar. 1995; Berkow, Ira. "Pro Basketball; Same Time, Next Year: Knicks Again Suspend the Volatile Mason." *New York Times.* 17 Mar. 1995.

20. Cronson, Don. Personal Interview. 6 Nov. 2017.

21. Fiedler, Scott. Personal Interview. 22 Mar. 2019.

22. Kriegel, Mark. "Riley Returns; Regrets Starks Passed On Pass." *New York Daily News.* 5 Sept. 1995.

23. Rubinstein, Barry. Personal Interview. 3 Sept. 2019.

24. Mannix, Chris. "Mike Breen." *The Crossover Podcast with Chris Mannix.* Sports.yahoo.com, 29 Nov. 2016. https://play.acast.com/s/theverticalpodcastwithchrismannix/espn-and-ny-knicks-broadcaster-mike-breen

25. Bunn, Curtis. Personal Interview. 16 Aug. 2019.

26. Oakley, Charles. Personal Interview. 8 May 2019; Skevich, Mark, and Yung, Trip. "Special Guest NY Knicks Legend Anthony Mason." *Real Fans Real Talk.* Youtube.com, 30 Dec. 2013. https://www.youtube.com/watch?v=F3k6OIzBMRc

27. Salmi, Bob. Personal Interview. 6 May 2019.

28. *Ibid.*

29. Araton, Harvey. "Sports of The Times;

Another Rebellion at Fort Riley." *New York Times.* 16 Mar. 1995.
30. Vecsey, Peter. Personal Interview. 9 Apr. 2019. Mason took karate lessons until he was 12, at which point his mother made him stop because she was worried about his temper. During his tenure with the Knicks, Mase remained a huge fan of kung fu movies.
31. Cronson, Don. Personal Interview. 6 Nov. 2017; Fiedler, Scott. Personal Interview. 22 Mar. 2019.
32. Masiello, Stephen. Personal Interview. 21 June 2019.
33. Fiedler, Scott. Personal Interview. 22 Mar. 2019.
34. *Ibid.*
35. Masiello, Stephen. Personal Interview. 21 June 2019.
36. Fiedler, Scott. Personal Interview. 22 Mar. 2019.
37. Lupica, Mike. "Ep. 91—Dave Checketts." *The Mike Lupica Podcast.* stitcher.com, 2 Mar. 2018. https://www.stitcher.com/podcast/compass-media-networks/mike-lupica-show/e/53547636
38. Mayo, Michael. "Fiedler Figure: 'Dad' to Two Top Athletes." *Sun-Sentinel.* 7 Aug. 2000.
39. Taylor, Phil. "Resurrection." *Sports Illustrated.* 27 Mar. 1995.
40. Brown, Clifton. "Looking Like Mike Again, Jordan Beats Knicks." *New York Times.* 29 Mar. 1995.
41. Ryan, Adam. "Episode 001: Bill Wennington—Three-time NBA Champion of the Chicago Bulls." *In All Airness.* Inallairness.com, 5 Oct. 2012. http://inallairness.com/air001-bill-wennington/
42. Checketts, Spence. "Jeff Van Gundy (Part 1)." *Reality Check with Spence Checketts.* Realitycheckpod.com, 8 Nov. 2018. https://player.fm/series/reality-check-with-spence-checketts/jeff-van-gundy-part-1-on-coaching-against-michael-jordan-great-knicks-rivalries-and-his-relationship-with-david-stern. At the time, Michael Jordan's 55 points were the most scored in a game at the current version of Madison Square Garden, which opened in 1968. Carmelo Anthony currently holds the record with 62 points.
43. Brown, Clifton. "1995 N.B.A. PLAYOFFS; Knicks Off and Running Out of the Starting Blocks." *New York Times.* 28 Apr. 1995.

44. No author provided. "Knicks Beat Cavaliers One Point at a Time." *Associated Press.* 2 May 1995.
45. Brown, Clifton. "1995 N.B.A. PLAYOFFS; Harper For Three...Yes! It's a Knicks-Pacers Rematch." *New York Times.* 5 May 1995.
46. Miller, Reggie, with Wojciechowski, Gene. *I Love Being the Enemy.* Simon & Schuster, 1995. Print.
47. Brown, Clifton. "PRO BASKETBALL; Mark Jackson Acquired By Pacers." *New York Times.* 1 July 1994.
48. *Winning Time: Reggie Miller vs. the New York Knicks.* Dir. Dan Klores. Perf. Reggie Miller, Cheryl Miller, Spike Lee, Patrick Ewing, and Donnie Walsh. ESPN Films, 2010. ESPN.
49. *Ibid.*
50. Miller, Reggie. "Hall of Fame Induction Speech." Naismith Memorial Basketball Hall of Fame. Springfield, Massachusetts, 7 Sept. 2012. https://www.youtube.com/watch?v=Xo5S7xJm594
51. *Winning Time: Reggie Miller vs. the New York Knicks.* Dir. Dan Klores. Perf. Reggie Miller, Cheryl Miller, Spike Lee, Patrick Ewing, and Donnie Walsh. ESPN Films, 2010. ESPN.
52. *Ibid.*
53. *Ibid.*
54. *Ibid.*
55. Smits, Rik. Personal Interview. 16 Apr. 2019.
56. No author provided. "1995 N.B.A. PLAYOFFS; Mason Wins Sixth Man Award." *New York Times.* 9 May 1995.
57. Miller, Reggie, with Wojciechowski, Gene. *I Love Being the Enemy.* Simon & Schuster, 1995. Print.
58. Brown, Clifton. "1995 N.B.A. PLAYOFFS; Knicks Breather Easier After Storming Past Pacers." *New York Times.* 10 May 1995.
59. Miller, Reggie, with Wojciechowski, Gene. *I Love Being the Enemy.* Simon & Schuster, 1995. Print.
60. Brown, Clifton. "1995 N.B.A. PLAYOFFS; Knicks Breather Easier After Storming Past Pacers." *New York Times.* 10 May 1995.
61. Brown, Clifton. "1995 N.B.A. PLAYOFFS; Ewing Sits, Then Vents Frustration." *New York Times.* 12 May 1995.
62. *Ibid.*
63. Brown, Clifton. "1995 N.B.A. PLAY-

OFFS; Now It's Knicks Who Need Incredible Comeback." *New York Times.* 14 May 1995.

64. Miller, Reggie, with Wojciechowski, Gene. *I Love Being the Enemy.* Simon & Schuster, 1995. Print.

65. Brown, Clifton. "1995 N.B.A. PLAY-OFFS; Now It's Knicks Who Need Incredible Comeback." *New York Times.* 14 May 1995.

66. Miller, Reggie, with Wojciechowski, Gene. *I Love Being the Enemy.* Simon & Schuster, 1995. Print.

67. *Ibid.*

68. *Ibid.*

69. *Ibid.*

70. Brienza, Chris. Personal Interview. Dec. 18, 2019.

71. Miller, Reggie, with Wojciechowski, Gene. *I Love Being the Enemy.* Simon & Schuster, 1995. Print.

72. *Winning Time: Reggie Miller vs. the New York Knicks.* Dir. Dan Klores. Perf. Reggie Miller, Cheryl Miller, Spike Lee, Patrick Ewing, and Donnie Walsh. ESPN Films, 2010. ESPN.

73. Miller, Reggie, with Wojciechowski, Gene. *I Love Being the Enemy.* Simon & Schuster, 1995. Print.

74. *Ibid.*

75. *Ibid.*

76. Steele, David. Personal Interview. 28 Aug. 2019.

77. *Winning Time: Reggie Miller vs. the New York Knicks.* Dir. Dan Klores. Perf. Reggie Miller, Cheryl Miller, Spike Lee, Patrick Ewing, and Donnie Walsh. ESPN Films, 2010. ESPN.

78. Brown. Clifton. "1995 N.B.A. PLAY-OFFS; Riley Says Dissension Spoiled the Knicks' Season." *New York Times.* 24 May 1995.

Chapter 12

1. Winderman, Ira. "Accusations Fly As Riley, Knicks Reveal Bitter Split." *Sun-Sentinel.* 4 Sept. 1995.

2. Heisler, Mark. *The Lives of Riley.* Macmillan, 1994. Print. Le Batard, Dan. "Pat Riley." *The Dan Le Batard Show—South Beach Sessions.* ESPN Radio, 6 Nov. 2014. http://www.espn.com/espnradio/play/_/id/11821514

3. Kriegel, Mark. "Escape From New York." *Esquire Magazine.* 1 Dec. 1995.

4. Araton, Harvey. "Sports of The Times;

Right Move For Riley And Knicks." *New York Times.* 16 June 1995.

5. Brown, Clifton. "PRO BASKETBALL; Riley Won't Make Any Guarantees on His Future." *New York Times.* 22 Mar. 1995.

6. Checketts, Dave. Personal Interview. 26 Feb. 2018.

7. Chass, Murray. "ITT-Cablevision Deal Reported to Buy Madison Square Garden." *New York Times.* 28 Aug. 1994.

8. Araskog, Rand. Personal Interview. 2 Oct. 2019.

9. Checketts, Dave. Personal Interview. 26 Feb. 2018.

10. Bunn, Curtis. "Pat Out of Control Riley Resigns As Knicks Coach In Management Power Fight." *New York Daily News.* 16 June 1995; Robichaux, Mark. "Cablevision Is Willing to Buy Half of Garden It Doesn't Own." *Wall Street Journal.* 19 Feb. 1997.

11. Gutkowski, Bob. Personal Interview. 9 Aug. 2019. Gutkowski had a contentious history with Cablevision from his days as president of MSG Network and could not work with them.

12. Araskog, Rand. Personal Interview. 2 Oct. 2019.

13. *Ibid.*

14. *Ibid.*

15. Checketts, Dave. Personal Interview. 26 Feb. 2018; O'Connor, Ian. "Losing Riley Doomed Knickbockers." *ESPN.com,* 25 June 2013. https://www.espn.com/new-york/nba/story/_/id/9418559/new-york-knicks-never-let-pat-riley-go

16. Checketts, Dave. Personal Interview. 26 Feb. 2018.

17. Gutkowski, Bob. Personal Interview. 9 Aug. 2019.

18. Vecsey, Peter. Personal Interview. 9 Apr. 2019.

19. Dick Butera, who negotiated Riley's contract with the Heat, believes the coach would have stayed in New York if he had been named team president.

20. Checketts, Dave. Personal Interview. 26 Feb. 2018.

21. Brown, Clifton. "ON PRO BASKETBALL; Barbs Are Exchanged After Divorce Is Final." *New York Times.* 4 Sept. 1995.

22. Brown, Clifton. "PRO BASKETBALL; Riley Quits Citing Differences With Management." *New York Times.* 16 June 1995

23. When Grunfeld contemplated leaving the Knicks to become president of the Bucks a couple of years earlier, Riley asked Gut-

kowski to retain Grunfeld, who he believed was the most knowledgeable basketball man in the organization.

24. Grunfeld, Ernie. Personal Interview. 3 Oct. 2019.

25. Kriegel, Mark. "What Failure Did to Pat Riley." *Deadspin.com*, 21 Apr. 2015. https://thestacks.deadspin.com/what-failure-did-to-pat-riley-1699254357; No author provided. "Remembering Riley's 'gutless' Knicks exit as he calls for LeBron's loyalty." *New York Post*. 20 June 2014.

26. Brown, Clifton. "PRO BASKETBALL; Riley Quits Citing Differences With Management." *New York Times*. 16 June 1995.

27. Van Gundy, Jeff. Personal Interview. 23 May 2019.

28. Starks, John. Personal Interview. 10 July 2019.

29. Kriegel, Mark. "Riley Returns; Regrets Starks Passed On Pass." *New York Daily News*. 5 Sept. 1995.

30. Starks, John. Personal Interview. 10 July 2019; Skevich, Mark. "Knicks Legend John Starks talks about 'The Dunk' over Jordan, Knicks, Ewing, Steph Curry, Spike Lee." *Real Fans Real Talk*. Youtube.com, 21 May 2016. https://www.youtube.com/watch?v=psS4tAdaWhM

31. Smith, Chris. "Hoops Genius." *New York Magazine*. 27 Nov. 1995.

32. Tomjanovich, Rudy, with Falkoff, Robert. *A Rocket at Heart*. Simon & Schuster, 1997. Print.

33. Brown, Clifton. "PRO BASKETBALL; Heat Says It Wants Riley, But Ball is in Knicks' Corner." *New York Times*. 20 June 1995.

34. Mallozzi, Vincent. "BASKETBALL; Knicks File Tampering Charges over Riley." *New York Times*. 30 June 1995.

35. *Ibid.*

36. Wohl also included Doc Rivers, who was still playing for the Spurs, on the list.

37. Wise, Mike. "Former Player, Coach and GM Dave Wohl." *The Mike Wise Show*. purehoopsmedia.com, 2 Sept. 2019. https://purehoopsmedia.com/former-player-coach-and-gm-dave-wohl/

38. Mallozzi, Vincent. "BASKETBALL; Knicks File Tampering Charges over Riley." *New York Times*. 30 June 1995.

39. Araskog, Rand. Personal Interview. 2 Oct. 2019.

40. Checketts, Dave. Personal Interview. 26 Feb. 2018.

41. *Ibid.*

42. *Ibid.*

43. Wise, Mike. "PRO BASKETBALL; Riley Sought Heat Contract Before Quitting Knicks." *New York Times*. 25 Aug. 1995.

44. Wise, Mike. "Former Player, Coach and GM Dave Wohl." *The Mike Wise Show*. purehoopsmedia.com, 2 Sept. 2019. https://purehoopsmedia.com/former-player-coach-and-gm-dave-wohl/

45. Wise, Mike. "PRO BASKETBALL; Riley Sought Heat Contract Before Quitting Knicks." *New York Times*. 25 Aug. 1995.

46. Wise, Mike. "PRO BASKETBALL; Book Is Closed on the Knicks-Riley Saga." *New York Times*. 8 Sept. 1995.

47. Butera, Dick. Personal Interview. 27 Aug. 2019.

48. *Ibid.*

49. *Ibid.*

50. *Ibid.*

51. Checketts, Dave. Personal Interview. 26 Feb. 2018.

52. Baker Katie. "It Was Like True, True Disdain for Each Other." *theringer.com*, 15 May 2017. https://www.theringer.com/2017/5/15/16045664/oral-history-nba-playoffs-new-york-knicks-miami-heat-1997-brawl-20-year-anniversary-96b8a5be329f

53. Checketts, Dave. Personal Interview. 26 Feb. 2018. Araskog does not recall having a conversation with Stern about the arbitration, though he conceded that at 87 years old his memory is not as sharp as it once was and deferred to Checketts' recollection.

54. Wise, Mike. "PRO BASKETBALL; For Riley, Knicks Get $1 Million and a No. 1 Pick." *New York Times*. 2 Sept. 1995. The draft pick Miami sent to New York originally belonged to Atlanta.

55. *Ibid.*

56. Butera, Dick. Personal Interview. 27 Aug. 2019.

57. Winderman, Ira. "Accusations Fly As Riley, Knicks Reveal Bitter Split." *Sun-Sentinel*. 4 Sept. 1995.

Chapter 13

1. No author provided. "Nelson Takes Blame For Being Fired By Knicks." *Associated Press*. 12 May. 1996.

2. Brown, Clifton. "ON PRO BASKETBALL; Knicks' Future Is Now, So Coach Must Be Proven." *New York Times*. 18 June 1995.

3. Wise, Mike. "PRO BASKETBALL; If Daly Decides to Become Coach, Knicks Want Some Strings Attached." *New York Times*. 22 June 1995.

4. *Ibid.*

5. Wise, Mike. "PRO BASKETBALL; Daly Tells the Knicks: Thanks, but No Thanks." *New York Times*. 24 June 1995.

6. Wise, Mike. "PRO BASKETBALL; If Daly Decides to Become Coach, Knicks Want Some Strings Attached." *New York Times*. 22 June 1995; Wise, Mike. "PRO BASKETBALL; In Search For a Coach, Knicks Talk With Nelson." *New York Times*. 21 June 1995.

7. Wise, Mike. "PRO BASKETBALL; In Search For a Coach, Knicks Talk With Nelson." *New York Times*. 21 June 1995.

8. Wise, Mike. "BASKETBALL; Nelson Vows to Rev Up Offense and Laugh Track." *New York Times*. 7 July 1995.

9. *Ibid.*

10. Hersch, Hank. "2 New York Knicks." *Sports Illustrated*. 23 Oct. 1995.

11. Nelson and Webber reconciled soon after the trade.

12. *Ibid.*

13. Araskog, Rand. Personal Interview. 2 Oct. 2019; Ostler, Scott. "Don Nelson on the Warriors, Webber and Weed." *San Francisco Chronicle*. 25 May 2018; Smith, Chris. "Hoops Genius." *New York Magazine*. 27 Nov. 1995. Araskog recalls being surprised that Nelson had three beers during their first lunch together. Nellie was later reprimanded by the league for bringing a beer to the interview room after a game as coach of the Warriors.

14. Wise, Mike. "BASKETBALL; Knicks Count on Master Salesman." *New York Times*. 2 Nov. 1995.

15. Coslov, Noah, and Stanko, Adam. "Bob Salmi." *Catch and Shoot*. Art119.com, 6 Mar. 2019. https://art19.com/shows/catch-and-shoot/episodes/314dc7f9-3833-48b5-b5c4-4c49fac98663

16. Smith, Chris. "Hoops Genius." *New York Magazine*. 27 Nov. 1995.

17. Heisler, Mark. "Armstrong Becomes Top Expansion Pick." *Los Angeles Times*. 25 June 1995.

18. Prosportstransactions.com .http://www.prosportstransactions.com/basketball/Search/SearchResults.php?Player=&Team=Knicks&PlayerMovementChkBx=yes&BeginDate=1991-4-23&EndDate=1999-4-21&submit=Search&start=75

19. Wise, Mike. "PRO BASKETBALL; Knicks Reward Mason's Effort With New Deal." *New York Times*. 22 Sept. 1995.

20. Cronson, Don. Personal Interview. 6 Nov. 2017. Wise, Mike. "Pro Basketball; Knicks Reward Mason's Effort With New Deal." *New York Times*. 22 Sept. 1995.

21. Smith, Chris. "Hoops Genius." *New York Magazine*. 27 Nov. 1995.

22. Wise, Mike. "PRO BASKETBALL; Knicks Reward Mason's Effort With New Deal." *New York Times*. 22 Sept. 1995.

23. Smith, Sam. "A Predictable Prediction From Knicks' Ewing." *Chicago Tribune*. 22 Oct. 1995.

24. Wise, Mike. "For an Outspoken Ewing, It's Back to Business." *New York Times*. 29 Sept. 1995.

25. Nelson, Don. "Nellie Ball." *theplayerstribune.com* 19 May 2016.

26. Wise, Mike. "For an Outspoken Ewing, It's Back to Business." *New York Times*. 29 Sept. 1995.

27. Berkow, Ira. *Autumns in the Garden: The Coach of Camelot and Other Knicks Stories*. Triumph Books, 2013. Print.

28. MacMullan, Jackie. "Van's the Man." *Sports Illustrated*. 18 Mar. 1996.

29. Starks, John with Markowitz, David. *My Life*. Sports Publishing LLC, 2004. Print.

30. Stanton, Barry. Personal Interview. 13 Jan. 2020.

31. Le Batard, Dan. "Pat Riley." *The Art of Conversation with Dan Le Batard*. ESPN, 24 Feb. 2019. https://www.youtube.com/watch?v=Q3o1BS5_kFc

32. Vecsey, Peter. Personal Interview. 9 Apr. 2019.

33. Le Batard, Dan. "Pat Riley." *The Dan Le Batard Show—South Beach Sessions*. ESPN Radio, 6 Nov. 2014. http://www.espn.com/espnradio/play/_/id/11821514

34. Baker, Katie. "It Was Like True, True Disdain for Each Other." theringer.com, 15 May 2017. https://www.theringer.com/2017/5/15/16045664/oral-history-nba-playoffs-new-york-knicks-miami-heat-1997-brawl-20-year-anniversary-96b8a5be329f

35. Le Batard, Dan. "Pat Riley." *The Dan Le Batard Show—South Beach Sessions*. ESPN Radio, 6 Nov. 2014. http://www.espn.com/espnradio/play/_/id/11821514

36. Starks, John with Markowitz, David. *My Life*. Sports Publishing LLC, 2004. Print.

37. Le Batard, Dan. "Pat Riley." *The Dan*

Le Batard Show—South Beach Sessions. ESPN Radio, 6 Nov. 2014. http://www.espn. com/espnradio/play/_/id/11821514

38. Wise, Mike. "PRO BASKETBALL; Knicks Defeat the Heat, but Fans Take on Riley." *New York Times.* 20 Dec. 1995.

39. Wise, Mike. "PRO BASKETBALL; Olajuwon and Rockets Rejected and Ejected." *New York Times.* 26 Nov. 1995.

40. Wise, Mike. "BASKETBALL; Knicks Have No Trouble Expressing Themselves." *New York Times.* 31 Dec. 1995.

41. *Ibid.*

42. Smith, Chris. "Hoops Genius." *New York Magazine.* 27 Nov. 1995.

43. Hahn, Alan. *New York Knicks: The Complete Illustrated History.* MVP Books, 2012. Print.

44. Checketts, Dave. Personal Interview. 26 Feb. 2018.

45. MacMullan, Jackie. "Van's the Man." *Sports Illustrated.* 18 Mar. 1996.

46. Wise, Mike. "PRO BASKETBALL; Oakley Returns to Knicks For a Look at the New Look." *New York Times.* 10 Mar. 1996.

47. Starks, John. Personal Interview. 10 July 2019.

48. Wise, Mike. "PRO BASKETBALL; Starks Criticizes Nelson's Coaching Style." *New York Times.* 28 Feb. 1996.

49. Wise, Mike, and Isola, Frank. *Just Ballin': The Chaotic Rise of the New York Knicks.* Simon & Schuster, 1999. Print.

50. *Ibid.*

51. Wise, Mike. Personal Interview. 23 Feb. 2018.

52. Childs, Chris. Personal Interview. 12 July 2019.

53. Davis, Hubert. Personal Interview. 29 Sept. 2017.

54. MacMullan, Jackie. "Van's the Man." *Sports Illustrated.* 18 Mar. 1996.

55. Wise, Mike. Personal Interview. 23 Feb. 2018.

56. D'Agostino, Dennis. *Garden Glory: An Oral History of the New York Knicks.* Triumph Books, 2003. Print.

57. Wise, Mike. "PRO BASKETBALL; Knicks Change Direction and Dismiss Coach." *New York Times.* 9 Mar. 1996.

58. Shouler, Kenneth. "To Fix the Knicks." *Cigar Aficionado.* Autumn 1996.

59. Gumbel, Bryant. "Don Nelson." *Real Sports with Bryant Gumbel.* HBO. Youtube.com, 21 June 2019. https://www.

hbo.com/video/real-sports-with-bryant-gumbel/2017/2017-episodes/june-2019/videos/don-nelson-bonus-clip

60. MacMullan, Jackie. "Van's the Man." *Sports Illustrated.* 18 Mar. 1996.

61. No author provided. "Nelson Takes Blame For Being Fired By Knicks." *Associated Press.* 12 May. 1996.

Chapter 14

1. Wise, Mike. "N.B.A. Playoffs; Van Gundy Guaranteed 2 More Years." *New York Times.* 22 May 1996.

2. Wojnarowski, Adrian. "Jeff Van Gundy." *The Vertical Podcast with Woj.* sports.yahoo.com, 10 Feb. 2016. https://sports.yahoo.com/news/the-vertical-podcast-with-woj—jeff-van-gundy-145814221.html

3. Van Gundy, Jeff. Personal Interview. 23 May 2019.

4. Wise, Mike. "Jeff Van Gundy of ESPN and ABC Sports." *The Mike Wise Show.* purehoopsmedia.com, 19 Aug. 2019.https://purehoopsmedia.com/jeff-van-gundy-of-espn-and-abc-sports/

5. Salmi, Bob. Personal Interview. 6 May 2019.

6. Van Gundy, Jeff. Personal Interview. 23 May 2019.

7. Wise, Mike, and Isola, Frank. *Just Ballin': The Chaotic Rise of the New York Knicks.* Simon & Schuster, 1999. Print.

8. MacMullan, Jackie. "Van's the Man." *Sports Illustrated.* 18 Mar. 1996.

9. Berlind, William. "Van Gundy: Warrior in Nebbish Clothing." *Observor.com,* 17 May 1999. https://observer.com/1999/05/van-gundy-warrior-in-nebbish-clothing/

10. Price, S.L. "Mourning After." *Sports Illustrated.* 11 May 1998.

11. Steinlight, Sammy. Personal Interview. 23 May 2019; Thibodeau, Tom. Personal Interview. 23 July 2019.

12. Berlind, William. "Van Gundy: Warrior in Nebbish Clothing." *Observor.com,* 17 May 1999.

13. Price, S.L. "The Last Laugh." *Sports Illustrated.* 30 Oct. 2000.

14. Berlind, William. "Van Gundy: Warrior in Nebbish Clothing." *Observor.com,* 17 May 1999.

15. Wise, Mike, and Isola, Frank. *Just Ballin': The Chaotic Rise of the New York Knicks.* Simon & Schuster, 1999. Print.

16. Salmi, Bob. Personal Interview. 6 May 2019.

17. Wojnarowski, Adrian. "Jeff Van Gundy." *The Vertical Podcast with Woj.* sports.yahoo.com, 10 Feb. 2016. https://sports.yahoo.com/news/the-vertical-podcast-with-woj—jeff-van-gundy-145814221.html

18. *Ibid.*

19. *Ibid.*

20. Mannix, Chris. "Mike Breen." *The Crossover Podcast with Chris Mannix.* Sports.yahoo.com, 29 Nov. 2016. https://play.acast.com/s/theverticalpodcastwithchrismannix/espn-and-ny-knicks-broadcaster-mike-breen

21. Donahue, Anthony. "Ep. 4: Marcus Camby." *33 and 7th: A New York Knicks Pod.* podcasts.apple.com, 2 May 2019. https://podcasts.apple.com/us/podcast/33rd-and-7th-a-new-york-knicks-pod/id1455564828

22. Dudley, Chris. Personal Interview. 20 Oct. 2017.

23. Wise, Mike and Isola, Frank. *Just Ballin': The Chaotic Rise of the New York Knicks.* Simon & Schuster, 1999. Print.

24. *Ibid.*

25. D'Agostino, Dennis. *Garden Glory: An Oral History of the New York Knicks.* Triumph Books, 2003. Print.

26. Barker, Barbara. Personal Interview. 20 Apr. 2018.

27. Wise, Mike and Isola, Frank. *Just Ballin': The Chaotic Rise of the New York Knicks.* Simon & Schuster, 1999. Print.

28. Starks, John with Markowitz, David. *My Life.* Sports Publishing LLC, 2004. Print.

29. Wise, Mike. "PRO BASKETBALL; Knicks Change Direction and Dismiss Coach." *New York Times.* 9 Mar. 1996.

30. Wise, Mike. "PRO BASKETBALL; The Knicks Players Agree That Nelson Had to Go." *New York Times.* 9 Mar. 1996.

31. Wise, Mike, and Isola, Frank. *Just Ballin': The Chaotic Rise of the New York Knicks.* Simon & Schuster, 1999. Print.

32. O'Connor, Ian. "For Crying Out Loud, New Knick Boss Has Biggest Gift." *New York Daily News.* 11 Mar. 1996.

33. Wise, Mike. "PRO BASKETBALL; So Much for Karma. Knicks Stomp Bulls." *New York Times.* 11 Mar. 1996.

34. Wise, Mike. "PRO BASKETBALL; Knicks Change Direction and Dismiss Coach." *New York Times.* 9 Mar. 1996.

35. Checketts, Dave. Personal Interview. 26 Feb. 2018.

36. Araton, Harvey. "Sports of The Times; The Kid Coach Makes All the Right Moves." *New York Times.* 11 Mar. 1996.

37. Isola, Frank. "Van's Had His Phil of Jackson." *New York Daily News.* 3 May 1996.

38. Price, S.L. "The Last Laugh." *Sports Illustrated.* 30 Oct. 2000.

39. Wise, Mike. "PRO BASKETBALL; Van Gundy Remembers Lessons in Loyalty." *New York Times.* 13 Apr. 1996.

40. Wise, Mike. "N.B.A. PLAYOFFS; Van Gundy Guaranteed 2 More Years." *New York Times.* 22 May 1996.

41. Markowitz, Dan. "Knicks Coach Brings Intensity to His Work." *New York Times.* 20 Apr. 1997.

42. Wise, Mike. "N.B.A. PLAYOFFS; Oakley Returns to Knicks Practice with a Visor and a Vengeance." *New York Times.* 24 Apr. 1996.

43. Hoffer, Richard. "Floor Leader." *Sports Illustrated.* 10 Feb. 1997.

44. Wise, Mike. Personal Interview. 23 Feb. 2018.

45. Cummings, D.L. "Knicks' Masked Bandit Oak Steals the Show." *New York Daily News.* 26 Apr. 1996.

46. Wise, Mike. "PRO BASKETBALL PLAYOFFS; Knicks Believe and Withstand a Garden Thriller." *New York Times.* 13 May 1996.

47. *Ibid.*

48. Wise, Mike. "N.B.A. PLAYOFFS; Knicks and Ewing Are All Heart, but It's Barely Beating." *New York Times.* 13 May 1996.

49. Wise, Mike. "N.B.A. PLAYOFFS; Van Gundy Guaranteed 2 More Years." *New York Times.* 22 May 1996.

50. Wise, Mike. "N.B.A. PLAYOFFS; Ewing Is Still Planning His Future with Knicks and Van Gundy." *New York Times.* 16 May 1996.

Chapter 15

1. Brown, Clifton. "ON PRO BASKETBALL; Quick as 1–2–3, the Knicks Grab a Shot at a Third Championship." *New York Times.* 15 July 1996.

2. Isola, Frank. "Money to Burn but Can Knicks Add an Igniter." *New York Daily News.* 9 July 1996.

3. "1996 NBA Draft." Basketballreference.com. https://www.basketball-reference.com/draft/NBA_1996.html

4. Wise, Mike. "PRO BASKETBALL; Knicks Go Forward in the First Round." *New York Times*. 27 June 1996.

5. *Ibid.*

6. Thomas, Etan. "John Wallace." *The Rematch with Etan Thomas*. Art19.com, 14 May 2017. https://art19.com/shows/the-rematch/episodes/edabb736-27e2-4f7b-a59b-2eb7fc89f18d

7. Isola, Frank. "Wallace Falls to Knicks Follow With McCarty and Dontae.'" *New York Daily News*. 29 June 1996.

8. Coincidentally, the first college recruiting letter Wallace received as a ninth grader, which he pinned on his wall, was from Van Gundy, when the coach was at Rutgers.

9. Wise, Mike. "PRO BASKETBALL; Knicks Deal Smith, and His Salary, to San Antonio." *New York Times*. 9 Feb. 1996.

10. Wise, Mike. "PRO BASKETBALL; Cash and Carry On at Trader Knick." *New York Times*. 19 Feb. 1996.

11. Moran, Michael. "PRO BASKET-BALL; The Dream Team Meets, as Miller Dreams of New York." *New York Times*. 2 July 1996.

12. Wise, Mike. "PRO BASKETBALL; New Knick Johnson Says Right Things." *New York Times*. 17 July 1996.

13. Withers, Tom. "Boxing Led to hoops for Rebels' Johnson." *UPI*. 1 Apr. 1990.

14. Montville, Leigh. "Out of the Hood." *Sports Illustrated*. 20 Apr. 1992.

15. *Ibid.*

16. No host provided. "Larry Johnson." NBA Inside Stuff. Youtube.com, Apr. 1993. https://www.youtube.com/watch?v=Md3FkVBAEOw

17. Salop, Andrew. "Episode 19— 'Grandmama' Larry Johnson Interview." *Combos Court*. Listennotes.com, 6 Aug. 2018. https://www.listennotes.com/podcasts/combos-court/episode-19-grandmama-larry-SszamN_UVo1/

18. Grimala, Mike. "Larry Johnson becomes first Rebel selected to college basketball Hall of Fame." Lasvegassun.com, 2 Apr. 2019. https://lasvegassun.com/news/2019/apr/02/larry-johnson-becomes-first-rebel-selected-to-coll/

19. Johnson, Larry and Sprewell, Latrell. "Connections: Larry Johnson and Latrell Sprewell." *Connections*. MSG Networks, 25 Oct. 2018. https://www.youtube.com/watch?v=LN4fC1Ntr-8

20. Hahn, Alan. "Season 1, Episode 16." *Knicks Fix Podcast*. Msgnetworks.com, 16 Mar. 14. URL not available; Johnson, Larry and Sprewell, Latrell. "Connections: Larry Johnson and Latrell Sprewell." *Connections*. MSG Networks, 25 Oct. 2018. https://www.youtube.com/watch?v=LN4fC1Ntr-8

21. Johnson, Larry, and Sprewell, Latrell. "Connections: Larry Johnson and Latrell Sprewell." *Connections*. MSG Networks, 25 Oct. 2018. https://www.youtube.com/watch?v=LN4fC1Ntr-8

22. Hahn, Alan. "Season 1, Episode 16." *Knicks Fix Podcast*. Msgnetworks.com, 16 Mar. 14. URL not available.

23. Verducci, Tom. "Back to Basics." *Sports Illustrated*. 10 Oct. 1994.

24. Nobody was more shocked by Johnson's contract than Checketts. "It was a big shock, and I think it was that way to everyone in the league," said Checketts. "No one ever expected Larry Johnson to suddenly become the richest player in the NBA—by far. By far!" He added, "There's never been a contract signed in the NBA that had the same ripple effect as Johnson's contract did." Verducci, Tom. "Back to Basics." *Sports Illustrated*. 10 Oct. 1994.

25. *Ibid.*

26. Wise, Mike. "PRO BASKETBALL; New Knick Johnson Says Right Things." *New York Times*. 17 July 1996.

27. Taylor, Phil. "A Real Stretch: Convinced at a secret face-to-face meeting that tarnished Latrell Sprewell was worth the gamble, the Knicks transformed themselves—for better or worse." *Sports Illustrated*. 2 Feb. 1999.

28. Cronson, Don. Personal Interview. 6 Nov. 2017.

29. Maull, Samuel. "Anthony Mason, China Club, Bouncers, Maitre d' Sued in Fracas" *Associated Press*. 1 May 1996. To nobody's surprise, Mason was arrested in Times Square at about 3 a.m. a few weeks after the trade when he engaged in a verbal altercation with a police officer regarding a parking ticket. It took 10 officers to restrain him. Lapointe, Joe. "Pro Basketball; Mason Spends Day in Jail After Scuffling with Police." *New York Times*. 25 July 1996.

30. Isola, Frank. "Mase Sulking: He's Mad Role Has Shrunk." *New York Daily News*. 29 Mar. 1996.

31. Van Gundy, Jeff. Personal Interview. 23 May 2019. Like other new Knicks before him, Johnson had a history with Oakley.

The two engaged in a scuffle in December 1995. No author provided. "New Fine Leveled Against Oakley." *New York Times*. 2 Dec. 1995.

32. Brown, Clifton. "PRO BASKETBALL; Free Agents Line Up In Force For Tip-Off." *New York Times*. 11 July 1996.

33. Lidz, Franz. "FAR AFIELD UNHAPPILY UPROOTED FROM THE BIGGEST CITIES IN THE NBA, VLADE DIVAC AND ANTHONY MASON ARE ADJUSTING TO CHARLOTTE" *Sports Illustrated*. 21 Oct. 1996.

34. Wise, Mike, and Isola, Frank. *Just Ballin': The Chaotic Rise of the New York Knicks*. Simon & Schuster, 1999. Print.

35. Checketts, Dave. Personal Interview. 26 Feb. 2018.

36. D'Agostino, Dennis. *Garden Glory: An Oral History of the New York Knicks*. Triumph Books, 2003. Print.

37. Steve Smith was the Knicks' third option at shooting guard.

38. Smith, Sam. "Nearly a Knick." *Chicago Tribune*. 13 Aug. 1997.

39. Lazenby, Roland. *Michael Jordan: The Life*. Little, Brown, 2014. Print.

40. *Ibid.*

41. Smith, Sam. "Nearly a Knick." *Chicago Tribune*. 13 Aug. 1997.

42. Falk, David. Personal Interview. 18 Aug. 2019.

43. Falk, David. Personal Interview. 18 Aug. 2019; Araskog, Rand. Personal Interview. 2 Oct. 2019.

44. Lazenby, Roland. *Michael Jordan: The Life*. Little, Brown, 2014. Print.

45. Smith, Samuel. "Re: Knicks book." Message to Paul Knepper. 21 Apr. 2019. Email.

46. Grunfeld, Ernie. Personal Interview. 3 Oct. 2019.

47. *Ibid.*

48. Brown, Clifton. "PRO BASKETBALL; A New Backcourt: Childs and Houston Join the Knicks." *New York Times*. 14 July 1996.

49. Winderman, Ira. "NBA Voids Howard Contract." *Sun-Sentinel*. 1 Aug. 1996.

50. Asher, Mark. "Juwan Howard Re-signs with Bullets." *Washington Post*. 6 Aug. 1996.

51. Brown, Clifton. "ON PRO BASKETBALL; Quick as 1–2–3, the Knicks Grab A Shot at a Third Championship." *New York Times*. 15 July 1996.

52. Devine, Dan. "BDL Interview: Allan Houston on what it's like to be a free agent." *Sports.yahoo.com*, 30 June 2010. https://sports.yahoo.com/bdl-interview-allan-houston-free-agent—nba.html

53. Robertson, Howard, and Larry Robinson. "My Life as an NBA Player and a New York Knick—Allan Houston." *A Little R&R on Sports Podcast*. Iheart.com, 31 Mar. 2017. https://www.iheart.com/podcast/156-a-little-rr-on-sports-podc-26962974/episode/my-life-as-an-nba-player-28073612/

54. Brown, Clifton. "ON PRO BASKETBALL; Quick as 1–2–3, the Knicks Grab A Shot at a Third Championship." *New York Times*. 15 July 1996.

55. Isola, Frank. "Sill Ill Will From Hill; Grant Won't Rush to End Houston Feud." *New York Daily News*. 19 Dec. 1996.

56. Brown, Clifton. "ON PRO BASKETBALL; Quick as 1–2–3, the Knicks Grab A Shot at a Third Championship." *New York Times*. 15 July 1996.

57. Bondy, Filip. "Knicks; Best Shot Allan Over Miller Was Right Choice." *New York Daily News*. 5 May 1998.

58. Isola, Frank. "Sill Ill Will From Hill; Grant Won't Rush to End Houston Feud." *New York Daily News*. 19 Dec. 1996.

59. Marolachakis, Stefan. "Reggie Miller on the Epic Rivalries of the '90s and the Lost Art of Not Making Friends." *Open Run*. stitcher.com, 16 Oct. 2017. https://www.stitcher.com/podcast/uninterrupted/open-run/e/51833992

60. Wojnarowski, Adrian. "Donnie Walsh." *The Vertical Podcast with Woj*. sports.yahoo.com, 23 Nov. 2016. https://sports.yahoo.com/news/vertical-pod-with-woj—donnie-walsh-180013834.html

61. *Ibid.*

62. Brown, Clifton. "PRO BASKETBALL; A New Backcourt: Childs and Houston Join the Knicks." *New York Times*. 14 July 1996.

63. Childs, Chris. Personal Interview. 12 July 2019; Brown, Clifton. "PRO BASKETBALL; A New Backcourt: Childs and Houston Join the Knicks." *New York Times*. 14 July 1996.

64. Isola, Frank. "Hubert Takes a Hike: Davis Dealt to Raptors For '97 First-Rounder." *New York Daily News*. 25 July 1996.

65. Davis, Hubert. Personal Interview. 28 Sept. 2017.

66. Harper, Derek. Personal Interview. 25 July 2017.

67. Roberts, Selena. "PRO BASKET-BALL; Knicks Seal Up Buck Williams." *New York Times*. 27 July 1996.

68. Brown, Clifton. "PRO BASKETBALL; Unsigned In Chicago: Good Coach with Karma." *New York Times*. 10 Mar. 1996.

69. Brown, Clifton. "'96–97 Bulls: Ready, Smart, Crafty." *New York Times*. 10 Oct. 1996.

70. Corey, Joel. "The inside story: How the Magic let the Lakers steal Shaquille O'Neal." *CBSsports.com*, 21 July 2016. https://www.cbssports.com/nba/news/the-inside-story-how-the-orlando-magic-let-the-lakers-steal-shaquille-oneal/

71. *Ibid.*

72. *Ibid.*

73. No author provided. "Forgotten Finals." *CBSsports.com*, 3 June 2014. https://www.cbssports.com/nba/feature/24559469/the-forgotten-finals

74. Checketts, Dave. Personal Interview. 26 Feb. 2018.

75. Corey, Joel. "The inside story: How the Magic let the Lakers steal Shaquille O'Neal." *CBSsports.com*, 21 July 2016. https://www.cbssports.com/nba/news/the-inside-story-how-the-orlando-magic-let-the-lakers-steal-shaquille-oneal/

76. Dwyer, Kelly. "Paying tribute to the NBA's 1996 offseason, the wackiest one by miles." *Sports.yahoo.com*, 8 July 2014. https://sports.yahoo.com/paying-needed-tribute-to-the-nba-s-1996-offseason—the-wackiest-one-by-miles-201944082.html?y20=1

77. *Ibid.*

78. *Ibid.*

Chapter 16

1. Wilbon, Michael. "MANY NICKS AND ALL KNICKS." *Washington Post*. 13 May 1997.

2. The NBA's fiftieth anniversary was a bit of a misnomer. The Basketball Association of America was formed in June 1946 to compete with the National Basketball League, which had existed since 1937. After the 1948–49 season, the two leagues merged to form the NBA.

3. No author provided. "NBA at 50: Top 50 Players." *NBA.com*, 3 Nov. 2017. https://www.nba.com/history/nba-at-50/top-50-players

4. *Ibid.*

5. Isola, Frank. "Checketts Raises Stakes; Forget the Second Round, Knicks Expected to Go 'Four' It." *New York Daily News*. 8 Oct. 1996.

6. Wise, Mike. "PRO BASKETBALL; The Knicks Are Off and Running at Camp." *New York Times*. 5 Oct. 1996.

7. Thibodeau, Tom. Personal Interview. 23 July 2019.

8. Wise, Mike. "PRO BASKETBALL; Ward Will Get Starting Nod at Point Over Childs." *New York Times*. 28 Nov. 1996.

9. Starks, John. Personal Interview. 10 July 2019.

10. Brown, Clifton. "An Angry Ewing Takes On the Fans." *New York Times*. 8 Dec. 1996.

11. *Ibid.*

12. Armour, Terry. "Jordan Goes to Town, Courtesy of Van Gundy." *Chicago Tribune*. 21 Jan. 1997.

13. *Ibid.*

14. D'Agostino, Dennis. *Garden Glory: An Oral History of the New York Knicks*. Triumph Books, 2003. Print.

15. Araton, Harvey. "Just Another Hot Night in Chicago." *New York Times*. 22 Jan. 1997.

16. Wise, Mike. "Jordan Does the Talking in Knicks' Silent Movie." *New York Times*. 22 Jan. 1997.

17. D'Agostino, Dennis. *Garden Glory: An Oral History of the New York Knicks*. Triumph Books, 2003. Print.

18. Cummings, D.L., and Frank Isola. "Childs, Oakley Tough on Mates." *New York Daily News*. 23 Jan. 1997.

19. Wallace, John. Personal Interview. 12 June 2019.

20. Wise, Mike. "In a War of Words, Ewing Has the Final Say." *New York Times*. 10 Mar. 1997.

21. Brown, Clifton. "ON PRO BASKET-BALL; When a Knick Victory Is Not Just a Victory." *New York Times*. 20 Apr. 1997.

22. *Ibid.*

23. Wise, Mike. "Loyal Ewing Has Van Gundy Clause." *New York Times*. 26 Feb. 1997.

24. Taylor, Phil. "NBA, Turning It Up as the NBA Playoffs Begin, the Stakes—and Intensity—Rise." *Sports Illustrated*. 5 May 1997.

25. Lupica, Mike. "Hot Shot Brings the Heat." *New York Daily News*. 29 Apr. 1997.

26. McCallum, Jack. "Road Kill." *Sports Illustrated*. 29 May 2000.

27. Price, S.L. "The Last Laugh." *Sports Illustrated*. 30 Oct. 2000.

28. D'Agostino, Dennis. *Garden Glory: An Oral History of the New York Knicks.* Triumph Books, 2003. Print.

29. Wallace, John. Personal Interview. 12 June 2019.

30. Van Gundy, Jeff. Personal Interview. 23 May. 2019.

31. Van Gundy, Stan. Personal Interview. 20 Aug. 2019.

32. *Patrick and Zo.* Dir. Jon Weinbach. Perf. Patrick Ewing, Alonzo Mourning, Jeff Van Gundy and Michael Wilbon. *Sports Illustrated*, 2016. SI.com. Web. 7 July 2016.

33. Easton, Ed. "Alonzo Mourning talks New York Knicks rivalry and relationship with Patrick Ewing." *empirewritesback.com*, 21 Nov. 2019. https://empirewritesback.com/2019/11/23/alonzo-mourning-talks-new-york-knicks-rivalry-relationship-patrick-ewing/

34. *Patrick and Zo.* Dir. Jon Weinbach. Perf. Patrick Ewing, Alonzo Mourning, Jeff Van Gundy and Michael Wilbon. *Sports Illustrated*, 2016. SI.com. Web. 7 July 2016.

35. Falk, David. Personal Interview. 8 Aug. 2019.

36. Harper, Zach. "*Patrick and Zo* Director Jon Weinbach." *Eye on Basketball Podcast.* CBSsports.com, 28 Apr. 2016 https://www.cbssports.com/nba/news/eye-on-basketball-podcast-patrick-zo-director-jon-weinbach/

37. Grunfeld, Ernie. Personal Interview. 3 Oct. 2019.

38. Heisler, Mark. "Mourning Turns Up with Heat." *Los Angeles Times.* 4 Nov. 1995.

39. Kolnick, Ethan, and Wittyngham, Chris. "Heat Stories: Tim Hardaway 'Always Basketball.'" *Five Reasons with Ethan and Chris.* Fivereasons.com, 5 Dec. 2018. https://fivereasons.podbean.com/e/heat-stories-tim-hardaway/

40. *Ibid.*

41. Wise, Mike. "Get Physical: Knicks and Heat Ready." *New York Times.* 7 May 1997.

42. *Ibid.*

43. Lupica, Mike. "Settled On Wrong Court." *New York Daily News.* 19 May 1997.

44. *Ibid.*

45. *Ibid.*

46. *Ibid.*

47. *Ibid.*

48. Van Gundy, Stan. Personal Interview. 20 Aug. 2019.

49. Kolnick, Ethan, and Wittyngham, Chris. "Heat Stories: Tim Hardaway 'Always Basketball.'" *Five Reasons with Ethan and Chris.* Fivereasons.com, 5 Dec. 2018. https://fivereasons.podbean.com/e/heat-stories-tim-hardaway/

50. D'Agostino, Dennis. *Garden Glory: An Oral History of the New York Knicks.* Triumph Books, 2003. Print.

51. Baker Katie. "It Was Like True, True Disdain for Each Other." *theringer.com*, 15 May 2017. https://www.theringer.com/2017/5/15/16045664/oral-history-nba-playoffs-new-york-knicks-miami-heat-1997-brawl-20-year-anniversary-96b8a5be329f

52. *Ibid.*

53. Van Gundy, Jeff. Personal Interview. 23 May. 2019.

54. Van Gundy, Stan. Personal Interview. 20 Aug. 2019.

55. Thorn, Rod. Personal Interview. 16 July 2019.

56. Baker Katie. "It Was Like True, True Disdain for Each Other." *theringer.com*, 15 May 2017. https://www.theringer.com/2017/5/15/16045664/oral-history-nba-playoffs-new-york-knicks-miami-heat-1997-brawl-20-year-anniversary-96b8a5be329f

57. Checketts, Spence. "Jeff Van Gundy (Part 1)." *Reality Check with Spence Checketts.* Realitycheckpod.com, 8 Nov. 2018. https://player.fm/series/reality-check-with-spence-checketts/jeff-van-gundy-part-1-on-coaching-against-michael-jordan-great-knicks-rivalries-and-his-relationship-with-david-stern

58. Thorn, Rod. Personal Interview. 16 July 2019.

59. Baker Katie. "It Was Like True, True Disdain for Each Other." *theringer.com*, 15 May 2017. https://www.theringer.com/2017/5/15/16045664/oral-history-nba-playoffs-new-york-knicks-miami-heat-1997-brawl-20-year-anniversary-96b8a5be329f

60. Winderman, Ira. "Judge Upholds Suspension of Four Knicks." *Sun-Sentinel.* 17 May 1997.

61. Baker Katie. "It Was Like True, True Disdain for Each Other." *theringer.com*, 15 May 2017. https://www.theringer.com/2017/5/15/16045664/oral-history-

nba-playoffs-new-york-knicks-miami-heat-1997-brawl-20-year-anniversary-96b8a5be329f

62. *Ibid.*

63. Isola, Frank. "Ewing's on the Line; Pat Guarantees Game 7 Victory." *New York Daily News.* 18 May 1997.

64. Lupica, Mike. "Settled On Wrong Court." *New York Daily News.* 19 May 1997.

65. Baker Katie. "It Was Like True, True Disdain for Each Other." *theringer. com,* 15 May 2017. https://www.theringer. com/2017/5/15/16045664/oral-history-nba-playoffs-new-york-knicks-miami-heat-1997-brawl-20-year-anniversary-96b8a5be329f

66. Lupica, Mike. "Ep. 91—Dave Checketts." *The Mike Lupica Podcast.* stitcher.com, 2 Mar. 2018. https://www.stitcher.com/podcast/compass-media-networks/mike-lupica-show/e/53547636

67. Baker Katie. "It Was Like True, True Disdain for Each Other." *theringer. com,* 15 May 2017. https://www.theringer. com/2017/5/15/16045664/oral-history-nba-playoffs-new-york-knicks-miami-heat-1997-brawl-20-year-anniversary-96b8a5be329f

Chapter 17

1. D'Agostino, Dennis. *Garden Glory: An Oral History of the New York Knicks.* Triumph Books, 2003. Print.

2. Janofsky, Michael. "Marv Albert Pleads Guilty and Is Dismissed by NBC." *New York Times.* 26 Sept. 1997.

3. *Ibid.*

4. *Ibid.*

5. Wise, Mike. "Van Gundy Rewarded with Pact into 2000." *New York Times.* 8 July 1997.

6. Wise, Mike. "Ewing, Vowing to Retire a Knick, Signs for 4 Years. *New York Times.*" 3 July 1997.

7. Wise, Mike. "N.B.A. PREVIEW '97-'98: End of Line for Dynasty?; Aging Bulls to Face Challenge from Several Teams." *New York Times.* 29 Oct. 1997.

8. Wise, Mike, and Isola, Frank. *Just Ballin': The Chaotic Rise of the New York Knicks.* Simon & Schuster, 1999. Print.

9. D'Agostino, Dennis. *Garden Glory: An Oral History of the New York Knicks.* Triumph Books, 2003. Print.

10. Wise, Mike, and Isola, Frank. *Just Ballin': The Chaotic Rise of the New York Knicks.* Simon & Schuster, 1999. Print.

11. Wise, Mike. "ON PRO BASKETBALL; Refusing to Whine, Oakley Soldiers On." *New York Times.* 1 Apr. 1998.

12. Bunn, Curtis. "CHILDS STARTS OVER—SOBER." *New York Daily News.* 21 Jan. 1996.

13. Berkow, Ira. "Sports of The Times; Childs Thinks He Can . . . and So Do the Nets." *New York Times.* 19 Feb. 1996.

14. Bunn, Curtis. "CHILDS STARTS OVER—SOBER." *New York Daily News.* 21 Jan. 1996.

15. Wise, Mike. "BASKETBALL; New Net Knows All About Fresh Starts." *New York Times.* 6 Jan. 1995.

16. *Ibid.*

17. Isola, Frank. "Meeting the New Knicks: 'Big 3' Complete Facelift." *New York Daily News.* 15 July 1996.

18. Childs, Chris. Personal Interview. 12 July 2019.

19. Elhassan, Amin. "Once a Knick Always a Knick, Chris Childs." *The Hoop Collective.* Truehooptv, 13 Feb. 2017. http://www.espn.com/blog/truehoop/post/_/id/74758/truehoop-pod-once-a-knick-always-a-knick-chris-childs

20. Roberts, Selena. "PRO BASKETBALL; Childs Steps Out of Lineup for Ward." *New York Times.* 25 Oct. 1997.

21. Childs, Chris. Personal Interview. 12 July 2019.

22. Popper, Steve. "PRO BASKETBALL; Childs Is Unfazed by Boos and Trade Talk." *New York Times.* 16 Jan. 1998.

23. Childs, Chris. Personal Interview. 12 July 2019.

24. Wise, Mike, and Isola, Frank. *Just Ballin': The Chaotic Rise of the New York Knicks.* Simon & Schuster, 1999. Print.

25. *Ibid.*

26. Barker, Barbara. Personal Interview. 20 Apr. 2018.

27. Berman, Marc. *Living Without Ew: The Crash of the Post-Ewing Knicks.* Albion Press, 2001. Print.

28. Broussard, Chris. "PRO BASKETBALL; Ward Refers Writers to Bible." *New York Times.* 22 Apr. 2001.

29. Berman, Marc. *Living Without Ew: The Crash of the Post-Ewing Knicks.* Albion Press, 2001. Print.

30. Schlosser, Keith. "Charlie Ward

reminisces about Knicks career, discusses relationship with Jeff Van Gundy and new book." *thesportsdaily.com*, 5 Mar. 2018. https://thesportsdaily.com/2018/03/05/knicks-guard-charlie-ward-interview-new-book-nba/

31. Isola, Frank. "Childs Shrugs Off Trade Rumors." *New York Daily News*. 16 Jan. 1998.

32. Roberts, Selena. "PRO BASKETBALL; Knicks Add Cummings to Fill a Hole." *New York Times*. 20 Feb. 1998.

33. Wallace, John. Personal Interview. 12 June 2019.

34. Williams, Herb. Personal Interview. 2 Sept. 2019.

35. Christie, Doug. Personal Interview. 13 June 2019.

36. *Patrick and Zo*. Dir. Jon Weinbach. Perf. Patrick Ewing, Alonzo Mourning, Jeff Van Gundy and Michael Wilbon. *Sports Illustrated*, 2016. SI.com. Web. 7 July 2016.

37. No author provided. "THE N.B.A. PLAYOFFS; Murdock Regrets a Gesture In the Emotion of the Moment." *New York Times*. 3 May 1998.

38. *Ibid*.

39. Roberts, Selena. "PRO BASKETBALL; Knicks, a Year Wiser, Stay Put for Fight." *New York Times*. 2 Feb. 1998.

40. No author provided. "Johnson Deal Is NBA's Biggest." *Chicago Tribune*. 6 Oct. 1993.

41. Price, S.L. "Mourning After." *Sports Illustrated*. 11 May 1998.

42. Sandomir, Richard. "THE N.B.A. PLAYOFFS; And in This Corner, The Play-by-Play." *New York Times*. 2 May 1998.

43. Elhassan, Amin. "Once a Knick Always a Knick, Chris Childs." *The Hoop Collective*. Truehooptv, 13 Feb. 2017. http://www.espn.com/blog/truehoop/post/_/id/74758/truehoop-pod-once-a-knick-always-a-knick-chris-childs

44. D'Agostino, Dennis. *Garden Glory: An Oral History of the New York Knicks*. Triumph Books, 2003. Print.

45. Elhassan, Amin. "Once a Knick Always a Knick, Chris Childs." *The Hoop Collective*. Truehooptv, 13 Feb. 2017. http://www.espn.com/blog/truehoop/post/_/id/74758/truehoop-pod-once-a-knick-always-a-knick-chris-childs

46. Wise, Mike, and Isola, Frank. *Just Ballin': The Chaotic Rise of the New York Knicks*. Simon & Schuster, 1999. Print.

47. Price, S.L. "Mourning After." *Sports Illustrated*. 11 May 1998; Smith, Sam. "Riley, Mourning Stuck in Same Sinking Boat." *Chicago Tribune*. 5 May 1998.

48. Wise, Mike, and Isola, Frank. *Just Ballin': The Chaotic Rise of the New York Knicks*. Simon & Schuster, 1999. Print.

49. Price, S.L. "Mourning After." *Sports Illustrated*. 11 May 1998.

50. D'Agostino, Dennis. *Garden Glory: An Oral History of the New York Knicks*. Triumph Books, 2003. Print.

51. Williams, Herb. Personal Interview. 2 Sept. 2019.

52. Isola, Frank. "Knicks Win Is One for the Ages: In Whole Game, Oak Branches Out." *New York Daily News*. 4 May 1998.

53. Price, S.L. "Mourning After." *Sports Illustrated*. 11 May 1998.

54. Roberts, Selena. "THE N.B.A. PLAYOFFS; Van Gundy and Riley Get Lecture from Stern." *New York Times*. 20 May 1998.

55. Price, S.L. "Mourning After." *Sports Illustrated*. 11 May 1998.

56. Smits, Rik. Personal Interview. 16 Apr. 2019.

57. Marolachakis, Stefan. "Reggie Miller on the Epic Rivalries of the '90s and the Lost Art of Not Making Friends." *Open Run*. stitcher.com, 16 Oct. 2017. https://www.stitcher.com/podcast/uninterrupted/open-run/e/51833992

58. Wise, Mike, and Isola, Frank. *Just Ballin': The Chaotic Rise of the New York Knicks*. Simon & Schuster, 1999. Print.

59. *Ibid*.

Chapter 18

1. Berkow, Ira. *Autumns in the Garden: The Coach of Camelot and Other Knicks Stories*. Triumph Books, 2013. Print.

2. Wise, Mike. "BASKETBALL; It's Their Ball, and N.B.A. Owners Call for Lockout." *New York Times*. June 30, 1998.

3. *Ibid*.

4. *Ibid*.

5. *Ibid*.

6. No author provided. "NBA LOCKOUT: DAY BY DAY." *New York Daily News*. 7 Jan. 1999.

7. Golianopoulos, Thomas. "'An Unmitigated Disaster: An Oral History of the Lockout-Shortened 1999 NBA Season." *theringer.com*, 19 Feb. 2019. https://www.theringer.com/nba/2019/2/19/18228706/

lockout-1999-season-san-antonio-spurs-new-york-knicks

8. *Ibid.*

9. During a Bulls-76ers game in 1987, Barkley elbowed Oakley, and Oak grabbed Barkley by the jersey before the two were separated. In 1994, during a Knicks-Suns game, Barkley smacked Oakley in the face after the two got tangled under the basket. Oakley tried to retaliate with a punch, but was grabbed from behind by a teammate. Two years later, the forwards exchanged punches during a preseason game after Oak shoved Barkley, then with the Rockets, to the floor.

10. Golianopoulos, Thomas. "'An Unmitigated Disaster: An Oral History of the Lockout-Shortened 1999 NBA Season." *theringer.com*, 19 Feb. 2019. https://www.theringer.com/nba/2019/2/19/18228706/lockout-1999-season-san-antonio-spurs-new-york-knicks

11. Vecsey, Peter. "Oak's Got Beef with Hill...And the NBA Better Step in Quickly." *New York Post*. 6 Apr. 2001.

12. Childs, Chris. Personal Interview. 12 July 2019.

13. Le Batard, Dan. "Charles Oakley." *Highly Questionable*. ESPN, 21 Oct. 2011. https://www.youtube.com/watch?v=KRGB6MrChjc

14. Vecsey, Peter. "Oakley-McInnis War Looks Far from Over." *New York Post*. 5 Dec. 2000.

15. Taylor, Phil, and MacMullan, Jackie. "To the Victor Belongs the Spoils." *Sports Illustrated*. 18 Jan. 1999.

16. *Ibid.*

17. D'Agostino, Dennis. *Garden Glory: An Oral History of the New York Knicks*. Triumph Books, 2003. Print.

18. Grunfeld, Ernie. Personal Interview. 3 Oct. 2019; Van Gundy, Jeff. Personal Interview. 23 May 2019.

19. Malone, Brendan. Personal Interview. 23 Aug. 2019.

20. Heisler, Mark. "Garden of Good and Evil." *Los Angeles Times*. 23 June 1999.

21. The NBA began keeping flagrant foul statistics in 1990.

22. Oakley, Charles. Personal Interview. 8 May 2019.

23. Smith, Chris. "Smile and You Lose." *New York Magazine*. 16 Apr. 2001.

24. Spears, Marcus. "The Nuggets Interviews: Marcus Camby." *The Denver Post*. 24 Feb. 2007.

25. *Ibid.*

26. Jacobs, Jeff. "Marcus Camby Joins City Legends in Hartford Public High School Hall of Fame." *Hartford Courant*. 16 Nov. 2011.

27. UMass' 1996 Final Four appearance was vacated because Camby accepted gifts from an agent. Taylor, Phil. "Tangled Web Marcus Camby Was Both Victim and Villain in his Illicit Dealings with Agents While at UMass." *Sports Illustrated*. 15 Sept. 1997.

28. *Ibid.*

29. Grunfeld, Ernie. Personal Interview. 3 Oct. 2019.

30. Konigsberg, Eric. "The Real Spree." *New York Magazine*. 19 Apr. 1999.

31. Wise, Mike, and Isola, Frank. *Just Ballin': The Chaotic Rise of the New York Knicks*. Simon & Schuster, 1999. Print.

32. Konigsberg, Eric. "The Real Spree." *New York Magazine*. 19 Apr. 1999.

33. *Ibid.*

34. Wise, Mike, and Isola, Frank. *Just Ballin': The Chaotic Rise of the New York Knicks*. Simon & Schuster, 1999. Print.

35. Konigsberg, Eric. "The Real Spree." *New York Magazine*. 19 Apr. 1999.

36. Hardaway, Tim. Personal Interview. 18 Mar. 2019.

37. Konigsberg, Eric. "The Real Spree." *New York Magazine*. 19 Apr. 1999.

38. Taylor, Phil. "Center of the Storm." *Sports Illustrated*. 15 Dec. 1997.

39. *Ibid.*

40. *Ibid.*

41. Konigsberg, Eric. "The Real Spree." *New York Magazine*. 19 Apr. 1999.

42. Sanderson, Wimp. Personal Interview. 10 May 2019.

43. The accommodations the University of Alabama provided for Sprewell were in violation of NCAA rules.

44. Sanderson, Wimp. Personal Interview. 10 May 2019.

45. *Ibid.*

46. *Ibid.*

47. Rapaport, Michael. "Episode 187: Latrell Sprewell." *I Am Rapaport Stereo Podcast*. Youtube.com, 2 Aug. 2016. https://www.youtube.com/watch?v=l5LgiYSnQ9E

48. D'Agostino, Dennis. *Garden Glory: An Oral History of the New York Knicks*. Triumph Books, 2003. Print.

49. *Ibid.*

50. Ibid.; Checketts, Dave. Personal Interview. 26 Feb. 2018; Grunfeld, Ernie.

Personal Interview. 3 Oct. 2019; Van Gundy, Jeff. Personal Interview. 23 May 2019.

51. Wise, Mike. "Spree-ality." The *New York Times Magazine*. 2 May 1999.

52. *Ibid.*

53. Wise, Mike, and Isola, Frank. *Just Ballin': The Chaotic Rise of the New York Knicks*. Simon & Schuster, 1999. Print.

54. Starks, John, with Markowitz, David. *My Life*. Sports Publishing LLC, 2004. Print.

55. Johnson, Larry, and Sprewell, Latrell. "Connections: Larry Johnson and Latrell Sprewell." *Connections*. MSG Networks, 25 Oct. 2018. https://www.youtube.com/watch?v=LN4fC1Ntr-8

56. Wise, Mike, and Isola, Frank. *Just Ballin': The Chaotic Rise of the New York Knicks*. Simon & Schuster, 1999. Print.

57. D'Agostino, Dennis. *Garden Glory: An Oral History of the New York Knicks*. Triumph Books, 2003. Print.

58. Starks, John, with Markowitz, David. *My Life*. Sports Publishing LLC, 2004. Print.

59. *Ibid.*

60. Rhoden, William. "Sports of The Times; 'I'm Sorry, So Sorry.' Really, I Am." *New York Times*. 23 Jan. 1999.

61. Steinlight, Sammy. Personal Interview. 23 May 2019.

62. McCallum, Jack. "Spree for All." *Sports Illustrated*. 15 May 2000.

63. Konigsberg, Eric. "The Real Spree." *New York Magazine*. 19 Apr. 1999.

64. Leland, John. "PLAYING CHESS WITH: Larry Johnson; Fierce Competition, From a Seated Position." *New York Times*. 1 Apr. 2001.

65. Donahue, Anthony. "Ep. 4: Marcus Camby." *33 and 7th: A New York Knicks Pod*. podcasts.apple.com, 2 May 2019. https://podcasts.apple.com/us/podcast/33rd-and-7th-a-new-york-knicks-pod/id1455564828

66. Donahue, Anthony. "The Knicks Blog Radio: Kurt Thomas and Jeff Van Gundy call in." *TKB Radio*. SNY.tv, 23 Sept. 2014. http://podbay.fm/show/719127068/e/1411493577?autostart=1

67. D'Agostino, Dennis. *Garden Glory: An Oral History of the New York Knicks*. Triumph Books, 2003. Print.

68. Siegel, Joel. "Oedipus at the Garden." *New York Magazine*. No date.

69. *Ibid.*

70. Price, S.L. "Lord Jim." *Sports Illustrated*. 6 Feb. 2007.

Chapter 19

1. Heisler, Mark. "Garden of Good and Evil." *Los Angeles Times*. 23 June 1999.

2. Armour, Terry. "Krause Breaks Silence About Bulls' Breakup. *Chicago Tribune*. 20 Jan. 1999.

3. Louis, Steven. "In the Knick of Time." theringer.com, 3 Apr. 2019. https://www.theringer.com/nba/2019/4/3/18293135/new-york-knicks-1998-99-patrick-ewing-larry-johnson

4. Wise, Mike, and Isola, Frank. *Just Ballin': The Chaotic Rise of the New York Knicks*. Simon & Schuster, 1999. Print.

5. *Ibid.*

6. D'Agostino, Dennis. *Garden Glory: An Oral History of the New York Knicks*. Triumph Books, 2003. Print.

7. *Ibid.*

8. Donahue, Anthony. "Ep. 4: Marcus Camby." *33 and 7th: A New York Knicks Pod*. podcasts.apple.com, 2 May 2019. https://podcasts.apple.com/us/podcast/33rd-and-7th-a-new-york-knicks-pod/id1455564828

9. Isola, Frank. "Charles Cheered as Knicks Hold On." *New York Daily News*. 17 Feb. 1999.

10. *Ibid.*

11. Brunson, Rick. Personal Interview. 12 Sept. 2017; Davis, Ben. Personal Interview. 7 Dec. 2017.

12. Wallace, John. Personal Interview. 12 June 2019.

13. Ballow, Jonah. Interview with Larry Johnson, Latrell Sprewell, Allan Houston, Marcus Camby and Kurt Thomas. Facebook. 3 Apr. 2017. 2:30 P.M. EST. https://www.youtube.com/watch?v=5VysQaWnmUY

14. Strickland, Erick. Personal Interview. 16 July 2019.

15. Dudley, Chris. Personal Interview. 20 Oct. 2017.

16. Barker, Barbara. Personal Interview. 20 Apr. 2018.

17. Brunson, Rick. Personal Interview. 12 Sept. 2017; Davis, Ben. Personal Interview. 7 Dec. 2017.

18. No host provided. "Marcus Camby Talks '96 Draft Class, Knicks, Raptors and More at Mitchell & Ness Store Opening." *Slam Magazine*. 19 Jan. 2017. https://www.youtube.com/watch?v=OERg-GpZiBI

19. Dudley, Chris. Personal Interview.

20 Oct. 2017; Wise, Mike, and Isola, Frank. *Just Ballin': The Chaotic Rise of the New York Knicks.* Simon & Schuster, 1999. Print.

20. Munson, Lester. "Paternity Ward." *Sports Illustrated.* 3 May 1998.

21. Firestone, David. "In Testimony, Patrick Ewing Tells of Favors At Strip Club" *New York Times.* 24 July 2001.

22. Soltis, Andy. "Strip-Club Boss: L.J. Sought Sex on the Menu." *New York Post.* 2 June 2001.

23. No author provided. "Sex, sports and the mob: The Gold Club trial." *CNN. com,* 15 June 2001. http://www.cnn.com/2001/LAW/06/15/gold.club.trial/index.html

24. Firestone, David. "In Testimony, Patrick Ewing Tells of Favors at Strip Club." *New York Times.* 24 July 2001.

25. Wise, Mike, and Isola, Frank. *Just Ballin': The Chaotic Rise of the New York Knicks.* Simon & Schuster, 1999. Print.

26. *Ibid.*

27. *Ibid.*

28. *Ibid.*

29. No author provided. "Tempers Flare (Again) in NY Win." *CBSnews.com,* 30 Mar. 1999. https://www.cbsnews.com/news/tempers-flare-again-in-ny-win/

30. Wise, Mike, and Isola, Frank. *Just Ballin': The Chaotic Rise of the New York Knicks.* Simon & Schuster, 1999. Print.

31. *Ibid.*

32. Brunson, Rick. Personal Interview. 12 Sept. 2017.

33. Steinlight, Sammy. Personal Interview. 23 May 2019.

34. Brunson, Rick. Personal Interview. 12 Sept. 2017.

35. *Ibid.*

36. Wojnarowski, Adrian. "Jeff Van Gundy." *The Vertical Podcast with Woj.* sports.yahoo.com, 10 Feb. 2016. https://sports.yahoo.com/news/the-vertical-podcast-with-woj—jeff-van-gundy-145814221.html

37. Wise, Mike. Personal Interview. 23 Feb. 2018.

38. Vecsey, Peter. "Ernie-Van Feud Goes Way Back." *New York Post.* 23 Apr. 1999.

39. Wise, Mike. Personal Interview. 23 Feb. 2018.

40. Vecsey, Peter. "Ernie-Van Feud Goes Way Back." *New York Post.* 23 Apr. 1999.

41. Berman, Marc. "VAN GUNDY TOSSES BOUQUET TO ERNIE." *New York Post.* 8 Nov. 1999.

42. Checketts, Dave. Personal Interview. 26 Feb. 2018; Wise, Mike. Personal Interview. 23 Feb. 2018.

43. Checketts, Dave. Personal Interview. 26 Feb. 2018; Wise, Mike, and Isola, Frank. *Just Ballin': The Chaotic Rise of the New York Knicks.* Simon & Schuster, 1999. Print.

44. Checketts, Dave. Personal Interview. 26 Feb. 2018.

45. *Ibid.*

46. Checketts, Dave. Personal Interview. 26 Feb. 2018.

47. Wise, Mike. "PRO BASKETBALL: NOTEBOOK; Ewing Pulls a Power Play to Help the Embattled Van Gundy." *New York Times.* 4 Apr. 1999.

48. Checketts, Dave. Personal Interview. 26 Feb. 2018

49. Checketts, Dave. Personal Interview. 26 Feb. 2018.

50. *Ibid.*; Wise, Mike, and Isola, Frank. *Just Ballin': The Chaotic Rise of the New York Knicks.* Simon & Schuster, 1999. Print.

51. Grunfeld, Ernie. Personal Interview. 3 Oct. 2019.

52. Wise, Mike, and Isola, Frank. *Just Ballin': The Chaotic Rise of the New York Knicks.* Simon & Schuster, 1999. Print.

53. Roberts, Selena. "PRO BASKETBALL; Checkbook Is Open, Chemistry Book Closed." *New York Times.* 11 Apr. 1999.

54. Checketts, Dave. Personal Interview. 26 Feb. 2018.

55. *Ibid.*

56. Wise, Mike, and Isola, Frank. *Just Ballin': The Chaotic Rise of the New York Knicks.* Simon & Schuster, 1999. Print.

57. *Ibid.*

58. No author provided. "Latrell Sprewell-AND1 Commercial." youtube.com, 31 Oct. 2008. https://www.youtube.com/watch?v=s6DYYh5f2sg

59. Roberts, Selena. "PRO BASKETBALL; Finally, Ewing Hits One, Knicks Win One." *New York Times.* 24 Apr. 1999.

60. No author provided. "Sports of The Times; One Huge Comeback for Checketts's Team." *New York Times.* 26 Apr. 1999.

61. *Ibid.*

Chapter 20

1. "The Garden's Defining Moments: Larry Johnson's 4-Point Play." *The Garden's Defining Moments.* 20 Mar. 2016.

https://www.msgnetworks.com/shows/the-gardens-defining-moments/

2. Houston, Wade. Personal Interview. 6 June 2019.

3. *Ibid.*

4. *Ibid.*

5. *Ibid.*

6. *Ibid.*

7. Wise, Mike, and Isola, Frank. *Just Ballin': The Chaotic Rise of the New York Knicks.* Simon & Schuster, 1999. Print.

8. *Ibid.*

9. Houston, Wade. Personal Interview. 6 June 2019.

10. Edwards, James L., III. "25th anniversary of the 1993 NBA Draft in Auburn Hills: An oral history of the night's top storylines from the Warriors, Magic, 76ers and Pistons." *theathletic.com,* 18 June 2018. https://theathletic.com/389689/2018/06/18/25th-anniversary-of-the-1993-nba-draft-in-auburn-hills-an-oral-history-of-the-nights-top-storylines-from-the-warriors-magic-76ers-and-pistons/

11. Wise, Mike, and Isola, Frank. *Just Ballin': The Chaotic Rise of the New York Knicks.* Simon & Schuster, 1999. Print.

12. Donahue, Anthony. "Latrell Sprewell." *33rd and 7th.* Vsporto.com, 11 Mar. 2018. https://vsporto.com/show/33rd-and-7th/

13. Perdue, Will. Personal Interview. 6 Aug. 2019.

14. Wise, Mike, and Isola, Frank. *Just Ballin': The Chaotic Rise of the New York Knicks.* Simon & Schuster, 1999. Print.

15. Hardaway, Tim. Personal Interview. 18 Mar. 2019.

16. Strickland, Mark. Personal Interview. 25 Sept. 2019.

17. Wise, Mike, and Isola, Frank. *Just Ballin': The Chaotic Rise of the New York Knicks.* Simon & Schuster, 1999. Print.

18. *Ibid.*

19. Roberts, Selena. "N.B.A. PLAYOFFS; Memories of Series Past Moderate the Knicks' Giddiness." *New York Times.* 14 May 1999.

20. Starks, John. Personal Interview. 10 July 2019; Wise, Mike, and Isola, Frank. *Just Ballin': The Chaotic Rise of the New York Knicks.* Simon & Schuster, 1999. Print.

21. Roberts, Selena. "N.B.A. PLAYOFFS; Memories of Series Past Moderate the Knicks' Giddiness." *New York Times.* 14 May 1999.

22. Wise, Mike, and Isola, Frank. *Just Ballin': The Chaotic Rise of the New York Knicks.* Simon & Schuster, 1999. Print.

23. *Ibid.*

24. D'Agostino, Dennis. *Garden Glory: An Oral History of the New York Knicks.* Triumph Books, 2003. Print; Ballow, Jonah. Interview with Larry Johnson, Latrell Sprewell, Allan Houston, Marcus Camby and Kurt Thomas. Facebook. 3 Apr. 2017. 2:30 P.M. EST. https://www.youtube.com/watch?v=5VysQaWnmUY

25. Hahn, Alan. *New York Knicks: The Complete Illustrated History.* MVP Books, 2012. Print.

26. Lupica, Mike. "Ep. 91—Dave Checketts." *The Mike Lupica Podcast.* stitcher.com, 2 Mar. 2018. https://www.stitcher.com/podcast/compass-media-networks/mike-lupica-show/e/53547636

27. Van Gundy, Jeff. Personal Interview. 23 May 2019.

28. Wise, Mike, and Isola, Frank. *Just Ballin': The Chaotic Rise of the New York Knicks.* Simon & Schuster, 1999. Print.

29. Checketts, Spence. "Dave Checketts (Part 2)." *Reality Check with Spence Checketts.* Realitycheckpod.com, 23 Nov. 2018. https://player.fm/series/reality-check-with-spence-checketts/david-checketts-part-2-on-leaving-the-jazz-working-for-the-league-and-eventually-the-knicks-organization-patrick-ewing-turning-the-knicks-into-a-contender-john-starks-pat-rileys-departure-for-miami-and-the-jeff-van-gundy-era

30. *Ibid.*

31. *Ibid.*

32. Strickland, Mark. Personal Interview. 25 Sept. 2019.

33. D'Agostino, Dennis. *Garden Glory: An Oral History of the New York Knicks.* Triumph Books, 2003. Print.

34. *Ibid.*

35. Wojnarowski, Adrian. "Jeff Van Gundy." *The Vertical Podcast with Woj.* sports.yahoo.com, 10 Feb. 2016. https://sports.yahoo.com/news/the-vertical-podcast-with-woj-jeff-van-gundy-145814221.html

36. "Beginnings: Latrell Sprewell." *Beginnings.* Youtube.com, 22 July 2018. https://www.youtube.com/watch?v=F0jn60OTZ3I

37. Wise, Mike, and Isola, Frank. *Just Ballin': The Chaotic Rise of the New York Knicks.* Simon & Schuster, 1999. Print.

38. *Ibid.*

39. Wise, Mike. "N.B.A. PLAYOFFS;

Checketts Admits He Met Jackson, Then Denied It." *New York Times*. 25 May 1999.
40. *Ibid.*
41. Wise, Mike, and Isola, Frank. *Just Ballin': The Chaotic Rise of the New York Knicks*. Simon & Schuster, 1999. Print.
42. Wise, Mike. "N.B.A. PLAYOFFS; Checketts Admits He Met Jackson, Then Denied It." *New York Times*. 25 May 1999.
43. *Ibid.*
44. Roberts, Selena. "N.B.A. PLAYOFFS; Knicks Put the Hawks Away and Breeze to Eastern Finals." *New York Times*. 25 May 1999.
45. Van Gundy routinely guzzled Diet Coke during games.
46. D'Agostino, Dennis. *Garden Glory: An Oral History of the New York Knicks*. Triumph Books, 2003. Print.
47. Hahn, Alan. *New York Knicks: The Complete Illustrated History*. MVP Books, 2012. Print.
48. Wise, Mike, and Isola, Frank. *Just Ballin': The Chaotic Rise of the New York Knicks*. Simon & Schuster, 1999. Print.
49. Roberts, Selena. "N.B.A. PLAYOFFS: CONFERENCE FINALS; This Time, Ewing Buries Miller and the Pacers." *New York Times*. 31 May 1999.
50. Wise, Mike, and Isola, Frank. *Just Ballin': The Chaotic Rise of the New York Knicks*. Simon & Schuster, 1999. Print.
51. *Ibid.*
52. *Ibid.*
53. Roberts, Selena. "PRO BASKETBALL; Hobbled Ewing Lights a Fire Under His Undermanned Team." *New York Times*. 4 June 1999.
54. Rhoden, William. "Sports of The Times; Bit Part Behind Him, Camby Does Star Turn." *New York Times*. 6 June 1999.
55. D'Agostino, Dennis. *Garden Glory: An Oral History of the New York Knicks*. Triumph Books, 2003. Print.
56. Thibodeau, Tom. Personal Interview. 23 July 2019.
57. Ballow, Jonah. Interview with Larry Johnson, Latrell Sprewell, Allan Houston, Marcus Camby and Kurt Thomas. Facebook. 3 Apr. 2017. 2:30 P.M. EST. https://www.youtube.com/watch?v=5VysQaWnmUY
58. Wise, Mike. "ON PRO BASKETBALL; Johnson Takes the Game Into His Hands." *New York Times*. 6 June 1999.
59. Wise, Mike, and Isola, Frank. *Just Bal-*

Ballin': The Chaotic Rise of the New York Knicks. Simon & Schuster, 1999. Print.
60. No author provided. "11.9 Seconds, and a Play to Remember." *msg.com*, 5 June 2019. https://blog.msg.com/2019/06/05/11-9-seconds-and-a-play-to-remember/
61. Louis, Steven. "In the Knick of Time." theringer.com, 3 Apr. 2019. https://www.theringer.com/nba/2019/4/3/18293135/new-york-knicks-1998-99-patrick-ewing-larry-johnson
62. Childs, Chris. Personal Interview. 12 July 2019.
63. Brunson, Rick. Personal Interview. 12 Sept. 2017.
64. Bucher, Ric. "I Got Stripes." ESPNMag.com, 3 Dec. 2001. http://www.espn.com/magazine/bucher_20011203.html
65. Wise, Mike, and Isola, Frank. *Just Ballin': The Chaotic Rise of the New York Knicks*. Simon & Schuster, 1999. Print.
66. *Ibid.*
67. *Ibid.*
68. Roberts, Selena. "N.B.A. PLAYOFFS; Knicks Shrug Off Adversity Once Again to Reach Finals." *New York Times*. 12 June 1999.
69. *Ibid.*
70. D'Agostino, Dennis. *Garden Glory: An Oral History of the New York Knicks*. Triumph Books, 2003. Print.
71. Wise, Mike, and Isola, Frank. *Just Ballin': The Chaotic Rise of the New York Knicks*. Simon & Schuster, 1999. Print.

Chapter 21

1. Hubbard, Jan. *One for San Antonio: The Spurs' First NBA Championship*. Rare Air Media, 1999. Print.
2. Broussard, Chris. "N.B.A. FINALS; No Vindication, Just Victories, for Popovich." *New York Times*. 15 June 1999.
3. Golianopoulos, Thomas. "'An Unmitigated Disaster: An Oral History of the Lockout-Shortened 1999 NBA Season." theringer.com, 19 Feb. 2019. https://www.theringer.com/nba/2019/2/19/18228706/lockout-1999-season-san-antonio-spurs-new-york-knicks
4. Evans, Paul. Personal Interview. 29 Mar. 2019.
5. Montville, Leigh. "Trials of David." *Sports Illustrated*. 26 Apr. 1999.
6. *Ibid.*
7. Wise, Mike, and Isola, Frank. *Just Bal-*

lin': *The Chaotic Rise of the New York Knicks*. Simon & Schuster, 1999. Print.

8. Hoffer, Richard. "Easy Does It: Tim Duncan's seemingly effortless dismantling of the Lakers shows that he's now the league's dominant big man" *Sports Illustrated*. 31 May 1999.

9. Perdue, Will. Personal Interview. 6 Aug. 2019.

10. Hubbard, Jan. *One for San Antonio: The Spurs' First NBA Championship*. Rare Air Media, 1999. Print.

11. McCallum, Jack. "Pop Art." *Sports Illustrated*. 29 Apr. 2013.

12. Hubbard, Jan. *One for San Antonio: The Spurs' First NBA Championship*. Rare Air Media, 1999. Print.

13. Perdue, Will. Personal Interview. 6 Aug. 2019.

14. *Ibid.*

15. MacMullan, Jackie. "Scarred, but Not Scared Despite the Concerns of the Spurs, Kidney Transplant Survivor Sean Elliott Is Determined to Return to the Court This Season." *Sports Illustrated*. 31 Jan. 2000.

16. Taylor, Phil. "Drive to Survive." *Sports Illustrated*. 28 June 1999.

17. D'Agostino, Dennis. *Garden Glory: An Oral History of the New York Knicks*. Triumph Books, 2003. Print.

18. Wise, Mike, and Isola, Frank. *Just Ballin': The Chaotic Rise of the New York Knicks*. Simon & Schuster, 1999. Print.

19. Hubbard, Jan. *One for San Antonio: The Spurs' First NBA Championship*. Rare Air Media, 1999. Print.

20. Araton, Harvey. "Sports of The Times; Combatants a Mystery Until Now." *New York Times*. 17 June 1999.

21. Wise, Mike, and Isola, Frank. *Just Ballin': The Chaotic Rise of the New York Knicks*. Simon & Schuster, 1999. Print.

22. *Ibid.*

23. *Ibid.*

24. Taylor, Phil. "Drive to Survive." *Sports Illustrated*. 28 June 1999.

25. *Ibid.*

26. *Ibid.*

27. Wise, Mike, and Isola, Frank. *Just Ballin': The Chaotic Rise of the New York Knicks*. Simon & Schuster, 1999. Print.

28. Taylor, Phil. "Drive to Survive." *Sports Illustrated*. 28 June 1999.

29. Brunson, Rick. Personal Interview. 12 Sept. 2017.

30. *Ibid.*

31. Roberts, Selena. "N.B.A. FINALS: NOTEBOOK; Johnson Insists Knicks Are Not 'Mainstream.'" *New York Times*. 23 June 1999.

32. Roberts, Selena. "N.B.A. FINALS: NOTEBOOK; Johnson Responds To Walton." *New York Times*. 25 June 1999.

33. Wise, Mike, and Isola, Frank. *Just Ballin': The Chaotic Rise of the New York Knicks*. Simon & Schuster, 1999. Print.

34. *Ibid.*

35. *Ibid.*

36. *Ibid.*

37. Dudley, Chris. Personal Interview. 20 Oct. 2017.

38. D'Agostino, Dennis. *Garden Glory: An Oral History of the New York Knicks*. Triumph Books, 2003. Print.

39. Kay, Michael. "Patrick Ewing." *CenterStage*. YES Network, 1 July 2011. https://www.youtube.com/watch?v=VEF1TBFkcRM

40. Childs, Chris. Personal Interview. 12 July 2019.

41. Wise, Mike, and Isola, Frank. *Just Ballin': The Chaotic Rise of the New York Knicks*. Simon & Schuster, 1999. Print.

42. Roberts, Selena. "PRO BASKETBALL; Knicks Pick a Project, but He's All of 7 Feet 2." *New York Times*. 1 July 1999.

43. *Ibid.*

44. Van Gundy, Jeff. Personal Interview. 23 May 2019.

45. Russillo, Ryen. "Spencer Checketts." *Ryen Russillo Show*. ESPN.com, 1 Aug. 2018. https://player.fm/series/the-russillo-show/spencer-checketts. The Cavaliers selected Ilgauskas with the 20th pick in 1996 after New York passed on him in favor of Wallace and McCarty with the 18th and 19th picks, respectively.

46. *Ibid.*

47. McGuire, Scott. Personal Interview. 15 Mar. 2019. Scott is the son of legendary Knicks player and coach Dick McGuire, whose number 15 is retired for him and Earl Monroe. "Dicky" was serving as a scout for the Knicks at the time and remained with the organization as a consultant until his death in 2010.

48. *Ibid.* Artest now admits he was hungover after a night of drinking.

49. Berman, Marc. "Scout Raves About 'Star' Porzingis, Avoids Dreaded Comparison." *New York Post*. 28 June 2015.

50. Wise, Mike. "BASKETBALL; Weis

Shows Some Flair but Needs Work." *New York Times.* 23 July 1999.

51. Borden, Sam. "For Frédéric Weis, Knicks' Infamous Pick, Boos Began a Greater Struggle." *New York Times.* 14 July 2015.

52. Johnson, DeMarco. Personal Interview. 3 May 2019.

53. Borden, Sam. "For Frédéric Weis, Knicks' Infamous Pick, Boos Began a Greater Struggle." *New York Times.* 14 July 2015.

54. Ian Mahoney, who was director of basketball operations and remains a good friend of Tapscott, believes "Tap" never had a shot at the job because his resume was not flashy enough for such a prominent role with the Knicks. Tapscott played college ball at Tufts University and coached at American University, not exactly marquee programs. He neither played nor coached at the professional level.

55. Checketts, Dave. Personal Interview. 26 Feb. 2018.

56. Frank worked as a consultant for the Knicks while Scott was with the Knicks.

57. Popper, Steve. "PRO BASKETBALL; Knicks Trying to Hire Old Checketts Friend Away from the Jazz." *New York Times.* 10 Aug. 1999.

58. D'Agostino, Dennis. *Garden Glory: An Oral History of the New York Knicks.* Triumph Books, 2003. Print.

Chapter 22

1. Roberts, Selena. "PRO BASKETBALL; Ewing Ready to Start, but He's Not Exactly Smiling." *New York Times.* 10 Dec. 1999.

2. Sportswriter Bill Simmons popularized "The Ewing Theory," which was created in the mid- to late 1990s by his friend Dave Cirilli. Cirilli was convinced that Ewing's teams at Georgetown and with the Knicks inexplicably played better without him when he was out due to injury or foul trouble. Although there was no statistical evidence to support the theory, the term gained popularity as Simmons applied it to other teams. He and Cirilli decided on two elements that must be met for "The Ewing Theory" to apply.

"A star athlete receives an inordinate amount of media attention and fan interest, and yet his teams never win anything substantial with him (other than maybe some early-round playoff series)."

"That same athlete leaves his team (either by injury, trade, graduation, free agency or retirement)—and both the media and fans immediately write off the team for the following season." Simmons, Bill. "Ewing Theory 101." ESPN.com, 21 July 2009. https://proxy.espn.com/espn/page2/story?id=1193711

3. Hersch, Hank. "2 New York Knicks." *Sports Illustrated.* 23 October 1995.

4. Roberts, Selena. "PRO BASKETBALL; Knicks Tell Sprewell a Trade Is Possible." *New York Times.* 15 Oct. 1999.

5. Roberts, Selena. "PRO BASKETBALL; $130,000 Fine Rankles and Surprises Sprewell." *New York Times.* 14 Oct. 1999.

6. Wise, Mike. "ON PRO BASKETBALL; As Season Starts, So Does a Quest for a Go-To Guy." *New York Times.* 3 Nov. 1999.

7. D'Agostino, Dennis. *Garden Glory: An Oral History of the New York Knicks.* Triumph Books, 2003. Print.

8. Roberts, Selena. "PRO BASKETBALL; Some W.W.F., Some N.B.A.: Sprewell vs. Warriors." *New York Times.* 17 Nov. 1999.

9. Roberts, Selena. "COLLEGE BASKETBALL; Knicks Win, and Sprewell Gloats." *New York Times.* 21 Nov. 1999.

10. Roberts, Selena. "PRO BASKETBALL; Sprewell Is Fined $10,000 by N.B.A." *New York Times.* 25 Nov. 1999.

11. Wise, Mike. "Hard Way Is the Only Way for Starks." *New York Times.* 7 Dec. 1999.

12. "The Garden's Defining Moments: Larry Johnson's 4-Point Play." *The Garden's Defining Moments.* 20 Mar. 2016. https://www.msgnetworks.com/shows/the-gardens-defining-moments/

13. Wise, Mike. "ON PRO BASKETBALL; Trade Takes Heart Out of the Garden." *New York Times.* 26 June 1998.

14. Roberts, Selena. "PRO BASKETBALL; Ewing Ready to Start, but He's Not Exactly Smiling." *New York Times.* 10 Dec. 1999.

15. Popper, Steve. "BASKETBALL; Knicks' Leaders Fall Short of Duties." *New York Times.* 3 Feb. 2000.

16. Popper, Steve. "PRO BASKETBALL; For Ewing, Benching Just Isn't A Big Deal." *New York Times.* 11 Jan. 2000; Roberts, Selena. "BASKETBALL; The Knicks' Ewing for the Wizards' Howard? Let the Talks (or Rumors) Fly." *New York Times.* 2 Feb. 2000.

17. Roberts, Selena. "BASKETBALL; Ewing Is Knicks' Center of Attention." *New York Times.* 7 Feb. 2000.

18. Roberts, Selena. "PRO BASKETBALL; Van Gundy to Coach All-Stars." *New York Times.* 31 Jan. 2000.

19. *Ibid.*

20. Elhassan, Amin. "Once a Knick Always a Knick, Chris Childs." *The Hoop Collective.* Truehooptv, 13 Feb. 2017. http://www.espn.com/blog/truehoop/post/_/id/74758/truehoop-pod-once-a-knick-always-a-knick-chris-childs

21. *Ibid.*

22. *Ibid.*

23. Childs, Chris. Personal Interview. 12 July 2019.

24. Roberts, Selena. "PRO BASKETBALL; After Trading Hits, the Raptors Fall." *New York Times.* 27 Apr. 2000.

25. Roberts, Selena. "PRO BASKETBALL; Raptor Coach Files Defamation Suit Against Camby." *New York Times.* 23 Apr. 2000.

26. Van Gundy, Stan. Personal Interview. 20 Aug. 2019.

27. Thibodeau, Tom. Personal Interview. 23 July 2019.

28. Baker Katie. "It Was Like True, True Disdain for Each Other." *theringer.com*, 15 May 2017. https://www.theringer.com/2017/5/15/16045664/oral-history-nba-playoffs-new-york-knicks-miami-heat-1997-brawl-20-year-anniversary-96b8a5be329f

29. Roberts, Selena. "PRO BASKETBALL; New Arena, Different Result for the Knicks in Miami." *New York Times.* 8 May 2000.

30. Roberts, Selena. "PRO BASKETBALL; Ward Carries Load Until Knicks Awake." *New York Times.* 10 May 2000.

31. Wise, Mike. "ON PRO BASKETBALL; Ewing Shows Knicks Both Sides of Coin." *New York Times.* 13 May 2000.

32. *Ibid.*

33. Hardaway, Tim. Personal Interview. 18 Mar. 2019.

34. Berkow, Ira. *Autumns in the Garden: The Coach of Camelot and Other Knicks Stories.* Triumph Books, 2013. Print.

35. Thibodeau, Tom. Personal Interview. 23 July 2019; Thomas, Kurt. Personal Interview. 18 Sept. 2017; Ducey, Kenny. "On his 54th birthday, here is our favorite Jeff Van Gundy story." *SI.com*, 19 Jan. 2016. https://www.si.com/extra-mustard/2016/01/19/jeff-van-gundy-jet-destroyed-car-story-knicks-heat

36. Berkow, Ira. *Autumns in the Garden: The Coach of Camelot and Other Knicks Stories.* Triumph Books, 2013. Print.

37. *Ibid.*

38. D'Agostino, Dennis. *Garden Glory: An Oral History of the New York Knicks.* Triumph Books, 2003. Print; Roberts, Selena. "PRO BASKETBALL; Knicks Hand Heat Familiar Fate, Ousting Rival for 3rd Year in Row." *New York Times.* 22 May 2000.

39. Roberts, Selena. "PRO BASKETBALL; Knicks Hand Heat Familiar Fate, Ousting Rival for 3rd Year in Row." *New York Times.* 22 May 2000.

40. *Ibid.*

41. Hardaway, Tim. Personal Interview. 18 Mar. 2019.

42. Hubbard, Jan. *One for San Antonio: The Spurs' First NBA Championship.* Rare Air Media, 1999. Print.

43. Le Batard, Dan. "Pat Riley." *The Dan Le Batard Show—South Beach Sessions.* ESPN Radio, 6 Nov. 2014. http://www.espn.com/espnradio/play/_/id/11821514

44. Le Batard, Dan. "Pat Riley." *The Art of Conversation with Dan Le Batard.* ESPN, 24 Feb. 2019. https://www.youtube.com/watch?v=Q3o1BS5_kFc

45. No author provided. "Knicks have heart, no legs in Game 1." *ESPN.com*, 23 May 2000. https://www.espn.com/nba/playoffs00/s/2000/0523/547308.html

46. Roberts, Selena. "PRO BASKETBALL; Doubly Defeating for Knicks." *New York Times.* 26 May 2000.

47. *Ibid.*

48. Broussard, Chris. "PRO BASKETBALL: NOTEBOOK; Rose Strong in Fourth." *New York Times.* 28 May 2000.

49. Roberts, Selena. "BASKETBALL; Knicks Put Pacers in a World of Pain." *New York Times.* 30 May 2000.

50. Popper, Steve. "PRO BASKETBALL; For Knicks, Everything Hurts but Pride." *New York Times.* 2 June 2000.

51. Roberts, Selena. "PRO BASKETBALL; Tired Man and Fresh Question." *New York Times.* 2 June 2000.

52. No author provided. "Are the Knicks a better team without Ewing?" *ESPN.com* via *Associated Press.* 2000. http://a.espncdn.com/nba/playoffs00/s/2000/0530/558183.html

53. Roberts, Selena. "PRO BASKET-BALL; Tired Man and Fresh Question." *New York Times.* 2 June 2000.

54. *Ibid.*

55. Roberts, Selena. "The Great Big Engine That Simply Couldn't." *New York Times.* 3 June. 2000.

56. Berman, Marc. *Living Without Ew: The Crash of the Post-Ewing Knicks.* Albion Press, 2001. Print.

57. Roberts, Selena. "Ewing's Aging, Injured and Unappreciated." *New York Times.* 4 June 2000.

58. Brunson, Rick. Personal Interview. 12 Sept. 2017.

59. Wallace, John. Personal Interview. 12 June 2019.

60. Berman, Marc. *Living Without Ew: The Crash of the Post-Ewing Knicks.* Albion Press, 2001. Print.

61. Wojnarowski, Adrian. "Patrick Ewing." *The Vertical Podcast with Woj.* sports.yahoo.com, 30 Mar. 2016. https://sports.yahoo.com/news/the-vertical-podcast-with-woj—patrick-ewing-140057572.html

62. No author provided. "Forgotten Finals." *CBSsports.com.* 3 June 2014. https://www.cbssports.com/nba/feature/24559469/the-forgotten-finals

63. Berman, Marc. "Ewing Says He's Shocked." *New York Post.* 23 Sept. 2000.

64. Donahue, Anthony. "The Knicks Blog Radio: Kurt Thomas and Jeff Van Gundy call in." *TKB Radio.* SNY.tv, 23 Sept. 2014. http://podbay.fm/show/719127068/e/1411493577?autostart=1; Roberts, Selena. "Ewing's Aging, Injured and Unappreciated." *New York Times.* 4 June 2000.

65. Falk, David. Personal Interview. 18 Aug. 2019; Falk, David. *The Bald Truth: Secrets of Success from the Locker Room to the Boardroom.* Gallery Books, 2009. Print.

66. Falk, David. Personal Interview. 18 Aug. 2019; Berman, Marc. *Living Without Ew: The Crash of the Post-Ewing Knicks.* Albion Press, 2001. Print.

67. Berman, Marc. *Living Without Ew: The Crash of the Post-Ewing Knicks.* Albion Press, 2001. Print.

68. Matthews, Wallace. "GOOD RIDDANCE TO THAT MENACING SCOWL." *New York Post.* 22 Aug. 2000.

69. D'Agostino, Dennis. *Garden Glory: An Oral History of the New York Knicks.* Triumph Books, 2003. Print.

70. *Ibid.*

71. Broussard, Chris. "Knicks Send Ewing to Sonics as 4-Team Deal Ends an Era." *New York Times.* 21 Sept. 2000.

72. D'Agostino, Dennis. *Garden Glory: An Oral History of the New York Knicks.* Triumph Books, 2003. Print.

73. Van Gundy called Ewing "the mortgage" because he "paid the bills" for the coach and a lot of other people for many years.

74. Donahue, Anthony. "The Knicks Blog Radio: Kurt Thomas and Jeff Van Gundy call in." *TKB Radio.* SNY.tv, 23 Sept. 2014. http://podbay.fm/show/719127068/e/1411493577?autostart=1; Eisen, Rich. "Jeff Van Gundy of ESPN Talks Knicks Legends Charles Oakley and Patrick Ewing." *The Rich Eisen Show.* thericheisenshow.com, 7 Apr. 2017. http://www.richeisenshow.com/2017/04/07/jeff-van-gundy-of-espn-talks-knicks-legends-charles-oakley-patrick-ewing-4717/

75. Berman, Marc. *Living Without Ew: The Crash of the Post-Ewing Knicks.* Albion Press, 2001. Print.

76. Hahn, Alan. *New York Knicks: The Complete Illustrated History.* MVP Books, 2012. Print.

77. Berman, Marc. *Living Without Ew: The Crash of the Post-Ewing Knicks.* Albion Press, 2001. Print.

Epilogue

1. Isola, Frank. "Houston Gets Six Years, $99M Richest Contract in Knick History." *New York Daily News.* 7 July 2001.

2. Checketts, Dave. Personal Interview. 26 Feb. 2018.

Dolan purchased the electronics chain The Wiz out of bankruptcy and Clearview Cinemas and placed both companies under Checketts' control.

3. *Ibid.*

4. *Ibid.*

5. Berman, Marc. *Living Without Ew: The Crash of the Post-Ewing Knicks.* Albion Press, 2001. Print. That summer, Dolan instituted a new media policy in which a public relations representative had to be present for any interview with a member of the organization. That employee would then report back to Jonathan Supranowitz, vice president of public relations, who took notes on every interview. Stories started coming out of

the Garden about public relations staffers eavesdropping on conversations between reporters and team executives. Knicks employees clammed up out of fear they would be reported for saying something critical of the organization. Reporters were denied access to players and those who were disparaging of the team were cut off from team communications. The atmosphere was unlike any other in the NBA. Mike Vaccaro of the *New York Post* called the Garden "a gulag."

6. D'Agostino, Dennis. *Garden Glory: An Oral History of the New York Knicks*. Triumph Books, 2003. Print.

7. Broussard, Chris. "PRO BASKETBALL; Knicks' Johnson Retires, Preferring to Fade Away." *New York Times*. 11 Oct. 2001.

8. Broussard, Chris. "PRO BASKETBALL; Resigning After 19 Games, Van Gundy Shocks the Knicks." *New York Times*. 9 Dec. 2001.

9. *Ibid.*

10. Van Gundy, Jeff. Personal Interview. 23 May 2019.

11. D'Agostino, Dennis. *Garden Glory: An Oral History of the New York Knicks*. Triumph Books, 2003. Print.

12. Price-Brown, Laura. "Lonely at Bottom / 433-game sellout streak ends as Knicks fall to 0–4." *Newsday*. 4 Nov. 2002.

13. No host provided. "Patrick Ewing's Basketball Hall of Fame Enshrinement Speech." *Official Hoophall*. Youtube.com, 17 Feb. 2012.https://www.youtube.com/watch?v=47IcYphP6ZE

14. O'Connor, Ian. "Past Still Defines Heat-Knicks Rivalry." ESPN.com, 27 Feb. 2011.

15. Checketts, Dave. Personal Interview. 26 Feb. 2018.

16. *Ibid.*

17. Le Batard, Dan. "Pat Riley." *The Art of Conversation with Dan Le Batard*. ESPN, 24 Feb. 2019. https://www.youtube.com/watch?v=Q3o1BS5_kFc

18. Berman, Marc. "Pat Riley's greatest regret not getting Patrick Ewing NBA championship with Knicks." *New York Post*. 25 Dec. 2015.

19. Araton, Harvey. "Pat Riley firmly in Magic's corner: 'He's a prodigal son of the Lakers.'" *Yahoosports.com*, 6 Mar. 2017. https://sports.yahoo.com/news/pat-riley-firmly-in-magics-corner-hes-a-prodigal-son-of-the-lakers-143108623.html

20. Begley, Ian. "I 'regret' quitting Knicks." *ESPN.com*, 28 June 2013. https://www.espn.com/blog/new-york/knicks/post/_/id/46245/van-gundy-i-regret-quitting-knicks

21. Van Gundy, Stan. Personal Interview. 20 Aug. 2019.

22. Wojnarowski, Adrian. "Patrick Ewing." *The Vertical Podcast with Woj*. sports.yahoo.com, 30 Mar. 2016. https://sports.yahoo.com/news/the-vertical-podcast-with-woj—patrick-ewing-140057572.html

23. Fans chanted Van Gundy's name when he covered NBA drafts at the Garden for ESPN, and the group Citigrass penned "The Ballad of Jeff Van Gundy," which lamented the coach's departure from New York.

24. Isola, Frank. "Smith's Shot at Success Goes In." *New York Daily News*. 1 June 2003.

25. Starks, John with Markowitz, David. *My Life*. Sports Publishing LLC, 2004. Print.

26. No author provided. "Over Jordan, Over Grant … A Classic Garden Moment Relived." *MSG.com*, 25 May 2018. https://blog.msg.com/2018/05/25/over-jordan-over-grant-a-classic-garden-moment-relived/

27. Curtis, Charles. "Brief history of Charles Oakley's feud with Knicks." *USA Today*. 9 Feb. 2017.

28. Kerber, Fred. "Security drags Charles Oakley out of Knicks game in unreal scene." *New York Post*. 8 Feb. 2017.

29. Kriegel, Mark (@markkriegel) "Anthony Mason was real New York: self-made, hard as hell, with a little crazy and a lot of great. Damn, he'll be missed." 28 Feb. 2015, 11:22 A.M. Tweet.

30. Cronson, Don. Personal Interview. 6 Nov. 2017.

31. Isola, Frank. "Allan Houston can't take the pain and retires in 2005." *New York Daily News*. 17 Oct. 2016.

32. *Ibid.*

33. Berman, Marc. "Say Spree Broke His Hand During Boat Fracas." *New York Post*. 4 Oct. 2002. Spree claimed he broke his hand while trying to steady himself on his boat, but Marc Berman of the *New York Post* reported the injury occurred when Sprewell attempted to punch a man and connected with a wall instead.

34. Broussard, Chris. "PRO BASKET-

BALL; Sprewell Helps Beat the Knicks, Then Taunts Them." *New York Times.* 24 Dec. 2003.

35. Reilly, Rick. "GETTING BY ON $14.6 MIL." *Sports Illustrated.* 15 Nov. 2004.

36. Held, Joey. "How to Choke Your Way Out of $100 Million—The Rise and Fall of Latrell Sprewell." *celebritynetworth.com*, 6 July 2015. https://www.celebritynetworth.com/articles/sports-news/choke-way-100-million-rise-fall-latrell-sprewell/

37. Marsh, Julia. "Larry Johnson Hasn't Paid $2.7K Dentist Bill." *New York Post.* 23 Mar. 2017.

38. Riley would return to coaching in December 2005 when he took over for Stan Van Gundy and led Miami to a championship that very season.

39. Ward, Charlie. Personal Interview. 5 Apr. 2019.

40. Hahn, Alan. "Season 1, Episode 16." *Knicks Fix Podcast.* Msgnetworks.com, 16 Mar. 14. URL not available Accessed 2 Aug. 2016.

41. Hardaway, Tim. Personal Interview. 8 Mar. 2019.

42. Childs, Chris. Personal Interview. 12 July 2019.

43. Checketts, Spence. "Jeff Van Gundy (Part 1)." *Reality Check with Spence Checketts.* Realitycheckpod.com, 8 Nov. 2018. https://player.fm/series/reality-check-with-spence-checketts/jeff-van-gundy-part-1-on-coaching-against-michael-jordan-great-knicks-rivalries-and-his-relationship-with-david-stern

Bibliography

Books

Araton, Harvey. *Crashing the Boards: How Basketball Won the World and Lost Its Soul at Home.* Simon & Schuster, 2005.

Araton, Harvey. *When the Garden Was Eden: Clyde, The Captain, Dollar Bill, and the Glory Days of the New York Knicks.* HarperCollins, 2011.

Berkow, Ira. *Autumns in the Garden: The Coach of Camelot and Other Knicks Stories.* Triumph Books, 2013.

Bondy, Filip. *Tip Off: How the 1984 NBA Draft Changed Basketball Forever.* Da Capo Press, 2007.

Berman, Marc. *Living Without Ew: The Crash of the Post-Ewing Knicks.* Albion Press, 2001.

D'Agostino, Dennis. *Garden Glory: An Oral History of the New York Knicks.* Triumph Books, 2003.

Falk, David. *The Bald Truth: Secrets of Success from the Locker Room to the Boardroom.* Gallery Books, 2009.

Falkoff, Robert. *The Inside Story of the '93-'94 Houston Rockets' Championship Season.* Gulf Publishing Company, 1994.

Feinstein, John. *The Punch: One Night, Two Lives, and the Fight That Changed Basketball Forever.* Little, Brown, 2002.

Finkel, Jon. *The Athlete: Greatness, Grace and the Unprecedented Life of Charlie Ward.* Archervision Inc., 2017.

Free Darko. *Free Darko Presents the Undisputed Guide to Pro Basketball History.* Bloomsbury USA, 2010.

Hahn, Alan. *New York Knicks: The Complete Illustrated History.* MVP Books, 2012.

Halberstam, David. *Playing for Keeps Michael Jordan and the World He Made.* Random House, 1999.

Heisler, Mark. *The Lives of Riley.* Macmillan, 1994.

Hubbard, Jan. *One for San Antonio: The Spurs' First NBA Championship.* Rare Air Media, 1999.

Jackson, Phil, and Rosen, Charley. *More Than a Game.* Seven Stories Press, 2001.

Lazenby, Roland. *Blood on the Horns: The Long Strange Ride of Michael Jordan's Chicago Bulls.* Addax Publishing Group, 1998.

Lazenby, Roland. *Michael Jordan: The Life.* Little, Brown, 2014.

McCallum, Jack. *Dream Team: How Michael, Magic, Larry, Charles and the Greatest Team of All-Time Conquered the World and Changed the Game of Basketball Forever.* Ballantine Books, 2013.

McCallum, Jack. *Golden Days: West's Lakers, Steph's Warriors, and the California Dreamers Who Reinvented Basketball.* Ballantine Books, 2017.

Miller, Reggie, with Wojciechowski, Gene. *I Love Being the Enemy.* Simon & Schuster, 1995.

Minas, Mick. *The Curse: The Colorful and Chaotic History of the L.A. Clippers.* 77 Publishing, 2016.

Olajuwon, Hakeem, with Knobler, Peter. *Living the Dream: My Life and Basketball.* Little, Brown and Company, 1996.

Pitino, Rick, and Reynolds, Bill. *Born to Coach: A Season with the New York Knicks.* NAL Books, 1988.

Riley, Pat. *The Winner Within: A Life Plan for Team Players.* Berkley Books, 1993.

Rivers, Glenn, and Brooks, Bruce. *Those Who Love the Game: Glenn "Doc" Rivers on Life in the NBA and Elsewhere.* Henry Holt & Co., 1994.

Simmons, Bill. *The Book of Basketball: The NBA According to the Sports Guy.* ESPN Books, an imprint of Random House Publishing, 2009.

Smith, Sam. *The Jordan Rules: The Inside Story of a Turbulent Season with Michael*

Jordan and the Chicago Bulls. Simon & Schuster, 1992.

Starks, John, with Markowitz, David. *My Life*. Sports Publishing LLC, 2004.

Tomjanovich, Rudy, with Falkoff, Robert. *A Rocket at Heart*. Simon & Schuster, 1997.

Wise, Mike, and Isola, Frank. *Just Ballin': The Chaotic Rise of the New York Knicks*. Simon & Schuster, 1999.

Newspapers, Magazines and Websites

Basketballreference.com
Chicago Tribune
ESPN.com
Los Angeles Times
New York Daily News
New York Magazine
New York Post
New York Times
Sports Illustrated

Movies

The Forgotten Finals. 2014. *Cbssports.com*. Web. 18 August 2016.

June 17, 1994. Dir. Brett Morgan. Perf. Marv Albert, Rex Beaber and Chris Berman. ESPN Films, 2010. ESPN.

This Magic Moment. Dir. Gentry Kirby and Erin Leyden. ESPN Films, 2016. ESPN.

Patrick and Zo. Dir. Jon Weinbach. Perf. Patrick Ewing, Alonzo Mourning, Jeff Van Gundy and Michael Wilbon. Sports Illustrated, 2016. SI.com. Web. 7 July 2016.

Winning Time: Reggie Miller vs. The New York Knicks. Dir. Dan Klores. Perf. Reggie Miller, Cheryl Miller, Spike Lee, Patrick Ewing, and Donnie Walsh. ESPN Films, 2010. ESPN.

Podcasts

Checketts, Spence. *Reality Check with Spence Checketts*. Realitycheckpod.com.

Donahue, Anthony. *TKB Radio*. SNY.tv.

Hahn, Alan. *Knicks Fix Podcast*. msgnet-works.com

Le Batard, Dan. *The Dan Le Batard Show*. ESPN Radio.

Lupica, Mike. *The Mike Lupica Podcast*.

Rapaport, Michael. *I Am Rapaport Stereo Podcast*.

Ryan, Adam. *In All Airness*. Inallairness.com.

Wojnarowski, Adrian. *The Vertical Podcast with Woj*. sports.yahoo.com

Personal Interviews

Rand Araskog (10/2/19)
Harvey Araton (2/13/18)
Stan Asofsky (4/25/20)
Barbara Barker (4/20/18 and 2/8/19)
Al Bianchi (9/18/17)
Rolando Blackman (1/6/18)
Anthony Bonner (9/26/17)
Chris Brienza (12/18/19)
Clifton Brown (2/12/18)
Gerald Brown (12/17/19)
Rick Brunson (9/12/17)
Curtis Bunn (8/16/19)
Dick Butera (8/27/19)
Michael Carter, Jr. (8/21/19)
Bill Cartwright (4/16/19)
Dave Checketts (2/26/18)
Chris Childs (7/12/19)
Doug Christie (6/13/19)
John Cirillo (12/20/19)
Jim Cleamons (9/4/19)
Don Cronson (11/6/17)
Terry Cummings (2/21/18)
Dave D'Alessandro (8/5/18)
Ben Davis (12/7/17)
Hubert Davis (9/29/17)
Peter DeBusschere (11/20/18)
Chris Dudley (10/20/17)
Mario Elie (4/23/19)
Paul Evans (3/29/19)
David Falk (8/18/19)
Scott Fiedler (3/22/19)
Matt Fish (7/16/19)
Corey Gaines (7/23/19)
Lewis Geter (7/23/19)
Ronnie Grandison (4/2/19)
Ernie Grunfeld (10/3/19)
Bob Gutkowski (8/9/19)
Lori Hamamoto (8/26/19)
Said Hamdan (6/13/19)
Leonard Hamilton (5/14/19)
Tim Hardaway (3/18/19)
Derek Harper (7/25/17)
Wade Houston (6/6/19)
Jaren Jackson, Sr. (5/2/19)
Stanley Jaffe (8/21/19)
Mike Jarvis (3/15/19)
DeMarco Johnson (5/3/19)
Bo Kimble (9/26/17)
Travis Knight (4/4/19)
Andrew Lang (6/25/19)

Ian Mahoney (4/15/19)
Brendan Malone (8/23/19)
Stephen Masiello (6/21/19)
Vernon Maxwell (6/7/19)
Xavier McDaniel (10/30/17 and 2/2/19)
Scott McGuire (3/15/19)
Carlton McKinney (6/6/19)
Charles Oakley (5/8/19)
Will Perdue (8/6/19)
Dave Robbins (4/29/19
Barry Rubinstein (9/3/19)
Bob Salmi (5/6/19)
Wimp Sanderson (5/10/19)
Mike Saunders (8/2/17)
Rik Smits (4/16/19)
Barry Stanton (1/13/20)
John Starks (7/10/19)
David Steele (8/28/19)
Sammie Steinlight (5/23/19)

Spencer Stolpen (9/16/19)
Erick Strickland (7/16/19)
Mark Strickland (9/25/19)
Tom Thibodeau (7/23/19)
Kurt Thomas (9/18/17)
Rod Thorn (7/16/19)
Rudy Tomjanovich (6/27/19)
Jeff Van Gundy (5/23/19)
Stan Van Gundy (8/20/19)
Peter Vecsey (4/9/19)
Suzyn Waldman (12/26/19)
Kenny Walker (5/5/20)
John Wallace (6/12/19)
Charlie Ward (4/5/19)
Gerald Wilkins (6/24/19)
Herb Williams (9/2/19)
Mike Wise (2/23/18)
Dave Wohl (5/8/20)
Ronnie Zeidel (12/16/19)

Index